Understanding World Christianity

Understanding World Christianity

Eastern Africa

PAUL KOLLMAN AND
CYNTHIA TOMS SMEDLEY

FORTRESS PRESS
MINNEAPOLIS

UNDERSTANDING WORLD CHRISTIANITY
Eastern Africa

Cover image: Christopher Roche/Getty Images
Cover design: Laurie Ingram

Print ISBN: 978-1-4514-7299-8
eBook ISBN: 978-1-5064-5147-3

The paper used in this publication meets the minimum requirements of American National Standard for Information Sciences — Permanence of Paper for Printed Library Materials, ANSI Z329.48-1984.

Manufactured in the U.S.A.

Contents

Introducing the Fortress Press Series Understanding World Christianity

The idea of a major project on world Christianity is timely. According to research from Pew, approximately two-thirds of the world's nations and territories are Christian majority.[1] Christianity continues to widen its global net, claiming the allegiance of well over two billion people. Of the ten largest national Christian populations—the United States, Brazil, Mexico, Russia, Philippines, Nigeria, China, Democratic Republic of the Congo, Germany, Ethiopia—only two are from the Western world. Around one-sixth of the human population holds membership in the Roman Catholic Church. The modern Pentecostal/Charismatic movement—only a century old—claims roughly 600 million people today. As Pew reports, "Christians are also geographically widespread—so far-flung, in fact, that no single continent or region can indisputably claim to be the center of global Christianity. A century ago this was not the case."

Of the eight cultural blocs of the world, Christianity is the largest religion in six of them: Latin America and the Caribbean, North America, Western Europe, Eastern Europe, Africa, and Oceania. Only in Asia and the Middle East is Christianity not the religion most people adhere to. However, some of the most important developments in world Christianity are happening in Asia, and the Middle East will forever be the land of Jesus—where the gospel was unleashed. Furthermore, Islam—by far the most dominant Middle Eastern faith—can scarcely be understood apart from the history it shares with Judaism and

1. See "Global Christianity—A Report on the Size and Distribution of the World's Christian Population," Pew Research Center, December 19, 2011, https://tinyurl.com/ycsffdt7.

Christianity. Christianity's influence in the world is profound, and there is little reason to think it is abating.

In the 1960s, esteemed church historian Stephen Neill began noticing that—for the first time in human history—there existed a truly *world* religion: Christianity. Neill was ahead of his time. Due to his globetrotting on behalf of the World Council of Churches, he was able to observe rather intimately how deeply Christianity was taking root in Africa and Asia, seemingly against all the odds. While the leviathan structure of European colonialism was collapsing, Christianity defied all predictions by indigenizing. Many thought that when the colonial administrators and missionaries left, Christianity would wither. But the opposite happened. When the Europeans and North Americans got out of the way, these people integrated the gospel into their cultures, into their own lands, on their own terms. And today, we are front-row observers to these events, many of which are still unfolding. Christianity is changing civilizations as civilizations change Christianity. These stories are fascinating, they are important, and they need to be told.

The Understanding World Christianity project addresses head-on the fact that many churches, colleges, and seminaries are struggling to come to terms with the reality that Christianity is now a worldwide faith, not just a Western one. There is a popular and hardened conception that Christianity is dependent upon the nations of Western Europe and North America. Some variants of the story prolong the worn-out narrative that Asia and Africa are being somehow held hostage by the white man's religion, and that Christianity has everything to do with colonialism and imperialism, and nothing to do with indigenization, freedom, and self-assertion. Thus, many students even take degrees in Christianity under a long-outdated curriculum: Christianity is born in the Middle East, Constantine makes it a Western faith, the Enlightenment ushers in a modern era, Christianity fades, and now we inhabit a *postmodern* world.

This Eurocentric paradigm is obsolete, for many reasons. First of all, Christianity has expanded terrifically. No longer is it centered in the West. It is now broadly spread out across the world, especially in Africa and Latin America. Second, the important modern European thinkers—Bonhoeffer, Tillich, Barth—who are typically required reading in Western seminaries do not adequately represent the world's Christians. Christianity is so much more diversified now. We are in great need of hearing the southern voices such as John Mbiti, Kwame Bediako, Oscar Romero, and M. M. Thomas. The Western academy needs to think more globally, given the striking changes the Christian faith has undergone in the last century. Third, in what some call an era of globalization, we are much more exposed to the non-Western world. Media, immigration, and increased international travel have made cultures intersect and cross-pollinate, creating a hybridity that was not so obvious a generation or two ago. This is especially the case for people who live in cities. Los Angeles, Dallas, Chicago, New York, and Miami are excellent examples of this diversification process, which has a trickle-down effect throughout America's smaller cities, towns, and villages. A woman in small-town New Mexico could very well have an Indian physician, a Vietnamese priest, and a Guatemalan housekeeper. These situations are increasingly common for the average American.

Thankfully, a corpus of research on Christianity's *global* history is proliferating, and there is a growing awareness that Christianity never was the exclusive possession of the Western world, and certainly is not today. In spite of the gains that have been made, there are fundamental questions that remain unaddressed or underaddressed. For example, what is the *meaning* of global Christianity? How will the drastic changes to Christianity's geography impact theology, mission, and ministry? Indeed, what does this new body of research have to say to the church? What can Christians do with this information? How must missionary work be reconceived? These are practical questions begging further investigation. It is critical that Christians respond to global Christianity in sensitive and thoughtful ways. The Understanding World Christianity series will equip specialists, leaders, and students with up-to-date, on-the-ground information that will help them get their heads around the stories and the data.

In the parable of the sower, Jesus described a scene where seed was scattered on various types of soil. Some seed was unproductive, but some produced bountifully. Similarly, at the beginning of the twenty-first century, Christianity flourishes in surprising places. The continent of Africa is half Christian. China and the former Soviet Union are opening up to Christianity after decades of oppression. The 266th pope is from Buenos Aires. Korea is home to some of the largest Christian congregations in the world. Meanwhile, in Christianity's old heartland—Western Europe—it appears faith is receding. Who could have foreseen these astonishing developments a century ago?

In the early years of the faith, when Christian gentiles began to outnumber believing Jews, the faith began to take on a decidedly different identity. Led by the apostles' ambitious missionary work, the early church adapted capably, and grew exponentially. Peter and Paul profoundly shaped "the Way" by fashioning it into an institution open to all people, all nationalities and ethnicities alike. It was a blended family par excellence, albeit with considerable growth pains. Today we stand at a similar crossroads. The Global South has become the new heartland of a faith that was anchored in the West for centuries. The composition of Christianity—easily the world's largest religion—is changing, right before our eyes.

An important question remains, however. Is it a *fait accompli* that Christianity will continue to move south, with little for the Western churches to do but watch?

Scholars such as Robert Wuthnow contend there is much that the churches in the Western world can do, and in fact are doing. In *Boundless Faith: The Global Outreach of American Churches*, he shows that American churches now spend $4 billion annually on overseas ministry, more than ever, and the number of "full-time missionaries serving abroad has increased steadily." In contrast to paternalistic models of the past, where the sending church was the clear authority, mission work today follows a collaborative paradigm, "through direct partnerships with overseas congregations, engaging in faster and more efficient transcultural communication, interacting with a sizable population of refugees and immigrants, and contributing to large-scale international humanitarian and relief organizations."[2] Our mental maps of missionaries flowing from the West to the rest must be updated, as Brazil, Korea, and Nigeria are now sending nations with robust missionary programs. India, Vietnam, and the Philippines provide hundreds of Roman Catholic priests to serve in the United States. Indeed, Christians from the Global South are globally engaged, and North American churches are wise to partner with them.

The Understanding World Christianity series will contribute to this robust conversation in key ways. It will interpret these monumental changes for a larger audience. It will engage critical questions arising from a global, interconnected Christian faith. And it will draw upon some of today's best specialists—familiar with Christianity on the ground in their respective geographies—in order to create authoritative and readable composites of what is happening. Authors for the series come from a range of ecclesial backgrounds, including Orthodox, Roman Catholic, mainline Protestant, Evangelical, and Pentecostal.

The new era of world Christianity is impacting global politics, higher education, Christian ministry paradigms, and countless charitable organizations. This project will help professors, pastors, students, and professionals understand that with the global spread of Christianity comes a new opportunity for sharing the ongoing story, informed by sensitivity to local and contextual differences. As our world flattens and as Christians globally become more interdependent, a rich complexity is developing. Worldviews are shifting, societies are transforming, and theologies are being rewritten. This project will help Christians to navigate through the differences more carefully and more thoughtfully.

Read more about the Understanding World Christianity series online at: fortresspress.com/uwc.

—Dyron Daughrity, General Editor
The Understanding World Christianity Series

2. Robert Wuthnow, *Boundless Faith: The Global Outreach of American Churches* (Los Angeles: University of California Press, 2010), 1–2.

Acknowledgments

A wide-ranging work of this sort necessarily draws upon numerous sources prepared by others. In the footnotes and bibliography, we have sought to acknowledge written works that we consciously used, yet it might be that we have failed to recognize sources we drew upon. If so, we apologize and are glad to specify dependence where it is less than sufficiently articulated.

In addition, the two of us have also benefited from a number of fruitful professional and personal relationships in the preparing of this volume.

We would like to thank Paulines Publications Africa, a publishing ministry of the Daughters of St. Paul, for permission to reprint a map from the 2nd edition (1998) of their book *2000 Years of Christianity in Africa: An African Church History by John Baur.*

Pamela Foltz carried out superb proofreading of early drafts.

Alison Fitchett Climenhaga read through most chapters, improving each with her careful and educated eye.

Emmanuel Katongole and Robert Dowd, CSC, read through chapters and offered helpful comments in the midst of revision.

Finally, we thank very much Dyron Daughrity, series editor, for inviting us into the Understanding World Christianity series, and our editors Emily Brower and Allyce Amidon at Fortress Press, who have been unfailingly helpful.

In addition, we both acknowledge debts of a more personal sort accumulated in the preparation of this volume. Cynthia would like to thank her husband Michael and sons Ashton and

Soren, as well as other family members, for their support of this project, which entailed many hours of work, often at the expense of time with loved ones. In addition, colleagues at Uganda Christian University in Mukono, Uganda, and Westmont College in Santa Barbara have assisted in countless ways.

Paul would like to thank colleagues at the University of Notre Dame who have helped bring this book to fruition, especially those at the Center for Social Concerns, where he has served as executive director. The research and writing of this book meant time away from the office and often away from campus, during which their generosity was crucial and much appreciated. He also thanks the Center for World Catholicism and Intercultural Theology at DePaul University, Chicago, where editing was finalized.

From both of us to these and many others, heartfelt thanks.

Paul Kollman, CSC, and Cynthia Toms Smedley

Abbreviations and Acronyms

AACC	All Africa Council of Churches
ACK	Anglican Church of Kenya (formerly Church of the Province of Kenya, or CPK)
AFER	*African Ecclesiastical Review*
AIC	African Initiated (or Independent) Church
AICN	African Israel Church Nineveh
AIM	Africa Inland Mission (later Africa Inland Church, AIC)
AIPC	African Independent Pentecostal Church
AMECEA	Association of Member Episcopal Conferences of Eastern Africa
ANC	African National Congress
AOC	African Orthodox Church
AOG	Assemblies of God
ATIEA	Association of Theological Institutions of Eastern Africa
ATR	African Traditional Religion (or African Religion)
CCAWT	Circle of Concerned African Women Theologians

CMS	Church Mission Society (formerly Church Missionary Society)
COBEA	Church of Bethlehem East Africa
CPK	Church Province of Kenya
CSC	Congregation of Holy Cross
CSM	Church of Scotland Mission
CSSp	Congregation of the Holy Ghost (or Spiritans)
DACB	Dictionary of African Christian Biography
DOAG	German East Africa Company
DP	Democratic Party (Uganda)
DRC	Democratic Republic of Congo
EATWOT	Ecumenical Association of Third World Theologians
ELCT	Evangelical Lutheran Church of Tanzania
ESEAT	Ecumenical Symposium of Eastern African Theologians
IBEAC	Imperial British East Africa Company
JCC	Jerusalem Church of Christ
KAU	Kenya African Union
KISA	Kikuyu Independent Schools Association
KY	Kabaka Yekka
LMS	London Missionary Society
LWF	Lutheran World Federation
MAfr	Missionaries of Africa (or White Fathers)
MHM	Mill Hill Missionaries
NCCK	National Council of Churches of Kenya
NEGST	Nairobi Evangelical Graduate School of Theology (now part of the African International University)

NGO	Nongovernmental Organization
OAIC	Organization of African Instituted Churches
OBE	Order of the British Empire
OSB	Order of St. Benedict
PCEA	Presbyterian Church of East Africa
PEFA	Pentecostal Evangelistic Fellowship of Africa
SCCs	Small Christian communities
SDA	Seventh-Day Adventist Church
SECAM	Symposium of Episcopal Conferences of Africa and Madagascar
TANU	Tanganyika African National Union
TEC	Tanzania Episcopal Conference
UMCA	Universities Mission to Central Africa
UPC	Uganda People's Congress
WCC	World Council of Churches
YCS	Young Christian Students
YWAM	Youth with a Mission

Introducing Christianity in Eastern Africa

VITAL, VARIED, AND VOLATILE

Christianity in eastern Africa—Kenya, Tanzania, and Uganda —is unmistakable. Its physical manifestations strike even casual visitors. Church steeples arise in the downtown areas of the nations' capitals and other large cities: the Catholic St. Joseph's Cathedral and the Anglican Christ Church in Zanzibar, for example, their Lutheran and Catholic counterparts in Dar es Salaam, and Anglican and Catholic cathedrals on prominent hills around Kampala. Colorful billboards insistently announce rallies for spiritual rebirth and renewal: "Night of Power: Come and Feel the Spirit" and "Jesus Is Lord: Claim Your Destiny Tonight." The slogans share the canvas with calmly beaming faces of evangelist preachers, mostly Africans, mostly males with an occasional female. Christian refrains like "Under the Good Shepherd's Care" and "Born Again Shoppe" decorate storefronts and festoon privately owned minivans serving as public transportation for many. In towns and villages, Christian churches have founded and sponsor prominent schools and hospitals, and an increasing number of banks and insurance agencies. And Christian-linked religious signifiers decorate believers' bodies, especially on Sundays—rosaries around the necks of Catholics, Bibles in the hands of Protestants, white robes or more colorful vestments on adherents of African-initiated churches.

Of course, this has not always been the case. In the larger arena of world Christianity, the eastern African branch is comparatively young. Christianity first arrived in the region only in the late fifteenth century with Catholic Portuguese explorers on their way around the Cape of Good Hope to Asia. The Portuguese departure in the early eighteenth century, after conflicts with local Africans, many of them Muslim, means that today's Christian communities trace themselves to the mid-nineteenth century. At that time, European Christian missionaries, Catholic and Protestant, returned to the region. Compared to the faith's presence in Ethiopia to the north, which dates at least to the fourth century, or to its even more ancient lineage in Egypt and Syria, eastern Africa's Christianity is of recent vintage indeed, like that of much of sub-Saharan Africa.

In less than two centuries, however, Christianity has developed remarkably in the region. Followers of Jesus have been a prominent social and political force in all three countries and, before each became an independent nation in the early 1960s, also in the territories they now occupy. In addition, the region represents a stronghold for many types of Christianity. By way of a broad introduction, one might highlight the *vitality*, the *variety*, and the *volatility* of Christianity in eastern Africa.

Christianity has demonstrated considerable *vitality* in eastern Africa. The many Christian-inspired buildings and billboards, rituals, rallies, and raiment point to deeper transformations in people's sense of themselves. It is apparent that missionary energies of the past two centuries have borne fruit: most of eastern Africa's people are now Christian. And besides the simple demographic realities, other registers indicate that vitality. Uganda's accession to Christian identity represents one of the most successful missionary efforts in history, both for Catholics and Anglicans. Tanzania is home to more Moravian Christians than any other country and to one of the largest groups of Lutherans in the world; a Tanzanian was the first African to head the Lutheran World Federation. Kenya houses the largest national group of Quakers and one of the largest of Seventh-Day Adventists. The East African Revival in the first half of the twentieth century transformed Christian practice across the region and extended beyond into neighboring African countries as well. Nairobi, Kenya's dynamic capital, hosts more Catholic seminarians than perhaps any other city in the world—with the exception of Rome itself. It also houses the headquarters of the All Africa Council of Churches and the Organization of African Instituted Churches. Eastern Africa produced the first sub-Saharan African Catholic bishop in modern times, and the first sub-Saharan African cardinal. Finally, Christian leaders from Uganda, Tanzania, and Kenya have also gone elsewhere as missionaries—emissaries of many forms of Christianity, including as Catholic priests and sisters.

This brief survey suggests that Christianity's evident vitality in the region has meant not uniformity but bewildering *variety*. Numerous ways to be Christian have arrived in eastern Africa and found a home, and others appeared there as Africans took Christianity's messages and symbols and put them to work in innovative ways. The Catholic Church and numerous internationally linked Protestant and Orthodox bodies have substantial presences in the region, and thousands of African-founded churches—many these days Pentecostal in style—also dot cities and countryside. Indeed, eastern Africa is one of the places in the world where the varieties of ways of embodying Christian identity stretch the sensibilities of Christians in the region and elsewhere, a laboratory of sorts possibly helping to define just what separates a Christian from a non-Christian way of being a religious person. Is the Ugandan-born church called the Holy Quaternity (which is not rooted in belief in the Trinity of Father, Son, and Holy Spirit) a truly Christian body? What about the Lord's Resistance Army, which terrorized northern Uganda in the 1990s and early twenty-first century and still, as of this writing, festers in the Central African Republic? Who is to say?

Finally, besides its variety, the vitality of the comparatively young Christianity of eastern Africa has also meant considerable *volatility*, some that Christians caused, some their presence has evoked. The arrival of Christianity destabilized the Indian Ocean coast even before the nineteenth-century return of Christianity to the region, as the Catholic convictions of the early-modern Portuguese—distinguishable, but impossible to separate, from their militarily buttressed commercial ambitions—drew intermittent and eventually triumphant resistance from the mostly Muslim Indian Ocean coast. The volatility itself expressed Christianity's vitality, perhaps most evident in the courage of believers facing persecution. The earliest African Christians in the region, linked to the early-modern Portuguese presence, remained few, yet in Mombasa some suffered martyrdom in the seventeenth century, dying for their faith.

Two centuries later, another pioneering group of African Christians defied their ruler, the *kabaka* (or king) of the kingdom of Buganda, and were put to death in gruesome ways. To this day, few Christian feasts anywhere attract as many as the hundreds of thousands who gather from across eastern Africa and beyond every June 3 to celebrate the martyrs of Uganda—Catholic and Anglican—at Namugongo, near Kampala, on one of Uganda's national holidays. Those martyrs partly explain the quick accession to Christian identity in their land, which within a half-century of their deaths was on its way to becoming a predominantly Christian country. Equally impressive were the remarkable lay catechists, many from that same kingdom of Buganda, who took the martyrs' message and memory across eastern Africa.

More controversially, over sixty years later ardent faith led numerous Kenyan Christians to refuse to participate in the Mau Mau movement linked to eventual Kenyan independence efforts. They, too, paid with their lives—a vitality seen by certain other Kenyans today as unpatriotic, even traitorous, but nonetheless faith-driven.

Not all examples of volatility, of course, imply dying for faith. In the postcolonial period, Kenya's Presbyterian theologian John Gatu proposed a missionary moratorium to promote local Christian self-reliance, which aroused international praise as well as denunciation.

Such vitality, variety, and volatility persist in thousands of Christian communities across the region, groups large and small that gather weekly or more to celebrate and transmit their faith. Christian churches retain their vitality—thankfully, usually without being persecuted. Christian bodies have a prominence in public life in all three of the region's countries and provide substantial human services such as education and healthcare. The variety of ways of being Christian in the region also shows no sign of abating, with new churches—some linked internationally, some more homegrown—appearing all the time. And the volatility persists, too, as Christians face antagonism from some Muslims at the Indian Ocean coast, some churches face accusations of corruption, and others galvanize protests against perceived political and economic abuses.

EASTERN AFRICA AND WORLD CHRISTIANITY

The term "world Christianity" has recently emerged in scholarship that examines Christianity. Among its many uses, the term promises first an attempted comprehensiveness beyond a prior narrowness—in opposition, for example, to an approach to Christianity that favors "the West," or prioritizes the actions of religious elites instead of ordinary believers, or males at the expense of females.

Besides its comprehensiveness, the term also connotes two perspectival shifts. One stresses contemporary Christian vigor as central to interpreting the Christian past, so that the goal becomes not simply historical understanding of all that has happened but allowing present realities to help determine how to tell the story of the past. Without ignoring the instigating role of past missionary activity from outside, for example, a world-Christianity approach to Christian history prioritizes the early and ongoing responses and initiatives of the evangelized, since they invariably embody the essence of Christianity moving forward into the present day. The second perspectival shift places local Christian manifestations in a self-consciously comparative framework appreciative of the larger world Christian movement past and present. This invites insights into specific regional and historic singularities, while also highlighting experiences that Christians elsewhere have shared.

The two authors of this book embrace the world-Christianity perspective in all three senses: more comprehensiveness, but also looking at the past mindful of the present as well as placing the local in relation to the global. In so doing, we recognize the difficulty of holding all three together. We are also keenly aware of our personal and professional limitations. Both Americans, neither of us comes from eastern Africa originally. We have lived in eastern Africa for limited amounts of time, and in particular places with distinct roles that shaped us and the story we tell.

Kollman, a Catholic priest and member of an international Catholic religious order, the Congregation of Holy Cross, first came to Nairobi in the late 1980s as a seminarian. He later returned during a doctoral program in African religions, then taught for two years at a Catholic seminary in Jinja, Uganda. He also carried out research leading to a dissertation and eventually a book on nineteenth-century Catholic evangelization in Zanzibar and coastal Tanzania. He has returned for longer and shorter visits, for teaching and research.

Toms Smedley visited eastern Africa in 2003 before returning to Uganda and living in Mukono at Uganda Christian University from 2004 to 2007. She served as associate director of the school's Uganda Studies Program. In that capacity she facilitated a number of North American students' engagement with eastern Africa, with a special attention to global health. Since then she has earned a doctorate in higher education and international development, during which she worked with leaders of nongovernmental organizations in eastern Africa. She continues to accompany US students to eastern Africa for educational experiences.

In preparing this volume we have drawn upon our experiences and ranged widely in our reading, mindful of our limitations and the innumerable debts we owe to the work of other scholars. In general, we have allowed both high-quality scholarship and perceived importance to world Christianity decide what to include and omit. Mindful of our debts, we nonetheless have not provided intensive documentation, instead allowing occasional footnotes to refer to only some of the numerous sources informing this book.

DEFINING EASTERN AFRICA

Though the term "eastern Africa" can refer to a much larger area—and does so in some United Nations terminology, for example—here it refers to Kenya, Tanzania, and Uganda. (It does not, therefore, include present-day Rwanda and Burundi, now part of a growing sense of an eastern African community.) From a strictly geographic point of view, this is a somewhat artificial designation, for these three countries do not constitute a region with obvious comprehensively delimiting natural boundaries. The choice to so define the term reflects a history linked to European colonialism and the eventual limits of what became British East Africa, since the Christianity in this region in particular reflects that shared history. To avoid colonial-era terminology, we have opted to use "eastern Africa" in this volume to describe the region to distinguish it from the oft-capitalized "East Africa." Yet we admit that a geographic designation and historical periodization linked to formal colonialism is not the only possible way to tell the story of Christianity in the region. It risks overlooking the specifically African ways of being-in-the-world not controlled by external events connected to Europe.[1] Still, that colonial history created a shared set of social and historical experiences, and also defines a region with shared cultural characteristics.

WHAT LIES AHEAD

We begin with the *geographical*, aware that Christianity arose in the region due to forces that depend on a geographical understanding, and because the limits and range of our subject matter only make sense in relation to the development of borders and frontiers that underwent historical transformation over time, some in close relation to specifically Christian-linked dynamics. Next comes a *chronological* chapter that explores the specifically Christian history of the region. Due to the regional specificities of how Christianity evolved in eastern Africa, it can be challenging to tell the story in a strictly chronological fashion. For example, the remarkable earliest unfolding of Christianity in Uganda has a coherence best maintained by not interrupting its narration with reminders of the challenges facing Christian mis-

1. For a good discussion, see Derek R. Peterson, "Culture and Chronology in African History," *The Historical Review* 50, no. 2 (2007): 483–97.

sionaries and African converts elsewhere over the same period. Still, there remain reasons beyond chronological order to intersperse various regional stories—especially since the same Christian denominations worked alongside (or against) each other in various places and did so with self-awareness of their coreligionists' struggles and successes.

The third chapter examines Christianity in the region through a *denominational* lens, building on the previous two chapters. The classification of types of Christianity suggested by the term "denominational"—though it can seem comparatively trouble-free in the case of larger, international bodies like Anglicans, Catholics, or Lutherans—is not objective science, especially when it comes to the churches founded by Africans themselves in eastern Africa and elsewhere. In addition, whereas in the past the smaller number of Christians in the region often possessed a deep self-awareness of their specific denominational affiliation—as well as the related insights about the kinds of Christians they were *not*—today many in the region participate in a variety of ways of being Christian in a single life, and often simultaneously.

The fourth chapter focuses on Christianity's role in the *social* and *political* realms of eastern Africa. Though necessarily revisiting content from the previous three chapters, it will deal more directly with contemporary issues facing Christians and their communities in the region. The turn to the specifically *theological* in chapter five foregrounds the practice of theology, informal and formal, in eastern Africa. The final chapter contains deeper looks at the *biographies* of influential or especially representative individuals whose experiences disclose significant aspects of Christianity in eastern Africa.

1.

Geographical

Eastern Africa: Christianity, the Land, and Its Peoples

Eastern Africa contains abundant geological and biological diversity, enjoying renown for possessing some of the world's most breathtaking sights. Tourists flock to majestic mountains in all three countries, enjoy Indian Ocean beaches, and observe wildlife in national parks. Though popularly appreciated, such features have less importance for the region's Christianity than mundane aspects of its geography that, with related historical forces, shaped past and present experiences of Christian believers and communities.

A world-Christianity perspective discloses constant regional interactions that shaped Christianity's unfolding, and Christian realities in eastern Africa likewise have depended upon changes elsewhere. These included early modern Portuguese exploration, the nineteenth-century European Christian missionary resurgence that overlapped with colonial-imperial expansion, Indian Ocean Christian dynamics linking European missionary groups throughout the region and bringing once-enslaved eastern Africans back from India, the two twentieth-century world wars, evangelical and Pentecostal renewal movements starting in the late nineteenth century, and initiatives for ecumenical rapprochement between Protestants and Catholics. As such historical trajectories reached the region, eastern African Christians absorbed and adapted them according to the particular circumstances in which local peoples lived, prayed, and believed. External historical forces shaped internal borders, political and religious, with important consequences for Christianity in eastern Africa.

DELIMITING EASTERN AFRICA

The region composed of Kenya, Tanzania, and Uganda totals 735,000 square miles, three times the size of California (Kenya, 224,000 square miles; Uganda, 147,000 square miles; Tanzania, 364,000 square miles). The current population is about 130 million people (Kenya, 45 million; Uganda, 40 million; Tanzania, 45 million). Lake Victoria, the world's second largest lake, lies at the center of the three countries, with Kenya to the north and east, Uganda to the north and west, and Tanzania to the south. The equator runs through the northern portion of Lake Victoria and across southern parts of Kenya and Uganda.

The borders between Kenya, Uganda, and Tanzania rarely coincide with defined physical markers, instead being the result of European colonialism. Yet if internal boundaries between them reflect historical contingencies, the eastern, southern, and western boundaries marking off eastern Africa itself consist mostly of discernible physical features.

Kenya and Tanzania border the Indian Ocean, which thus creates most of the eastern limit of eastern Africa. Exceptions include a considerable vertical stretch of Kenya's eastern border with Somalia and islands belonging to each country that sit off the coast. The region's southern border lies at the Ruvuma River, south of which lies Mozambique.

The western border of the region is more complex. Its southern part consists mostly of two lakes, Lake Tanganyika and Lake Malawi, at Tanzania's western boundary, which separate Tanzania from Malawi, Zambia, and the Democratic Republic of Congo (DRC). To Tanzania's northwest, more historically contingent boundaries mark off Burundi and Rwanda from Tanzania and also, in the latter case, southwestern Uganda. The western border of Uganda and the northwestern border of the region is made up largely of two additional ample lakes, Lake Edward and Lake Albert, along with two mountain ranges: the Virunga Mountains south of Lake Edward and the Rwenzori Mountains between the lakes. These features mark most of Uganda's border with the DRC, but the northern part is more arbitrary, extending to the west of the Albert Nile (a section of the Nile River) so that three northwestern districts of present-day Uganda jut into the DRC.

The region's northern border separates Uganda from South Sudan—an independent country only since 2011—and Kenya from the southeast corner of South Sudan and Ethiopia. Those boundaries occasionally align with rivers, but mostly derive from historical factors instead of geographic logic.

Christianity's story in eastern Africa has not obeyed the region's internal or external borders. Christianity came from outside—mostly the Indian Ocean, also some from the north. Missionary efforts, too, Africans' and others', have transcended borders. Territories assigned to Catholic missionary groups, for example, spilled from Sudan into northern Uganda, and from Tanzania into Rwanda and Burundi. Earnest evangelizers associated with the East African Revival moved from Rwanda to Uganda, then throughout the region and beyond. More recently, refugees into and out of the region have brought Christians elsewhere in—Rwandese, Burundian, and Sudanese—and taken eastern African Christians out—Ugandans to Sudan, for example. And today nearly every sizeable Christian group in eastern Africa partakes in international networks creating global relationships that transcend regional and national borders. The borders, however, remain important in shaping the unfolding of Christianity in the region.

GEOGRAPHIC AND DEMOGRAPHIC FEATURES

All three countries have islands populated for centuries. Kenya's and Tanzania's are mostly in the Indian Ocean. Tanzania prominently includes Zanzibar, a term from the Persian for "black," *zanj*, referring to the island of Zanzibar itself, whose main town is also called Zanzibar, as well as the collectivity that includes the island of Zanzibar along with Pemba and other smaller islands nearby. The ancient port of Mombasa represents Kenya's most important Indian Ocean island, and unlike Zanzibar it is quite close to the coast. Both Mombasa and Zanzibar served as gateways for Europeans' (and thus Christianity's) reentry into the region in the nineteenth century, nearly a century and a half after the Portuguese departure.

As Muslim strongholds for centuries, the Indian Ocean islands' importance to Christianity is mostly historical, and their Christian population, like that of the coast, remains small. Yet because they were entry points for missionaries until recently, both Mombasa and Zanzibar, like other sites at the coasts of Kenya and Tanzania, housed the earliest Christian missionary presence. Catholics, Anglicans, and Lutherans have most of their earliest cathedrals at the coast or offshore islands: at Zanzibar, Mombasa, or Dar es Salaam, a mainland port founded by the Sultan of Zanzibar in the late nineteenth century before European colonialism had formalized. The Sultan's new port-city on the *tanga*, Swahili for "coast," became the first capital of Tanganyika (*nyika* means "wilderness" in Swahili), and, after Zanzibar joined in 1964, Tanzania. Both the Kenyan and Tanzanian coasts remained important staging areas for missionary expansion through independence in the early 1960s. Meanwhile, Tanzania's capital moved inland to Dodoma in 1973.

All three countries also claim islands in Lake Victoria. Tanzania's Ukerewe Island and those belonging to Uganda, especially the Ssese Islands, have the largest populations and greatest historical significance. The populations on these lake islands are small and, like most of the rest of each country, mostly Christian, with the predominant type of Christianity in each usually traceable to early missionary influence.

Eastern Africa's climate, landscape, flora, and fauna all drew Europeans, including Christian missionaries, into the region beginning in the nineteenth century. The weather is pleasant for, despite the equatorial setting, the typical inland altitudes make the region's climate relatively mild for the most part. Thus, though coastal regions near the Indian Ocean and low-lying plains are predictably warm and humid, Europeans found most of the region comfortable and attractive. Its largely pleasant climate meant that, unlike western Africa, eastern Africa never became reputed as "a white man's grave," a difference that drew missionaries even though mortality rates could be high, largely due to malaria.

It was also interesting land, for a variety of reasons. All three countries share Lake Victoria's shores, long sources of food and livelihood for coastal residents as well as a curiosity for geographers. At the lake's northern edge, Jinja, Uganda marks one claimed starting point of the White Nile, which forms the world's longest river with the Blue Nile in Khartoum before heading north to Egypt. Lake Tanganyika, the world's second deepest lake, houses one of the world's most diverse collections of fish. Other Rift Valley lakes in Uganda help designate Africa's "Great Lakes region," that is, Uganda and Tanzania, as well as Rwanda, Burundi, and eastern DRC.

The Rift Valley itself, a deep depression in the earth's surface formed as the eastern African tectonic plate separated from the rest of the continent, runs south from the Dead Sea in Israel/Palestine across Ethiopia and into northern Kenya. There it splits, with its eastern branch entering Tanzania from Kenya, while the western branch crosses into Uganda. This fissure creates dramatic scenery for travelers, who descend into and rise out of it as they traverse the region. Its fertile floor also permits agricultural bounty, another draw, along with scientific curiosity and evangelizing zeal, for nineteenth-century Europeans: explorers, colonialists, investors, and Christian missionaries.

Africa's three highest mountains are located in eastern Africa: Mount Kilimanjaro in Tanzania, Kenya's eponymous Mount Kenya, and Mount Margherita, part of the Ruwenzori range in western Uganda. These mountains, along with Mount Elgon on Uganda's eastern border with Kenya, have long shaped local ecologies and held abundant populations, also attracting explorers, missionaries, and, today, tourists. The mountainous regions of each country possess numerous microclimates.

In addition, Europeans wanted to understand the notable wildlife. Some of the world's largest migrations of large mammals occur in the region, making it a revered destination for safari-goers to the present day. The Serengeti, stretching over the border between Tanzania and Kenya, is particularly notable, while the world's largest inactive, intact, and unfilled volcanic caldera, the Ngorongoro Crater, allows unique wildlife viewing. Such places were underpopulated, making them less interesting to Christian missionaries as sites of evangelization, but descriptions of the land and its animals featured in much missionary writing, including that which sought to gain financial support.

In response to the physical beauty, European visitors, including missionaries, have long extolled eastern Africa. Africans, too, have appreciated their land. Thus, Kenyan writer Ngugi wa Thiong'o in his classic novel *The River Between* depicts a character admiring its lushness: "The land was fertile. It was the whole of Gikuyu country from one horizon embracing the heavens to the other hidden in the clouds."[1] Tensions with European colonizers over land seizures in the nineteenth and twentieth centuries thus naturally also led to some African accusations that missionaries shared in the processes that disempowered and disenfranchised them.

Today's production capacities also have relationships to Christianity. In some places, temperate conditions generate abundant agricultural productivity. These include tea and coffee, whose cultivation began in colonial times and often with missionary support. The region's mineral resources do not equal neighboring DRC or southern Africa, yet small amounts of precious metals have been mined in Tanzania, and Uganda has had considerable copper and cobalt production. Oil was discovered in western Uganda in 2006, and moves are being made toward extraction. Ethical issues linked to the extraction of natural resources have increasingly been part of Christian theological reflection.

1. Ngugi Wa Thiong'o, *The River Between* (Nairobi: Heinemann, 1965), 2.

HUMAN PREHISTORY AND ETHNO-LINGUISTIC DIVERSITY

Eastern Africa represents one of the oldest places on earth where *Homo sapiens* emerged. From there—in the Rift Valley or nearby, perhaps southern Ethiopia—our species populated the globe through migrations starting between fifty and a hundred thousand years ago, according to a narrow accord among scholars.

The origins of the region's ethnic and linguistic differences are the subject of great debate and such differences also shaped the emergence of Christianity in the region, helping to determine missionary strategies and African responses to evangelization. The presence of extreme DNA diversity among a few peoples suggests that these groups, socially marginalized at present and less Christian than other neighboring groups, represent the region's (and thus maybe the world's) oldest more or less homogeneous populations. These include hunter-gatherers in eastern Uganda and northern Tanzania, and so-called Pygmoid people-groups currently residing in southwestern Uganda as well as Rwanda and the DRC. Along with southern Africa's Kalahari Desert residents, the Khoi-San, these peoples might be the remote ancestors of everyone else, including their mostly Bantu neighbors. Recent research suggests that nearly one quarter of the specifically human DNA in some such African groups is found nowhere else in the world.[2]

Both cultural practices and economic production differentiate eastern African people groups, and Christianity evolved in relationship to such differences. People's livelihoods overlapped with their ethno-linguistic identity in the region in obvious ways, and missionary practices selectively targeted groups based on language and culture. Self-identified cattle-keepers, sometimes called pastoralists and at times claiming to shun agricultural cultivation, have long predominated in northeastern

2. C. A. Lambert and S. A. Tishkoff, "Genetic Structure in African Populations: Implications for Human Demographic History," *Cold Spring Harbor Symposia on Quantitative Biology* 74 (2009): 395–402. See the discussion of the research of Sarah Tishkoff in *Nature* 488 (August 2012): 8, https://tinyurl. com/y8d7gnpr.

Uganda and much of Kenya, along with parts of Tanzania. Meanwhile agriculture predominates in southern and western Uganda, central Kenya, and northern and western Tanzania. In the latter regions, Christianity has tended to grow more quickly. Yet both population groups keep cattle, which play a large role in cultural practices of exchange like marriage across the region. Ocean-coastal and lakeside populations have long supplied their diets through fishing and trade—including trade extending for millennia to the Middle East and Asia for those at the Indian Ocean coast.

Language families, linked partially with biological homogeneity and shared cultural features, also differentiate the region's peoples. Most eastern Africans speak a language in the Bantu language family, linked to a prehistorical migration from Cameroon, with reasons for historical distinctions in language and culture hard to know since oral traditions vary. Bantu languages include Kenya's Kikuyu and Kamba, Uganda's Baganda and Banyoro, and Tanzania's Chagga and Nyamwezi—among whom most today are Christian. Bantu speakers are believed to have displaced preceding hunter-gatherers and cultivated the Lake Victoria Basin between two and three millennia ago. Bantu speakers also became proficient metallurgists specializing in iron smelting—a skill that proved profitable following their migration into southern parts of Uganda. In coastal eastern Africa, the Bantu tongue Swahili became the dominant language, with many Arabic-linked words, and its use has spread, reinforcing shared cultural and linguistic features with most of the region's other inhabitants. This has created a set of Bantu-linked ways of speaking and behaving common across much of eastern—as well as much of central and southern—Africa.

Yet not all the peoples speak Bantu languages. About a quarter of the region's people speak a Nilotic language like Luo or Acholi, the result of historical factors—likely migration patterns from Sudan—whose details elude historical precision. This shaped Christianity's evolution, since both Protestant and Catholic missionaries drew on the Bantu-Nilotic distinction in developing evangelizing strategies. They generally favored Bantu groups, whose more centralized political organization and (once having learned one Bantu language) less daunting linguistic barriers made conversions appear more attainable. Finally, there are small numbers of speakers of other language groups—Cushitic-language users in northern Tanzania, for example, and a larger number of Maa-linked speakers related to other Nilotic speakers. Most are pastoralists who have long been seen as resistant to Christian evangelization. These linguistic variations overlap loosely with the cultivation and husbandry differences, since a disproportionate number of so-called pastoralists speak non-Bantu languages and live in northern Kenya and Uganda, and in northern Tanzania, too. Such regions are sparsely populated, mostly with such traditional cattle-keepers.

The national boundaries separating the countries of eastern Africa do not respect these linguistic and ethnic divisions in any direct way. Instead the nations' borders are mostly traceable to European colonial impact beginning in the nineteenth century. Yet these ethnic and linguistic identities have been central to the unfolding of Christianity in eastern Africa, organizing missionary strategy and affecting how Christianity was received and transformed. Missionaries organized their practices in relationship to groups as they discerned them, and African peoples responded to Christianity in relationship to those they thought of as sharing their culture and language.

POLITICS AND COMMERCE IN EASTERN AFRICA PRIOR TO EUROPEAN CONTACT

Frontiers and boundaries—geographically based or not—have of course shaped the region and its peoples, including political developments. Waterways brought the first visitors to the region and also allowed eastern Africans to venture out. The Indian Ocean coastal peoples of today's Kenya and Tanzania have long engaged in transoceanic trading, as mentioned in classical sources like the Periplus of the Erythraean (or Red) Sea, a first-century Greek description of many ancient ports including those of the Indian Ocean. Global trade is attested to as well by coins and pottery traceable to the Roman Empire and ancient China. Intercontinental connections also exposed the region to other languages, notably Arabic, whose words shaped about one-third of Swahili. These trade connections also brought Islam to the region by the ninth century and allowed the political powers of the coast—increasingly Muslim—to expand their influence inland through trade. The coastal region of eastern Africa also first encountered Europeans through Portuguese contact starting in the late fifteenth century, leading to Portuguese trading posts in Kilwa, Mombasa, Zanzibar, and smaller sites along the coast.

Intermittent local resistance finally pushed the Portuguese out by the early eighteenth century, yet it was not only Europeans who sought control over the eastern African coast. By the time of nineteenth-century western European contact, Zanzibar's regime, which had come from Oman earlier in the century, claimed power over much of eastern Africa, though in practice their control was tenuous and contested.

The longstanding presence of Islam at the coast has meant that though Christian missionaries came to eastern Africa through Zanzibar and Mombasa, the growth of Christianity there and at the coast has been slow from the beginning. Even the most determined nineteenth-century European missionaries accepted that large-scale conversions lay inland, away from Islamic influence. Their appraisal has been fulfilled, with the populations of coastal Kenya and Tanzania, along with the islands off each nation's coast, remaining largely Muslim, while Christianity has become the majority religion nearly everywhere else.

This set of historical and geographical realities forges an interesting contrast with the geographic and religious situation shaping Islam and Christianity in western Africa. There ancient Muslim polities arose after believers crossed the Sahara from northern Africa, occupying the northern parts of what are today Nigeria, Ghana, and countries further north. Thus, when European Christian missionaries arrived at the Atlantic coast in the early modern period, they did not face the entrenched coastal Islamic populations of eastern Africa. Consequently, in the religiously divided countries of western Africa, coastal regions have become primarily Christian, while the interior remains more Muslim. The converse is true in eastern Africa, with the Indian Ocean coast primarily Muslim and the interior largely Christian. The concentration of Muslims in each region also shaped the unfolding of colonialism later, as Europeans discouraged Christian missionaries from active proselytizing in Muslim regions—in eastern and western Africa—one consequence being that Christianized areas developed greater educational, industrial, and healthcare infrastructures. In western Africa, that has meant greater indices of development in the areas *near* the Atlantic Ocean, while in eastern Africa the areas *away* from the Indian Ocean have better health and education standards.

Inland the shaping of eastern African political and cultural realities by geography prior to European contact eludes easy generalizations, but its results affected developing Christianity. Precolonial societies and states knew boundaries delineated by rocks, hills, and water points such as rivers, streams, and swamps. People migrated from ancestral homelands, crossed boundaries, and settled in new lands, redefining their collective identities in relationship to new locales.

Centuries of historical change prior to written records created numerous small-scale political identities before European contact in the nineteenth century—overlapping and sometimes interlinked chiefdoms with occasional attempts to consolidate political power by ambitious local populations or potentates. At times rather short-lived dynasty-like polities, depicted as kingdoms, emerged in some places, as among the Shambaa of northeastern Tanzania.[3] Most areas, however, developed less centralized polities—small-scale groups loosely linked to similar bodies through language, culture, and trade. Older scholars distinguished rather firmly between so-called "acephalous" (literally "headless") and "centralized" political orders, a distinction these days seen as overdrawn and latent with racist-evolutionist overtones. Recognizing those limitations in the terms, nonetheless many of the peoples of eastern Africa gravitated toward something like the former rather than the latter.

When the European incursion came in the latter nineteenth century, however, the situation differed rather dramatically in the so-called Great Lakes region of southern and western Uganda and northwestern Tanzania—as well as Rwanda and

3. Steven Feierman, *Peasant Intellectuals: Anthropology and History in Tanzania* (Madison: University of Wisconsin Press, 1990).

Burundi. In those areas, for reasons subject to historical dispute, larger-scale political entities developed. Nineteenth-century Europeans encountering these peoples unhesitatingly recognized some as "kingdoms," a designation only rarely conferred on polities elsewhere in eastern Africa. Hierarchical caste-like social order, bureaucratic-monarchical ruling structures, dynastic self-understandings, and historical claims of a lengthy multigenerational past among ruling families featured famously among the Baganda, the people of the kingdom of Buganda, and also among other Great Lakes peoples. Their hierarchical solidarity—that is, a naturalized identification with political rulers—proved advantageous when Christian missionaries arrived. Such centralized kingdoms witnessed historically momentous large-scale conversions starting in the late nineteenth century, with people following their kings into Christianity.

By the mid-nineteenth century, a foreign trading presence was growing in the region around Lake Victoria, connected to Swahili traders from the Indian Ocean and, to a lesser degree, traders from the Sudan. As distinctive kingdoms emerged, their interregional trading also increased. The kingdom of Buganda in what is now south-central Uganda forged especially strong relations with Arab traders from Zanzibar, trading cotton and guns for slaves and iron. In addition, Buganda practiced a system of kingship by clan lottery and proved unique in its primary economic reliance on agriculture as opposed to cattle. Each factor contributed to the maintenance of comparatively equitable social relations and political stability. The resultant internal cohesiveness of the Baganda kingdom allowed it to serve as a refuge to peoples suffering the instability and power struggles within other regional kingdoms. Further, the high degree of centralization within the Bagandan system of organization —around a single king, or *kabaka*—provided a strong base for expansion, particularly in comparison to the nearby Bunyoro-Kitara kingdom in what is today western Uganda, whose widening boundaries led to a decentralization of power and lack of royal oversight.

Growth in fishing on Lake Victoria also helped Buganda

to grow as an economic and cultural force. Trade around the lake had long existed, and by the seventeenth century, coastal peoples began to venture to the lake's islands to increase their catch when they could not get enough fish along the bays. The kabakas soon organized fishing expeditions, which took royal-sponsored fishermen further to unknown islands where more fish might be caught. Luganda, the language of Buganda, became widely spoken by the traders, eventually becoming the commercial language. These trade routes allowed fishermen from Uganda to exchange various commodities with their Nilotic- and Bantu-speaking neighbors, including iron ornaments like bangles, leg-rings, armbands, and earrings, along with bananas, salt, and fish, as well as slaves, many of whom were taken to Zanzibar.

In addition to novelty items, coastal traders also brought religion, and Islam assumed an early following in some parts of eastern Africa. Although in competition with later Christian efforts, Islam expedited various social changes that proved beneficial for future Christian ideas and frameworks. Islam exposed local peoples to the notions of a single God, a holy book, and strong moral imperatives, and also emphasized literacy. Christianity later mobilized the printing press and other resources to capitalize even more on fascination with literacy. In addition, an early nineteenth-century change in the Baganda kingdom had separated the role of king and high priest in the local religion. This allowed the kabaka to explore Islam (and later Christianity) without undermining his ongoing, if less central, religious role in the traditional religion.

Nineteenth-century European explorers drew attention to these advanced kingdoms in "the heart of darkest Africa," especially in Buganda—sprawling courts, sophisticated regional networks linking local chiefs to the royal center, formal ceremonies reminiscent of Versailles and Buckingham Palace, and a monarchical genealogy that counted generations back further than Queen Victoria's. Soon the political centralization of the peoples in the Great Lakes region attracted the attention of missionaries, Protestant and Catholic. Both groups had toiled, briefly first at the coast and in the regions between the coast and the Great Lakes, where less centralized polities were the norm, with disappointing results. Former slaves constituted most of their early converts. The presence of these kingdoms further inland, however, led missionaries to imagine large-scale conversions as in Europe's first millennium, when the baptism of monarchs presaged the Christianization of their peoples. To a degree rare in world history, such hopes came to fulfillment, first and most swiftly in Uganda, especially in the kingdom of Buganda, where both Anglican and Catholic converts emerged very quickly after initial contact with European missionaries in the 1870s, and where large churches of both denominations were already in place by the early twentieth century.

THE BACKGROUND OF CONTEMPORARY POLITICAL BOUNDARIES

Kenya, Tanzania, and Uganda each have a distinct history that forged its current boundaries, mostly traceable to the colonialism that ended with the independence they received from the United Kingdom. Uganda received formal independence in 1962 and Kenya in 1963. Tanzania was formed in 1964, after independence was given first to Tanganyika—the continental part of the current country of Tanzania—that then joined Zanzibar, which had also formally been given independence. "Tanzania" was a neologism, the "Tan" joined with the "Zan." In all three cases there were preliminary steps—elections, Commonwealth membership, and conferral of self-rule—that predated formal independence. Early elections, especially in Uganda, sowed seeds of later political unrest. In none of the cases do the formal present boundaries of the country go back further than the late nineteenth century, when European colonial activity began in eastern Africa.

Though the borders themselves depended on the so-called "scramble for Africa" in which European powers carved up the continent, the claims of the Sultan of Zanzibar to the hinterland opposite on the mainland provided the framework for many aspects of the region's eventual colonial and then post-independence borders. Having moved their royal residence from Oman to Zanzibar by 1840, succeeding sultans made claims leading to a proliferation of treaties and agreements, formal and informal, with local political entities, many of whom existed only briefly. Other coastal rulers, like those inland, paid intermittent attention to Zanzibari claims to overrule, which likewise were intermittently enforceable. Yet such claims from Zanzibar could at times extend to much of eastern Africa, even though aside from sponsoring and arming caravans that brought slaves and ivory to the coast from inland areas, the sultans often had little authority over the region, especially before the 1860s. Nonetheless, much of the borders of what are today Kenya and Tanzania draw upon the Sultan's earlier claims.

Already by the mid-nineteenth century, a number of European and other countries had representatives in Zanzibar overseeing their national interests in the region, mostly linked to trade. As missionaries arrived in the latter nineteenth century, such diplomatic posts supported and defended missionaries, and also loosely sponsored scientific and exploratory caravans from the coast.

Diplomatic presence led to exploration, which brought Christian missionaries from Europe. Famous English explorers leading expeditions into eastern Africa included Richard Burton and John Speke in 1857 and 1858, then later Speke and James Grant in 1863, leading to the European discoveries of Lake Tanganyika and Lake Victoria (then called Victoria Nyanza). The 1869 opening of the Suez Canal made travel to eastern Africa easier and Henry Morton Stanley, who in 1871 found the lost English missionary doctor David Livingstone in western Tanzania, returned a few years later to circumnavigate the two lakes. Livingstone himself died soon after in Zambia, and his desiccated body, carried for thousands of miles by his African colleagues, embarked for England from Bagamoyo, an Indian Ocean port in Tanzania where Catholics had founded a renowned mission in 1868.

The European press and political leaders followed the explorers' achievements and only later did formal colonial rule take place. The impetus for European engagement in eastern Africa thus drew upon varying impulses alive in the nineteenth century: zeal for evangelization, scientific and geographic curiosity, search for economic gain through resource exploitation, humanitarian concerns especially to counter the slave trade, and, perhaps most significantly, European rivalries in which eastern Africa became another theater for competition—especially as others sought to counter the British. Such rivalries led to the partition of the Sultan's supposed territories—and those claimed by other rulers in, for example, the Great Lakes region—by the British and the Germans. Final arrangements depended on agreements between European powers, which received and made concessions elsewhere in Africa—and sometimes beyond —as international jostling assigned huge swathes of the globe to governments in London, Paris, Lisbon, Brussels, and Berlin.

THE SCRAMBLE FOR AFRICA IN EASTERN AFRICA: POLITICAL AND RELIGIOUS

The earliest missionaries into nineteenth-century eastern Africa arrived connected to their own homes and the lands of their missionary agencies. In Kenya, this meant the United Kingdom for the Anglican Church Missionary Society (CMS), which sent the German Lutheran Johannes Krapf and associates in 1844, as well as for Thomas Wakefield and other British Methodists, who arrived in 1862. In Tanzania, it was first the French Catholic Church for the Spiritan (or Holy Ghost) missionaries who came to Zanzibar in the early 1860s, moving to the coast at Bagamoyo in 1868. Anglicans linked to the Universities' Mission to Central Africa (UMCA) came to Zanzibar in 1864 after a failed mission further south on the Zambezi River. In the 1870s, a more ambitious contingent of CMS missionaries came to Uganda, spurred by explorer Henry Morton Stanley's reports of a "civilized" kingdom in the heart of Africa—the Baganda in today's Uganda. The CMS was soon followed inland by a second Catholic missionary society to enter eastern Africa, the Missionaries of Africa, commonly known as the White Fathers. Mostly French like the Spiritans, the Missionaries of Africa also worked in inland Tanzania.

Rivalries between these missionaries occurred naturally, with denomination and nation coinciding as European contentions played out, first rather inconsequentially at the Indian Ocean, later with more dramatic consequences in Uganda as Anglican and Catholic missionaries and their followers reprised a global French-British rivalry. The impetus for the fuller transfer of European political rivalries into the region, however—and a direct cause of contemporary national boundaries—came with German explorer-adventurer Carl Peters, founder of the Society for German Colonization in 1884. Peters's activities in eastern Africa included dubious treaties with local rulers in Tanzania, eventually giving rise to the German East Africa Company (DOAG) in 1885. The 1884–85 Berlin Conference, which gathered fourteen European powers under the German Chancellor Otto von Bismarck's lead to discuss Africa's future and set rules for European engagements, had formalized German inclusion in the colonial-imperial scramble for Africa. The British, then embarking on a decades-long rivalry with Germany, responded with their own organization in pursuit of commercial interests, the Imperial British East African Company (IBEAC), centered in Mombasa and soon represented in Uganda. In each case, these commercial bodies laid the ground for formal colonial over-rule—the Germans in Tanganyika and the British in Kenya and Uganda.

Through a series of treaties between the Germans and British, and at times between each and the increasingly marginalized Zanzibari Sultan or even less powerful local rulers, eastern Africa over time was parceled out between the two European nations. In 1887, the Zanzibar Sultan conferred his claimed lands in Kenya to the IBEAC, and over the next years Germany assumed control over what would be called Tanganyika, forcing the Sultan to cede the entire mainland. Meanwhile the British took steps to control Uganda through the IBEAC, though soon the Foreign Office assumed direct control over both the future Uganda and Kenya, initially called the East Africa Protectorate, later the Protectorate of Uganda and, after 1920, the Crown Colony of Kenya. In 1890, the Heligoland-Zanzibar Treaty confirmed British influence in Zanzibar, while the Germans were given a small bit of land in what is now Namibia as well as Heligoland—a onetime British territory in the North Sea near

Germany. This meant German confinement of its claims in eastern Africa to the mainland of Tanganyika.[4]

Various rebellions against German overrule in Tanganyika arose starting in the late 1880s, each crushed, and the British squelched uprisings in Uganda and Kenya as well. After the 1896 Anglo-Zanzibari War, the shortest in recorded history—forty-seven minutes—British shelling of the fortress at Zanzibar led to the reluctant Sultan's surrender, not to mention 500 Zanzibari casualties. As Africa entered the era of high imperialism, with nearly the entire continent under European control, eastern Africa was effectively partitioned as the British East Africa Protectorate and German East Africa.

The borders of Kenya, Uganda, and Tanzania were mostly set by the dawn of the twentieth century. The Uganda railroad reached Nairobi from Mombasa in 1899, Lake Victoria at Kisumu in Kenya two years later, and Kampala in 1930. The Germans followed suit, so that railways connected major cities in Tanganyika by 1910. World War I saw significant conflict in the region, with thousands of Africans impressed by colonial officials in the British and German areas. Bloody battles ensued on land and sea, with guerilla tactics employed, at great cost to Africans on both sides. At war's end, the Germans lost control of their African possessions, with Tanganyika passing under British administration due to a League of Nations mandate. Uganda's territories were augmented by the addition of districts west of the Nile River, including the current West Nile. The political scramble for Africa, for the most part, ended.

Overlapping with political processes eventuating in British East Africa, however, had also been a similar ecclesial scramble. The largest and constant fault-line arose between Catholic and Protestant missionaries, and sometimes between their African followers across the region. Different Protestant groups also, however, opposed one another—even differing groups of Anglicans, as more evangelical, low-church CMS missionaries opposed the Anglo-Catholic, high-church UMCA. Most, however, eventually accepted comity agreements to respect each other's territory—exceptions being especially hard-charging

4. German East Africa also included what are today Rwanda and Burundi and a small bit of what is northern Mozambique, all relinquished after World War I.

evangelicals and later Pentecostals. Catholics theoretically could not accept such agreements with Protestants, though in practice they often did so.

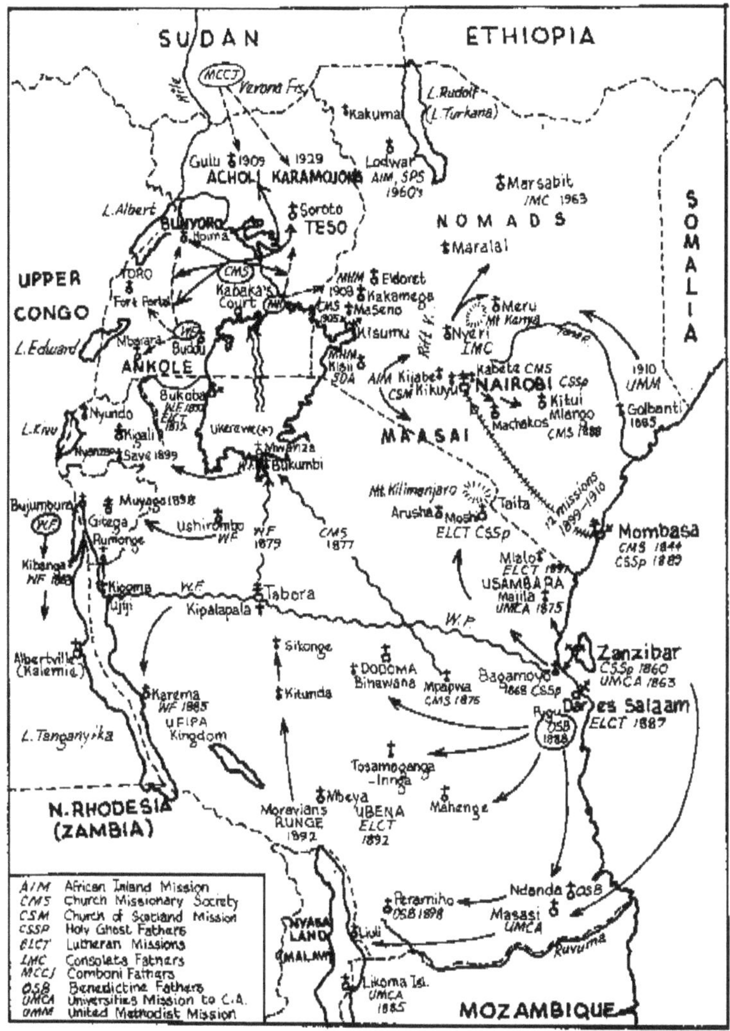

Missionary Foundations in East Africa

Catholics also disagreed among themselves. Both the Spiritans, first at the coast of eastern Africa, and Comboni missionaries, who eyed eastern Africa after moving down from Sudan beginning in the nineteenth century, expressed dismay when the White Fathers received permission in the 1870s to work in western Tanzania and Uganda. Later, early twentieth-century Spiritans in Kenya bitterly watched Consolata missionaries receive Rome's permission to evangelize central Kenya, which they had eyed for their own work. The conferral of southern Tanganyika on German Benedictines—linked to German colonial control—drew less ire from the Spiritans. And the White Fathers themselves agreed, with varying degrees of reluctance, to welcome British-based Mill Hill missionaries to eastern Uganda and western Kenya. Catholic orders and societies later coming to work in the region, whether male or female, all did so by working under the authority of these six first Catholic groups or, in the case of some male societies, by taking over territory first assigned to one of the six.

The complex unfolding of the Vatican's demarcations of missionary territories to differing groups in the region can be bewildering, as are terms describing the units conferred. Partly this resulted from theoretical medieval papal claims to global control clashing with the political realities of nation-states in the modern world and related ecclesiastical realities. Propaganda Fide, the Vatican's mission office founded in 1622, assigned mission territories in places not governed by treaties with Catholic monarchs—which meant all of eastern Africa. And over several centuries a system of evolving titles for mission territories had been developed. Initial assignments defined *apostolic prefectures*, which, as they grew, became *apostolic vicariates* that had the equivalent of a bishop in a mission territory, and finally evolved into proper dioceses. In practice, the granting of permission to evangelize particular groups, varying rates of growth in missionized areas, changing political realities on the ground, and the vagaries of Vatican politics created labyrinthine arrangements. Changing Catholic jurisdictions usually made little difference on the ground, but at times they shaped Christian experiences quite decisively—for instance during times of war and resulting changes in political overrule, when missionaries from a declared enemy nation found themselves in unfriendly territory and suffered expulsion or internment.

EASTERN AFRICA UNDER COLONIAL CONTROL

Colonialism cemented political control by Europeans, who sought to rule indirectly through indigenous agents like the kabaka of Buganda when possible. Christianity helped at times, lending legitimacy to local rulers like the kabaka. Colonial overrule also joined Christianity in binding eastern Africa into the German and British empires, with education an important accompanying process. This political incorporation along with skills derived from schooling aroused and allowed resistance of various sorts, with consequent uprisings and violent suppressions. It also brought some new resources to the region—infrastructure like railways, medicines, other technologies—and people, both Europeans and others like Indians from south Asia linked to the British Commonwealth. Among the earliest Catholics in eastern Africa, for example, were immigrants from Goa, the Portuguese colony in western India, long a Catholic stronghold and a source for British colonial skilled labor. Kenya in particular also became a favored settlement colony for the British, especially veterans of World War I, and many Germans settled in Tanganyika prior to World War I. This large-scale immigration—like that in South Africa—created tensions with local populations and, at times, with missionaries seeking to protect converts from labor impressment and other colonial indignities.

Considerable disruptions to Christian missions occurred during World War I, with mission stations destroyed in Kenya and Tanganyika. British and French missionaries in Tanganyika suffered internment or expulsion before the German defeat, and German missionaries faced the same treatment after. World War II saw few changes in borders—German and Italian missionaries were interned, however—and Tanganyika's status changed to a United Nations trust territory under British control. Though in retrospect the move to independence for all three countries in less than two decades—as with most of the rest of the colonized world—looks inevitable, in fact the British desire to relinquish colonial overrule in eastern Africa was anything but coherent or unanimous. Nor did eastern Africans view colonialism in the same way. Frustrations at colonial overrule along with the provision of a fine colonial education to a few created a group in eastern Africa anxious to take their place among the nations of the world. Nearly all were educated by Christian missionaries. Meanwhile, over the same years, colonial officials had selectively relied on local rulers in their policy of indirect rule, with the British rather boldly inventing local monarchies in this effort, for instance among the Basoga in eastern Uganda. Some new monarchs feared a loss of authority in an independent nation.

Amidst the variety of anti-colonial movements in eastern Africa, two deserve special mention: the Maji Maji uprising in southern Tanganyika from 1905 to 1907, and the Mau Mau emergency in Kenya, which ran from 1952 to 1959. In both cases, land seizures and disenfranchisement of local peoples occurred beforehand. In the first case, German incursions prompted resistance, and in the second, English settlers in Kenya took land for their plantations largely from the Kikuyu, who formed the largest part of the Mau Mau insurgents.

GEOGRAPHIC DYNAMICS IN THE POST-INDEPENDENCE PERIOD

The present-day boundaries of the countries of eastern Africa have not formally changed since independence. Their borders, however, have been sites of important historical processes and events at times over the past five decades, at times with implications for Christian belief and practice.

Dynamics at these borders have taken different forms. Much of the activity has been unrelated to Christianity in any obvious way. For instance, when Idi Amin declared war on Tanzania in 1978, claiming historical rights to the Kagera region in Tanzania's far northwest, his invasion prompted a war that toppled him, with Tanzanian troops aided by Ugandan dissidents taking Kampala in April 1979. Similarly, religious considerations had no obvious role in small-scale border clashes at overland border posts between Uganda and Kenya in the 1980s.

On the other hand, Christianity has been active at those borders as well. Church-linked relief agencies have played key roles in caring for refugees who entered the region fleeing violence in their homes. Some of that violence has had religious overtones. Such refugee situations have included Rwandese and Burundians who came to all three countries starting in the 1960s and continuing through the 1990s, Congolese who have entered Uganda, and Sudanese (and more recently, South Sudanese) coming mostly to Uganda and Kenya. Christian agencies that have responded include Protestant groups like Lutheran World Relief, Mennonite Central Committee, and World Vision, along with Catholic groups like Caritas International, US-based Catholic Relief Services, and the Jesuit Refugee Service. In turn, Ugandans fleeing their own country's violence in the 1970s and 1980s, especially in the north, fled to Sudan for refuge.

***

These geographic and geopolitical issues linked to the boundaries and borders of eastern Africa and its constituent countries have naturally played an important role in the unfolding history of Christianity in the region, to which we now turn.

2.

Chronological

Christianity's Unfolding in Eastern Africa

The history of Christianity in eastern Africa can be told from a number of distinct yet interrelated perspectives: as a stage in the unfolding of the world Christian movement understood as a global phenomenon; as an important aspect of the religious lives of people who have dwelled in the current countries of Uganda, Kenya, and Tanzania; as the myriad localizations of a world religion in a loosely defined region with many distinct local histories and dynamic sociocultural matrices; and as the proliferation of numerous Christian social forms shaped by people subject to particular historical and social forces over time. This chapter will focus on broad historical trends and dates that mark events of significance for Christianity in eastern Africa and adopt a perspective that is shaped by world Christianity.[1]

1. Choosing how to tell this story from a world-Christianity perspective presupposes awareness of what has already been written on the history of Christianity previously with regard to eastern Africa. Fortunately, the history of Christianity in the entire continent has, in the past few decades, been the subject of several important single-volume studies, mostly in English. Four indispensable sources in English are: John Baur, *2000 Years of Christianity in Africa: An African Church History*, 2nd ed. (Nairobi: Daughters of St. Paul, 1998); Adrian Hastings, *The Church in Africa: 1450–1950* (Oxford: Oxford University Press, 1994); Elizabeth Isichei, *A History of Christianity in Africa: From Antiquity to the Present* (Grand Rapids: Eerdmans, 1995); and Bengt Sundkler and Christopher Steed, *The History of the Church in Africa* (Cambridge: Cambridge University Press, 2000). They are relied upon throughout the

A world-Christianity perspective in this chapter emphasizes four things. First, it *foregrounds impactful missionary practices* that had effects in the creation of what has become African Christianity. Instead of emphasizing missionary heroism or perfidy, the focus will be placed on transmission, reception, and appropriation rather than individual or collective valor or failure. Second, it *underscores the role of eastern Africans* in the formation of Christian communities and takes a broad view of Christian belonging and identity that is both ecumenical and inclusive of diverse perspectives. Third, it seeks to understand precisely *how current Christian realities emerged from the past*, appreciating the roles of particular human agency among a variety of social forces in that emergence. Fourth, it comparatively *locates eastern African Christian history in relation to other ways in which Christianity has evolved*, in Africa and elsewhere. This does not mean necessarily adopting the theological perspectives associated with the traditional discipline of church history. It does mean treating Christian phenomena in eastern Africa in light of patterns arising in other places and times as Christianity has developed.

This chapter is divided into six sections that will organize the history of Christianity in eastern Africa over time, beginning with the Portuguese story at the coast in the early modern period, through the experiences leading up to colonialism, and into the post-independence realities for Christianity in Kenya, Tanzania, and Uganda.

chapter. In addition, there are a few studies that address particular aspects of Christian history in eastern Africa. Roland Oliver, *The Missionary Factor in East Africa* (London: Longman, Green, 1952) remains a valuable summary of the missionary effort, while one of the few works since then to take a regional view is the edited collection of Thomas Spear and Isaria N. Kimambo, eds., *East African Expressions of Christianity* (Oxford: James Currey, 1999).

The postcolonial period has seen decisive changes in the dominant perspective guiding historical studies of Christianity in Africa. The earliest works prioritized the formation of Christian institutions and highlighted the role of European missionaries, while since independence there have appeared more nationalist histories, often underscoring the Christian role as abetting or impeding the nation-state's emergence. Some of the nationalist historical accounts denigrated missionaries as cultural imperialists and willful beneficiaries of colonial overrule. Both the earlier hagiographies and overt nationalist approaches yield insights, yet both also miss important aspects of the story of Christianity in Africa, in eastern Africa and elsewhere, aspects that a world-Christianity perspective on the past seeks to capture.

PORTUGUESE PRESENCE, LATE FIFTEENTH TO EARLY EIGHTEENTH CENTURY: A THWARTED START

It is possible that Christians from Egypt, Ethiopia, or other places where Christianity had roots from earlier times reached contemporary eastern Africa before the late fifteenth century, leaving no records yet discovered.[2] In recorded history, however, the first Christians to arrive in eastern Africa were Portuguese sailors led by Vasco da Gama, who landed at the Swahili port of Malindi, now part of Kenya, in 1498.

In other parts of Africa, notably the kingdom of the Kongo (in present-day Angola and the Democratic Republic of the Congo), and even to the south of eastern Africa in what is today Mozambique, Portuguese-sponsored Catholic missionary efforts bore considerable fruit. Portuguese attention to their eastern African possessions, however, was intermittent and never included extensive settlement and ambitious political overrule. Still, over those centuries, clergy often were present—a few Franciscans are reported to have been in Mombasa between 1505 and 1513.[3] Aside from modest pastoral care for the children of unions between local women and Portuguese sailors and officials, however, they did little missionary work among local people. Notably, St. Francis Xavier, the first Jesuit missionary, stopped in Malindi on his way to India in 1542.

In the later sixteenth century, organized resistance from local Swahili-speaking Muslims arose, especially around Mombasa, supported by Ottoman attacks against Europeans led by the famous Turkish admiral Mir Ali Bey in the Indian Ocean. In response, Mombasa itself and Zanzibar became two prominent Portuguese sites for ongoing fortification, with Mombasa's Fort Jesus an imposing landmark to this day. In the same period, the religious order called the Augustinians, who had other res-

2. On the Portuguese in eastern Africa, see Carlos Alonso, *A History of the Augustinians and the Martyrs of Mombasa (1568–1698)* (Nairobi: Paulines Publications, 2007), and Loreen Maseno, "Christianity in East Africa," in *The Routledge Companion to Christianity in Africa*, ed. Elias Kifon Bongmba (New York: Routledge 2016), 109–10.

3. Alonso, *History of the Augustinians*, 15.

idences throughout the Indian Ocean, established in Mombasa the first Catholic monastery in eastern Africa, and in the seventeenth century, several future local sultans received education there. The Augustinians both served the Portuguese settlers and, at times, sought to convert local peoples. Still, armed conflict occurred episodically, punctuating decades of relative stability and commercially beneficial coexistence.

Important moments for the subsequent history of Christianity in the region during the back-and-forth history of Portuguese eastern Africa are few, so that the Portuguese and Catholic endeavor in eastern Africa plays a small role in the story of world Christianity. One episode deserving mention, however, was the so-called "Massacre of the Martyrs of Mombasa" in 1631, in which a Portuguese-appointed local king, a convert to Christianity, turned on the Iberians, killing many. Their cause for canonization was begun, then abandoned for several centuries before being renewed in the 1990s by the Augustinians.

Eventually the Portuguese retook Mombasa, but their triumph was short-lived. After a series of back-and-forth campaigns over several decades, with coastal Muslims periodically calling on the Sultan of Oman for help, the Iberians were expelled for good in the early eighteenth century. They were confined to what became Portuguese East Africa, and then in 1975 came to be the independent nation of Mozambique.

The expulsion removed a formal European political and Christian religious presence from eastern Africa. Aside from a few Portuguese-based words found in Swahili, such as *padri* (priest), *meza* (table), and *mvinyo* (wine), there was little long-term impact from the Portuguese period on eastern Africa and its Christianity. Representatives of Christian churches would not return formally for nearly a century and a half.

NEW BEGINNINGS AT THE INDIAN OCEAN COAST: EASTERN AFRICA ENCOUNTERS THE MODERN MISSIONARY MOVEMENT, 1844 TO THE LATE 1870S

A variety of factors help explain Christianity's near-absence in eastern Africa from the early eighteenth to the mid-nineteenth centuries. Protestant interest in missionary activity appeared slowly and focused elsewhere, while Catholic missionary activity also remained diffused. In addition, broader European circumstances limited resources and inclination toward evangelization in eastern Africa itself. These included ongoing awareness of Muslim strength in the region, intra-European military and political conflicts, and preoccupation with exploration and lucrative colonization in the Americas and Asia. European and Christian attention to eastern Africa grew, however, with the rise of Protestant missionary energy, the revitalization of Catholic mission, the end of the Napoleonic conflicts, and humanitarian interest in stopping the region's slave trade.

Nineteenth-century missionaries entering eastern Africa, nearly all from Europe, reflected their times. Resembling like-minded Christian evangelizers in western Africa, the ambitious among them dreamed of inaugurating a chain of mission stations across the continent, bringing the light of the gospel and other benefits. They recalled Europe's history of Christianization, when the conversion of monarchs fostered the creation of Christian nations from the fourth to the fourteenth centuries. Many among them also sought to end the slave trade and bring former slaves to Christ—though rarely with the focused zeal of missionaries in western Africa. The British Protestants in particular were buoyed by the confident providentialism of the Victorian age: "they did believe that it was their task to reorder African religion, politics, society, and economy in ways decided by them and for a good as defined by them."[4] German Protestant missionaries could also carry a similar self-confidence linked to

4. Roy Bridges, "The Christian Vision and Secular Imperialism: Missionaries, Geography, and the Approach to East Africa, c. 1844–1890," in *Converting Colonialism: Visions and Realities in Mission History, 1706–1914*, ed. Dana Robert (Grand Rapids: Eerdmans, 2008), 46.

their burgeoning new nation-state, while Catholics, regardless of nationality, tended to more modest aims linked to spiritual goals.

Ordinarily both Catholic and Protestant missionaries came to Africa expecting little from Africans themselves, and some never moved beyond such narrowness of vision. Others, however, grew in their understanding of those they had come to serve. They rarely sought European political overrule deliberately, yet were predisposed to accept it given their backgrounds, becoming what one analyst calls "incidental imperialists."[5] All of them partook in a wave of European Christian missionary energy that only ebbed in the latter twentieth century.

At the heart of the modern missionary movement lay the late eighteenth-century appearance of new voluntary missionary associations among Protestants in Europe, notably in the United Kingdom. Those that would play an important role in evangelizing eastern Africa include two Anglican groups: the low-church Church Missionary Society (CMS), founded by evangelical Anglicans in 1799; and the higher-church Universities' Mission to Central Africa (UMCA), founded in 1857 with a more Anglo-Catholic outlook. In the later nineteenth century, a number of Protestant societies also appeared in Germany whose members would start their work primarily in German East Africa.

The Catholic Church likewise underwent a nineteenth-century missionary revival, a period witnessing the restoration of the Jesuits in 1814 after their 1773 papal suppression, as well as the election of mission-minded popes. Older religious orders like the Congregation of the Holy Spirit (or the Holy Ghost Fathers, or Spiritans) in France experienced renewal while new missionary societies appeared. A number of new men's congregations founded in the mid- to late nineteenth century joined the Spiritans in evangelizing eastern Africa. These included the Missionaries of Africa (or "White Fathers," after the color of their habit), also originally French, founded by Cardinal Lavigerie; the Comboni missionaries (or Verona Fathers) as well as

5. John H. Darch, *Missionary Imperialists? Missionaries, Government and the Growth of the British Empire in the Tropics, 1860–1885* (Milton Keynes, UK: Paternoster, 2009), 237–46.

Consolata missionaries from Turin, both of whom were mostly Italian; Mill Hill missionaries, centered in the United Kingdom but with many Dutch members; and missionary Benedictines of St. Ottilien, in Germany. Along with them came congregations of Catholic sisters—some new, some older—who would serve in eastern Africa. First came the *Filles de Marie* ("Daughters of Mary") from the Indian Ocean islands, later also the "White Sisters" who worked with the White Fathers, and various groups of Franciscans. Just as importantly, Catholic laypeople founded organizations for financial support of overseas missions, notably the Society of the Propagation of the Faith at Lyons in 1822, which has provided resources for Catholic missionary work in eastern Africa from the mid-nineteenth century until the present.

MODERN MISSIONARIES ENTER EASTERN AFRICA, 1844 TO 1870

Already by the 1840s, mission-minded leaders among both Protestants and Catholics sought to evangelize eastern Africa. The first European missionary to arrive in the region itself after the Portuguese departure was the German-born Johannes Krapf, who came under the sponsorship of the Anglican CMS after several years serving as a missionary in Ethiopia. Krapf arrived in Mombasa in 1844 and settled nearby at Rabai, the first of an anticipated chain of mission stations across Africa. A gifted linguist and committed explorer, Krapf traveled extensively over the next thirty years, codifying languages and writing descriptions of the flora, fauna, and geography of the region. His actual missionary exploits were more modest: a few converts, nearly all from the margins of society—a common trend—such as onetime slaves, abandoned women, and those with physical disabilities like Mringe, his first convert. They lived with him at the small Rabai mission station. In 1846, Krapf was joined by fellow German and CMS missionary Johannes Rebmann. Together they represented the entire formal Christian missionary presence in what would become Kenya for sixteen years, until a group of Methodists settled nearby at Ribe in 1862.

To the south, two years earlier, in 1860, French Catholic priests from the Indian Ocean island of Réunion—northeast of Madagascar—arrived in the city of Zanzibar. Zanzibar's population was diverse: Africans, most of them slaves; Arabs, many from Oman; Indians of a bewildering variety; and a few Europeans. Bustling due to trade in goods and human beings, Zanzibar's population grew to 150,000 by the mid-nineteenth century—perhaps 70,000 in Zanzibar town—of whom 60,000 were slaves.

As had the Protestants further north, the Catholics in Zanzibar—initially French-speaking diocesan clergy from Réunion, soon joined by nuns of the *Filles de Marie*, most of whom were of mixed African-European parentage—focused their missionary zeal on slaves. They gathered the dying, baptizing many, and they made purchases at Zanzibar's busy slave market to relieve slaves' misery and to create a Christian community of Africans, Zanzibar being at the time one of the world's last open sites of human trafficking.[6] They also discreetly welcomed those escaping slavery, proceeding carefully with their endeavors because the local Omani Muslim rulers had interests in protecting the slave-dependent economic well-being of the island.

The impetus for Catholic engagement was augmented considerably in 1862 when the Congregation of the Holy Ghost (or Spiritans) received responsibility for the Zanzibar mission from Propaganda Fide, the Vatican's missionary office. The Vatican also established the Apostolic Prefecture of Zanzibar, the official Catholic designation of a territory on its way to becoming a diocese with a bishop. The Spiritans, an older religious order that had served the monarchy as clergy in French colonies prior to the French Revolution, had been revitalized in France by a union with another order founded by François Libermann, who then assumed leadership. By the 1860s they were growing in Europe, drawing members from beyond France. They also

6. For a fuller discussion of the Spiritan evangelization of slaves, see Paul V. Kollman, *The Evangelization of Slaves and Catholic Origins in Eastern Africa* (Maryknoll, NY: Orbis, 2005). Whether the missionaries thought of the slaves they purchased as free is a contested issue. Kollman's view is that their preferred term for such people, the "children of the mission," suggests their unease with modern notions of freedom and their preferences for a view of human flourishing in which belonging to the church was paramount.

worked in Réunion and, on arriving in Zanzibar in 1863, they expanded the mission begun a few years earlier. They continued the work with those once enslaved, many of whom were children, establishing rudimentary schooling, including some technical training. With the *Filles de Marie* they also staffed a clinic-hospital, which cared for both Africans and the growing expatriate community.

In 1868, the Spiritans established a larger mission on the coast near Bagamoyo, the starting point for most of Zanzibar's caravans into the African hinterland. The Catholic mission in Bagamoyo became a renowned mission station over the next decades. Sisters joined there, too, helping to create a large physical presence that persists to this day. Thousands of Africans came to Bagamoyo, most of them former slaves, and before long the Spiritans used their new converts to establish mission stations in the interior of what is today Tanzania. Conversions of local people remained very few.

Meanwhile in 1864, Anglicans linked to the Universities' Mission to Central Africa (UMCA) also arrived in Zanzibar and established a presence after a failed attempt to found a mission further south, in what is today Malawi. The UMCA had been founded in Great Britain in response to the preaching of the famous explorer and missionary David Livingstone, who vividly described the horrors of the slave trade and the promise of African regeneration found in the three C's—Christianity, commerce, and civilization. Bishop Tozer led the first group, giving way to Edward Steere, who became a translator and expert on the KiSwahili language. Near Zanzibar town, the UMCA soon founded both a slave settlement at Mbweni and, in 1869, St. Andrew's College at Kiungani, the first site for higher education in eastern Africa. Shortly afterward, the UMCA established missions on the mainland: in 1875 at Magila, inland from Tanga to the north of Bagamoyo, and in 1876 at Masasi,[7] to the south, just north of Mozambique. Several former slaves who came to the UMCA became prominent early Christians, including John Swedi, who in 1879 became the first eastern African ordained in

7. On Masasi's founding, see R. G. P. Lambourn, "Zanzibar to Masasi in 1876: The Founding of the Masasi Mission," *Tanganyika Notes and Records* 31 (1951): 42–46.

any denomination when he became a deacon; Cecil Majaliwa, who in 1890 became the first eastern African Anglican priest; and James Mbotela, who worked with Anglican missionaries among the Kamba in Kenya.

The Catholic mission at Bagamoyo, along with the Anglican missions at Mbweni and Masasi, were early and noteworthy examples of what became the standard missionary strategy for both Catholics and Protestants in eastern Africa, as it was elsewhere in Africa, for most of the century: the mission station from which Christian activity radiated. On a sizeable piece of land granted by local authorities (often linked to the Sultan of Zanzibar, especially if near the coast), missionaries oversaw the building of residences for themselves, a place for worship, classrooms, workshops, and often a clinic. Agricultural fields surrounded the buildings, along with animals for food and plowing, and the labor of residents sustained the missions. From such centralized stations, missionaries and their assistants—usually Africans with linguistic skills and some rudimentary training from the missionaries—preached and taught in the countryside. Much of their energy also was focused on the former slaves who were almost always among the mission station's first African residents in the nineteenth century.[8] The mission sought to protect their Christians from temptations from Islam and passing European traders and explorers, who appreciated assistants who could speak both African and European languages. Over time, the missions of both Catholics and Protestants also housed schools for specialized training for catechists, teachers, and, eventually, clergy, with Catholics also preparing some for religious orders as nuns or brothers in the consecrated life. Africans living at such places often chafed at missionary discipline and sought to escape or expand their liberties, leading missionaries at Bagamoyo and Masasi to build prisons.

8. See Robert W. Strayer, *The Making of Mission Communities in East Africa: Anglicans and Africans in Colonial Kenya, 1875–1935* (London: Heinemann, 1978), and Kollman, *Evangelization of Slaves*.

ANTI-SLAVERY EFFORTS, 1860S–1890S

As Catholic and Protestant missions grew, eastern Africa increasingly drew the attention of Europeans anxious to stop the slave trade, especially the British. Some abolitionists claimed that missionary purchases of slaves only stimulated the seizure and sale of eastern Africans, a charge missionaries rebutted with mixed results. In 1873, Sir Bartle Frere (1815–1884), former governor of Bombay in India, came as an official visitor of the British crown to investigate the problem of slavery and the slave trade in the region. Frere's report, supplemented by threats of embargo and naval action against the Sultan, prompted the formal closing of the Zanzibar slave market in 1873. In 1879, the UMCA mission opened an imposing cathedral supposedly on the site of that slave market, Christ Church, which still looms over Zanzibar's Stone Town today.

Besides reporting on the slave trade, Frere also evaluated missionary efforts in the region. The Catholic mission at Bagamoyo drew his fulsome praise for its practical orientation:

> I can suggest no change in the general arrangements of the institution, with any view to increase its efficiency as an industrial and civilizing agency, and in that point of view I would recommend it as a model to be followed in any attempt to civilize or evangelize Africa.[9]

Frere, however, criticized the work of the CMS and the Methodists in Kenya as too evangelical and impractical. Their leaders, he thought, scorned the "industrial and worldly element" he found essential and which he admired among the Catholics, thus "exciting the admiration, without securing the imitation, of the people around [them]."[10]

In the wake of Frere's report, the Anglicans—in a joint undertaking by the more "low church" CMS in Kenya and "high church" UMCA centered in Zanzibar—founded a settlement

9. Sir Bartle Frere, Correspondence concerning the mission of Sir Bartle Frere, 1873 (Archives of the Congregation of the Holy Ghost, Chevilly-Larue, France. Box 196bi, #3), 122.

10. Frere, Correspondence, 123; Norman R. Bennett, *Studies in East African History* (Boston: Boston University Press, 1963), 161.

called "Freretown," named after Frere himself, near Mombasa in 1875 as a Christian community of former slaves. Among the first settlers were those called "Bombay Africans," onetime slaves originally from eastern Africa freed in the Indian Ocean world who had been settled near Bombay in India at a CMS mission. This practice of settling slaves freed at sea in India, which began in 1847, ended when eastern African missions linked to the British emerged in 1864. Nineteenth-century abolitionism not only led to the new Christian colony but, buoyed by missionary links across the Indian Ocean, supplied it with some of its earliest residents. The establishment of Freretown allowed expansion, with a similar colony of both Bombay Africans and more recently freed slaves at the original mission at Rabai. By the early 1890s, Freretown had 145 Bombay Africans and 900 liberated slaves, while Rabai had 3000 residents.[11]

In the late 1870s, Catholic missionaries of the Missionaries of Africa, or White Fathers, arrived in Zanzibar after their founder, Cardinal Lavigerie, secured Vatican approval to evangelize large parts of the interior of Africa. They aspired to fight slavery closer to where Africans were seized and to that end sought to establish missions much further inland than their fellow Catholics, the Spiritans, had ventured. Large caravans of missionaries along with hundreds of porters trekked from the coast, seeking places for new missions where amenable political forces, available water, fertile soil, and a sizeable population to evangelize promised possibilities for new Christian communities. Eventually they made their way to western Tanzania and to Uganda, where they had heard of peoples ready for evangelization. Later they came with Papal *zouaves*, consecrated soldiers who would assist them in fighting the slave trade.

Preceding the White Fathers by less than two years to Uganda were Anglicans of the CMS, who came from Mombasa in 1877. Both the Catholics and the Protestants had read in Europe the accounts describing the kingdom of Buganda given by journalist and explorer Henry Morton Stanley. Though the White Fathers, for their part, drew motivation from abolitionist sentiments, both Catholic and Protestant responses to Stanley's tales

11. Sundkler and Steed, *History of the Church in Africa*, 553.

led to the first widespread missionary effort in eastern Africa not directed at former slaves, and one of the most significant Christian missionary successes of all time.

TO THE GREAT LAKES: UGANDA FROM 1877 TO 1900

In April 1875, Stanley arrived in Kampala at the court of the kabaka, or king, of Buganda, Mutesa I, along with a UMCA-trained former slave from Zanzibar, Dallington Scopion Maftaa. Stanley's reports in European newspapers later that year excited missionary imaginations, telling of a place, that, as Adrian Hastings puts it, was "highly populated, effectively governed, and very welcoming"[12]—quite different from the comparatively inhospitable lands between the Indian Ocean and the Great Lakes. Maftaa remained behind when Stanley left, and translated some of the Bible into KiSwahili using Arabic script. He thus set the stage for the CMS missionaries, led by a Scottish engineer named Alexander Mackay, who soon arrived: first an advance party briefly in June 1877, then in larger numbers in November 1878.

Mackay and his fellow missionaries soon found themselves explaining the advantages of Christianity to the wily Mutesa and other officials. The locals knew Islam, which had been gaining a foothold, as well as their own ubiquitous and pervasive religion, which in important ways reinforced royal authority. Then in February 1879, the Catholics appeared: two members of the Missionaries of Africa, Father Simon Lourdel and Brother Amans Delmas. Lourdel would compete with Mackay for Mutesa's affections for the next few years, joining the Arab Muslims who had for several years also vied for preference at the court. Meanwhile, other White Fathers had remained in Tanganyika, near the south coast of Lake Victoria.

Interreligious conversations at the court attracted the attention not only of Mutesa, who skillfully played the three groups off each other, but more importantly of the young palace apprentices whom the missionaries called "pages." These were often sons of prominent chiefs from among the Baganda or

12. Hastings, *Church in Africa*, 372.

neighboring groups. Their curiosity already piqued by Islam and literacy, these ambitious youths soon gravitated toward the European missionaries. The European Christians meanwhile attacked each other. Catholics accused Protestants of historical tendencies toward treason and disloyalty, while Protestants charged Catholics with idolatry and, as they were French, of coming from a country renowned for killing its kings—a charge designed to draw Mutesa to the Anglicans. Meanwhile, both missionary factions expressed astonishment at the earnest zeal of the young men who came to them. Cardinal Lavigerie, founder of the Missionaries of Africa, had forbidden any baptisms prior to a four-year catechumenate of preparation, yet Lourdel baptized eight in 1880, then in 1882 eight more. The Anglicans, equally insistent on persistent evidence of conversion, nonetheless baptized a group in 1882 and many in 1883.

Mutesa's manipulations at the court among the religions—at times even allowing three-way debates among Muslims, Protestants, and Catholics—reflected his resistance to foreign domination, either by Muslims from the north or east, or from the British and French European powers represented through their missionaries. He was also likely genuinely curious. In late 1882, however, he expelled the White Fathers, and Mackay, too, was kept at arm's length from court for extended periods. Meanwhile both the Anglican and Catholic cohorts among the pages and other Baganda grew, with few missionaries present.

The sudden death of Mutesa in 1884 brought his son, the young and less stable Mwanga, to the throne. Though Mwanga invited the missionaries back, he also proved sensitive to perceived challenges to his authority. His sensitivity led to tragic consequences when the newly appointed CMS bishop, James Hannington, began to travel to Uganda after his ordination as bishop at Freretown in May 1885. His approach toward Buganda in October 1885 took him on an unprecedented overland route across Kenya—all previous missionaries had come from the south, across Lake Victoria, and lore among the Baganda warned of visitors from the east. Mwanga perceived a threat that needed to be contained. Royal instructions to stop the bishop—their imprecision allowing the kabaka dubious "plausible deniability" in the aftermath—led to Hannington's death after arrest. A fearful Mwanga, worried about the implications, ordered the killing of one of the leading converts, the Catholic Joseph Mukasa Balikuddembe, who had warned against the bishop's murder and became the first of the eventual Uganda Martyrs who would be canonized. Also killed were Anglican converts Nuwa Seruwanga, Marko Kakumba, and Yusufu Lugalama.[13] In early 1886, a newly baptized Baganda princess in turn destroyed symbols of her royalty, and Christian pages ceased complying with the kabaka's requests for sex. These events set the stage for the June 3, 1886 killing of thirty-one pages, Catholic and Protestant, at Namugongo, near Kampala.[14] Some pages were spared entirely, others were tortured but lived, and the persecution wound down fitfully over time. These killings may have eased the kabaka's anxieties temporarily, but the creation of martyrs, Anglican and Catholic, whose heroism defied royal violence in the eyes of many witnesses, helped erode Mwanga's authority. In 1888 he was deposed by a joint effort of Muslims and Christians.

The next few years saw complex political maneuverings, with alliances formed and undone as political divisions within the Baganda, and in turn with their neighbors, led to much fighting. British traders linked to the Imperial British East Africa Company (IBEAC) in Kenya also pursued their commercial interests through multiple and shifting alliances. Not all missionaries welcomed the European presence uncritically. Mackay himself remarked, placing slavery's history in relation to what he perceived around him, "In former years the universal aim [of Europeans] was to steal the African from Africa. Today the determination of Europe is to steal Africa from the African."[15]

In the political turmoil of the late 1880s, the Muslims first upended the Christians, many of whom sought refuge in the Ankole kingdom to the west while the missionaries were seized

13. Kevin Ward, *A History of Global Anglicanism* (Cambridge: Cambridge University Press, 2006), 167.

14. For Catholic perspectives on the Uganda Martyrs, see J. F. Faupel, *African Holocaust: The Story of the Uganda Martyrs* (New York: P. J. Kenedy, 1962), and A. Tarcis Nsobya, *The Uganda Martyrs Are Our Light* (Kisubi, Uganda: Marianum, 2006).

15. Hastings, *Church in Africa*, 432.

and sent away. Mwanga, too, fled from the Muslims and claimed to be a Christian believer, seeking refuge with the White Fathers at their mission at Bukumbi on the south shore of Lake Victoria in present-day Tanzania. Soon he was convinced to lead the Ankole-based Christian refugees back to Kampala, where fierce fighting led to a Christian victory in 1890 and the taking of the capital.

The cooperation among the Christians in their fight against the Muslims was short-lived. In that fight, important Christian leaders, Catholic and Protestant, died—including some of those best able to hold the two groups together. Other ecclesial and political transitions also occurred. The missionary pioneers Mackay and Lourdel both died. In addition, Captain Lugard of the IBEAC arrived, along with Anglican Alfred Tucker, the first bishop to reach Buganda.

Internecine trials soon beset the Christian Baganda. The Catholic party, called the *Bafaransa* due to the local pronunciation of the "French" missionaries who had brought the faith, soon split with the Anglicans, called the *Bangereza* from "English." An 1892 fight, the "Battle of Mengo," was decided by the superior weaponry—supplied by Lugard—on the Anglican side, with strident protests lodged by Paris to London afterward. The nascent and soon-to-be-formalized British colonial power reinforced Anglican political superiority. In the aftermath, Catholics were first restricted to Buddu county, wherein lay the city of Masaka. Meanwhile the new Catholic bishop, Jean-Joseph Hirth, and Tucker, his Anglican counterpart, developed an enmity. The unclear authority of the IBEAC in Uganda gave way to formal British protectorate status for Uganda in 1894, reinforcing the official Anglican connections to the kingdom of Buganda.[16]

Most importantly for Christian history, however, many Baganda had forged a strong Christian identity—as Catholics and Protestants—without colonial overrule. Even though formal numbers of the baptized remained only several thousand, they were fervent, with thousands more wanting to join. The ter-

16. The best recent account of the process by which Uganda came under British colonial rule can be found in D. A. Low, *Fabrication of Empire: The British and the Uganda Kingdoms, 1890–1902* (Cambridge: Cambridge University Press), 2009.

ritory that would become Uganda, especially the kingdom of Buganda, was on its way to being a Christian nation as the Baganda and other peoples nearby flocked to both confessions. The institutionalizing of Christianization, with a deep split between the Catholics and the Anglicans, began in earnest.

The next few years saw each church body expand its reach into different parts of what would later be the country of Uganda, and beyond. Women outnumbered men among converts,[17] yet, given traditional roles of women in the region as well as missionary predilections in their accounts, the actions of males dominate the comments of European and local observers and thus the historical record. Baganda converts like Apolo Kagwa among the Anglicans and Stanislaus Mugwanya among the Catholics grew into prominent political and religious figures upon whom both missionaries and colonial leaders depended.[18] Lay catechists in both groups, mostly male Baganda, zealously crossed linguistic and cultural boundaries to spread the faith. In 1891, the CMS's Bishop Tucker set aside six men for the task, and by 1894 there were 290 lay agents working for the CMS, 2,199 in 1902, and 3,882 in 1922.[19] Famous catechists included Apolo Kivebulaya, who worked for the CMS in western Uganda and Congo with the so-called pygmies of the forest regions, and Yohana Kitagana, a Catholic who evangelized in the southwest, in Kigezi. Lay evangelists from Uganda also preached outside the territory's borders, in Kenya, Tanganyika, Rwanda, and Burundi.

Each side sought to bring chiefs and subchiefs to its particular Christian confession. Catholics, worried that Anglican favoritism linked to growing British control of Uganda would sideline them even more, worked to bring to the region the British Catholic missionary group called the Society of St. Joseph, known as the Mill Hill missionaries after the London suburb where their headquarters were located. Mill Hill, many

17. Elizabeth E. Prevost, *The Communion of Women: Missions and Gender in Colonial Africa and the British Metropole* (Oxford: Oxford University Press, 2010), 99.

18. Asavia Wandira, *Early Missionary Education in Uganda: A Study of Purpose in Missionary Education* (Kampala: Makerere University Department of Education, 1972), 86–87.

19. Wandira, *Early Missionary Education*, 89–90.

of them British but over time even more populated by Dutch priests and brothers, received Catholic authority in the region of eastern Uganda and what is now western Kenya in 1895, while the White Fathers maintained authority over western Uganda. The Mill Hill bishop, Henry Hanlon, had his cathedral on Nsambya Hill in Kampala, while the White Fathers' cathedral was on nearby Rubaga Hill. Meanwhile, the Anglican cathedral stood on a third hill, Namirembe.[20]

Besides training and encouraging lay catechists, both Catholics and Anglicans also invested in education of a more secular sort. This created groups of literate believers and encouraged publications of Christian periodicals and other materials in Luganda (the language of the Baganda). In 1897, a CMS missionary, George Pilkington, working with a group of Anglican Baganda led by Henry Wright Duta, completed the Bible in Luganda, and in the process fostered a distinctly evangelical piety among some of his coworkers.[21] Three decades later this born-again spirituality blossomed for thousands of believers during the East African Revival. Meanwhile, both Catholics and Anglicans developed huge, African-led educational programs for the education and preparation of people for baptism.

All of this energy meant that a professionalized, literate, and zealous elite was being formed on both sides, with Catholics larger in number and the Anglicans, helped by increasingly formalized British overrule, occupying most of the indigenous leadership positions in the developing colony. In 1900, the British colonizers forged the Uganda Agreement with select local leaders, which gave the Baganda limited autonomy under the British, cemented the political roles of other kingdoms and chieftainships, and formalized territorial arrangements that stipulated numbers and locations of Anglican and Catholic chieftainships. In place until 1955, it was prompted by the ill-fated attempts of certain Baganda to rally around Mwanga, their deposed kabaka, to push out the British. A minority of disaffected Catholics had supported Mwanga, and the new redistribution sought to allay Catholic frustrations. The arrangement,

20. Robert O'Neil, *Mission to the Upper Nile: The Story of St. Joseph's Missionary Society in Uganda* (London: Mission Book Service, 1999), 19–35.

21. Ward, *History of Global Anglicanism*, 168.

with districts predominantly either Anglican or Catholic, created a status quo of sorts, though the Anglican-Catholic rivalry played out in countless local settings, sometimes violently, for decades to come. Meanwhile the CMS divided its diocese between Uganda and Kenya in 1899 in recognition of the new political boundaries.

As Adrian Hastings notes, Buganda was the only place in Africa that saw both large-scale movements of Africans to Christianity before colonial overrule and the continuance of mass conversions after colonialism was imposed.[22] Both Catholics and Anglicans developed formidable Christian colonial churches with impressive infrastructures of parishes, schools, catechetical training centers, and eventually clinics and hospitals. Soon clergy were being formed locally and before long they assumed administrative authority. Both Catholics and Anglicans grew catechetical programs to train young and old to adopt the faith, with legions of catechists to assist expatriate missionaries. Both also developed presses, publishing books and regular newsletters in Luganda that fed the growing interest in literacy and Christian scholarship among their adherents.

Yet the two groups had slightly different priorities that shaped how they developed. Huge Catholic parishes developed in Buddu county around Masaka, with massive main churches at the central parish centers and numerous surrounding outstations, with similar programs later in neighboring kingdoms to the west of the protectorate. The White Father bishop, Henri Streicher, appointed in 1897 and retiring only in 1933, presided over enormous growth in western and central Uganda in Catholic institutions. Streicher emphasized the creation of indigenous priests and members of religious congregations, the expansion of parishes, and knowledge of local languages among missionaries. He founded a seminary at Katigondo near Masaka in 1911, which became an important regional center for Catholic formation of clergy.[23] The White Fathers, assisted by the White

22. Hastings, *Church in Africa*, 464.

23. John Mary Waliggo, "The Catholic Church in the Buddu Province of Buganda, 1879–1925" (diss., Cambridge University, 1976); John Mary Waliggo, *A History of African Priests: Katigondo Major Seminary, 1911–1986* (Kampala: Marianum, 1988); and John Mary Waliggo, "The Bugandan Christian Revolution: The

Sisters, a group of nuns affiliated with them, in 1910 founded the *Bannabikira* ("daughters of the Virgin"), an indigenous religious order of women, and in 1927 also the *Bannakaroli* ("sons of Charles," referring to Charles Lwanga, leader of the Catholic Uganda martyrs), a group of religious brothers. In 1913, the first two Baganda Catholic priests were ordained.

The CMS-inspired Anglican churches across the region also expanded, stressing earlier than the Catholics the need for literacy in English for an anticipated group of indigenous leaders, and developing Christian monarchies where possible. Influential missionaries sought to follow the three-self formula of former CMS director Henry Venn, according to which the missionary goal was a self-governing, self-supporting, and self-propagating church. Over time this goal's advocates overcame resistance from CMS missionaries skeptical due to more paternalistic instincts, so that the Anglican Church in Buganda approximated Venn's ideal more than almost anywhere else. If Catholic spirituality took shape in rosaries and medals, devotions and processions, the Anglican emphasis on biblical literacy and formal education encouraged the creation of a well-educated Baganda elite. Helped by Bishop Tucker over the protests of other missionaries, Ugandan Anglicans received their own church constitution and ordained numerous indigenous clergy.[24] Neighboring kingdoms also developed leaders whose royal connections and Anglican religious identity overlapped.

THE MISSIONARY EVANGELIZATION OF EASTERN AFRICA, 1870S TO 1914

Though the rapid Christianization of southern and western Uganda, and especially the kingdom of Buganda, was unique

Catholic Church in Buddu, 1879–1896," in *Christianity and the African Imagination: Essays in Honour of Adrian Hastings*, ed. David Maxwell with Ingrid Lawrie (Leiden: Brill, 2002).

24. For a discussion of this process, see Holger Bernt Hansen, *Mission, Church and State in a Colonial Setting: Uganda, 1890–1925* (New York: St. Martin's, 1984), and Prevost, *Communion of Women*, 111–12.

—and not only in eastern Africa—missionary activity continued elsewhere in the region over the same years, with new efforts undertaken as zealous male and female missionaries came from Europe and eventually North America. Some of the most important efforts, Catholic and Protestant, were led not by expatriate missionaries, however, but by catechist-evangelizers from central Uganda who moved to other parts of Uganda and beyond, spreading the Christian message. Responses to the Christian message varied, but the African evangelizers tended to create Christian communities more effectively than expatriate missionaries.

Closer to the Indian Ocean, in regions that would become Kenya and Tanzania, Catholic and Protestant evangelization in the nineteenth century remained centered on the mission stations at Bagamoyo, Freretown, Mbweni, and elsewhere. These large institutions gathered fleeing slaves while also serving as staging areas for new missions founded further inland. Besides the European missionaries there, the early African Christian leaders in such places also often had international roots, which could create tensions with missionaries. Some were onetime slaves from further inland; others came through existing Protestant and Catholic networks that funneled them to eastern Africa. Prominent among the Anglicans were the Bombay Africans, while others, Catholic and Protestant, came from earlier missions to the south, from Ethiopia, or from Indian Ocean islands. Eventually the strategy of enclaving, in which missionaries formed villages of their first converts, many of them slaves, receded, but it remained common as a way to start new missions into the early twentieth century.

The kinds of missionaries in eastern Africa diversified beginning in the late nineteenth century with the arrival of new groups, Protestant and Catholic. Missionaries of the London Missionary Society (LMS), another evangelical British group not linked to the Church of England, had reached Lake Tanganyika from Zanzibar in 1876. This was before both the CMS and the White Fathers moved toward Uganda, but the LMS soon withdrew, its missions assumed by the Moravians who came in the wake of German colonial overrule in the early 1890s. Other groups also arrived at the coast in the late 1870s. Most followed the pattern of their Catholic and Protestant predecessors like the UMCA, White Fathers, and Spiritans, establishing centers near Mombasa, Zanzibar, or Dar es Salaam to serve as staging grounds from which to equip missionaries heading inland.

On the Catholic side, Bagamoyo continued to serve the Spiritan goals as a place of forming and sending groups of African Catholics, most former slaves, to start new missions along with missionaries. After founding a number of such missions with Christian villages inland from the coast in Tanganyika, groups from Bagamoyo reached Mombasa in the late 1880s, the first ongoing Catholic presence of missionaries in Kenya. There they met a small number of Catholics from Goa in India before moving inland to establish another short-lived mission. Brought by the British to serve the colonial regime, Goans became important Catholics in eastern Africa through the colonial period and beyond, especially in major cities like Nairobi, Dar es Salaam, Mombasa, Zanzibar, and Jinja.

In the early 1890s, the Spiritans arrived around Mount Kilimanjaro in Tanganyika, where a formidable Catholic presence emerged among the Chagga.[25] Meanwhile, the White Fathers, firmly in place in Uganda, continued to expand their work in western Tanganyika, moving from there into what are now Rwanda, Burundi, and the Democratic Republic of Congo.

In 1887, prompted by German presence that culminated in the establishment of German East Africa, a third Catholic group arrived, joining the Spiritans and White Fathers. Benedictine missionaries linked to St. Ottilien monastery near Munich came with the support of colonial officials anxious to bring their countrymen into the region to balance the mostly French Catholic missionaries already present on the ground. The Benedictines began in Dar es Salaam, then founded a station at Pugu nearby in 1888, where they tried to work among the Zaramo. Anticolonial resistance to German encroachment led to the killing of the superior and several other religious in 1889. The rebels apologized afterward, explaining that the monks' earnest cultivation efforts made it hard to distinguish missionaries from colonizers.

25. Anza A. Lema, "Chaga Religion and Missionary Christianity on Kilimanjaro: The Initial Phase, 1893–1916," in *East African Expressions of Christianity*, ed. Thomas Spear and Isaria N. Kimambo (Oxford: James Currey, 1999).

The monks returned the same year. They soon built St. Joseph Cathedral in Dar es Salaam, begun in 1896 and completed in 1902, though their main energies moved away from the Muslim coast. Following an invitation from the local Ngoni chief, in 1898 the Benedictines founded what became a very large and famous mission at Peramiho in the southwest of the territory, near Songea. Missionary Benedictine Sisters from Tutzing in Germany soon joined them. From Peramiho, the monks went out and the surrounding area was soon dotted with other churches. In 1906 the Benedictines founded a second major monastery at Ndanda, also in southern Tanganyika yet closer to the coast near Lindi.

The increased German presence also occasioned new groups of Protestant missionaries.[26] A small group of Bavarian Lutherans had worked in Kenya among the Kamba from 1881, but more importantly the developing German colonial presence beginning in the mid-1880s naturally also brought many German missionary societies to what became German East Africa. Three groups were prominent—the Leipzig Mission, and two others that in English have long been called "Berlin I" and "Berlin III"—each linked to different Protestant bodies in Germany, with differing balances of Lutheran, Calvinist, and evangelical tendencies.[27] Eventually the CMS ceded its missions near Mount Kilimanjaro to the Leipzig Mission. Meanwhile, the Anglicans maintained centers at the coast such as the CMS's Freretown and the UMCA's Zanzibar, and at inland missions like Magila and Masasi, while also establishing newer mission stations inland.

The CMS colony at Freretown near Mombasa faced a number of challenges prior to the formal establishment of British colonial rule over Kenya.[28] Some came from the colony's neighbors, local

26. Carl J. Hellberg, *Missions on a Colonial Frontier West of Lake of Victoria: Evangelical Missions in North-West Tanganyika to 1932*, trans. Eric Sharpe (Uppsala, Sweden: Gleerups, 1965); Marcia Wright, *German Missions in Tanganyika, 1891–1941: Lutherans and Moravians in the Southern Highlands* (Oxford: Clarendon, 1971); Klaus Fiedler, *Christianity and African Culture: Conservative Protestant Missionaries in Tanzania, 1900–1940* (Leiden: Brill, 1996).

27. Isaria N. Kimambo, "The Impact of Christianity among the Zaramo: A Case Study of Maneromango Lutheran Parish," in *East African Expressions of Christianity*, ed. Thomas Spear and Isaria N. Kimambo (Oxford: James Currey, 1999), 64.

28. Frederick Cooper, *Plantation Slavery on the East Coast of Africa* (New Haven:

African and Arab leaders who disliked its practice of welcoming runaway slaves and linked the economic disruption caused by missionary enfranchisement with developing British colonial overrule. They initiated armed attacks, in which African Christians defended their settlement, even though they too resented British overrule at times.

Different Christian groups followed different paths as they grew, depending on local conditions as well as colonial and missionary processes. Ethnic and linguistic groups with settled agricultural practices and clear political boundaries tended to welcome Christianity more easily than smaller-scale groups and those whose settlements were short-term due to nomadic herding practices. New groups of missionaries tended to focus their inaugural efforts on what they perceived to be a single ethnolinguistic group, marking their territory by constructing buildings on land they received, and then learning the local spoken language.

In both the acquisition of land and their linguistic endeavors, missionaries initiated and catalyzed complex social processes. Besides securing their own land for church-building and other development, missionaries commonly assisted their preferred local leaders to consolidate regional hegemony under eventual European colonial control, a process facilitated by the scripting of a single language from a variety of local dialects. In a number of kingdoms now part of modern Uganda, the conversion of the king or paramount chief—or at least his welcome of the missionaries—led to the widespread adoption of Christianity by the local people, with the leader usually Anglican, and the lesser chiefs Catholic. Missionaries tried to replicate this pattern elsewhere, too, so that certain regions—southern and western Uganda, central Kenya, and northern, northwestern, and southwestern Tanganyika—had converts rather quickly. Places where Christianization proceeded rapidly also saw the development of local literate cultural identity due to widely circulated Christian writ-

Yale University Press, 1977); Frederick Cooper, *From Slaves to Squatters: Plantation Labor and Agriculture in Zanzibar and Coastal Kenya, 1890–1925* (New Haven: Yale University Press,1980); Strayer, *Making of Mission Communities*; Fred Morton, *Children of Ham: Freed Slaves and Fugitive Slaves on the Kenyan Coast, 1873–1907* (Boulder, CO: Westview, 1990).

ings in the vernacular, especially the Bible. Other regions, however, had lower or no Christian growth.

The early twentieth century saw a deepening of colonial control over the region, German and British, which created boundaries that meant increasingly distinct Christian histories among the areas that would become the countries of Kenya, Uganda, and Tanzania. British initiatives to build a railway from Mombasa to Nairobi, then on to Uganda, allowed easier moves inland by missionary groups. Similar German efforts facilitated transportation into Tanganyika. Soon there were missionaries in most regions of eastern Africa. There was resistance to encroaching European control, but anti-colonial insurrections rarely targeted missionaries and most were quickly quelled.

Across the region, the scale of the positive initial local reception to Christianity reflected a combination of factors: the creativity of missionary strategies that drew on cultural awareness of local peoples, African perceptions of the new religion's advantages in the colonial situation, promises of spiritual well-being both in the present and the future that appealed to indigenous values, and inscrutable personal and communal convictions. One chief evangelized by Catholics praised the missionaries who came, exclaiming "You are our coast," the implication being that his people prized connections to the comparatively cosmopolitan world of Zanzibar that Christianity offered. Another had a dream in which bearded white visitors in dark garb would come—and soon arrived cassock-wearing, hirsute Europeans. At times local prophets claimed to have foreseen the European arrival, with visions of "pale invaders." This could increase the welcome accorded missionaries. In addition, drought, disease (both among humans and cattle), and subsequent famine brought people to missions, as did local warfare, whether among Africans or with Europeans.

The most important factor determining local reception of Christianity remained a large group of the already converted, as in Buganda. These forerunners there and elsewhere pursued the lion's share of evangelization of those who followed them into the faith. Yet not everywhere in eastern Africa saw the development of such a group of early converts, who usually signaled the beginning of a robust Christian presence. Of course, they were not the only factor determining Christianity's shape. Each of the territories that became British East Africa saw different missionary groups enter, different paths into colonial overrule, different kinds of local responses, and different resulting shapes of Christianity. Regions within each territory also saw considerable variations in missionary activity, colonial experience, and reactions to evangelization.

***

British colonial control in *Kenya* evolved in the early twentieth century, from the initial commercial presence of the Imperial British East Africa Company between 1885 and 1895, to formal control by the Foreign Office. The Christian missionary presence expanded amid these changes. Significant inland missions appeared in the protectorate (in 1920, Kenya was named a Crown Colony) later than in Tanganyika, yet Kenya, especially through its Indian Ocean port of Mombasa, became the main gateway into the region for many new Protestant missionary groups, including those that settled around Mount Kilimanjaro in northern Tanganyika. This is one explanation for the diversity of Christian forms in Kenya to this day compared to Uganda and Tanzania. Much of Kenya's north, still thinly populated, lacked a Christian presence, but the eastern, central, and western parts slowly filled with missionaries. The Kamba, an ethno-linguistic group close to the coast that was not heavily Islamized, had eight missionary bodies evangelizing them by the early twentieth century including Bavarian Lutherans, who arrived in 1881; Catholic Spiritans from 1889; and Scottish Presbyterians. Missionary efforts toward Mount Kilimanjaro in German East Africa sometimes began from Kenya, other times from the southern part of the German territory.

Central Kenya, especially the Kikuyu and neighboring groups the Embu and Meru, also drew considerable missionary attention.[29] The first mission among them, a Church of Scotland Mission (CSM), was founded in 1898 and developed into

29. David P. Sandgren, *Christianity and the Kikuyu: Religious Divisions and Social Conflict* (New York: Peter Lang, 2000); John Karanja, "The Role of Kikuyu Christians in Developing a Self-Consciously African Anglicanism," in *The Church Mission*

the Presbyterian Church of East Africa (PCEA). Certain ardent Kikuyu converts also served as effective catechists, not unlike their Baganda counterparts to the west. Such zealous local agents traveled the railroad to evangelize from Mombasa to Nairobi, and eventually on to Kisumu in western Kenya at Lake Victoria. Nairobi, bolstered as a railroad hub, grew into a missionary headquarters for most missionary bodies, with not only the Presbyterians and Anglicans, but also Methodists, Catholics, and many smaller groups establishing themselves there.

Another group working among the Kamba from 1895 was the Africa Inland Mission (AIM), led by its American founder Peter Cameron Scott. AIM was eastern Africa's first "faith mission," a term for missionary bodies that eschew any social reform efforts, focusing instead on spiritual conversions oriented toward eternal life. Such groups, many American and inspired by the conversionist preaching of revivalists like Dwight Moody and the missionary zeal of Hudson Taylor's China Inland Mission, soon reached around the globe. Scott and most of the other Kenyan-based AIM missionaries were quickly dead of disease, yet the mission persisted and expanded to work among the Maasai, later becoming the Africa Inland Church.[30]

Catholic efforts in Kenya had begun in Mombasa, then moved quickly to Nairobi, and, as noted already, in both places Goans provided Catholic lay leadership. Not far from Nairobi, Kiambu grew into a Catholic stronghold and the Spiritans founded a notable school for boys at Kabaa, among the Kamba. In addition, their cultivation of coffee, first begun in Tanganyika, was the first in Kenya. Consolata missionaries soon supplemented the Spiritans, and their assumption of Catholic missionary responsibility for much of central Kenya led initially to Spiritan dismay. Priding themselves on the vigor with which they made daily visits to local households, by 1909 the Consolatas oversaw their own Vicariate of Kenya, which did not include Nairobi—the colonial capital being part of the Mombasa Vicariate under

Society and World Christianity, 1799–1999, ed. Kevin Ward and Brian Stanley (Grand Rapids: Eerdmans, 2000), 257–59.

30. Richard Waller, "They Do the Dictating and We Must Submit: The Africa Inland Mission in Maasailand," in *East African Expressions of Christianity*, ed. Thomas Spear and Isaria N. Kimambo (Oxford: James Currey, 1999).

direction of the Spiritans.[31] Soon the Consolatas were welcoming young men and women who wanted to become priests and nuns.

Western Kenya received most of its initial missionaries from Uganda to the west. These included Catholic Mill Hill missionaries, who established missions among the Luo, Luhya, and eventually Kisii speakers who formed the largest groups, and CMS-linked Anglicans, who made their headquarters in Maseno, which straddled Luo and Luhya speakers. Eventually there were also Quakers from the US who settled in Kaimosi from 1902, and Seventh-Day Adventists, who came in 1906. Also present were Canadian Pentecostals, South Africa–based Apostolics, and other small groups.

The different Protestant groups in Kenya sought to cooperate, eventually establishing a ten-mile rule according to which new missionaries agreed to respect territory in such a radius from a founded mission station. Cooperation also took place in translation of the Bible and in writing hymns in local languages. By 1910, certain farsighted missionaries envisioned more ambitious ecumenical cooperation, and in 1913 a group gathered at Kikuyu for a conference that tentatively agreed to form a Federation of Missions that would respect each other's liturgical practices, even to the point of allowing intercommunion.[32] When notices were sent to missionary sending agencies, however, Bishop Frank Weston of Zanzibar, a UMCA-linked missionary wary of the "low-church" CMS Anglicans in Uganda and Kenya, accused the two CMS bishops of heresy and schism. Though the archbishop of Canterbury disagreed with Weston's accusations, he disallowed the Federation. Five years later, however, the same groups formed an "Alliance of Protestant Missions," which led to Alliance institutions for medical training, theological formation, and later the famous Alliance High School, soon Kenya's best secondary school. No Africans were

31. Gabriele Soldati, *The Pioneer: The African Adventure of Benedict Falda* (Rome: Istituto Missioni Consolata, 1991); Giovanni Tebaldi, *Consolata Missionaries in the World (1901–2001)* (Nairobi: Paulines Publications, 1999), 57–87.

32. Colin Reed, "Denominationalism or Protestantism? Mission Strategy and Church in the Kikuyu Conference of 1913," *International Bulletin of Missionary Research* 37, no. 4 (2013): 207–12.

invited to be involved in these arrangements, only European missionaries.

***

Similar missionary occupation occurred to the south in the larger mainland African territory comprised of *Tanganyika*, which in 1891 became German East Africa after the German government took over from the German East Africa Company, as well as *Zanzibar* and other Indian Ocean islands. Understandably, German missionary groups, Protestant and Catholic, played an increasing role as formal colonialism took hold in Tanganyika. Among Catholics, the German Benedictines expanded in the southern part of the country after their 1887 arrival, while the mostly French Missionaries of Africa (White Fathers) continued in the north and west, maintaining the mission begun simultaneously with their work in Uganda. Meanwhile the Spiritans, who had begun at Zanzibar and coastal Tanganyika, continued at the coast and expanded around Mount Kilimanjaro along with their Lutheran counterparts. The Kilimanjaro region became Christianized comparatively quickly. Lutherans dominated some parts, with schools, churches, and catechetical programs, while some of the vast slopes of the mountain came to resemble Masaka in Uganda: huge churches, numerous outstations, and an impressive Catholic culture. Over time the Spiritan missionaries became more Irish and Dutch than French, and eventually American Spiritans arrived, who work in northern Tanzania to the present.

The Protestant missionary presence changed even more with the German arrival. Anglicans were already present: the high-church UMCA at Zanzibar and the coast, and the low-church CMS inland, supplemented by Baganda converts. One notable example was Nathaniel Mudeka, nephew of Kabaka Mutesa who had first welcomed the missionaries into Uganda. Mudeka's missionary work among the Sukuma of central Tanganyika, begun in 1891, gathered large numbers of converts.[33] The arrival of German missionaries with the German colonial presence led to

33. Hastings, *Church in Africa*, 468.

changes among Anglicans. CMS missionaries mostly yielded to German groups, retreating to what was then Northern Rhodesia (now Zambia), Kenya, and Uganda. The UMCA for its part remained centered at British-controlled Zanzibar, also keeping its early missions on the continent. Beginning in 1908, Frank Weston served as UMCA bishop of Zanzibar. From there he temporarily sidelined the bold ecumenical efforts in Kenya, as noted already, and he also defended local peoples against labor impressment by British colonizers, penning *Serfs of East Africa* in their defense. Older missions on the mainland, such as at Masasi, also grew.[34]

Meanwhile the new German Protestant missionary groups evangelized throughout the colony. By 1891, German Moravians had established themselves in the southern center of the territory, the so-called Southern Highlands, and other groups worked with different populations throughout the colony. Among these were the groups called Berlin I and III at the coast and in the Southern Highlands, the Leipzig mission near Kilimanjaro, and Seventh-Day Adventists to Mwanza on Lake Victoria, coming from Kenya in the early twentieth century.

In many places, the earliest converts were onetime slaves who had been educated and catechized at missions near the coast, or who had found their way to new missions as they were established. They were usually different in culture and language from the local people. Over time, however, local peoples became converts, sometimes in large numbers. Sizeable Christian populations appeared around Mount Kilimanjaro among the Chagga—both Catholic and Lutheran, with villages and entire areas of the mountain firmly allied with one or the other, distributions still in place. Catholicism, Lutheranism, and Anglicanism took hold among the Haya on the far side of Lake Victoria. Meanwhile in southern Tanganyika other smaller groups like the Fipa and Ngoni mostly became Catholic,[35] with neighboring peoples joining the German Protestant missions nearby.

Political changes shaped religious transformation, with education and healthcare attracting people to the faith. Large-scale

34. Ward, *History of Global Anglicanism*, 173–75.

35. Kathleen R. Smythe, *Fipa Families: Reproduction and Catholic Evangelization in Nkansi, Ufipa, 1880–1960* (Portsmouth, NH: Heinemann, 2006).

conversion among the Ngoni and some of their neighbors only began after the Germans crushed the anti-colonial Maji Maji uprising of 1905–1907. In that armed resistance movement, the rebels' belief that drinking sacred water (*maji* in KiSwahili) would make them invulnerable failed to deflect the colonizers' lethal weaponry.[36] Missionaries tended to be spared anti-colonial violence, but the Benedictines lost a bishop, Cassian Spiess, OSB, and four other monks in the Maji Maji fighting, and two Catholic sisters also were killed by rebels.

***

By 1915, *Uganda* was the largest and strongest site for the Catholic Church in Africa, with an estimated 135,000 converts, and its Anglican counterpart, the Church of Uganda, was equally famous.[37] Understandably, the remarkable success that had begun with the kingdom of Buganda made it a hopeful model for the rest of the missionaries in the British colony of Uganda. In some other places to the west, east, and north, catechist-evangelizers, many of them lay believers who were Baganda, led successful missionary efforts. In western Uganda especially, there were other existing kingdoms when missionaries arrived. The usual model saw the king become Anglican under CMS leadership, while other leaders and most of the peasants joined the Catholic Church over time. Thus by the early twentieth century, the monarchies west of Buganda had formally become Christian, with narratives of royal conversion to the faith not unlike the European countries of the first millennium.[38] At times, Baganda Christian elites could be perceived as culturally arrogant—some have even referred to their stance as "sub-imperialism" due to their tendency to look down on their neighbors—but where their arrogance did not create resistance

36. Marcia Wright, "Maji-Maji: Prophecy and Historiography," in *Revealing Prophets: Prophecy in Eastern African History*, ed. David M. Anderson and Douglas H. Johnson (London: James Currey, 1995).

37. Jonathan Hildebrandt, *History of the Church in Africa: A Survey* (Achimota, Ghana: Africa Christian Press, 1987), 190.

38. Hastings, *Church in Africa*, 474.

their linguistic abilities and cultural awareness made them more effective than European missionaries.

Northern Uganda, where large-scale indigenous political organizations were less present than in southern and western parts of the colony, and where the mostly Nilotic cultures and languages were quite different from the mostly Bantu south, also drew Catholic and Protestant emissaries. Eventually the Catholic presence was embodied by the Comboni missionaries (or Verona Fathers), who had come initially from the north in Sudan.[39] The first Protestant missionaries in the area came from Kenya's Africa Inland Mission, yet soon CMS efforts coming from Buganda into the north meant that there too the Catholic-Anglican rivalry emerged.

The rivalry only intensified the impressive institutional growth of both Catholics and Anglicans throughout Uganda, who built schools and new missions at a rapid pace mostly in close cooperation with colonial authorities, though colonial-missionary tensions could emerge.[40] Perhaps most notably, both groups successfully formed clergy, with twenty Ugandan Anglican clergy by 1900 and ten Ugandan Catholic clergy by 1920—the latter an especially unusual feat given expectations of clerical celibacy, education in Latin, and years of study.

Catholics and Anglicans predominated in Uganda, but other Christian-linked religious forms also appeared. In 1913, the Church of One Almighty God emerged, also known as the Bamalaki sect after its leader Malaki Musajjakawa, who led mostly former Anglicans in combining local beliefs, Christianity, and elements of Judaism, as well as resisting European medicine. One notable Malakite was Semei Kakungulu, a fascinating figure who earlier had helped the British take control of eastern Uganda, thus helping the CMS expand there. Later he became alienated from missionary Christianity and dispirited by colonial overrule. In 1917 Kakungulu founded his own group, the Abayudaya, and he and several hundred Ugandans became Jewish, a community that exists to this day. One Englishwoman in Uganda, Mabel Ensor, broke away from the Anglican Church

39. Mario Cisternino, *Passion for Africa: Missionary and Imperial Papers on the Evangelisation of Uganda and Sudan, 1848–1923* (Kampala: Fountain, 2004), 276–398.

40. Hansen, *Mission, Church and State*, 156–60.

after her accusation of immorality against an African pastor earned her a rebuke for disloyalty. She founded the Mengo Gospel Church in 1928.[41]

The Malakites and Ensor's group were among the few African independent churches (AICs) to appear in eastern Africa in this period, with many others emerging later especially in western and central Kenya. Indeed, compared to early twentieth-century western and southern Africa, eastern Africa saw few AICs until after World War I. One reason might be the role of the Baganda catechists, which gave African Christians ample chance to exercise religious leadership—for lack of chances for African Christian leadership in mission-founded churches often gave rise to AICs.

Another factor explaining the comparative lack of AICs in early twentieth-century eastern Africa might well have been the advantages linked to missionary Christianity in the emerging colonial order. Schools connected to the missions provided skills of literacy and numeracy that in turn provided employment, and independent churches lacked schools—at least until later in the colonial period. Indeed, early eastern African Christians tended not to resist colonialism, so that the most important anti-colonial movements that took religious shape before World War I tended to be overtly anti-Christian. These included Muslim-led resistance to the Germans in late nineteenth-century coastal Tanganyika, Maji Maji in Tanganyika from 1905 to 1907, Mumboism in 1913 in Kenya near Lake Victoria, and the Yakan cult among the Lugbara of northern Uganda in 1919, which, like Maji Maji, used magic medicines for defense against bullets.

FROM WORLD WAR I TO INDEPENDENCE, 1914 TO THE EARLY 1960S

World War I (1914–1918) reached violently into eastern Africa, which saw considerable naval and ground conflict, mostly between the forces of the United Kingdom and those connected to Germany. Some Christian missions suffered as local popula-

41. Wandira, *Early Missionary Education in Uganda*, 105.

tions avoided fighting, or their personnel fled conflicts or faced internment by colonial authorities due to their national origins. In many missions both Catholic and Protestant, however, Africans assumed new authority when missionaries withdrew, often with positive results for the development of African Christian leadership. Not a few missionaries were astonished to find flourishing Christian faith communities when they returned.

The end of the war led to eventual British control over the entire region under a League of Nations mandate. When German power ceased, the British, French, and other missionaries they had removed from their territory returned quickly to what was soon Tanganyika. More slowly, interned and removed German missionaries themselves returned to eastern Africa in the 1920s.[42]

Compared to World War I, World War II (1939–1945) disrupted eastern Africa and its Christians less since the region never became an extended military theater. International Protestant missionary cooperation had grown in the 1920s, and this helped make leadership-transfer arrangements easier when personnel were removed. Some missions were again disrupted, while financial and other support for missions from overseas shrank. More importantly, a number of African Christians served overseas with British forces in Europe and in Asia, and they returned with a new global awareness that shaped their faith and their political aspirations.[43] They lent voice and self-confidence to anti-colonial sentiment prompted by ongoing loss of land and growing desires for self-determination.

Violent resistance to colonialism was rare after World War I in eastern Africa until the 1950s, when certain Baganda sought greater authority for their kabaka and, in Kenya, the Mau Mau uprising took place. These political movements often attacked Christianity as well, which was understandable given how a considerable number of missionaries who remained wary of

42. The British in this case were more generous than the French and Belgians, who disallowed the return of German missionaries to their African territories after the war. For discussions, see Hellberg, *Missions on a Colonial Frontier*; Wright, *German Missions in Tanganyika*; Fiedler, *Christianity and African Culture*.

43. James R. Brennan, *TAIFA: Making Nation and Race in Urban Tanzania* (Athens: Ohio University Press, 2012).

African leadership in their churches stubbornly clung to control. Their stances ranged from paternalistic caution to outright racist belittling. A few missionaries, however, were more supportive of eventual independence, political and ecclesial, and anticipated conferral of authority.

In the five decades prior to independence, granted to each country in the early 1960s, Christianity's trajectories in eastern Africa grew more numerous and diversified. According to Bengt Sundkler, in 1920 Protestants in eastern Africa numbered 235,000, the Catholics 600,000, while by 1960 those numbers had grown to 2.5 and 5 million, respectively.[44] Growth occurred among existing groups, Protestant and Catholic, across the region, as Catholic priests, sisters, and religious brothers from the early religious orders, along with missionaries connected to existing Protestant churches—Anglicans, Lutherans, Presbyterians—continued to come into the region from European countries throughout the first half of the twentieth century.

New groups of Christian missionaries also arrived. Small groups linked to global Pentecostalism's first wave in the early twentieth century arrived throughout eastern Africa beginning before World War I, and the Salvation Army came to Kenya in 1921. Orthodox Christianity also appeared in eastern Africa, coming both with Greek immigrants to some places, and, more interestingly, in response to local aspirations for a venerable form of Christianity not linked to existing missionaries—and thus to colonial overrule—by Ugandan and Kenyan Christians.[45]

New Catholic religious orders of men and women arrived and received territory for their work. When German missionaries were withdrawn from Tanganyika after the British took over, non-German Catholic missionaries were brought in. Italian Consolata missionaries, some of whom had been working in Kenya, came to Iringa in the southern Highlands in 1919, even-

44. Sundkler and Steed, *History of the Church in Africa*, 846.

45. Stephen Hayes, "Orthodox Mission in Tropical Africa," *Missionalia* 24 (1996): 383–98; Ciprian Burlacioiu, "Expansion without Western Missionary Agency and Constructing Confessional Identities: The African Orthodox Church between the United States, South Africa, and East Africa (1921–1940)," *Journal of World Christianity* 6, no. 1 (2016): 82–98.

tually establishing a large presence in Tosamaganga.[46] Other Catholic groups followed later: Passionists to the south-central part of the country in 1933; Pallottines to Mbulu in the 1940s; and the US-based Maryknoll missionaries to Musoma in 1946.[47] To Uganda came American Catholics like Sacred Heart Brothers in 1931 to the north to run schools with the Combonis and in 1948 doing the same with the Consolatas in central Kenya, and the Congregation of Holy Cross in the west of Uganda, taking over what would become the dioceses of Fort Portal, Hoima, and Kasese from the Missionaries of Africa.

More new groups came especially after World War II, while longstanding missionary organizations moved into new territories within the region. On the Catholic side the Irish Kiltegan Fathers, or Society of St. Patrick, arrived in 1952 (today recognized for fostering the development of Kenya's outstanding long-distance runners at their secondary schools), along with the nuns of the Medical Missionaries of Mary and US-based Vincentian brothers. Just before independence came new groups of Pentecostals. To Uganda alone came the Full Gospel Church in 1959, Conservative Baptists in 1961, and in 1962 the Assemblies of God, the Elim Missionary Assemblies, and the Southern Baptists.[48] Meanwhile Consolata missionaries went to Somali-linked groups near the Kenyan border, while the Maasai in Kenya were evangelized by the Mill Hill missionaries and also the Protestant Africa Inland Mission.

Besides the new arrivals and new mission territories, several other trends embodied the dynamism of these years, each of them very important in a world-Christianity perspective. First, already by 1938, Christians amounted to 8 percent of Kenya, 10 percent of Tanganyika, and 25 percent of Uganda,[49] and the institutional structures of many existing Christian bodies grew in size in response to growing numbers of converts, with

46. Tebaldi, *Consolata Missionaries in the World*, 105–20.

47. Michael C. Kirwen, "Africans in Global Mission," in *Exploring the Future of Mission in Africa: In Celebration of Maryknoll's 100 Years in Mission*, ed. Laurenti Magesa and Michael C. Kirwen (Nairobi: Maryknoll Institute of African Studies, 2012), 10.

48. Adrian Hastings, *A History of African Christianity, 1950–1975* (Cambridge: Cambridge University Press, 1979), 165.

49. Oliver, *Missionary Factor in East Africa*, 236.

the establishment of schools becoming a priority for nearly all the Christian churches. Consequently, more opportunities for African leadership appeared in mission-founded churches, with the training of numerous catechists, teachers, and ordained ministers, as well as members of religious orders for Catholics. Second, the East African Revival, linked to an earlier movement in Rwanda and drawing on evangelical Keswick theology and the revivalistic energy of the faith missions, transformed many Protestant Christian bodies across eastern Africa, beginning in Uganda in the late 1920s and spreading to Kenya, Tanganyika, and beyond. The global impact of the East African Revival continues to be felt. Third, African independent churches also emerged prominently in the region, notably in central and western Kenya, beginning around the time of World War I and continuing to the present.

GROWTH AND CONSOLIDATION IN MISSIONARY-FOUNDED CHRISTIAN CHURCHES IN THE FIRST HALF OF THE TWENTIETH CENTURY

Missionary strategies, Catholic and Protestant, usually continued the already operative pattern of identifying distinct peoples by language and culture, and seeking to evangelize them by establishing missions, outstations, and schools in their midst. Missionaries implicitly drew advantages from the British colonial principle of indirect rule, which theoretically sought to govern by empowering indigenous political authorities. This colonial policy cohered not only with missionary strategy but also with the structural-functionalist methodology of most anthropologists of the period who also tried to understand cultures in a systematic way.

Reinforcing local chiefs allowed colonial control with fewer Europeans on the ground, supposedly protected local cultures, *and* fostered easier evangelization. In practice, it could lead to colonial promotion of dubious authorities and the formation of new ethnic-cultural identities.[50] Indirect rule was a strategy that

50. Gabrielle Lynch, *I Say to You: Ethnic Politics and the Kalenjin in Kenya*

local peoples sometimes found paternalistic and, perhaps unintentionally, inclined to keep them economically underdeveloped. The policy also encouraged missionaries to work through indigenous political authorities. And where a single form of missionary Christianity was present, together with what looked to colonial and missionary eyes like a relatively coherent political order and single ethnic identity, homogeneity of Christian belonging and practice sometimes developed over time. Missionaries liked to work with single-language groups, seemingly united people groups sometimes converted more or less together, and the colonial order preferred the perceived resulting coherence and stability.

Regarding the types of missionaries present in each region, Uganda remained distinctive in the near-monopoly of two types of Christians: Catholics and CMS-linked Anglicans, both of whom grew throughout the twentieth century. There were small groups of Orthodox Christians who had once been Anglicans, as well as Muslim strongholds from earlier trading posts or former colonial soldiers from Sudan who settled after their service, and a few places that saw short-lived resurgences of traditional religion. But Catholics and especially Anglicans were ascendant. The latter operated throughout the protectorate, having among their converts most of the elites, including kings and chiefs. For their part, Catholics developed three distinct regions, each linked to the dominant male missionary group: the center and west under the direction of the White Fathers, the east led by Mill Hill missionaries, and the north overseen by Comboni missionaries. Different groups of Catholic sisters, often at first linked by predominant national origin to the male missionary order dominant in that area, assisted throughout the protectorate, providing education and medical care. Rivalries developed between Catholics and Anglicans, sometimes based on local competition among chiefs. They could be bitter, playing out in the establishment of mission stations, the adminis-

(Chicago: University of Chicago Press, 2011); Julie MacArthur, "The Making and Unmaking of African Languages: Oral Communities and Competitive Linguistic Work in Western Kenya," *Journal of African History* 53, no. 2 (2012): 151–72; Derek R. Peterson, *Ethnic Patriotism and the East African Revival: A History of Dissent, c. 1935–1972* (Cambridge: Cambridge University Press, 2012).

tration of schools, and in seeking colonial support for social projects.

In Kenya and Tanganyika, along with Zanzibar, there were more diverse groups of Christians than Uganda. In Kenya, a large number of different Christian bodies gathered adherents especially in the center and west of the country, while the remote north and the Islamized Indian Ocean coast saw little Christian growth. The railroad and settler presence led to dispersed bodies of Protestants throughout the country. Presbyterians and Anglicans were the largest of the Protestant groups, with western Kenya full of smaller bodies like the Seventh-Day Adventists, Quakers, and various faith missions.

In Tanganyika, Anglicans continued to grow, mostly under UMCA leadership near the coast, where they began, and at other places where missions had been founded. The CMS had yielded to German missionary societies before World War I. Still, CMS-sponsored Australians came to central Tanzania and gathered many new believers. Meanwhile the largest number of Protestants in Tanganyika remained the Lutherans, who were linked to the several different German missionary societies' originating work.

In both Kenya and Tanganyika, as in Uganda, three major groups of male missionaries had formal responsibility for the Catholic presence. In Kenya, the Spiritans operated in the east and around Nairobi, the Consolatas in the center, and Mill Hill missionaries in the west. In Tanganyika, leadership remained with the White Fathers in the west, the Benedictines in the south, and the Spiritans in the east and northeast. Everywhere religious sisters worked alongside the men, chiefly in healthcare and education.

International changes in the broader Protestant and Catholic world affected Christianity in eastern Africa. On the Protestant side, ecumenical cooperation grew somewhat fitfully. On the one hand, the 1910 Edinburgh Conference represented a high-water mark for Protestant ecumenical missionary idealism, gathering many leaders, especially from the US and Great Britain, who embraced the goal of bringing the world to Christ in one generation. Ironically, many leaders set their hopes on China especially, with Africa deemed unlikely to show much progress quickly.[51] Though such idealism took a hit in World War I, ecumenical cooperation began again before too long, with areas like eastern Africa natural laboratories for interdenominational missionary cooperation. The International Missionary Council—founded in 1921 and a seedbed for the later World Council of Churches, with which it merged in 1961—tried to build upon Edinburgh's ideals. It turned its attention to Africa, and a one-week conference addressing missionary work on the continent took place at Le Zoute, Belgium in 1926. One German delegate noted, "Nowhere in the world has the Church such an overwhelming importance as in Africa,"[52] and many urged the churches to provide education that respected African culture while debating the advisability of forcible attacks on native practices like polygamy. European "specialists" on Africa, missionaries and academics, dominated the proceedings, and only five of the 220 delegates present were black Africans. In retrospect, one cannot help but note the absence not only of African participants but also of any discussion of theological education in Africa, something that would preoccupy mission leaders after World War II.

On the Catholic side, African leadership remained in its infancy. Papal encyclicals had long pushed for native clergy, as well as indigenous religious brothers and sisters, but in eastern Africa efforts had shown few results in most places by the 1920s. Masaka in Uganda, home of Katigondo Seminary and where the White Father bishop Henri Streicher had exerted such energy on behalf of indigenous priests, was an exception. It received the first sub-Saharan African bishop, Joseph Kiwanuka, in 1939, the culmination in a process that made Masaka nearly free of missionaries. This was unprecedented: a Catholic diocese under sub-Saharan African control.

Propaganda Fide, the Vatican's office for missionary activity, took special interest in Africa, too, seeing possibilities for Catholic growth. The 1920 beatification of the Uganda Martyrs galvanized Catholic energy in the region, as did the Vatican-proclaimed 1925 Jubilee year, one of the periodic such obser-

51. Andrew F. Walls, *The Cross-Cultural Process in Christian History* (Maryknoll, NY: Orbis, 2001), 63–66.

52. Sundkler and Steed, *History of the Church in Africa*, 634.

vances—with missionaries promoting both events as occasions for large and elaborate celebrations. The Vatican's representative, or apostolic delegate, visited British East Africa in 1930, which led to the founding of the Legion of Mary, a lay devotional movement that gathered many, especially women, into devotional prayer groups. Edel Quinn became a traveling evangelist for the Legion of Mary in eastern Africa beginning in 1936 and traveled across the region founding local chapters in Kenya, Tanganyika, Uganda, and beyond before her death in Nairobi in 1944. The Holy Year of 1950 proclaimed by Pope Pius XII saw Archbishop Mathew of Mombasa push numerous devotional activities like the rosary and the Legion of Mary across eastern Africa.[53]

Throughout the 1950s, new papal encouragement led to more African bishops. No longer was the region's Catholic administration under the control of Propaganda Fide's assignments of missionary groups to their territories, called the practice of *ius commissionis*. Instead, ordinary diocesan structures slowly appeared. A new crop of missionaries also came from Europe, called *Fidei Donum* priests after the papal encyclical that called for them to assist the church's move toward local self-determination. Unlike earlier missionaries, they were diocesan priests who volunteered to work in Africa.

Amid the growth of Christian churches, the end of World War I prompted British colonizers as well as missionaries Protestant and Catholic to focus on the building of schools, both for the purposes of evangelization and developing the colonies in eastern Africa by providing an educated populace. Already by the end of the nineteenth century, small schools existed at nearly every mission. The standard model that developed throughout eastern Africa—as in many other places—saw so-called "central schools" at the large mission stations and "bush schools" near the many small chapels affiliated with the main stations. The pace was set in Uganda, where both Anglicans and Catholics had already developed extensive networks of primary education by the early twentieth century. In addition, secondary education for the elites, with a focus on training

53. Hastings, *History of African Christianity*, 54–55.

clergy and other religious workers, emerged there, drawing young men—and soon, women—from all over the protectorate. Compared to Uganda, the expansion of schools throughout the colony was slower in Kenya, and slower still in Tanganyika, yet in both places missionaries established impressive institutions. Along with schools, mission-founded hospitals appeared in the larger towns, with rural clinics at mission stations.

THE EAST AFRICAN REVIVAL FROM 1929 TO WORLD WAR II

The most important religious movement that occurred amid the growth of mission-founded Christianity in twentieth-century eastern Africa was the East African Revival, whose forms are traceable to late nineteenth-century evangelical spiritual currents of the Keswick movement in the United Kingdom.[54] The Revival's precise beginning in eastern Africa has been ascribed to a fateful 1929 meeting in Rwanda between an Anglican missionary doctor, Joe Church, and an African orderly, Simeon Nsibambi. In their encounter, the two men confessed their faith to each other and studied the Bible intensely, leading to a deeper friendship with Jesus and between them. Their gathering and subsequent partnership were repeatedly described at evangelical gatherings thereafter, thereby creating a pattern of public confession and testimony that, along with the Luganda hymn *Tukutendereza Yesu* (meaning "We praise you Jesus" in Luganda), epitomized revivalist rallies for the next four decades.

Despite the celebrated interracial story of friendship marking the Revival's formal beginnings, there had been predecessors, that is, outbreaks of public confessions of sin during rallies that featured personal testimony of Jesus's salvation. These occurred in southern Tanganyika in 1916 and ten years later among

54. On the Revival, see the brief summaries in Mark A. Noll, *The New Shape of World Christianity: How American Experience Reflects Global Faith* (Downers Grove, IL: InterVarsity, 2009), 169–87, and Maseno, "Christianity in East Africa," 115–16. For a fuller discussion, see the essays in Kevin Ward and Emma Wild-Wood, eds., *The East African Revival: History and Legacies* (Burlington, VT: Ashgate, 2012), as well as relevant sections of Peterson, *Ethnic Patriotism*.

Quakers in western Kenya, and were linked to Spirit-led movements that would end up leading to African independent churches. The Revival traceable to the physician Church, Nsibambi, and later Nsibambi's brother-in-law William Nagenda, however, expanded in unprecedented ways, soon moving across eastern Africa. Teams of preachers journeyed from Uganda and Rwanda to Tanganyika, Kenya, and beyond, creating new leaders who themselves traveled the railroads. They preached the need to be saved by Christ, urging believers beyond the perceived formalism and dead intellectual focus of *kusoma* (KiSwahili for "reading") Christianity—that is, the Christianity of established churches linked to literacy and schooling. In addition to invigorating passive Christians, revivalists, called the *Balokole* or "saved ones" in Luganda (*Walokole* in KiSwahili), also targeted alleged remnants of traditional beliefs, such as recourse to fetishes, ethnic food taboos, and alleged practices of witchcraft.

The revivalists also targeted so-called "modernism" in scriptural interpretation, which led to controversies with missionary educators at local centers for theological scholarship. In 1941, a group of students at the Anglican seminary in Mukono, Uganda, a CMS bastion, were expelled due to their vociferous disagreements with the warden, whose supposed liberal theology they felt undermined his orthodoxy. William Nagenda was among their leaders, and a little over a decade later, Nagenda and Joe Church visited the US, where they were celebrated by Billy Graham and others. By the mid-twentieth century, the revival style had become the norm for Protestant Christianity in many places in eastern Africa, though it was never without its critics, both among missionaries and African believers wary of such enthusiasms.

AFRICAN-LED CHURCHES IN EASTERN AFRICA BEFORE THE 1960S

Compared to elsewhere in Africa, eastern Africa was slow to develop African-initiated churches (AICs).[55] In addition, none have grown to the size of famous ones in western and southern Africa like South Africa's Zion Christian Church or Nigeria's Redeemed Church of God in Christ.

Besides their relative small scale, three other distinctive features mark the appearance of AICs in eastern Africa. First, far fewer AICs have appeared in Uganda and Tanzania than in Kenya.[56] The few that arose in colonial Tanganyika were linked to larger AICs in Nyasaland, today Malawi.[57] In Uganda, they coalesced around royal figures like the kabaka of Buganda, thus were often less Christian and more rooted in an earlier religious expression. One example was the Bataka movement of the late 1940s and early 1950s, which was led by a former Catholic seminarian and brought together educated Ugandan citizens and a few progressive chiefs to push for more self-rule against British colonialism, missionary Christianity, and traditional Baganda politics.[58]

The larger AIC presence in Kenya compared with its neighbors can be attributed to several factors. First, the greater European settler population in Kenya increased African frustrations, which manifested themselves in religious fervor against missionary control. Second, there were a greater number of Protestant groups in the Crown Colony, which heightened awareness of competing ways of being Christian. Kenya also had fewer Catholics than the other two colonies, and early AICs most commonly arose among peoples evangelized by Protestants. The hierarchical self-understanding of the Catholic Church seems to

55. Such churches have been variously described as Africa independent, indigenous, instituted, or initiated churches—hence the usefulness and/or ambiguity of the acronym AICs.

56. For a summary of Kenyan AIC origins, see Marko Kuhn, *Prophetic Christianity in Western Kenya: Political, Cultural and Theological Aspects of African Independent Churches* (Frankfurt am Main: Peter Lang, 2008), 33–39.

57. Hastings, *History of African Christianity*, 78–79.

58. Hastings, *History of African Christianity*, 33–34.

prompt less secession. The greater presence of AICs in Kenya also, however, might reflect the particular cultural frameworks of the peoples in Kenya among whom such AICs have arisen—mainly Kikuyus and Luos, both lacking the centralized political leadership that was common in other parts of the Great Lakes region. Political instincts rooted in cultural identity sometimes predispose subgroups to fissure instead of maintaining unity, and this arguably played out in the Christian sphere as well.

The cultural and historical forces that shaped AICs in eastern Africa raise a second feature, which is that, unlike western and southern Africa, few of the AICs in eastern Africa took the so-called "Ethiopian" form. This term refers to a typology of AICs developed by Bengt Sundkler in the 1940s.[59] Sundkler noted that some AICs resembled mission-founded churches but simply had African leadership—the Ethiopian type—while others took on rather different features in their religious practices and leadership styles—the Zionist type. Sundkler's typology has its flaws, yet the absence of Ethiopian-style churches in eastern Africa compared to southern or western Africa invites an explanation. It may be that opportunities for African leadership present in Catholicism and Anglicanism in eastern Africa, especially in Buganda—rare examples of openness to indigenous agency in missionary-founded churches—lessened the drive to establish Ethiopian-type AICs.

Where Ethiopian-type AICs appeared in eastern Africa, they did so in response to what was felt to be excessive missionary control. One famous example arose among the Kikuyu of Kenya after missionary attempts to suppress so-called female circumcision,[60] also known as female genital mutilation, which was linked to initiation into adulthood for girls among the Kikuyu, as male circumcision was for boys. The Christians who left missionary churches in the late 1920s among the Kikuyu had all

59. For a discussion of Sundkler's methodology and influence, see Paul V. Kollman, "Classifying African Religions Past, Present, and Future: Part One. Ogbu Kalu and the Appropriation of Pentecostalism," *Journal of Religion in Africa* 40, no. 1 (2010): 3–32.

60. This is a common practice in much of Kenya and Tanzania that involves the surgical removal of female genitalia and is linked to becoming an adult.

sorts of grievances, many connected to loss of land, but only in response to the missionary crackdown on female circumcision did the African Independent Pentecostal Church (or AIPC, which despite its name was not Pentecostal in today's sense), appear. The AIPC was instrumental in the rise of the Kikuyu Independent Schools Association (KISA) and similar groups in the late 1920s and early 1930s. Both the AIPC and KISA followed missionary patterns in religious and educational style, thus fitting the designation "Ethiopian."

The history of the AIPC connects to a third distinctive feature of AIC-linked activity in eastern Africa, which was the appearance of Orthodox Christianity in Uganda and Kenya. This affiliation with Orthodoxy suggests an eastern African predilection to loyalty to venerable Christian bodies and practices of ecclesial conformity to global norms—a predilection not as clearly visible elsewhere in Africa. The option for joining the global communion of the Orthodox churches is, of course, in an overt sense the antithesis of the move toward independency as normally understood. Yet central Kenya's AIPC, beginning as an AIC, itself later joined the Orthodox communion out of a concern for the validity of its ordinations after it left missionary control. This move was at once a move toward independency in light of eastern Africa's existing religious situation—since the Orthodox were before that not present in eastern Africa except perhaps in isolated individuals from Europe—*and* an attempt to embrace a global Christian identity with an august tradition. In addition, it arose amid conditions reminiscent of those that prompted Ethiopian AICs elsewhere, such as perceptions of missionary curtailing of African Christian leadership.[61]

Similar instincts had earlier led certain Ugandan Christians, previously Anglicans, to seek connection to global Orthodoxy, beginning in 1919. Among them Reuben Spartas was a leader from 1932 until his death in 1982, and in 1946 he visited Alexandria, where the Patriarch appointed him Vicar General of Africa.[62] Spartas was jailed several times, the last from 1950 to 1953 after involvement with the Bataka modernizers resisting

61. Hayes, "Orthodox Mission"; Burlacioiu, "Expansion."

62. Hastings, *History of African Christianity*, 33; Burlacioiu, "Expansion," 85–91.

colonial overrule, yet his longer-term impact lay in the Orthodox leadership he provided to a small group of fellow Ugandan believers. Over time, both the Ugandan and Kenyan bodies of Orthodox Christians, at first under the authority of external Orthodox bodies, formed their own national hierarchies.

INDEPENDENCE IN THE EARLY 1960S AND ITS AFTERMATHS

THE CHURCHES PREPARE FOR INDEPENDENCE, 1945 TO THE EARLY 1960S

The end of World War II saw many missionary efforts to renew their churches with new recruits and the training of thousands of Africans for church leadership as teachers, catechists, ordained ministers—and, for Catholics, male and female members of religious orders. Churches also were shaped by white settler mobilization efforts to preserve and advance colonial control, all the while recognizing the appearances of proto-nationalist groups in all three countries.

The late 1950s saw nearly all mission-founded churches in eastern Africa aware of the likely coming of independence for Uganda, Kenya, and Tanganyika (soon to be Tanzania). In his influential 1957 book *Church and Politics in Africa*, CMS missionary John V. Taylor, outstanding chronicler of Anglican efforts in Uganda, urged missionaries to support movements for independence, and most groups intensified efforts to place Africans in leadership positions. Among Catholics, efforts on behalf of what was called the "lay apostolate"—that is, empowerment of the laity as Catholic leaders—began before the Second Vatican Council of 1962–1965, especially in Uganda under the leadership of the Canadian White Father Yves Tourigny, who helped organize a Lay Apostolate Council in every diocese by 1956.[63] Similar Catholic efforts took place through the formation of the Catholic Social Guild in Tanganyika. Many Protestant groups

63. W. B. Anderson, *The Church in East Africa: 1840–1974*, trans. Maureen Eyles (Dodoma, Tanzania: Central Tanganyika Press, 1977), 166.

across eastern Africa had long had programs of a similar nature already in place.

Catechists remained central to evangelization across eastern Africa, while critical observers noted the poor quality of their training.[64] Bishop Joseph Blomjous, a White Father who served as bishop of Mwanza through the early independence years, sought to increase catechists' effectiveness among Catholics, starting a new catechetical training center at Bukumbi, site of the earliest White Father mission in Tanzania.

Formal programs for education and training for ministry had also long been underway among Catholics and Protestants, with many of the programs organized for Protestants having an ecumenical shape building on missionary cooperation. These intensified as awareness of independence's imminence grew. Mukono in Uganda, St. Paul's in Kenya, and the Lutheran seminary at Makumira in Tanganyika emerged as institutional centers for formation of clergy and catechists. Still, there was a way to go. Four Anglicans had been ordained bishop at Namirembe Cathedral in Kampala in 1955, but they were junior or went elsewhere to serve. In 1960 there were still no black Anglican bishops heading dioceses in eastern Africa, only seven assistant bishops.[65] After independence, however, the days of expatriate bishops were numbered, and by the 1980s nearly all bishops in Protestant churches were Africans.

On the Catholic side, strongholds in Masaka in Uganda, Moshi in Tanganyika, and Nyeri in central Kenya grew as sites where many young men and women were being formed into priests, nuns, and religious brothers. Though Masaka had an African Catholic bishop from 1939 in Kiwanuka, African bishops remained very rare into the 1960s. There was one from among the Fipa in the diocese of Karema, Charles Msakila. More momentously, the priest Laurean Rugambwa (1912–1997), born in Tanganyika but trained at Katigondo Seminary in Uganda, became bishop of a small diocese in the northwestern part of the country in 1952. He later became cardinal archbishop of Bukoba in 1960, the first African cardinal appointed. At the Sec-

64. Hastings, *History of African Christianity*, 113–14.
65. Hastings, *History of African Christianity*, 112–13.

ond Vatican Council, Rugambwa often spoke on behalf of the few indigenous African bishops present. At the council proceedings, the bishops of eastern Africa were organized by the White Father Blomjous and the American Holy Cross bishop of Fort Portal, Vincent McCauley, both of whom hosted meetings in Rome to discuss the proceedings.[66] By the time Rugambwa retired in 1985, the majority of Catholic bishops in eastern Africa were African. Today the rare expatriate bishop serves in a missionary setting where indigenous clergy remain few or amid a pastoral crisis that makes naming an African priest difficult—as in the wake of the 1994 Rwandan genocide for Uganda's neighboring border diocese of Kabale, where the Canadian White Father Robert Gay became bishop in 1996.

In all three countries-to-be, Christian leaders, most still expatriates, issued letters and guidelines calling for responsible Christian citizenship in the new nations.[67] Most touched on the themes of social commitment to advances in education and healthcare, the need for integrity in public life, and urged resistance to sectarian tendencies based on religion, region, or ethnicity. Ominously, however, Archbishop Kiwanuka's 1961 letter that urged monarchs to live within constitutions in the anticipated new nation enraged the kabaka, who responded by arresting the priest-rector of Kampala's Catholic cathedral.[68]

In Kenya and Tanganyika, religious differences played only minor roles in the run-up to independence. In Uganda, however, the embryonic political parties of the emergent country reflected longstanding intra-Christian rivalry, with the mostly Anglican Uganda People's Congress (UPC) and the mostly Catholic Democratic Party (DP) dominant by the late 1950s.

A preliminary election prior to formal independence chose the DP's Benedict Kiwanuka, a Catholic, as first minister, a sign that he would be the first president of independent Uganda, for Catholics were the majority faith in the country. Loyalists

66. Richard Gribble, *Vincent McCauley, C.S.C.: Bishop of the Poor, Apostle of East Africa* (Notre Dame, IN: Ave Maria, 2008), 221–27.

67. See the discussion in Hastings, *History of African Christianity*, 148–53, which discusses the Tanganyikan bishops' 1953 letter *Africans and the Christian Way of Life* and their 1960 *Unity and Freedom in the New Tanganyika.*

68. Hastings, *History of African Christianity*, 153.

to the kingdom of Buganda who had founded their own party called the Kabaka Yekka (KY, "kabaka alone"), however, had boycotted the preliminary election. Their subsequent participation in the formal first election after independence drew away enough voters from the DP for the UPC's Milton Obote to ally with the KY, giving Obote the inaugural presidency. Some see Uganda's subsequent political unrest and tragic death toll—the kabaka deposed and exiled by Obote in 1966, then Obote's overthrow by Amin in 1971, the bloody years of Amin's regime, then Obote's return after Tanzania ousted Amin in 1978–79, with Museveni deposing Obote in the mid-1980s after another bloody civil war—traceable to that ethnically and religiously inflected election.[69] Uganda's civil unrest between 1971 and 1985 led to the death of hundreds of thousands. Christian churches suffered at the hands of Amin and Obote, with both Catholic and Protestant leaders, lay and ordained, assassinated.

CHRISTIAN CHURCHES IN THE NATION-STATES OF KENYA, TANZANIA, AND UGANDA, 1960S TO THE PRESENT

Meanwhile, Christianity has remained an important force in all three countries, adapting to the new nation-states in a variety of ways. The Mau Mau uprising of the 1950s led some to anticipate an anti-Christian backlash in Kenya upon independence—after all, some church leaders had worked to "cleanse" onetime believers of the taint of the Mau Mau oaths, in what some CMS-linked Anglicans called the "Moral Rearmament Movement" featuring forced public confession[70]—but it was little felt. In all three countries, most mission-founded Protestant churches gained self-rule, taking their part in denominational global networks. If they were churches with bishops, nearly all developed an entirely African episcopacy. The Anglican churches in Kenya, Tanzania, and Uganda, for example, have national struc-

69. John Mary Waliggo, "The Catholic Church and the Root Cause of Instability in Uganda," in *Religion and Politics in East Africa*, ed. Holger Bernt Hansen and Michael Twaddle (Athens: Ohio University Press, 1995).

70. Ward, *History of Global Anglicanism*, 181.

tures instead of formal dependency on Canterbury. Similarly, in the mid-1950s Tanganyika's northern province of Lutherans formed an autonomous national body, with Stefano Moshi the first African to be the leading bishop in 1958. In 1963 he became head of the newly formed Evangelical Lutheran Church of Tanganyika (later Tanzania). In 1971, Kenya's Africa Inland Mission became the Africa Inland Church, somewhat later than other Protestant bodies. National Catholic bishops' groups also arose in all three countries, with new dioceses formed on a regular basis since independence. Some local church leaders, notably Kenya's John Gatu, a Presbyterian, famously called for a missionary moratorium, arguing that it was needed if the churches of Africa were to grow into maturity.[71]

A variety of international Christian lay movements—some linked with particular churches, others more ecumenical—have been present in eastern Africa over the past century, and many have grown since independence. These include the Scripture Union, an evangelical movement founded in nineteenth-century England to bring the Bible to all. Its African headquarters are in Nairobi, and all three countries in eastern Africa have chapters. Other evangelical movements present in eastern Africa have included Youth with a Mission (YWAM), Youth for Christ, and Campus Crusade for Christ (now known as Cru in the US). Catholic organizations for laypeople since the 1950s include Catholic Action, along with particular groups like a number organized for women and men in parishes, as well as Young Christian Workers and Young Christian Students (YCS). Many remain prominent in Catholic circles, and YCS, like the Scripture Union, remains common in secondary schools across eastern Africa.

Eastern Africa's role as a center of emerging world Christianity has been enhanced by its hosting of a number of international Christian events in the late twentieth and twenty-first centuries. These include the rallies of international evangelists like Reinhard Bonnke of Germany at various times since the 1980s, many preachers from Nigeria and Ghana, as well as from the US and

71. Isichei, *History of Christianity in Africa*, 325–27.; Sundkler and Steed, *History of the Church in Africa*, 959.

other western countries. In 1969, Pope Paul VI visited Uganda amid the first tour by a pope of sub-Saharan Africa. At the new shrine of the Uganda Martyrs in Namugongo, near Kampala, he consecrated a number of bishops and announced to the African Christians assembled that they "were now missionaries to yourselves." In 1975, the World Council of Churches held its General Assembly in Nairobi, with 664 delegates and many observers.[72] In 1984, the Catholic Church held an international Eucharistic Congress in Nairobi, indicative of the city's importance for the worldwide faith. Pope John Paul II visited all three countries in eastern Africa during his pontificate, drawing throngs to Kenya in 1980, 1985, and 1995; to Tanzania in 1990; and to Uganda in 1993. Pope Francis visited Uganda in November 2015. Catholics and other eastern Africans flocked to see the popes, suggesting the excitement they felt at these global Christian events.

Besides such events, continental and international Christian organizations have also made their home in eastern Africa, with Nairobi becoming a regional hub and global center of Christianity. The All Africa Council of Churches (AACC), linked to the World Council of Churches, held its first meeting in Kampala in 1963. Today representing around 120 million Christians in Africa—that is, most of the so-called mainline Protestant churches, as well as the Orthodox and some AICs—its headquarters moved to Nairobi after a few years in Zambia. The Association of Evangelicals in Africa, linked to the World Evangelical Alliance and housing many churches wary of the WCC due to perceptions that it lacks evangelical fervor, is also headquartered in Nairobi. Nairobi also is home to the continental offices of the Organization of African Instituted Churches (OAIC), which represents AICs. The churches listed in the East Africa OAIC region number nearly one hundred, with about half located in Kenya, one third in Tanzania, and the smallest number in Uganda.[73] The headquarters of the regional association of the Roman Catholic Church, the Association of Member Episcopal

72. J. W. Hofmeyr, "Mainline Churches in the Public Space, 1975–2000," in *African Christianity: An African Story*, ed. Ogbu Kalu (Trenton, NJ: Africa World, 2007), 317.

73. See "East Africa Region," Organization of African Instituted Churches, https://tinyurl.com/y8n62jtw.

Conferences of Eastern Africa (AMECEA), a constituent member of the continent-wide Symposium of Episcopal Conferences of Africa and Madagascar (SECAM), is also located in Nairobi, representing thirteen countries from Ethiopia to Zambia.

Church music in all three countries began to reflect African musicality in the independence period, and each major denomination now has a hymnal with mixed hymnody in the local vernaculars and international languages. Swahili hymns are especially well developed since it is the most common language for worship across eastern Africa. Tanzania pioneered Swahili hymnody in Makumira among Lutherans, and from Father Mbunga in Peramiho,[74] and the 1984 Eucharistic Congress gave a great boost to Kenya's Swahili-language Catholic song production.

Traditional Christian emphases on education and healthcare have continued in the post-independence era. New issues faced by churches across the region have included the growing urbanization of eastern Africa, which created new social problems and opportunities to which churches have responded with new forms of urban ministry. Importantly, eastern Africa became one of the global centers in the explosion of cases of HIV/AIDS from the early 1980s. Efforts to fight HIV/AIDS galvanized new cooperative efforts among Christian groups to treat the disease and halt its spread, building on ecumenical cooperation that had been spurred by independence.[75]

As noted, Uganda's Catholic-Anglican tensions had been particularly sharp in the colonial period, but even before independence bishops cooperated a bit, forming a Joint Christian Council. When Paul VI visited in 1969, Anglican Bishop Leslie Brown joined him at the Uganda Martyrs' Shrine in Namugongo.[76] More recently, Pope Francis visited the Anglican martyrs' shrine when he visited Namugongo in November 2015. Still, local tensions did not lessen to a great extent until the Amin years, when all suffered. Since then, despite local rivalries, major leaders of Uganda's two largest churches have worked together on a number of initiatives. Besides cooperating on HIV/AIDS

74. Anderson, *Church in East Africa*, 179.

75. Anderson, *Church in East Africa*, 170.

76. Sundkler and Steed, *History of the Church in Africa*, 1018.

education and treatment, they have addressed the longstanding violence in the north of the country, sought expansion of schooling, and condemned corruption. In Kenya and Tanzania, inter-Christian cooperation has been somewhat easier, with especially impressive cooperation among Lutherans, Catholics, and Muslims in Bukoba in Tanzania since the 1960s.[77]

Tanzania also witnessed the institutional strengthening of all the larger churches. In addition, the writings and policies of Julius Nyerere, self-consciously shaped by the social outlook deriving from his Catholic faith, have a historical significance unique in eastern Africa—and beyond. His February 1967 Arusha Declaration along with other writings articulated a path toward self-reliance and development that avoided Cold War alternatives. His thought drew on the progressive Catholic social teaching of his missionary friends, especially Father Dick Walsh, onetime headmaster at St. Mary's in Tabora, where Nyerere had taught, who later became the Catholic Secretary for education in Tanganyika.[78] By the early 1970s, some of the socialist aspects of Nyerere's policy of *ujamaa* (Swahili for "familyhood") drew criticisms from both firm anti-communists and those who foresaw economic perils. Critics included some of his fellow Catholics after Nyerere chastised the Catholic countries of Europe like Spain and Italy as lagging behind the mostly Protestant nations of northern Europe.[79] The Catholic bishops' 1970 pastoral letter, a translation of a 1932 anti-communism encyclical, in turn angered the President. Still, though bishops' groups were divided over *ujamaa*, most of the country's Christian leaders—Catholic and Protestant—embraced the philosophy and policies that Nyerere espoused. The nationalization of schools that followed in the wake of the Arusha Declaration drew little complaint.

77. Sundkler and Steed, *History of the Church in Africa*, 1016.

78. Frieder Ludwig, *Church and State in Tanzania: Aspects of a Changing Relationship, 1961–1994* (Leiden: Brill, 1999), 32. For a fuller discussion of the Catholic background of Nyerere's ideas, see John C. Sivalon, "Roman Catholicism and the Defining of Tanzanian Socialism: 1955–1985" (PhD diss., University of Toronto, 1990).

79. Ludwig, *Church and State in Tanzania*, 102–5.

PENTECOSTAL GROWTH IN EASTERN AFRICA IN THE POST-INDEPENDENCE PERIOD

As in other places in Africa, eastern Africa has witnessed the expansion of Pentecostal-charismatic Christian forms since the 1980s to the present. There had been precursors,[80] many of them subsumed by or connected to the East African Revival, but over recent decades churches that are formally Pentecostal in structure and sometimes in global connection have grown while new ones have appeared. In addition, styles of prayer shaped by Pentecostalism—prominent healing ministries, deliverance from spirits, ecstatic prayer, and large rallies with vibrant preaching and praise-and-worship music—have increasingly featured in mainstream Protestant and Catholic churches alike, leading to large charismatic movements, especially among Catholics. None of the Pentecostal churches of eastern Africa approach the size of counterparts in Nigeria or Ghana, yet the major cities of the region all have very large urban churches that are locally founded and others connected to international Pentecostal churches like the Assemblies of God.

Yet Pentecostalism in eastern Africa is not without its particular features. One commentator has noted the unique predominance of Nordic Pentecostal preachers in the region.[81] Others note the close affinities between African traditional religions and Pentecostal practices and describe the Pentecostalization of nongovernmental organizations in places like eastern Uganda.[82] A distinctive aspect of Pentecostalism in Kenya has been the appearance of strong women leaders. As Philomena Mwaura, a Kenyan Catholic theologian, has shown, women like Margaret Wanjiru, founder of the Jesus Is Alive Ministries in 1993, and Teresia Wairimu of Faith Evangelists Ministries, appeal to Kenyans who feel powerless in the face of contemporary urban

80. Anderson, *Church in East Africa*, 168–70.

81. Martina Prosén, "Pentecostalism in Eastern Africa," in *The Routledge Companion to Christianity in Africa*, ed. Elias Kifon Bongmba (New York: Routledge, 2016).

82. Martin Lindhardt, ed., *Pentecostalism in Africa: Presence and Impact of Pneumatic Christianity in Postcolonial Societies* (Leiden: Brill, 2015); Ben Jones, "Pentecostalism and Development in Sub-Saharan Africa: In the Office and in the Village," in *Pentecostalism in Africa*, ed. Martin Lindhardt (Leiden: Brill, 2015).

realities, especially women like themselves.[83] Many of these female pastors and preachers began in churches where their leadership was unwelcome. By either joining Pentecostal churches or starting their own, they found a distinctive voice with which to empower others with the life of the Spirit. Some have also sought training as evangelists in Nigeria, Ghana, or the US.

As with the appearance of AICs earlier in the twentieth century, Kenya has likely seen a larger growth in Pentecostalism than Uganda and Tanzania. Given the political turmoil of the 1980s and 1990s, some commentators saw these Christian movements contributing to Kenya's stagnation, with Pentecostalized religion developing into a civil religion uncritically supportive of the corrupt regime of President Daniel Arap Moi. Moi, a member of the Africa Inland Church, began his career with a low-profile Christian identity, but in the 1980s began to parade his Christian credentials buoyed by his AIC participation and his annunciations of his saved status at rallies led by the international preacher Reinhard Bonnke. For political scientist Paul Gifford, such behavior showed the danger of Christian piety at the service of political domination. Gifford and others also have argued that Pentecostalism encourages individualism that undermines social ties among African families as well as social intolerance of groups like Muslims and other non-Christians, and marginalized groups like gays and lesbians.[84] Others have defended African Christians against such accusations on the grounds of African cultural values, saying that conflating Pentecostalism with the so-called Prosperity Gospel overlooks a variety of ways that faith inspires believers.[85]

83. Philomena Njeri Mwaura, "Gender and Power in African Christianity: African Instituted Churches and Pentecostal Churches," in *African Christianity: An African Story*, ed. Ogbu Kalu (Trenton, NJ: Africa World, 2007), 373; Damaris Parsitau, "'Arise, Oh Ye Daughters of Faith': Women, Pentecostalism, and Public Culture in Kenya," in *Christianity and Public Culture in Africa*, ed. Harri Englund (Cambridge: Cambridge University Press, 2011).

84. Paul Gifford, *Christianity, Politics, and Public Life in Kenya* (New York: Columbia University Press, 2009), Paul Gifford, *Christianity, Development and Modernity in Africa* (London: Hurst, 2015), John A. Chesworth, "Fundamentalism and Outreach Strategies in East Africa: Christian Evangelism and Muslim *Da'wa*," in *Muslim-Christian Encounters in Africa*, ed. Benjamin F. Soares (Leiden: Brill, 2006), 159–86.

85. Ogbu Kalu, ed., *African Christianity: An African Story* (Trenton, NJ: Africa World, 2007). This is also a theme of several contributors to Harri Englund, ed.,

***

Many of the issues touched on in this chapter are linked to specific denominations, the sociopolitical role of Christianity in eastern Africa, and theological developments that will be considered in the next three chapters.

Christianity and Public Culture in Africa (Cambridge: Cambridge University Press, 2011).

3.

Denominational

Christianity's Varieties in Eastern Africa

As the chronological survey in the previous chapter shows, a variety of Christian forms have existed in eastern Africa, and proliferation has only increased over the last few decades. In particular, African-initiated churches (AICs) have mushroomed, both homegrown and Pentecostal-linked churches from western and southern Africa, which in turn have encouraged new ways to be Christian. Nonetheless, longstanding denominational distributions remain in place. So-called mainstream Christian denominations linked to early missionary activity remain strong across the region. Roman Catholics constitute the largest single group in all three countries, and significant Anglican-linked bodies are also present in each. In addition, Lutherans, Presbyterians, Moravians, Quakers, Seventh-Day Adventists, and other international Christian groups have substantial presences in one of the countries—though at the same time they are nearly absent elsewhere.

A number of interrelated factors help explain contemporary denominational distributions in Kenya, Uganda, and Tanzania. *First*, the nature of the religious field for initial evangelization has played a prominent role in certain places. Thus, there are areas in eastern Africa where a certain missionary group, Protestant or Catholic, made an early sizeable effort without a competing Christian group and no large Muslim presence. In that region the first Christian group usually remains numerous with local people linked to that denominational identity by reputation and self-attribution. Presbyterian missionaries from Scotland, for instance, arrived in east-central Kenya in the colonial period and, where they worked, a sizeable number of Presbyterians live to this day. Similarly, late nineteenth-century German Moravian missionaries came to southern German East Africa, and today contemporary Tanzania houses the largest number of Moravian believers of any country, mostly in the south.

A *second* factor, linked to the first, revolves around the ethnic identity of people within regions. European missionaries newly arrived in a certain place often sought facility in a language that they perceived to allow access to the people nearby who could understand it, or who in light of translation came to regard it as their own. Translation usually took place in a complex and contentious relationship with other missionaries and expatriates, as well as local believers whose assistance was underacknowledged. This process often brought a language forged from local variations to a standardized written form. Consequently some ethnic groups, united by language and linked to particular locales, have widespread shared Christian affinities. Many Lutherans, for example, live on the slopes of Mount Kilimanjaro, and most are Chagga, remnants of the efforts of German Lutheran missionaries who first reached the area in the 1890s. Similarly, a large number of Quakers—members of the Society of Friends—live in Western Kenya, linked to the initial efforts of British and American missionaries who worked among peoples today known as the Kisii, Luo, and Luhya, among whom African Quaker leaders quickly appeared.

Population movements responding to historical forces represent a *third* factor that shapes denominational distribution today. The coasts of Kenya and Tanzania, for instance, have been largely Muslim for centuries and thus Christians remain comparatively few. In larger cities along the Indian Ocean, however, migration from other parts of the region has brought many Christians. The Christian identities of the incoming migrants—their journeys motivated by concerns such as political unrest at home, illness and the desire for better medical care, or the search for education or employment—shape the nature of Christianity in cities like Mombasa and Dar es Salaam. Certain neighborhoods there, and in other large cities like Nairobi, have taken on a distinctive ethnic identity, at times with a preponderant religious identity linked.

Variations in the oppressive nature of the colonial experience have arguably shaped denominational distributions, a *fourth* factor. Kenya, for example, suffered the harshest colonial experience during the British colonial period, and perhaps 20 percent of its Christians belong to AICs, whereas Uganda and Tanzania have only 3.7 percent and 1.9 percent AIC membership among their Christians.[1]

A *fifth* factor determining denominational distributions lies in the emergence of strong religious figures from among African believers—galvanizing African leaders of mission-founded churches as well as charismatic pioneers who founded African-initiated churches. Such men and, at times, women, gathered Christians of different ethnic groups together into an existing ecclesial body, or brought new churches into being. Eastern Uganda, for instance, has seen a diversity of Christianities rare in the rest of the country, some traceable to an early leader named Semei Kakungulu. Kakungulu, after embracing a variety of ways to be Christian late in his life, even founded a community of Jews. Similarly, charismatic individuals or small groups of visionaries lie at the origins of most of the AICs of western Kenya, where many have originated.

Reliably determining numbers of adherents to different religious bodies is a notoriously difficult task. International efforts such as those linked to the Pew Foundation or the World Christian Database offer estimates, yet so, too, do individual denominations, which obviously have their own interests as they count themselves. In addition, as in many other places, fixed religious identity has become hard to mark among eastern Africans, with many Christians worshiping and participating in a number of different Christian (and other religious) bodies simultaneously.

1. Laurenti Magesa, *What Is Not Sacred? African Spirituality* (Maryknoll, NY: Orbis, 2013), 103.

A growing number of Christian congregations, in eastern Africa as elsewhere, also proclaim their nondenominational status. Finally, labels like "Pentecostal" and "evangelical" when affixed to Christians sometimes identify a particular denomination, such as the Assemblies of God, while other times they refer to a style of Christian practice that can attach itself to denominations that are not otherwise seen as formally "Pentecostal" or "evangelical." For example, the Catholic Church in all three countries, like other larger and internationally linked Christian churches in eastern Africa, has a sizeable charismatic movement with officially recognized status. Its adherents are thus simultaneously Catholic and Pentecostal—often labeled "charismatic" in accord both with their self-description and a growing scholarly consensus. Thus, they can be double-counted, which makes comparison and accuracy problematic. What is offered here by way of estimates of denominational membership thus must be viewed as provisional.

While attention will be given to historical developments, this chapter prioritizes present-day denominational circumstances and is organized in a country-by-country fashion.

KENYA

Kenya's population of 45 million is currently estimated to be 82 percent Christian, with Protestants 47 percent, Catholics 23 percent, and other Christians 12 percent. About 11 percent of the country is Muslim. Catholics thus number between 10 and 11 million in the country, with the breakdown of other prominent denominations as follows: 4.5 million in the Anglican Church of Kenya (or ACK), 4–5 million in the Presbyterian Church of Eastern Africa (PCEA), and 14 million counted as "renewalists," that is, people practicing Christian forms roughly described as Pentecostal, charismatic (Christians who worship in a Pentecostal manner but remain in other churches, such as the Catholic or Anglican Church), or neo-Pentecostal, with the largest such group the Assemblies of God (perhaps 1.5 million). Other sizeable denominations include the Africa Inland Church, with 2.5 million; Seventh-Day Adventists, 350,000; and Quakers (or Society of Friends), 130,000. Compared to Uganda and Tanzania, Kenya has a larger number of African independent churches, and new groups appear all the time.

The Protestant presence in Kenya is more diverse than in either Uganda or Tanzania. It began with the efforts of the Church Mission Society of the Anglican Church at the coast in the 1840s, and soon gathered other groups. In 1862, Thomas Wakefield led a group of British Methodists to the coast of the Indian Ocean who settled in Ribe. Other Protestant groups soon followed, most beginning among the Kamba, a people who were a few days' journey from the heavily Muslim coast. Bavarian Lutherans came in 1881, followed soon by Scottish Presbyterians, who also worked in central Kenya, and the Africa Inland Mission from the US in the 1890s.

Beginning in the 1880s, the short-lived Imperial British East African Company (IBEAC) handed out large tracts of land to both Protestant and Catholic missionaries, often near an existing missionary presence, sometimes inaugurating the presence. Such properties, besides guaranteeing the missions a place moving ahead, also linked particular denominations to the people living near, since local Africans tended to join the missionary groups that made contact. When the IBEAC gave way to direct control from the British Foreign Office, missions found themselves holding considerable property, circumstances noticed by Africans who felt disenfranchised by colonial-era land seizures.

The *Anglican Church in Kenya* only took that name in 1998, after many years linked to the worldwide Anglican Communion as the Church Province of Kenya (CPK).[2] Anglicanism in the country derives from the first missionary efforts in eastern Africa in the modern era, begun by Johann Ludwig Krapf and Johann Rebmann of the low-church[3] Anglican Church Mission Society (CMS) in 1844 and 1846, respectively. Their translations into Swahili and other local languages of a few books of the Bible

2. See their website: "Church History," Anglican Church of Kenya, https://tinyurl.com/y7py8qe6.

3. The term "low-church" refers to tendencies among Anglicans that moved away from Catholic concerns with formal liturgy and bishops toward more evangelical styles of worship and congregational leadership. In contrast, "high-church" or "Anglo-Catholic" refers to those among Anglicans with a more formal liturgical and ecclesiastical style.

were groundbreaking, as were their explorations in the region. A man with physical disabilities who came to their mission before dying, Mringe, was the first convert to be baptized in 1853. The CMS sponsored work among slaves starting in the 1870s, linked to simultaneous work by the high-church Anglican Universities' Mission to Central Africa (UMCA) at Zanzibar. These Anglican efforts earned international recognition, especially with the establishment of freed-slave settlements in Rabai and Freretown, both not far from Mombasa.

An Anglican diocese, "Eastern Equatorial Africa," was formed in 1884, covering Uganda, Kenya, and Tanzania. James Hannington was sent from Great Britain as the first bishop. Hannington was killed on his way to Uganda by agents of the kabaka (or king) of Buganda, but before that he ordained ex-slaves Ishmael Semler and William Jones, the first Africans ordained in eastern Africa. Both were "Bombay Africans," slaves freed at sea who had first been sent to India, then returned to eastern Africa in the 1860s to assist Rebmann at Rabai.[4] More concerted training for African evangelists began at Freretown in 1889, and in 1898 the diocese of Mombasa was founded, covering what is Kenya and northern Tanganyika.

Anglicans arrived in central Kenya at Kabete in 1900 and a few years later they cooperated with other missionary groups in the translation of the Bible into Kikuyu. Meanwhile Anglicans also worked on translations into Swahili (a New Testament came in 1909, with the entire Bible finished by 1914) and the western Kenyan language of Luo beginning in 1900.

As Nairobi grew, it became a center for Protestant cooperation in matters such as Bible translation, eventually leading to what is today the ACK (Anglican Church of Kenya) Language and Orientation School. Anglicans also played a key role in other ecumenical efforts toward missionary cooperation, sometimes over the protests of UMCA bishops like Zanzibar's Frank Weston, who resisted intercommunion with non-Anglicans that was planned at a 1913 meeting. After a delay and modification due to the ruling of the archbishop of Canterbury, the process continued more slowly, eventually leading, however, to the

4. Strayer, *Making of Mission Communities*, 15.

famous Alliance High School near Nairobi, founded in 1926. One famous CMS missionary in Nairobi was George Burns, an Australian former boxer and policeman who led the church in the city with a strong hand from 1905 to 1932.[5] In western Kenya, CMS Archdeacon Walter Edwin Owen (1879–1945) was a noted defender of Africans against colonial abuses, though he never questioned the colonial enterprise.

Various structural changes and milestones have affected Kenya's Anglican presence. In 1930, the CMS divinity school moved from Freretown to Limuru, in the highlands near Nairobi, what is today part of St. Paul's University, formerly St. Paul's United Theological College, which was founded in 1954 together with Methodists and Presbyterians. Other events of note include the separation of Tanganyika from the diocese of Mombasa in the late 1920s, the inauguration of Anglican missions in northern Kenya beginning in the 1930s, collaborating with other Protestant groups to form the Christian Council of Kenya in 1943, multiple translation projects that fostered ecumenical cooperation, and in 1955 the ordination of the first Kenyan Anglican bishops Festo Olang' and Obadiah Kariuki. Olang' became the first Kenyan archbishop in 1970. Other international Anglican groups like the Church Army, which pursues evangelization and social welfare, have also entered the country. International Anglican meetings have also been hosted in Kenya, and today there are twenty-nine dioceses for the 5 million or so Kenyan Anglicans.

The most important theological and spiritual current shaping Kenyan Anglicanism has been the East African Revival, which came from Rwanda and Uganda in the 1930s. Revivalists from Rwanda first arrived in 1937, and by 1938 Kenya had its own rallies. Kenya's Anglican leaders have usually been deeply shaped by the East African Revival.

Methodists in Kenya are few, but they have a long presence in the country. In 1862, a group of missionaries sent by the United Methodist Free Churches of Great Britain arrived in Mombasa. Inspired by Krapf's reports and led by Thomas Wakefield, who was soon joined by Charles New, they settled at Ribe nearby.

5. Sundkler and Steed, *History of the Church in Africa*, 559–60.

Soon came three Sierra Leonean missionaries sent by Methodists linked to western Africa.[6] For decades, Wakefield enjoyed a strong reputation for hospitality and cooperation among his fellow missionaries and explorers, but converts were rare, and Methodists have never become numerous in Kenya. Still, in 1967 the Methodist Church in Kenya became independent of the British Methodist Church, with membership at about 8000. And the Kenyan Methodist Sam Kobia became General Secretary of the World Council of Churches in 2003.[7]

Today twelve synods govern the church, one of which is located in Uganda, and they claim a growth rate of nearly 8 percent per year. Numbers of adherents were not available, but they remain comparatively low. Nonetheless, churches exist throughout the country and they work among most of Kenya's ethnic groups. In addition, Methodists sponsor over 140 schools, a large hospital and several clinics, polytechnic and educational training centers, as well as the Kenya Methodist University, which had its first graduating class in 1997 and now sends out several thousand per year from its main campus in Meru and branches in five other locations across the country. In addition, Kenya's Methodists cooperate with other groups in sponsoring St. Paul's University, previously St. Paul's Theological College, in Limuru.[8]

The *Presbyterian* Church of East Africa (PCEA) traces its origins to the desires of early officials of the Imperial British East Africa Company (IBEAC), Sir William Mackinnon and Alexander Low Bruce, to found a mission linked to the Church of Scotland. In 1891, IBEAC-financed missionaries left Great Britain and arrived in Mombasa. James Stewart, founder of a famous Church of Scotland mission in Lovedale, South Africa, arrived to assume leadership, and soon he led a journey to start a mission in Kibwezi among the Kamba, focusing on agricultural development. Illness drove them further from the coast, toward the

6. Sundkler and Steed, *History of the Church in Africa*, 555.

7. Dana Robert, *Christian Mission: How Christianity Became a World Religion* (Chichester, UK: Wiley-Blackwell, 2009), 74.

8. "Methodist Church in Kenya," World Council of Churches, https://tinyurl.com/y9earpt5; "About the Methodist Church," The Methodist Church in Kenya, https://tinyurl.com/y9u8ngje; "Synod Structure," The Methodist Church in Kenya, https://tinyurl.com/yagkwakb.

highlands of central Kenya, where they founded new missions among the Kikuyu near what is today Nairobi. In 1898 they took the name the Church of Scotland Mission (CSM), soon founding a large mission at Thogoto, a name whose origins lie in the local Kikuyu attempts to pronounce the word "Scot." The school at Thogoto educated Johnstone Kamau, an activist for African rights who later took the name Jomo Kenyatta and became Kenya's first president. Smaller missions were established elsewhere, including in Nairobi. The first native elders were ordained in 1920 and six years later saw the ordination of the first African pastors: Musa Gitau, Benjamin Githieya, and Joshua Matenjwa. St. Andrew's in Nairobi was the prominent Presbyterian church in the colonial capital, and it remains there today.

The most famous Presbyterian missionary in the colonial period was John Arthur (1881–1952), who arrived in Kenya in 1906, and who helped forge the ecumenical cooperation that culminated in a famous 1913 conference at Kikuyu with other Protestant missionary leaders. Though the initial ambitions for unity were delayed, first by the criticisms of Frank Weston, leader of the high-church (UMCA) Anglicans in Zanzibar, and then by World War I, the Alliance of Protestant Missions was eventually established in 1918. Like CMS Archdeacon Owen, Arthur resisted the forced conscription of Kenyans into the British force in World War I, eventually founding his own group of "native carriers" and serving as its captain in an effort to protect them. He also defended Africans against arbitrary land seizures by the British and was longstanding headmaster of Alliance High School. In the late 1920s, he was among the leaders of the missionary campaign to stop clitoridectomy, or female genital mutilation, in central Kenya, resistance to which led to independent schools and churches, especially among the Kikuyu.

Subsequently Presbyterians contributed to St. Paul's United Theological College in Limuru, Alliance High School, and various medical missions all linked to the Alliance, which included Episcopalians and Methodists as well. US Presbyterians have assisted in Kenya since the expulsion of several missionaries from Sudan in the late 1950s. They have supported the expansion of medical services, including the reestablishment of a hospital in

Kikuyu in 1990, and helped found the Christian Organizations Advisory Trust in 1975 to train church leaders in business practices. John Gatu, a PCEA leader who taught at St. Paul's and famously called for a moratorium on missionaries to Africa in the 1970s, studied theology at Princeton in the US.[9]

Currently the PCEA has fifty-four presbyteries divided into five regions and hundreds of parishes in east and central Africa, most in Kenya, with two in Tanzania, where the PCEA went in 1950. They total perhaps 4 million in the region, with nearly all in Kenya.

Today Kenya has perhaps 350,000 *Seventh-Day Adventists* (SDAs), making it, with the US, Tanzania, Zambia, Malawi, and Rwanda, among the largest national groups in the world.[10] The first two missionaries, Canadian-born Arthur Carscallen (1879–1964) and Peter Nyambo (d. 1968), an African teacher from Nyasaland (now Malawi), arrived in Mombasa in 1906 and soon headed to the eastern side of Lake Victoria. They had met in England, where Nyambo went after meeting the Adventist leader Joseph Booth in Nyasaland, but Nyambo soon left Kenya for home. Carscallen stayed, founding a string of missions over the next thirteen years before leaving Kenya. In 1913, he set up a printing press and published in English and Luo, a language he was the first to write, later producing a grammar and Luo New Testament.[11]

Today the SDAs run Adventist University outside Nairobi, as well as many other schools and medical clinics, most in western Kenya where most adherents live. Nairobi is also headquarters of the East-Central Africa Division of the global General Conference of Adventists. Recent growth has taken place in Tanzania and Uganda, but the majority of eastern Africa's SDAs are Kenyan. These include Elder Blasious Ruguri, who was educated at Andrews University in Michigan and elected president

9. William B. Anderson, "Africa," in *A History of Presbyterian Missions, 1944–2007*, ed. Scott W. Sunquist and Caroline N. Becker (Louisville: Geneva, 2008), 234–55.

10. "2015 Annual Statistical Report," Seventh-Day Adventist Church, last revised August 8, 2017, PDF, https://tinyurl.com/ycu7rsye.

11. "Carscallen, Arthur Asa Grandville," Dictionary of African Christian Biography, https://tinyurl.com/y9tgtmpl.

of the East-Central Africa Division in 2010, then reelected in 2015.[12]

Kenya has more *Quakers* than any other nation, about 150,000.[13] Their origins lie with American Quaker missionaries Arthur Chilson, Edgar Hole, and Willis Hotchkiss who arrived in eastern Africa in 1902, settling about twenty miles from Kisumu at Kaimosi in western Kenya, where they founded a mission. Most Quakers still live in western Kenya. The first missionaries taught the local Kavirondo people, who eventually were differentiated into the Bantu Kavirondo (later, Luhya) and Nilotic Kavirondo (later, Luo). Quakers focused first on the Maragoli, one of the Luhya peoples. By 1919 there were 200 converts among the Maragoli.[14] A 1914 printing press and Bible translation led to consolidation of the Maragoli dialect of Luhya. By 1929 the New Testament in the language of the Maragoli was complete,[15] with the Friends Bible Institute opened in 1942, while the whole Bible was translated in 1951. In addition, a clinic was built by 1919,[16] becoming a formal hospital in 1941. Other medical work included a colony organized for treating those with leprosy.

In 1946, the first meeting of the East Africa Yearly Meeting of Friends took place. In 1964 it spread into Uganda and later into Tanzania, where an earlier Quaker effort had taken place linked to English Quakers on the island of Pemba, which is part of Zanzibar. The missionaries to Pemba had pursued abolition and amelioration of the lot of former slaves. Ironically, their efforts had complex consequences for those they sought to help. Missionary efforts overlapped with and, at times, competed with the slaves' own efforts to mitigate their vulnerability after the 1897

12. Stephen Chavez, Wilona Karimabadi, and Marcos Paseggi, "6 Newcomers among 13 Division Presidents," Adventist News Network, July 7, 2015, https://tinyurl.com/y8l4jv4w.

13. "World Distribution of Quakers, 2012," QuakerInfo.com, https://tinyurl.com/ya7tzp9l.

14. Kenda Mutongi, *Worries of the Heart: Widows, Family, and Community in Kenya* (Chicago: University of Chicago Press, 2007).

15. Herbert Kimball and Beatrice Kimball, *Go into All the World: A Centennial Celebration of Friends in East Africa* (Richmond, IN: Friends United, 2002), 33.

16. Kimball and Kimball, *Go into All the World*, 28.

Emancipation decree.[17] Quakers remain numerous, especially in western Kenya, where they resemble more evangelical Quaker bodies elsewhere.

Kenya's *Africa Inland Church* had as its precursor the Africa Inland Mission (AIM), founded by Peter Cameron Scott, who came to Kenya in 1895 and died the next year. Linked to missionary supporters in Philadelphia, AIM worked among the Kamba in eastern Kenya before spreading to other parts of the country.[18] In 1943, AIM became the Africa Inland Church, adopting its own constitution in 1952. In 1995, AIC celebrated its centenary at the Moi International Sports Centre in Nairobi. Then President Daniel Arap Moi, an AIC member who counted on AIC support during his rule in Kenya, was an honored guest.[19] Linked to the AIM was the Gospel Mission Society, which began in Kiambu starting in 1902. It trained Harry Thuku, an early agitator for African self-determination who worked to protect African land from European seizure. He was imprisoned in 1922 by the British.

The *Catholic* presence in Kenya is related to places where the earliest three European-based missionary groups operated. In the area around Nairobi and to its east, all the way to the Indian Ocean, Spiritans—first mostly French, then later Irish—arrived in the late nineteenth century after beginning in what is today coastal Tanzania and Zanzibar.[20] Before long, Italian missionaries of the Consolata Fathers, centered in Turin, arrived in Kenya, ostensibly to head north into Ethiopia to work among what were then called the Galla (today, the Oromo). In fact, much to the Spiritans' chagrin, the Consolata missionaries stayed in central Kenya, founding missions among the Kikuyu, Embu, and Meru, as well as, more slowly, in regions to the north. In western Kenya, Mill Hill missionaries, who began working alongside the White Fathers in Uganda, eventually received missionary

17. Elizabeth McMahon, *Slavery and Emancipation in Islamic East Africa* (Cambridge: Cambridge University Press, 2013).

18. Waller, "They Do the Dictating."

19. "About Us: Background," Africa Inland Church Kenya, https://tinyurl.com/ybr6ywy9.

20. Cothrai Gogan, *History of the Holy Ghost Mission in Kenya* (Nairobi: Paulines Publications, 2005), 13–21.

responsibility for eastern Uganda as well as western Kenya. Their territory soon was divided by the colonial-era boundary between the Uganda Protectorate and the Crown Colony of Kenya.

Until the early twentieth century, the tiny Catholic presence in Kenya remained under the control of the Catholic diocesan see of Northern Zanzibar, except for the west, which remained instead connected to the Catholic Church in Uganda as part of the Mill Hill mission territory. The Consolata areas of central Kenya received semi-formal autonomy in 1905, and the Mill Hill western areas of Kenya received similar status in 1925. Spiritan areas remained connected to Tanganyika and Zanzibar. No formal diocese was established in Kenya itself until 1953, when dioceses were set up in Nairobi and Kisumu, under the Spiritans and Mill Hill missionaries respectively, as well as in Meru and Nyeri, under the Consolatas. Prior to that, ecclesial structures of the apostolic prefecture and apostolic vicariate, steps in the move toward a diocese governed by the Vatican's missionary office Propaganda Fide, organized the Catholic presence.

Catholics grew in central Kenya during the Mau Mau revolt. Some see the reason as the national background of the missionaries present, for the two groups of Catholic missionaries—the Consolatas, who were Italian, and the Spiritans, who were mostly Irish—differed from the British colonizers, and Africans noted the difference. In addition, some have suggested that Catholic practices of confession provided the moral cleansing that imprisoned Mau Mau captives needed after the taboo-violating oathing ceremonies that featured in the movement's initiation processes.

As elsewhere in eastern Africa, the changes in Catholic jurisdictions in Kenya have been many, and they are ongoing as the church responds to new realities. Today there are four metropolitan sees—that is, those with an archbishop: Nairobi, Kisumu, Mombasa, and Nyeri. Connected to each are a number of dioceses, with the total of dioceses and archdioceses reaching twenty-four. The archbishop in Nairobi generally receives a cardinal's hat, a sign of the city's importance. Other important Catholics in the country include the apostolic nuncio, the pope's diplomatic representative, who in accordance with tradition is a bishop and never a citizen of the country where he serves.

Beginning in the middle of the twentieth century, a number of other Catholic religious orders have come to Kenya, receiving jurisdiction of parishes, schools, hospitals—or receiving other responsibilities—first from the original three missionary groups and later the bishops. In the last forty years or so, Nairobi has become a major center for the formation of Catholic clergy and consecrated religious in Africa, with over fifty religious orders and missionary societies training men and women in the archdiocese. Most also seek to have a pastoral presence, so schools and parishes are also often run by such groups. Major institutions include many seminaries and certain hospitals; the Catholic University of Eastern Africa, which is organized by AMECEA, the Catholic bishops' association of eastern Africa; and Hekima University, run by the Jesuits. The Basilica of the Holy Family, completed in 1960, prominently appears on Nairobi's skyline.

Global *Pentecostalism* has a strong presence in Kenya, the first place in eastern Africa to encounter the movement in the early twentieth century.[21] At that time, missionaries carrying the message, many from the US and linked to the Azusa Street mission in Los Angeles, went around the world preaching new life in the Spirit. Clyde Miller, linked to Charles Parham's Pentecostal ministry in Topeka, Kansas, arrived in western Kenya and founded Nyang'ori mission in 1907, at first hoping that the Spirit would allow hearts to respond to Christ even if he only preached in English. Miller later sold the mission to two other Pentecostal missionaries, a married couple, Otto and Marian Keller, a German and Canadian, respectively. Marian and her first husband, Karl Wittich, had come with the Canadian Assemblies of God to Tanganyika, and after her husband's death, she continued to work as World War I broke out. Fleeing to Kenya, she met Otto, who had been her husband's friend in Detroit. After purchasing Miller's mission, they established numerous

21. "Historical Overview of Pentecostalism in Kenya," Pew Research Center, August 5, 2010, https://tinyurl.com/y7ljpyom.

congregations in western Kenya over the next decades, effectively founding the Assemblies of God in eastern Africa.[22]

Growth through the twentieth century was steady but slow, exploding in the independence period as global Pentecostal currents came to Kenya and the rest of eastern Africa. In 1957, American preacher T. L. Osborn founded a ministry in Mombasa, from which Pentecostals moved to the rest of Kenya and beyond. The Assemblies of God came to Nairobi in the 1960s, and churches proliferated afterward, some local, some with global connections.

The regime of Daniel Arap Moi (1978–2001) saw divisions among Kenya's churches, with Catholic leaders and those of most mission-founded Protestant churches calling for multiparty democracy, and many evangelical and Pentecostal leaders supporting Moi and the single-party state. Pentecostals came under fire from some Kenyans for their uncritical support of Moi, who became an unpopular dictator. Still, they have grown. International Pentecostal preacher T. D. Jakes drew a million people to a rally in Nairobi in 2006. A Pentecostal style also shapes Catholics and Protestants belonging to other churches, many of whom participate in formal movements like the Catholic Charismatic Renewal.

Compared to its neighbors, Kenya has been home to the most *African-Initiated Churches* (AICs) in eastern Africa, most of them from the western and central parts of the country.[23] The earliest accounts that exist of many AICs come from European missionaries frustrated by the preliminary manifestations of rebellion among converts. Many AICs only later recounted their own origins in official narratives. Very commonly such formalized founding narratives tell of mission-trained catechists or teachers receiving visions from a spirit or the Holy Spirit. Such churches are thus often labeled "Roho" churches (from the KiSwahili word for "spirit"), and these Roho churches are especially common in western Kenya. Due to their simultaneous emergence in the 1920s and 1930s in colonized Africa, scholars have linked

22. Kalu, *African Christianity*, 301. See also "Keller, Marion and Otto (A)," Dictionary of African Christian Biography, https://tinyurl.com/yc9ts8na.

23. Kuhn, *Prophetic Christianity in Western Kenya*, 33–39.

Kenya's Roho churches to the Aladura churches of Nigeria and Zionist churches in South Africa.[24]

Sometimes, as in Kaimosi in western Kenya, Roho movements began with missionary encouragement linked to global Pentecostal growth, and then gradually grew beyond missionary control, eventually rejecting oversight by expatriates. At Kaimosi, Arthur Chilson, a leader of the Friends African Mission, or Quakers, first welcomed the enthusiasm of his western Kenyan converts. Later, however, those converts rejected the doctrinal guidelines he sought to enforce, eventually forming the African Church of the Holy Spirit in 1933. Today it numbers between 500,000 and a million members in Kenya and belongs to the World Council of Churches. As noted on the WCC website on the church, "Members are identified by a cross on their clothes."[25]

Other times outright rebellion against missionary control stands at the origin of an AIC, with those forming the new church either leaving of their own accord or forced to secede after accusations of false doctrines or practices. A common pattern involves the death of a heroic forerunner—often linked to colonial violence—galvanizing those who come after. The origins of the Ruwe Holy Ghost Church among the Luo follow this pattern, with Alfred Mango's death in a fire in 1913 remembered later as the church founded in his name grew, starting in the 1920s. It is one of three similar Roho churches headquartered in Nyanza Province, western Kenya, the other two being the Musanda Holy Ghost Church of East Africa and the Cross Church of East Africa.[26]

Another prominent church that emerged from western Kenya in the early mid-twentieth century is African Israel Church Nineveh, which appeared under the leadership of the Pentecostal Christian David Zakayo Kivuli in the early 1940s after visions

24. For example, Afe Adogame and Lazio Jafta, "Zionists, Aladura and Roho: African Instituted Churches," in *African Christianity: An African Story*, ed. Ogbu Kalu (Trenton, NJ: Africa World, 2007).

25. "African Church of the Holy Spirit," World Council of Churches, https://tinyurl.com/ybasjkvx.

26. Cynthia Hoehler-Fatton, *Women of Fire and Spirit: History, Faith, and Gender in Roho Religion in Western Kenya* (Oxford: Oxford University Press, 1996); Adogame and Jafta, "Zionists, Aladura and Roho," 274–75.

and miraculous appearances of water from a rock near his home. Drum-led processions of members in white robes characterize this church, which is very visible in Nairobi and elsewhere. Most of its members are Luhya and Luo, both groups from western Kenya.

Central Kenya also saw various AICs appear in colonial times. The African Independent Pentecostal Church (AIPC), discussed in the previous chapter, was linked to the controversy over female genital mutilation and independent schools, later joining the global Orthodox communion. In addition, the *Arathi* appeared around the same time. This church, linked to local Kikuyu prophet-healers, drew upon traditional teachings along with Christian aspects in forming their movement with a variety of small communities composing it.[27] In *Facing Mount Kenya*, Jomo Kenyatta referred to them as *Watu wa Mungu*, or "people of God." Their descendants are today dubbed the Wakorino (or Akurinu), a visible group in Kenya due to their white turbans and gowns. Their pacifism and refusal to engage colonialism made them very suspect among the British, and three members were shot in 1934, accused of trespassing after having entered a forest to pray. Instinctively sectarian, at times they have been linked to Kikuyu separatist impulses.

Many colonial-era AICs faced repression from colonial authorities who saw in religious restiveness the potential for political unrest. This was certainly true of many of the Roho churches and the Arathi in colonial Kenya, whose practices included challenging land-grabs by colonizers, resisting the use of European currency, refusing European medicine and education, and wearing distinctive garb (often white robes), all of which aroused suspicion. The Dini ya Msambwa, "religion of ancestors" in the Bukusu dialect of the Luhya in western Kenya, emerged in the 1940s under the leadership of Elijah Masinde, a onetime Quaker. Not formally Christian, Masinde's movement drew on certain Christian beliefs and traditional ancestral veneration to resist colonial demands for taxes and other perceived

27. Francis Kimani Githieya, "The Church of the Holy Spirit: Biblical Beliefs and Practices of the Arathi of Kenya, 1926–1950," in *East African Expressions of Christianity*, ed. Thomas Spear and Isaria N. Kimambo (Oxford: James Currey, 1999).

abuses, and fought the Kenyan police in 1950, with twenty killed, including four police officers.[28]

Even late in the colonial era, a new AIC could occasion violence, as was the case for the origins of the Church of Christ in Africa, commonly known as the Johera, founded by Archbishop Matthew Ajuoga in 1957. The Johera originally were the largest revivalist group within the CMS-linked Anglican Church in western Kenya, yet efforts to constrain them in the 1950s led to the exodus of numerous congregations and clergy, as well as thousands of Anglicans. They were led by Ajuoga, who maintained a style and structure of worship quite similar to the Anglicans, yet in the process churches were destroyed and the colonial police were drawn in.[29]

Most AICs, whether emerging in eastern Africa or elsewhere, derive from Protestant Christianity. Western Kenya, however, has also been the origin of one of the largest AICs traceable to Catholic evangelization, the Legio Maria or Maria Legio church. Like most of the Roho churches, Maria Legio, officially the Legio Maria of African Church Mission, began among the Luo of western Kenya, but it was unusual since it emerged among fervent Catholics. Their spirituality had been shaped by the Legion of Mary as preached by Irish laywoman Edel Quinn beginning in 1936.[30]

Already by the 1930s, local Kenyans claimed to have witnessed Mary appearing to them, and a movement arose. Over the next decades the movement grew, sometimes in tension with the Catholic Church though also in close collaboration with many local parishes. In 1963, however, a group among the Kisii formally left the Catholic Church, led by Simeo Ondeto as well

28. Hastings, *History of African Christianity*, 32–33; Sundkler and Steed, *History of the Church in Africa*, 890–91.

29. Hastings, *History of African Christianity*, 127. The Church of Christ in Africa is thus more of an Ethiopian than Zionist type of AIC, using the typology of Bengt Sundkler described in the chronological chapter. For a fuller explanation of Ajuoga and his church, see the remarkable study by George Pickens, *African Christian God-Talk: Matthew Ajuoga's Johera Narrative* (Dallas: University Press of America, 2004).

30. There is ample material on this movement and on its founders and leaders. Much is mutually contradictory, however, and the online sources are particularly hard to interpret. For an analysis, see Matthew Kustenbauder, "Believing in the Black Messiah: The Legio Maria Church in an African Landscape," *Novo Religio* 13, no. 1 (2009): 11–40.

as—it is claimed—a woman identified as Mama Maria, whose visions were linked to the Fatima appearances and the linked "secrets" of Mary that allegedly occurred in 1917. Some were arrested for plotting violence, but released. Later another early leader, Gaudencia Aoko, claimed the actual early leadership of the church with Ondeto, and condemned his supposed excesses. The current officialized narrative of the church emphasizes Ondeto and, secondarily, Regina Owitch also known as Mama Maria. Ondeto is seen by a large number of adherents to be the incarnate Son of God and a Black Messiah who lives forever, despite his apparent death in 1992.

Over time, Legio Maria's beliefs and rituals have departed from traditional Christianity more and more. The church's practices combine traditional Catholic aspects like the Latin Mass and the rosary with public healing and myths about female ancestral figures among the Luo to whom the Virgin Mary is linked. Features of faith include an intricate hierarchy under a pope, with cardinals, archbishops, and bishops below him; strong beliefs in Ondeto's dying and rising in 1958, making him for some analysts an archetypal "Black Messiah"; apparitions of the Virgin Mary to Luo believers beginning in the 1920s; and self-conscious connections made by adherents between those apparitions and the ones at Fatima in Portugal in 1917.[31] They have a central shrine at Got Kwer in western Kenya, known as "the Mount of Atonement." Besides being present especially in Kenya, the church is also present throughout eastern Africa and in neighboring regions. Its adherents number perhaps one million.

One distinctive aspect of Kenya's AICs and overlapping Pentecostal churches lies in the leadership roles women have taken. Theologian Philomena Mwaura has analyzed women-led AICs in Kenya in a number of publications, describing the personal experiences of the women in question. Mary Akatsa, founder of the Jerusalem Church of Christ in 1985, and Bishop Margaret Wanjiru, who established Jesus Is Alive Ministries in 1993, came to their positions in different ways.[32] Akatsa had a Pentecostal

31. Hastings, *History of African Christianity*, 177–78; Kuhn, *Prophetic Christianity in Western Kenya*, 39–45.

32. Mwaura, "Gender and Power in African Christianity"; Philomena Njeri

background and in 1982 felt a call to a healing ministry while living in a low-income Nairobi neighborhood. Wanjiru was raised Anglican but claims to have been introduced to witchcraft as a young girl. Later converted during the crusade of a Nigerian evangelist, she founded her ministry before leaving it for international preaching a few years later. These female AIC leaders adopt varying media strategies, differ in their relationship to mission-founded churches and their links to Kenya's ethnic groups, and also address Kenya's social problems in diverse ways in their preaching. The very fact of having prominent women in religious leadership challenges assumed social hierarchies, though at times the message of women preachers can reinforce traditional gendered social expectations.

TANZANIA

Tanzania is a relatively new label, forged from the name for the continental portion of the country, Tanganyika, and the islands comprising Zanzibar, at the time of their formal union after Tanganyika's independence and Zanzibar's sudden and violent revolution in 1964. Of the current population of perhaps 45 million, 20 million are deemed Christian, 20 million Muslim, and 5 million as either unreligious or in other religious groups, the largest being African traditional beliefs.

Christians and Muslims, though nearly equal in the country, are not evenly distributed. Islam has a long presence at the Indian Ocean coast and adjacent islands. Zanzibar until 1964 was formally an independent country led by the Oman-linked Sultan of Zanzibar, though the British had actual control. It had long been the gateway for a variety of Christian groups coming not only to Tanganyika but to eastern Africa as a whole. The Christian presence there, however, as along the entire Indian Ocean coastline, remained very small until quite recently, since most people remained Muslim.

Mwaura, "Gendered Appropriation of Mass Media in Kenyan Christianities: A Comparison of Two Women-Led African Instituted Churches in Kenya," in *Interpreting Contemporary Christianity: Global Processes and Local Identities*, ed. Ogbu U. Kalu and Alaine Low (Grand Rapids: Eerdmans, 2008).

The Christian presence in contemporary Tanzania, predominantly inland from the Indian Ocean, has sizeable numbers of Catholics and Anglicans, as well as one of the largest national populations of Lutherans in the world. In addition, there are quite a few Moravians connected to their early missionary practice. In the past several decades, Pentecostal churches have grown as part of the global growth of this form of Christian belonging and practice, though they remain small compared to some other African countries.

Roman Catholics comprise over half of Tanzania's Christian population, 10 or 11 million. The largest Catholic densities lie in places where the first three male Catholic missionary bodies operated and had success, founding institutions that persist to this day. The Spiritans, or Holy Ghost Fathers, who began their efforts at Zanzibar and then coastal Tanganyika, achieved large breakthroughs in numbers of converts around Moshi in the north beginning in the early twentieth century. Today the diocese of Moshi has a large number of Catholics, with priests, sisters, and brothers from there all over the rest of the region as well. Most of the region's people are Chagga, and certain areas of the slopes of Mount Kilimanjaro are almost uniformly Catholic, with very large churches dating back to the early twentieth century.

The Missionaries of Africa, or White Fathers, started working in western Tanganyika beginning in the late 1870s. They found great success among several groups. Perhaps the largest single group of Catholics among those they evangelized are among the Haya people on the western side of Lake Victoria, today mostly the diocese of Bukoba, with converts too among the Nyamwezi and Sukuma in central Tanganyika. They also drew many converts among the Fipa people in the southwestern part of the country, near Lake Tanganyika's eastern shore, who mostly reside in the diocese of Sumbawanga. Like the Chagga around Moshi, the Fipa and, to a lesser extent, the Haya, are largely Catholic. The White Fathers' earliest mission at Bukumbi on Lake Victoria, founded by the same group, some of whose members established the Catholic Church in Uganda in 1879, became the site of a model catechetical center in 1957 founded by the visionary Bishop Joseph Blomjous of Mwanza (1908–1992).

Finally, in the late 1880s, German Benedictines came to what was soon to be German East Africa, founding missions near the coast around Dar es Salaam, but soon concentrating their efforts in the southern part of the territory. They founded large monasteries, first at Peramiho near Songea, later at Ndanda near Lindi. Around Peramiho especially, numerous Africans, many Ngoni, joined them after the crushing of the 1905–1907 Maji Maji rebellion in which the Ngoni figured prominently. Peramiho, like Moshi, Bukoba, and Sumbawanga, has long been seen as a strong center of Catholicism.

Catholics evince considerable vitality in contemporary Tanzania, with bishops often seen as national leaders and intra-Catholic conflicts part of national news. All major cities in the country have Catholic bishops who quite naturally become local leaders. The strong Catholic identity and regular Catholic practice by the country's most famous leader and first president, Mwalimu (KiSwahili for "teacher") Julius Nyerere, made Muslims and many other Christians wary at times. Yet Nyerere usually overcame any suspicions of sectarian loyalties during his more than two decades as Tanzania's chief executive. In fact, some of the strongest criticism of his policies came from Catholic leaders in the 1970s and 1980s, and he often complained about Catholic resistance to his African socialism compared to the cooperation he enjoyed from Protestant churches.

The Catholic Church in Tanzania today is structured with six archdioceses, each headed by an archbishop: Dar es Salaam, Arusha, Mwanza, Tabora, Songea, and Dodoma. Under each of these are between three and eight dioceses, with a total number of dioceses and archdioceses at thirty-four. Though Dodoma is the national capital officially, the archbishop of Dar es Salaam, as head of the largest and most important city, has tended to have pride of place among the bishops. Today the current officeholder, Polycarp Pengo (b. 1944), is the only one that enjoys the position of cardinal, which means that he serves as an elector of the pope. The national organization of the Catholic bishops is the Tanzania Episcopal Conference (TEC), founded in 1956, with headquarters in Dar es Salaam. Like the Catholic episcopal conferences of Uganda and Kenya, TEC belongs both to the Association of Member Episcopal Conferences in Eastern Africa (AMECEA) and the Symposium of Episcopal Conferences of Africa and Madagascar (SECAM).

Besides its institutional infrastructure, the Catholic presence in Tanzania, as elsewhere in eastern Africa, includes substantial medical and educational service. Many hospitals and schools founded by the church have been formally nationalized, though the abrupt nationalization process undertaken after independence has been softened somewhat. Besides the numerous dispensaries and clinics linked to the Catholic Church, distinguished Catholic hospitals include St. Joseph in Peramiho, founded in the 1890s in Dar es Salaam and moved to its present location in the early twentieth century; Tosamaganga hospital in Iringa; St. Francis in Ifakara, founded by Swiss sisters in 1921 and now a regional medical center; Bugando Medical Centre in Mwanza, founded in the late 1960s; and St. Francis in Turiani, near Morogoro, founded in the early 1960s.

The Catholic Church in Tanzania, as elsewhere in eastern Africa, has prioritized the formation of small Christian communities within Catholic parishes. This innovation in parish life, inspired by similar movements in Latin America and inaugurated in eastern Africa within the diocese of Musoma in the 1960s, has spread across the country. Such groups meet weekly, reflecting on the Bible in light of their own experiences, and seeking to live their faith more fully through deeper communal life and shared prayer, including action on behalf of justice. There are now at least 90,000 small Christian communities within Catholic parishes in eastern Africa.[33]

Tanzania's Catholic Church has not been free of controversy. Beginning in the late 1960s, one Tanzanian priest, Fr. Felician Nkwera (b. 1936), began to achieve fame as an alleged healer, working primarily in the south of the country. Featuring fervent devotion to the Virgin Mary, his ministry became institutionalized as the Marian Faith Healing Centre, attracting people

33. Joseph G. Healey and Jeanne Hinton, eds., *Small Christian Communities Today: Capturing the New Moment* (Maryknoll, NY: Orbis, 2005). See also James Jay Carney and Krystina Kwizera-Masabo, "Tanzania: Introduction," Catholics and Cultures, last updated December 8, 2016, https://tinyurl.com/y89l2cmd.

from around the country, across eastern Africa, and beyond. In the late 1980s Catholic authorities began to pressure Nkwera and his movement, which had ties to ultraconservative global Catholic groups, to refrain from healing without permission. He was ordered to move to Dar es Salaam in 1990, where he continued in popularity, and shortly afterward was excommunicated for refusing to abide by hierarchical efforts to curtail what the bishops saw as a dubious practice. Eventually he appealed to the Tanzanian courts, who allowed him to practice his ministry despite the excommunication.[34]

Anglicans in Tanzania today total about 2.5 million, comprising twenty-seven dioceses, one of them in Zanzibar, the rest on the mainland. Compared to Uganda and Kenya, the Anglican presence in Tanzania is smaller and Anglicans have been less influential, both in the colonial period and since independence. This is largely due to German overrule from the 1880s to 1918, when a number of Protestant missionary groups from Germany arrived and took over Anglican missions.

Tanzanian Anglicanism derives from two different historical origins, stemming from the two different Church of England–linked voluntary mission agencies that sent missionaries from Great Britain beginning in the nineteenth century. The Universities' Mission to Central Africa, or UMCA, arrived first in Zanzibar in 1864 after a failed attempt on the Zambezi River in what is today Malawi. Like the Catholics who had arrived a few years earlier, they focused their efforts on slaves, ransoming and educating them in Zanzibar and later settling them at missions on the mainland. Some of those missions, such as at Masasi, became quite famous even if the Christians there, as in Zanzibar, remained few. To this day, Christ Church in Zanzibar, built near the site of the Zanzibar slave market that was officially closed in 1873, looms over Zanzibar's Stone Town.

While the UMCA was a "high church" or Anglo-Catholic body, for the most part, the Church Missionary Society (CMS; later the Church Mission Society) was low church in its ori-

34. See Katharina Wilkens, "Mary and the Demons: Marian Devotion and Ritual Healing in Tanzania," *Journal of Religion in Africa* 39, no. 3 (2009): 295–318; Katharina Wilkens, *Holy Water and Evil Spirits: Religious Healing in East Africa* (Berlin: Lit Verlag, 2011).

entation—that is, more evangelical in its style—and founded a half-century before the UMCA in the United Kingdom. The CMS began work in Kenya twenty years before the UMCA came to Zanzibar, then also went to Uganda in 1877 with great success ensuing. Meanwhile, the CMS began in a smaller and slower way in western Tanganyika in 1878. In a short time, however, conversions linked to the CMS were faster than for the UMCA, mostly due to the absence of Muslims in the areas where they worked. The coming of German missionaries with German colonialism in the 1880s led to some inter-missionary conflicts, and eventually many of the UMCA and CMS missions passed into the hands of one of the German mission societies as the result of cooperative arrangements.

Tanzanian Anglicans resemble others in Africa in their tendency toward social conservatism compared to Anglicans in the UK and Episcopalians in the US, which has led to tensions in the Anglican Communion over the past several decades. Disagreements over the role of women as church leaders, especially priests and bishops, and the welcome accorded to gay clergy have led to public divisions. Certain Anglican or Episcopalian congregations in the US and UK that share their African coreligionists' doubts about the legitimacy of global Anglican positions on these matters have sought to be tied in communion with dioceses in Uganda, Tanzania, as well as Nigeria, which has the largest Anglican population in Africa. In some ways, these conflicts are quite new, but in other ways they are a new version of an older conflict already found in the CMS/UMCA split in Tanganyika. According to Kevin Ward, there were rumors in the colonial period "that the UMCA advised their adherents to attend the Catholic church if they moved to a CMS area [Catholics being considered closer to the bishop-friendly, formal liturgy of the UMCA], and the CMS advised joining the Moravians or Lutherans if their members found themselves in UMCA territory [since the Moravians and Lutherans had less formal liturgy and more congregational ecclesial preferences]."[35]

Compared to Tanzania's Lutherans and Moravians, Anglicans were slower to embrace African leadership. In 1960, for exam-

35. Ward, *History of Global Anglicanism*, 175.

ple, the heroic white anti-apartheid activist Trevor Huddleston became bishop of Masasi, coming from South Africa, and serving until 1968 while becoming a close friend of Julius Nyerere. A split with the Kenya-headquartered Anglican Province of East Africa in 1970 led to John Sepeku being named first Anglican archbishop of Tanzania.

Lutherans in Tanzania comprise just over six million, making them one of the largest Lutheran national constituencies in the world and the second-largest group of Christians in Tanzania. Nearly all of them belong to the Evangelical Lutheran Church in Tanzania (ELCT), which began as the Federation of Lutheran Churches in Tanganyika in 1938 when seven different Lutheran-linked bodies came together. Today the ELCT has twenty-two dioceses encompassing the country, two of which were founded in 2013.[36]

Like other sizeable groups of Lutherans in Africa—in Namibia and Cameroon, (though not Ethiopia, which was not colonized but has the largest Lutheran population in the world)—those seven bodies were traceable to German missionary activity beginning in the late nineteenth century, when the newly united German state established a colonial empire in Africa. In German East Africa, three different missionary agencies played large parts. Not all the missionaries were strongly Lutheran, since Calvinist and Pietist orientations also shaped some of them, and since there was cooperation among Lutheran and evangelical traditions in Germany at the time, both domestically and in missionary work overseas.

First to come was what became known, due to multiple similar groups, as Berlin III, with the formal title the Evangelical Missionary Society for East Africa. They arrived in Dar es Salaam in 1887, founding a station at Kigamboni. Next came Berlin I, formally called the Society for the Advancement of Evangelistic Missions amongst the Heathen, which first worked in South Africa. They settled in the Southern Highlands of what is today Tanzania, their first station being at Ipagika—today in the ELCT diocese of Konde. Over time they cooperated closely with the Moravians. In 1893, the strongly Lutheran Leipzig

36. Evangelical Lutheran Church in Tanzania, http://www.elct.org.

Mission Society arrived in German East Africa, opening a station in Old Moshi, at Kidia.

As with other missionary groups, efforts began with missions near the coast. Their best success in terms of numbers of conversions, however, followed a typical pattern: better results among non-Islamized populations further inland, among settled populations instead of nomads, and among those with more rather than less centralized political structures. Yet there were obstacles, with two Lutheran missionaries and several African assistants killed by local peoples near Arusha in 1896.[37] Violent anti-colonial resistance such as among the Hehe in the early 1890s and the Maji Maji uprising of 1905–1907 undid short-lived missionary advances, yet the onset of German colonial control led to growth in most areas where missionaries were active. Among Chagga speakers around Kilimanjaro and Haya speakers west of Lake Victoria the largest Lutheran communities arose, and it is in these areas that the largest number of Lutherans persist.

The end of the formal German colonial presence in the wake of World War I and the subsequent detention and then removal of German missionary personnel led to disruption at many of the German missionary foundations. Many missionaries returned in the 1920s, however, to discover their mission-founded churches led by newly empowered African converts. One notable missionary, Bruno Gutmann, is widely heralded as a pioneer in appreciating African culture as a basis for establishing an African Christian church. Though the practical impact of his ideas faced opposition both from his fellow missionaries and some African converts who wanted better access to education and literacy—which Gutmann saw as threatening to traditional African culture—he is admired for his embrace of the Chagga culture especially and its potential as the basis of the Christian faith of Chagga believers.[38]

The interwar years saw growth among Lutherans in Tanganyika, with missionaries coming in support from the US as well as from strongholds of global Lutheranism in northern

37. Thomas Spear, *Mountain Farmers* (Berkeley: University of California Press, 1997), 65–68.

38. Ernst Jaeschke, *Bruno Gutmann: His Life, His Thoughts, and His Work* (Arusha, Tanzania: Makumira, 1985); Fiedler, *Christianity and African Culture*, 28–130.

Europe.[39] World War II led to detention of the German missionaries, but less disruption than World War I. The influx of missionaries and resources before and after helped extend the church into most of the British colony. The Swede Bengt Sundkler (1908–1995), a famous historian of Christianity in Africa and a professor at Uppsala, was from 1937 until 1945 a missionary among the Haya in northwestern Tanganyika. After a stretch teaching in Sweden, he returned to be the first bishop of Bukoba from 1961 to 1964. His 1974 book *Bara Bukoba* describes missionary activity and the subsequent growth of the Lutheran Church in Tanzania with the move from missionary to African leadership.[40]

Lutherans in Tanzania have founded and built impressive educational and healthcare institutions. The Tumaini University of the ELCT runs four constituent colleges, namely Makumira (in Arusha), Kilimanjaro Christian Medical College (in Moshi), Dar-es-Salaam College, and Iringa University College. The ELCT also sponsors the Lutheran Junior Seminary in Morogoro, and a network of twenty-three hospitals and more than 140 dispensaries across the country. Lutherans were central in an ecumenical effort with Anglicans and Moravians, supported by funds from the US-based Good Samaritan Foundation, to found the Kilimanjaro Christian Medical Centre in Moshi, an impressive teaching and research hospital. Today there are twenty-five Lutheran dioceses in Tanzania.

Tanzania's Lutherans also have for the past half-century played a strong role in global Lutheranism, carrying out missionary work, for instance, in Zaire (now the Democratic Republic of Congo) and Kenya, both now independent Lutheran national bodies. One of their leaders at the time of Tanzania's independence, Josiah Kibira, served from 1977 to 1984 as the first African to lead the Lutheran World Federation (LWF), the most important international Lutheran body, to

39. For an interesting study of American Lutheran missionaries in twentieth-century Tanganyika and Tanzania, see John S. Benson, *Missionary Families Find a Sense of Place and Identity: Two Generations on Two Continents* (London: Lexington, 2015).

40. On Sundkler, see Marji Liisa Swantz, *Beyond the Forestline: The Life and Letters of Bengt Sundkler* (Leominster, UK: Gracewing, 2002).

which the ELCT belongs.[41] It also participates in the Lutheran Communion in Central and Eastern Africa. The current presiding bishop of the ELCT, Alex Malususa, is the vice-president of the LWF for Africa, one of the seven international vice-presidents.

Tanzanian *Moravians* remain few compared to these larger groups, yet they now total perhaps 500,000 adherents out of 750,000 worldwide, thus by far the most numerous national group in the world. Also known as the Unitas Fratrum (United Brethren) and the Herrnhut community (after the headquarters in Herrnhut, Germany), Moravians have grown quite a bit since their 1891 arrival in southern German East Africa. They now have five dioceses and represent the fourth-largest Christian body in Tanzania. Their earliest mission at Rungwe soon gathered many and when the London Missionary Society withdrew from German East Africa in 1897, they conferred their mission on the Moravians. In the wake of colonial control and the end of the Maji Maji rebellion, locals joined the Moravians, so that two provinces arose in the south. The provinces together began a theological college in the 1960s to train ministers, which today is called Teofilo Kisanji University, located in Mbeya, after the first African bishop. Kisanji (1915–1982), who assumed office in 1966 at a service where Tanzania's Anglican and Lutheran bishops also participated, had previously supported independence as a member of TANU. What were then four provinces came together to form the Moravian Church in Tanzania in 1986 and became a recognized Unity Synod by the international Moravians in 1988.

A number of other Christian denominations have small presences in Tanzania. Seventh-Day Adventists number perhaps 300,000, having grown from small numbers into a sizeable folk church in certain parts of the south of the country.[42] Many of the newer and smaller groups are Pentecostal in their style. Pentecostals arrived in small numbers in the 1920s, with other outside groups coming in the intervening years, including from the US and Sweden. A significant national presence appeared only

41. Ludwig, *Church and State in Tanzania*, 3.

42. See Stefan Höschele, *Christian Remnant—African Folk Church: Seventh-Day Adventism in Tanzania, 1903–1980* (Leiden: Brill, 2007).

in the 1970s. Some of the Pentecostal groups are linked to global networks like the Assemblies of God, while others are more local. Pentecostals grow most quickly in urban settings, where Tanzanian Christians come into new environments due to pursuit of education or employment. Far from their home churches, which are often Catholic, Moravian, Anglican, or Lutheran, they are drawn by the vitality of Pentecostal worship, warm hospitality, and the presence of young people. One estimate puts the number of Pentecostal believers at between 3 and 4 million today. Participants in AICs, many but not all of them Pentecostal in style, probably total slightly fewer, with some obvious overlap between the two classifications.

UGANDA

Christian missionaries arrived later to what is today the country of Uganda than to either Kenya or Tanzania, but the spread of Christianity occurred there more rapidly than in the other two countries of eastern Africa. Today Uganda's population of 40 million is at least 85 percent Christian, with Catholics and Anglicans the two largest groups. Catholics number perhaps 16 million, Anglicans 14 million. The overwhelming number of the two groups is due to several factors, beginning with the enormous colonial growth of both. In addition, both groups successfully allowed African leadership comparatively early, so that reasons for schism arguably were less present. Then the success and vitality of the East African Revival also allowed chances for many forms of Christian leadership and worship especially within Uganda's Anglican Church, which likely lessened inclinations toward schism found elsewhere in Africa. These two bodies' dominance in Uganda was then reinforced in the regime of Idi Amin in the 1970s. Other Christian bodies faced legal obstacles to their missionary activity, since Amin contended that Ugandan religious identity had to be Muslim, Anglican, or Catholic. This kept numbers of other groups quite small.

Over the past three decades, however, other groups of Christians have grown, spurred by outside missionary activity as well as the leadership of Ugandan Christians. In particular, Pentecostal forms of Christianity have expanded in Uganda. In the recent past, national legislation attacking same-sex relationships and same-sex orientation have made global headlines, with the government's actions linked to mobilization by Uganda's Christian leaders, many of them from the newer groups. Some of those opposed to such legislation blame its originating impulse on conservative Christian missionaries from the US.

Both the Catholic and Anglican churches in Uganda appeared in the late 1870s when first the Anglican CMS and then the Catholic Missionary of Africa (White Father) missionaries arrived at the court of the kabaka of Buganda. The tumultuous politics of the next two decades culminated in British colonial control and the securing of the Anglican Church as a type of national church in much of the country. Catholics, likely more numerous countrywide, dominated the area around Masaka and were present nearly everywhere else, though usually Anglicans occupied the roles of kings and major chiefs. Both churches expanded through the twentieth century, developing impressive medical and educational institutions and networks of dioceses and parishes. Ugandans served in important leadership roles beginning in the 1930s in both churches, though up to independence most of the bishops remained European.

The dominance of the two large churches did not mean absence of other Christian-linked religious innovation. One famous rebel against existing religious conventions was Semei Kakungulu, who left the CMS in frustration over British limits to his authority, eventually founding a small group of Jewish Ugandans. Another, Reuben Mukasa Spartas, resisted the paternalism of Anglican missionaries in the early twentieth century, eventually becoming an Orthodox priest linked to the Greek Orthodox Church.[43] Similar links were made in Kenya in the mid-twentieth century, and in 1958 the East African diocese linked to the Greek Church was formed.[44] Numbers, however, remained small and today there are few Orthodox Christians in either country.

The *Anglican* Church of Uganda originated with CMS

43. Sundkler and Steed, *History of the Church in Africa*, 635–36.

44. Hayes, "Orthodox Mission in Tropical Africa," 383–98; Burlacioiu, "Expansion," 82–98.

missionaries who arrived in 1877, soon taking up residence near the kabaka of Buganda. In competition with French Catholic missionaries who soon followed and joining Muslims who were also present, the Anglicans grew tremendously during the turmoil of the next decades, with complex episodes of conflict eventuating in their triumph as the official colonial church. Led by notable missionaries Alexander Mackay and later Bishop Alfred Tucker, they developed a strong group of local Anglican leaders, including the historian and ethnographer Apolo Kagwa, who also served as regent and prime minister (or *katikkiro*) to several kabakas from 1890 to 1926. In Uganda, the CMS struggled over the issue of church constitution, which would give the Anglicans there limited self-rule. Such a constitution was supported by Bishop Tucker due to his confidence in Baganda Christians but by few other missionaries, even after its final approval in 1909.

Famously, Uganda's Anglicans developed a unique set of close relationships between the monarchies in the southern part of the country, all of them formally Anglican, and the colonial regime. The royal link in Buganda with the colonial regime, like that of the later king of neighboring Rwanda to the Belgians, remained especially tight. As with the queen of England, the kabaka maintained a formal ceremonial role in the Anglican Church in Uganda, and he also maintained formal political authority in the parliament, or *Lukiiko*, of Buganda. Real power, however, remained in both cases with foreigners: the bishops and the British colonial governor. In addition, *katikkiros*, or royal councilors, like Apolo Kagwa became close confidantes to the colonial regime as well as Anglican missionary leaders. Finally, the traditional Bagandan levels of chieftainship and subchieftainship in local constituencies mapped onto Anglican parochial structures. As late as the 1950s, CMS leaders in London played a role in Uganda's colonial politics. In 1953 the Ugandan governor, Andrew Cohen, exiled Kabaka Mutesa II amid scandal and political agitation for Buganda's independence, and CMS director Max Warren helped facilitate his return and an end to political unrest in 1955.

Of course, Anglican engagement in Uganda centrally concerned evangelization. Famous Anglican Baganda catechists like Apolo Kivebulaya (1864–1933) spread the faith across the colony and elsewhere in eastern Africa. Anglicans also founded schools like King's College, Budo, which opened in 1906 and trained national leaders. CMS missionaries were also instrumental in the formation of the colonial medical system.

The East African Revival arose most fervently among Uganda's Anglicans. Most of the saved ones, or *Balokole*, never left missionary-founded churches like the Anglican Church of Uganda, largely due to the leaders like William Nagenda who valued the ecclesial assumptions of Anglicanism. Yet the style of the Revival, with its features of personal empowerment through the Spirit, wariness about entrenched clerical authority, frequent pacifism, and intrinsic rejection of formal strictures that shackled enthusiasm, naturally stretched the sensibilities of many missionary leaders, especially those invested in the values of *kusoma* (or "reading") Christianity. Though most Ugandan Anglicans who adopted Revival-style spirituality remained in the church, the Revival also informed many of the independent Christian movements arising in eastern Africa both before and after the Revival's officialized beginnings, and such movements are at least as equally important for world Christianity as the Revival itself. The liturgical style of contemporary Pentecostalism in eastern Africa also often resembles the enthusiasm of the East African Revival.

The Anglican Church in Uganda has been the subject of landmark scholarship in the study of African Christianity. John V. Taylor, an Anglican missionary priest in Uganda beginning in 1945, was an influential leader. He later offered a historical perspective on the Church of Uganda with firsthand accounts based on his service in Mukono, site of the major Anglican theological college. He also wrote a book, *Primal Vision* (1963), that has become a classic interpretation of traditional African spirituality. He later returned to England to become secretary of the Church Missionary Society, then bishop of Winchester in 1973. Taylor's work built on previous research on Baganda religion by missionary-anthropologist John Roscoe and especially groundbreaking writings of Baganda intellectuals like Apolo

Kagwa. The Anglican Church in Uganda continues to hold global significance. Today the archbishop of York in the UK is the Ugandan-born John Sentamu, who assumed his post as the second-most important Anglican bishop, after the archbishop of Canterbury, in 2005.[45]

Uganda's *Catholics*, like the Anglicans, trace their presence in the country to missionaries who arrived in the late 1870s. The tumult of those first decades produced a body of strong lay Catholics energized by Catholic piety and identity, considerable interest among Ugandans to join the priesthood and consecrated religious life, and a sense of grievance toward the Anglicans who were favored in the colonial system. Prominent among the leaders of Uganda's Catholics in the days of early colonialism was Stanislaus Mugwanya (d. 1938), a Catholic counterpart to the Anglican Apolo Kagwa, one of the earliest proponents of formal education in Uganda, a regent for the child kabaka, and also a local judge until 1921.

Catholics were initially restricted to Masaka in the wake of armed conflict between Ugandans linked to the Anglicans and those allied with the Catholics in the early 1890s. Missionaries with help from chiefs like Mugwanya turned it into a stronghold where Catholic practices dominated life as in few other places in Africa, beginning by the late 1890s. Eventually Catholics spread throughout Uganda. Like the Anglicans, Catholics too founded schools, first St. Mary's at Rubaga, later moved to Kisubi in 1924, and given over to the Brothers of Christian Instruction.

In the mid-1890s, the White Fathers split their mission with the British-based Mill Hill missionaries, who had been founded a few decades earlier as a missionary body in the English Catholic Church. This decision was prompted by the White Fathers' and Ugandan Catholic conflicts with the British colonial presence and its Anglican allies—Europe's conflicts transferred into eastern Africa—since the Catholics sought to protect their interests as British colonialism took hold. The Mill Hill missionaries took responsibility for the eastern part of Uganda and western Kenya.

45. Robert, *Christian Mission*, 74–75.

They founded a famous school, St. Joseph's of Namilyango, in 1906.[46]

Meanwhile in the north the Verona missionaries—or Combonis—had come from Egypt through Sudan by 1910 and established the Catholic Church there.[47] Impressive linguistic work was carried out by the Comboni missionary Joseph Crazzolara (d. 1976), who published grammars and dictionaries in at least five different languages of northern Uganda and southern Sudan. All three groups of male missionaries—the White Fathers, Mill Hill, and Combonis—worked closely with groups of sisters.

In Masaka, a deep institutionalization of Catholicism took place. Founded in the 1890s, the White Fathers' seminary at Katigondo was the first to succeed in an ongoing way in eastern Africa when in 1913 two priests were ordained after years of training in philosophy and theology, much of it in Latin. Many others stood in line behind them. Unlike the Anglicans, who were closely linked to the colonial effort and whose elites usually became the colony's indigenous leaders—of course, always under British control—Catholics expanded among the peasantry, with Catholic piety a potent carrier of a fervent folk Catholicism. By the early 1920s, one Catholic mission in Masaka had an African superior, and the completion of Rubaga cathedral in Kampala in 1925, which could seat 5000 worshipers, signaled Catholic ambitions. The inaugural groups of African sisters and African brothers, the *Bannabikira* and *Bannakaroli*, founded in 1910 and 1927 respectively, drew scores of young women and men. Meanwhile, a charismatic Irish Franciscan sister who partnered with Mill Hill missionaries beginning in 1902, Mother Kevin, founded the Little Sisters of St. Francis in 1926.[48]

A remarkable step came in Masaka in 1934, years before nearly every other Catholic diocese in Africa, when all the parishes in the diocese were handed over to African priests, with only the bishop remaining a European missionary. The natural next step came in 1939, when Joseph Kiwanuka, who had studied canon law in Rome, became the first African bishop in sub-Saharan Africa. Kiwanuka remained the only one for twelve

46. O'Neil, *Mission to the Upper Nile*, 19–36.

47. Cisternino, *Passion for Africa*, 340–73.

48. O'Neil, *Mission to the Upper Nile*, 81.

years. There was no black African Anglican bishop on the continent, and the Church of Uganda got its first African Anglican bishop only in 1947.

Northern Uganda remained somewhat isolated culturally from the rest of the country, and the uneven development of the north compared to the rest of the territory has been one source of unrest in Uganda's history. The missionary-led growth of the Christian churches, however, resembled trends elsewhere in Uganda. Gulu developed as a Catholic center under the leadership of the Comboni missionaries, while the Anglicans grew as well under CMS leadership.

Paul VI's visit to Uganda in 1969 followed upon the canonization of the Uganda Martyrs in 1964. On that occasion he consecrated the shrine to the Martyrs at Namugongo, which today is a destination for pilgrims worldwide, especially on the Martyrs' feast of June 3, when several million gather for worship. The pope consecrated a number of bishops for Africa, sending a strong message of support to the church. Subsequent popes have also visited Uganda.

There are four Catholic archdioceses in Uganda: Kampala, Tororo, Gulu, and Mbarara, with nineteen dioceses total. Numerous religious congregations, male and female, operate throughout the country, many of them originating in Uganda.

As in Tanzania, the past few decades have seen the proliferation of *Pentecostal* churches in Uganda. Emerging in the early 1960s, the first congregations were initially belittled as *biwempe* churches, from the Luganda word for papyrus, indicative of the shoddy quality of their gathering spaces. After persecution during the Amin years, they have grown enormously since the 1980s, with large churches now in Kampala like the Makerere Full Gospel Church, the Miracle Centre Cathedral, and the Watoto Church (formerly Kampala Pentecostal Church).

As elsewhere in Africa, they have a distinctive style of prayer, with a large emphasis on healing. Many Christians today pray both with Pentecostals and in the church of their family origins—likely Anglican or Catholic—so that counting Pentecostals precisely is difficult. Yet they have also grown at the expense of the historic churches and now number 4 million.

4.

Sociocultural

Christianity and Social Transformation in Eastern Africa

Across eastern Africa, Christian individuals and communities have long been formidable political, economic, and social actors. Beginning in the nineteenth century, Christian missionaries from Europe catalyzed extensive social change while tying their growing missions into global Christian networks, Protestant and Catholic. New sources of power linked with the European/ Christian presence unleashed countless local changes that are hard to quantify. Besides fostering formal political transitions, Christianity empowered and disempowered various people organized by gender, age, marital status, genealogical connection, and other factors as social circumstances underwent transformation.

Missionaries and their messages had diverse and complex effects. They sought to provide social services like healthcare and education across the region, leading to widespread literacy by the latter twentieth century and bringing new technologies and other resources into the region. Christian churches still run thousands of schools, hospitals, and clinics throughout eastern Africa. The role of service provision in undermining eastern African resistance to colonial overrule, however, was no doubt considerable. Today, with most African churches led by

Africans, the missionary role of service provision is less, of course, while healthcare and education in all three countries take multiple forms, many non-Christian.

Since independence, the sociopolitical roles of Christianity in eastern Africa have gotten even more complicated. As Christian forms have multiplied, their functions have also increased and diversified. Formal political power may be muted, for few political parties self-identify as Christian and there are no formal national churches, as the Anglican Church of Uganda operated in the colonial period. Yet important social goods like education and healthcare continue to be delivered by Christian bodies, and the diversity of Christian bodies has generated equally diverse social and political roles for them. Amid such complexity, in the face of economic distress and frustration at national politics, Christian leaders remain very influential—indeed, at times, have been outspoken proponents of political change, especially in Kenya. One could make the case that colonial officials kept Christianity more controlled than, at certain key times, post-independence leaders have. Moreover, Christian discourses operate in the public sphere, legitimating and de-legitimating political processes, economic policies, and various social programs.

This chapter will summarize the social, political, and economic roles played by Christianity in eastern Africa. The first part of the chapter—organized around the precolonial, colonial, and postcolonial periods in an historical overview—examines Christianity's roles in formal political changes. This will be followed by a thematic section describing other transformations that overlapped with political transitions: Christianity-linked dynamics related to changes in education, health, and other indices of social development, as well as ways that a Christian presence modified understandings of social realities like language, ethnicity, and gender. A final section of the chapter will address the relationship between contemporary Christianity and notions of development operative in eastern Africa.

CHRISTIANITY'S IMPACTS ON FORMAL POLITICAL CHANGES IN EASTERN AFRICA

THE PRECOLONIAL PERIOD

Portuguese contact did not introduce eastern Africa to the world, for the region had long been integrated into the global economy, yet it led to important changes in the region. For instance, the Omani rule in Zanzibar formally in place by the early mid-nineteenth century, more than a century after the Europeans were driven out, is arguably traceable to the earlier Portuguese incursions, which prompted efforts by local Muslims and their allies to expel the Iberians. In addition, even though most slaves taken from eastern Africa fell into Muslim hands, the Portuguese presence also likely expanded enslavement practices due to increased global trade in spices that the slaves helped cultivate, and in ivory that the enslaved carried from inner regions to the coast. Thus, the eventual increase in human trade can arguably be traced to forces unleashed by European Christians.[1]

The effects of the Portuguese coastal presence on peoples inland is hard to assess. Few Portuguese ventured into the hinterlands, yet access to cotton cloth, advanced weapons, and gunpowder from the coast changed political relations wherever such international trade developed.[2] Finally, the Portuguese brought maize to the coast of eastern Africa, and today the crop is ubiquitous in eastern Africa and a staple in many diets.

As Europe's attention to eastern Africa grew in the nineteenth century after the tumult of the Napoleonic wars died down, other historical changes unfolded in the region. Besides the

1. For discussions see Alice Bellagamba, Sandra E. Greene, and Martin Klein, eds., *African Voices on Slavery and the Slave Trade* (Cambridge: Cambridge University Press, 2013), and Gwyn Campbell and Alessandro Stanziani, eds., *Bonded Labour and Debt in the Indian Ocean World* (London: Pickering & Chatto, 2013).

2. For further background see Isaria N. Kimambo, *Penetration and Protest in Tanzania: The Impact of the World Economy on the Pare, 1860–1960* (London: James Currey, 1991); Jean-Pierre Chrétien, *The Great Lakes of Africa: Two Thousand Years of History*, trans. Scott Straus (New York: Zone Books, 2003); and Marek Pawelczak, *The State and the Stateless. The Sultanate of Zanzibar and the East African Mainland: Politics, Economy and Society, 1837–1888* (Warsaw: University of Warsaw, 2010).

growth of Zanzibar as a regional power, there were myriad other examples of religious movements, political consolidations and disintegrations, and the development of dynamic trading networks, all of which fostered social change. The early nineteenth-century rise of the Zulu Kingdom in southern Africa had repercussions to the north, in the southern part of today's Tanzania, for it caused new people groups to enter the region to escape the unrest.

The nineteenth-century expansion of European power around the globe met eastern Africa amidst these internal transformations. Along with Europeans in pursuit of knowledge, as well as economic and political power, came Christian bodies anxious to spread the gospel. In light of eventual European colonial control over most of the world—including eastern Africa—by the early twentieth century, it is easy to think of missionaries and imperialism as operating hand-in-hand. At times, missionaries did come in only after Europeans had cemented their authority, thus with colonial-imperial approval. Africans recognized the shared interests between missionaries and colonial authorities, which shaped evangelization in harmful ways. Yet in eastern Africa—and many other places—numerous missionaries preceded the economic and political processes associated with formal colonialism.

European contact, bringing new forms of Christianity and leading to colonial overrule, altered the slave-based economies of lucrative plantations and rewarded those who were quicker to adapt to new political realities. Local rulers able to harness trade, education, and European protection could advance their interests against their rivals. At the formal level of political engagement, the mostly French Catholic and mostly British Protestant missionaries served additionally as emissaries of their countries of origin. They were thus also sometimes proxies in their home countries' ongoing rivalry. Eastern Africa was a theater for this political rivalry until the 1880s, when French aspirations for a global colonial presence looked elsewhere. The later-coming German and already-present British colonizers divided eastern Africa among themselves.

Missionaries' political effects were no doubt shaped by their national origins. More importantly, missionary actions and perspectives inevitably reflected their relationships with existing political authorities in eastern Africa itself, who had interests and often considerable power of their own. Those coming before colonial overrule thus faced negotiations with African political leaders as they sought sites for their missions, as well as scope and direction for their ministries.

For example, the earliest missionaries like the Protestants Krapf and Rebmann negotiated with local chiefs in founding their missions, as did later groups that would make a deeper mark. Catholics and Anglicans coming to Zanzibar in the 1860s, for instance, pursued and received permission from the Sultan of Zanzibar to found their missions in Zanzibar's Stone Town. Their provision of education and healthcare for their charges—many of them ex-slaves—as well as the expatriate population and local elites, made them very useful as the Sultan sought to expand his influence. They also brought new cultural forms. An Anglican missionary, Edward Steere, not only translated some of the Scripture into Swahili and composed a simple grammar for the language; he also prepared simplified Swahili versions of Shakespeare's plays.[3] Nonetheless, the missionaries were unable to preach publicly among the local population, and they accepted this restriction, focusing on slaves whom they received and ransomed. As they moved to places elsewhere on the island of Zanzibar they continued to negotiate with the Sultan for mission and school sites, and similar formalities occurred on establishing their first mainland missions.

The European pressure to end the slave trade—first through interdiction of slave-trading ships, later the campaign to stop the open trade in slaves that was taking place at the Zanzibar slave market until the 1873 British-forced closure—had economic and political repercussions in eastern Africa. Missionaries, especially Protestants, were among the keenest proponents of abolition, so that even though the maritime interdiction practices and a parliamentary visit were formal government actions by Great Britain, Christian motivation was obvious. Slavery continued as an institution well into the twentieth century, yet the Sultan of

3. See the book review of Edward Wilson Lee's 2017 book *Shakespeare in Swahililand: Adventures with the Ever-Living Poet*, in the *Economist*, March 19, 2016, 91.

the time, Barghash, saw his influence diminish as his economic power shrank. This made him and his successors more vulnerable to colonial manipulation, culminating in overrule—by Germans inland in the eventual Tanganyika, by the British at the Kenyan coastal regions claimed by the Sultan and at Zanzibar. Slave raids continued in the interior, though less openly.[4]

As Christian bodies moved inland, the nature of the administrative authority operative in most areas grew murkier. The Sultan's lessening grip led many local leaders to vie for control in a rapidly transforming political landscape. The growing European presence rendered the nature of political power only more difficult to interpret and negotiate. Much of the nineteenth century witnessed the intermittent and unpredictable operation of competing political claims that could be alternatingly Arab, European, and African, with variable means of enforcement of claims to authority. If the violence of the slave trade rendered local security always tenuous, open warfare between formal armies was rarely continuous. Even the so-called Mirambo War, named after a ruler of the Nyamwezi who fought coast-based Arabs in north-central Tanganyika from the 1870s to his death in 1884, was more a series of episodes than an ongoing engagement. One might argue that such conflicts, small and large, grew in number due to the European-caused and Christianity-motivated attenuation of the Sultan's grasp, but it is hard to be certain.

Even where no overt conflicts arose, or where local peoples showed disinterest in Christianity, the appearance of a mission station created a physical setting from which a Christian presence radiated, and station establishment thus had social, political, and economic repercussions. These depended on a variety of factors, including the degree of stability of local political authority, the types of missionary activities pursued, and the proximity of other sources of power such as trading partners and European officials. Africans linked to those respective missions themselves had their lives transformed through education, change in their livelihoods due to new agricultural and trading practices, and sometimes migration within eastern Africa and beyond, among myriad other factors.

4. Darch, *Missionary Imperialists?*, 209–36.

THE COLONIAL PERIOD

In Uganda, missionary successes affected the Buganda kingdom profoundly even before formal colonial overrule. Mutesa, the kabaka (Luganda for "king") at the time of Anglican and Catholic contact in the late 1870s until his death in 1884, skillfully played the Christian rivals off each other. He also parried the Muslims who were in his court, all the while managing his own power vis-à-vis many other sources of political authority. His unstable son and successor, Mwanga, lacked his father's savvy, failing to hold together his authority, then persecuting Christian converts among the court pages. The martyrdoms of the late 1880s and Mwanga's increasing unpredictability led to a coup by Buganda's Muslims and Christians, who cooperated to overthrow the young kabaka. Then followed war between the Muslims and Christians, which after the Muslim defeat eventuated in conflict between the two groups of Christian-affiliated Ugandans. The Anglican triumph, aided by British guns, set the stage for the coming of colonial overrule and cemented the protected status of the two major Christian bodies in the colonial order, with the Anglicans formally above the Catholics due to their connection to the British colonial apparatus.[5]

By 1894, the British had proclaimed a formal protectorate status over Uganda, and the Catholic-Anglican rivalry prompted each group to develop its missions, along with healthcare and educational institutions linked to them, over the next decades. The British control led to what political scientists, following the British themselves, call "indirect rule," in which the colonial overlords cemented the authority of the kabaka in Buganda and similar rulers over the territory's other kingdoms, ruling through them and supporting them if they supported the colonial regime. It was a truncated and often awkward political system to be sure, part "invention of tradition," part building on existing loyalties, and a great deal of improvisation in practice.[6]

People's identities often became linked to their Christianiza-

5. For a recent summary, see Low, *Fabrication of Empire*.

6. For a critical discussion of the process and effects of indirect rule, see Mahmood Mamdani, *Citizen and Subject: Contemporary Africa and the Legacy of Late Colonialism* (Princeton: Princeton University Press, 1996).

tion. Kings in what was to become Uganda, possessing varying degrees of local legitimacy, usually converted to Anglican Christianity. Local chiefs either followed them, chose to be Catholic, or occasionally remained non-Christian or became or remained Muslim, thus embodying a semi-official, semi-loyal "opposition." Peasants and others found themselves embraced by developing Christian institutions for education and colonial economic structures. Such processes developed ethnic identity in a British colony, as royal conversions formed monarchs whose authority was buttressed by the colonial regime.

Such royal conversions included *Omukama* (or King) Kasagama of Toro in western Uganda, who converted in 1896, and who ruled from 1891 to 1928, receiving the Order of the British Empire (OBE) in 1918 for his help in fighting the Germans in eastern Africa. A less propitious outcome befell *Mukama* (again, King) Kitehimbwa of Bunyoro, who converted in 1899 with his sister and regent.[7] Kitehimbwa struggled for legitimacy during the period when his predecessor Kabalega resisted the British, and then later was deposed for resisting the British introduction of supposedly more loyal Baganda chiefs to rule parts of Bunyoro, Buganda's traditional enemy.[8] In 1902, *Mugabe* (King) Kahaya of Ankole converted with his chief minister Mbaguta and, though he, like Kasagama, received the OBE in 1918, he was never a vigorous ruler and died an inconsequential figure in 1944.[9]

Ankole remained outside the four "official" monarchies of the British territory of Uganda: Toro, Bunyoro, Buganda, and Busoga. The latter was formed in 1906 when the British united previously disparate chiefdoms east of Buganda under an officially sanctioned king, or *kyabazinga*.[10] The 1900 Uganda agreement meant that Busoga, a region that long had been preyed upon by Buganda, was removed from the larger kingdom's

7. Hastings, *Church in Africa*, 469.

8. See "The Rise of Sub-Imperialism and Its Rejection in Bunyoro," *Daily Monitor*, April 13, 2012, https://tinyurl.com/y98j74ua.

9. Hastings, *Church in Africa*, 469.

10. These four monarchies persisted until their dissolution by the first president, Milton Obote, in 1966, and have been reintroduced since the 1990s by the Museveni regime, their political power legally restricted. Ankole's official status as a monarchy within Uganda, before 1966 and today, remains contested.

political control and linked to the British colonial authority directly.[11] Other kingdoms similar in culture across the border in German East Africa saw comparable processes of Christianization among Great Lakes peoples, for instance the Haya people west of Lake Victoria, whose eight kings suddenly became Christian in 1919 and 1920.[12] Most such royal accessions to Christianity were, like Buganda's, toward Anglicanism. Catholics later approached lesser chiefs or younger brothers, whose clients and relatives then were likely to become Catholic.

Indirect rule and the ongoing Christianization of Uganda led to the systematic centralization of power in Christian kings' hands. Commoners or peasants—*bakopi* in Luganda, the language of Buganda, *bairu* in the other Bantu languages of the kingdoms—were progressively disempowered as colonialism reinforced royal authority and the local chiefs allied to it, to the detriment of traditional checks on such power that commoners had wielded before colonial rule.

Turning to Tanzania, starting in the mid-1880s, German encroachment on eastern Africa began, first through dubious treaties with supposed African rulers, who "agreed" to hand over their authority for various gifts and concessions. Such agreements culminated in a sweeping one with the Zanzibar Sultan in 1888 that, buttressed by a German naval threat directed at Zanzibar's port, effectively ceded the entire mainland to the Germans. This led to a militarized German presence at the Indian Ocean coast of Tanganyika.

Unlike in Uganda, in Tanzania and Kenya sizeable Muslim populations faced colonial encroachment and accompanying Christian missionization. Muslim responses varied, with faith sometimes forging bonds that resisted the European colonizers, especially near the Indian Ocean. Unlike western Africa, however, there were no large Muslim political bodies with whom the Europeans had to negotiate, and no large and enduring pan-Muslim alliances grew at the coast. In fact, African Muslims often lived in tension with Arabs like the Sultan of Zanzibar and

11. Rhiannon Stephens, *A History of African Motherhood: The Case of Uganda, 700–1900* (Cambridge: Cambridge University Press, 2013), 177–78.

12. Hastings, *Church in Africa*, 474.

others from Oman. Those Muslims who were literate, usually due to their involvement in coastal trade, became favored colonial officials for the Germans, who occasionally found mission-educated African Christians too haughty. Over time, Christian and then colonial growth in education led to Christian advances at Muslim expense.

Though Muslim resistance to colonialism was rarely widespread, one important moment of armed resistance has come to be called the "Abushiri War," due to the Arab leader, Bushiri, who rallied coastal Arabs and Swahilis against the Germans, as well as against some Christian missions, in the late 1880s. The Catholic missionaries at Bagamoyo faced a complex role. Most were French, but they had Alsatian roots and could speak German, too, and thus played the role of go-between in the conflict. This led a few to be accused of spying on the African rebels for the Germans.[13] Eventually Bismarck sent a German force that, with African soldiers under German officers, crushed the rebellion and hanged Bushiri.

Unlike the British, the Germans were less inclined to indirect rule, and other groups in German East Africa also rebelled, the most famous being the Maji Maji uprising in 1905–1907, focused in the south of the territory after land was seized. Other battles took place near Kilimanjaro. In these cases, Christian missionaries often found themselves in delicate positions, anxious to protect their own converts and to minimize destruction at their missions, and to defend their rights to evangelize openly. The violence of German suppressions eventually quelled instincts to resist, but it also led to scandals in Germany, which had waged an even more violent campaign in what is today Namibia against the Herero, possibly the first modern genocide. The years after 1907 until the dawn of World War I saw the Germans spend heavily in developing Tanganyika's infrastructure and educational sector. Many Africans subsequently served with the Germans during World War I, often forced to be porters.

British control in Kenya likewise came in stages, foreshadowed by the formation of the Imperial British East African Company (IBEAC) to defend trading interests in 1888. Already

13. Kollman, *Evangelization of Slaves*, 198–99n11.

there were numerous missionary groups at the coast and inland among the Kamba, beginning in the early 1880s.

A rebellion against the encroaching IBEAC in 1895–96, called the Mazrui rebellion after the leading Muslim family of the Kenyan coast, saw the CMS mission at Freretown and other missions face armed attacks organized and sponsored by disgruntled plantation owners and other landlords. A number of African Christians showed heroism defending the mission and its residents, at Freretown and elsewhere. Africans at independent former-slave colonies like Fuladayo, some of whose residents were Christians who had once served the missionaries—for example, as porters on caravans—also fought Muslim plantation owners. At the same time, many of the former slaves at Freretown also bristled at the stern order imposed on them and fled to other settlements.

Western Kenya, which for a while was attached to Uganda, also saw armed resistance, notably by the Nandi people between 1895 and 1902. As in Tanganyika, missionaries often had to balance their desire to keep their converts safe and to minimize damage from military interventions with the need to maintain good relations both with encroaching colonizers and local political powers.

World War I

Savage fighting took place during World War I in the region, as the Germans of Tanganyika were attacked by Belgians from Congo, the British from Kenya and the south, and by South Africans. Eastern Africans themselves suffered considerably, with thousands dying from disease and combat after they were pressed into the war by German and British colonial militaries. Commerce, agriculture, and local health all suffered. Protestant missionaries in Kenya organized their own people into porters to form a "Carrier Corps" for the British, with eventually 22,000 Ugandans and Kenyans joining the cause. Germans had their own recruitment of thousands of Africans from Tanganyika, where most of the fighting took place, while Zanzibar's bishop recruited many for the British effort. After the war, both Nairobi and Dar es Salaam developed neighborhoods called "Kariakoo," a corruption of "Carrier Corps," which indicated the background of many of the first residents who received plots in the settlements after their military service.

Missions were disrupted in many places during the Great War. On the Catholic side, clergy and religious from other European countries pitched in to replace Germans interned in Tanganyika after their defeat, especially Italian Consolatas and Swiss Capuchins. Protestants made numerous arrangements to cover lost personnel, though they lacked the centralized authority of the Catholics, which made organizing coverage more difficult. Tanganyikan Lutherans among the Haya, for instance, bristled when their mission came under Wesleyan control. This led to schism that was healed only in the early 1930s.[14]

The war's end meant several things. First, a population decline in the region that took place between 1880 and 1920 due to epidemics, famine, and social dislocations began to reverse itself. Most areas recovered beginning in the 1920s, though some places continued to suffer demographic stagnation due to unrest, ongoing disease, or heightened colonial impacts from intense exploitation of natural resources that required a larger military presence to contain local resistance.[15]

Second, the end of the war led to British control over the region, and some German missionaries once in Tanganyika did not return. Peace allowed the resumption of certain development efforts, with missionaries supporting the colonial establishment of educational and health systems. As elsewhere, missionaries engaged local political authorities, yet Tanganyika had little of the royal infrastructure for indirect rule that the British used in Uganda.

14. John Iliffe, *A Modern History of Tanganyika* (Cambridge: Cambridge University Press, 1979), 260; Hastings, *History of African Christianity*, 51; Hastings, *Church in Africa*, 490.

15. Shane Doyle, *Crisis and Decline in Bunyoro: Population and Environment in Western Uganda, 1860–1955* (Athens: Ohio University Press, 2006).

After the Great War

In a 1918 rare show of unanimity, the three bishops of Uganda—the Anglican and the two Catholic, one of the White Fathers, the other of Mill Hill—wrote a letter to the colonial governor asking for support in reinforcing the Christian identity of the colony, which they felt was waning. Heroes of the age of martyrs were dying and zeal eroding, while polygamy and other misbehavior kept many chiefs from full communion. The governor demurred, saying the colonial role included civilizing not Christianizing, and the Anglican bishop in 1921 excommunicated the Bagandan king for misconduct. Similar actions were taken against chiefs in Bukoba to the south in Tanganyika, culturally resembling the Great Lakes monarchies of Uganda, and where Catholics and Anglicans also were many.

In the 1920s, the British intermittently pursued educational reform, economic empowerment, and improvements in health across the region. Increasingly the need for African labor and revenue led colonial officials to rely on the African leaders they supported, including those with dubious local legitimacy, to tax and secure the labor of local peoples. Some missionaries in turn attacked colonial policies that preyed upon their Christians; others avoided political engagement.

All the while, nascent proto-nationalist and anti-colonial sentiments simmered, often among the mission-educated of eastern Africa. Mission-trained Kenyans like Harry Thuku and Johnstone Kamau (later taking the name Jomo Kenyatta) organized their grievances into political bodies, drawing upon their education and often utilizing Christian-linked language of liberation and salvation to challenge British rule. Thuku led the East Africa Association from 1921, with lukewarm missionary support. It eventually gave way to the Kikuyu Central Association following Thuku's 1922 arrest and nine-year exile after a Nairobi protest in which twenty Africans were shot.

More firmly linked to missionary Christianity was the Kavirondo Taxpayers Welfare Association, which gathered western Kenyans under the direction of the CMS's Archdeacon Walter Edwin Owen (1879–1945), who had arrived in 1918 after a decade in Uganda. Owen's association coalesced anti-colonial sentiment on behalf of "native rights" against colonial abuses like labor impressment and land seizures. His calls for improvement of colonial policy still fell short of questioning British control, and in fact, according to some analyses, legitimated coercive labor practices with reference to supposedly traditional communal working practices.[16] By 1931, seventeen Europeans resided in Kenya and their contempt for missionary advocacy on behalf of native peoples grew bitter, with Owen called a Bolshevik and dubbed "Archdemon Owen" for his defense of Africans' rights. Over time, however, missionary advocacy against European excesses eased, and colonialism settled into regular patterns, with mission churches benefiting from the stability to grow.

Yet local anger did not go away, and Christianity sometimes stood accused of collusion with African disenfranchisement, often with good reason. After all, supported by colonial decree, German or British, the early missionary groups at times received large swathes of land, much of it of course seen by local peoples as theirs. In Kenya, for example, the Church of Scotland Mission received 64,000 acres near Kibwezi, much of which they sold to develop eventually into sisal plantations.[17] Such conferrals grew much smaller over time, with the eventual British policy to set aside a sizeable tract for Catholics and Anglicans in the major towns of Uganda or Kenya, often a square mile. To this day many cathedrals, seminaries, schools, and clinics—as well as bishops' residences—sit on that land, which often includes a hill. German policy in Tanganyika, built upon by the British, was similar. Understandably, especially in parts of Kenya where European settlers eventually became numerous, the formal Christian presence was linked by Africans to European expropriation of traditional territory. As one Kikuyu proverb had it, "the missionary is no different from the settler."

In the late 1920s, Protestant missionaries in central Kenya mobilized to stop the female excision-linked practices sometimes called "female circumcision." Also known today as "female geni-

16. See Opolot Opia, *Communal Labor in Colonial Kenya: The Legitimization of Coercion, 1912–1930* (New York: Palgrave Macmillan, 2012), which argues that such traditional practices were "invented" as part of colonial policy.

17. Hastings, *Church in Africa*, 426.

tal mutilation" (FGM), these practices were common among the Kikuyu, and linked to initiation. Local resistance to the missionary campaign, perhaps planned with a proto-nationalist awareness to unite people in defense of cultural tradition, culminated in the departure of many Kenyan believers from Presbyterian and other churches. The CMS and Catholics were less rigid and suffered fewer losses of members. The departures generated a movement to start independent schools, since those whose daughters underwent the procedure were kept from missionary education. The bitter conflict divided Africans among themselves, something that manifested itself later in the Mau Mau uprising of the 1950s.[18]

World War II did not see overt fighting in eastern Africa like World War I, though the internment of German and Italian missionaries disrupted missions in all three countries. Missionaries also had a hard time traveling to and from the region. In the mid-1940s, decommissioned World War II-era naval vessels carried hundreds of European missionaries into eastern Africa as mainline Protestants and Catholics sought to shore up their presence.[19]

Approaching Independence

In the postwar period, British attempts to reinforce their control faced challenges of various sorts. Pan-Africanist sentiments oriented toward self-rule had decades-old roots, though eastern Africa had fewer such leaders than western or southern Africa. Still, Jomo Kenyatta was present at the Pan-African Congress in Manchester that took place in October 1945, and soon thereafter he returned to Kenya after fifteen years away. He had been in Europe pursuing an advanced degree in anthropology from the University of London, writing his ethnographic study of the Kikuyu titled *Facing Mount Kenya*, and building networks with European social progressives, including flirtations with the

18. Sandgren, *Christianity and the Kikuyu*; Wangari Muoria-Sal, Bodil Folke Frederiksen, John Lonsdale, and Derek Peterson, eds., *Writing for Kenya: The Life and Works of Henry Muoria* (Leiden: Brill, 2009).

19. Personal communication, Rev. Theodore Winkelmolen, CSSp, Morogoro, Tanzania, August 1998.

Soviet Union. In 1947, Kenyatta succeeded Harry Thuku as head of the Kenya African Union. Other eastern Africans also studied in Europe after the end of World War II, including Uganda's Benedict Kiwanuka and Tanganyika's Julius Nyerere, both committed Catholics who took leadership positions in their new nations.

Many groups opposing colonialism emerged with religious motivations. Some, like the Bataka movement among the Baganda in Uganda and western Kenya's Dini ya Msambwa, were ethnically based and sectarian, and each of these led to riots and deaths amid colonial suppression. Others, like the Tanganyika Africa National Union (TANU), led by Nyerere from its founding in 1954, and the Kenya African Union (KAU), resembled political parties in the making, which in retrospect they were.

Still, cities in eastern Africa remained places of rather stark racial segregation through the 1950s. This shaped Christian practice profoundly, since Catholic and Protestant churches were often racially—or, if African, ethnically—homogeneous instead of integrated. In Nairobi, for example, only the end of Mau Mau led Catholic leaders to question the segregation of most of the Catholic parishes as either Asian (Goan), European, or African.

Unsurprisingly, therefore, in Uganda and Kenya anti-colonial movements often attacked Christianity as well, something only spurred by the stubborn clinging to control by a considerable number of missionaries who remained wary of African leadership in their churches and over the colonies. Stances ranged from paternalistic caution to outright racist belittling. Some missionaries, however, were more supportive of eventual independence, political and ecclesial, even if they did not always see all the implications. In Tanganyika, Catholic missionaries were split; the White Fathers excommunicated members of TANU, while its founder Nyerere drew support from the Maryknoll missionaries from the US.[20] The late Nigerian church historian Ogbu Kalu, from a pan-African perspective, speaks of European church leaders "waltzing with nationalists" in the years up to and

20. Ludwig, *Church and State in Tanzania*, 31–32.

just after independence, an apt description for eastern Africa's experiences.[21]

Kenya's Mau Mau uprising of 1952–1958 was the most important anti-colonial movement in eastern Africa in the latter twentieth century. Many Africans died during Mau Mau, both accused rebels at the hands of the English colonial authorities and African (especially Kikuyu, and especially those linked to the East African Revival) Christians loyal to their faith at the hands of the Mau Mau fighters. Though European deaths were widely reported in Europe, they were under 100, while African deaths numbered in the thousands. As Adrian Hastings noted, Mau Mau was both an anti-colonial revolt and a civil war, with the vast majority of deaths on both sides Kenyans. Christians, including missionaries, were linked with both sides.[22] Churches also protested against the brutality of the colonial suppression of the movement, with the CMS leader Cecil Bewes a strong voice condemning Home Guard abuses during Mau Mau.[23] In fact, many Kenyan Christians, communities and even individuals, were divided internally, both sympathetic to the cause of independence yet also disturbed by the anti-Christian tone of Mau Mau, which often drew upon supposedly venerable Kikuyu religious traditions in intentionally shocking oathing rituals designed to enforce loyalty to the cause. Henry Muoria (1914–1997), for instance, was an earlier writer for the Kikuyu Christian journal *Muigwithania*, which means "the reconciler," whose first editor was Johnstone Kamau—later, Jomo Kenyatta. Over time, Muoria continued to see the value of Christianity as a way toward greater Kikuyu—and Kenyan—self-reliance, while Kenyatta himself stressed the loss of land since the coming of Christianity and colonialism.[24]

Tanganyika and Uganda saw less violent resistance leading up to independence, yet it was not insignificant. In Tanganyika,

21. Kalu, *African Christianity*, 309–12.

22. Hastings, *History of African Christianity*, 87, 102–3.

23. Hastings, *History of African Christianity*, 94; Timothy H. Parsons, *The Second British Empire: In the Crucible of the Twentieth Century* (Lanham, MD: Rowman & Littlefield, 2014); Timothy Yates, with Stephen Skuce, *Twentieth-Century Missiology: Issues and Thinkers* (Calver, UK: Cliff College Publishing, 2014), 59–75.

24. Muoria-Sal, Frederiksen, Lonsdale, and Peterson, *Writing for Kenya*.

ill-conceived British agricultural schemes aroused protests in certain places.[25] In Uganda, considerable resistance to British rule coalesced among the Baganda around the kabaka, before and especially after his deportation in 1953 due to his alleged undermining of colonial control. Max Warren, global Christian leader and the CMS secretary in London at the time, played a role in securing the kabaka's return from exile in 1955 in negotiations with colonial officials.[26]

CHRISTIANITY'S POLITICAL ROLE IN POSTCOLONIAL EASTERN AFRICA

Christianity's formal role in politics of the postcolonial period has been less obvious than during colonialism, but it has been considerable. As mostly elsewhere in Africa, the first presidents in the newly independent nations were mission-trained Christians: Uganda's Milton Obote and Kenya's Jomo Kenyatta were nominal Protestants, Tanzania's Julius Nyerere a committed Catholic. All three ruled with little overt reference to religion, however, as mostly have their successors.

In Uganda, the differing identities of the two major political parties as primarily Catholic or Anglican, traceable to colonial tensions, arguably contributed to tragic violence from the late 1960s until the 1980s. This was mostly due to their inability to cooperate, which allowed rulers to commit atrocities without concerted religiously based opposition. In contrast, religiously linked parties have been rare in Kenya and Tanzania, except for a few Muslim parties at the coast. In all three countries, efforts to outlaw other parties than the ruling party have drawn occasional protests from religious leaders, as governing political forces changed their "parties" into "movements," ostensibly for national unity.[27]

Nor have Kenya or Tanzania suffered as much political unrest

25. Hastings, *History of African Christianity*, 6.

26. On the CMS role, see Kevin Ward, "The Church of Uganda and the Exile of Kabaka Muteesa II, 1953–1955," *Journal of Religion in Africa* 28, no. 4 (1998): 411–49, and Parsons, *Second British Empire*, 138–40, 175–76.

27. Ludwig, *Church and State in Tanzania*, 66.

as Uganda since independence. Still, the sudden end of the Arab regime in Zanzibar in 1964, which led to the forming of Tanzania as the island nation joined mainland Tanganyika, occasioned two weeks of bloodletting with 14,000 dead. Until recently, however, the Muslim coast and Indian Ocean islands have been mostly peaceful in Tanzania.

Kenya's internal violence has been considerable, yet mostly occurred over land, not religion, as ethnic tensions coupled with political opportunism yielded massacres, refugees, and displacement, extensively so in the early 1990s. Like those earlier land clashes, Kenya's post-election unrest in 2007–2008 was more ethnic than religious. More recent larger violent episodes—those at the coast or in the border regions near Somalia, and the Westgate Mall massacre in Nairobi in 2014—occurred due to Islamist activity.

Early independence leaders expected churches to support the ruling regime. Churches complied, being what one observer called "extravagantly deferential" to new African-led governments.[28] All three countries' regimes violated civil liberties through arrests of political opponents and the curtailing of press freedoms—with little opposition from Christian bodies in the 1960s and 1970s through most of the 1980s. The imposition of Tanzania's theoretically laudable *ujamaa* program meant displacement of landowners and led to resistance by those anxious to protect their property and corresponding violent enforcements. There was little church criticism.[29]

Uganda's churches became an exception to deference to the national government in the later Amin years, when his violent rule led to the deaths of thousands. Though both Catholic and Anglican leaders had, like many foreign governments, originally welcomed him, many later criticized the regime. The overthrow of Obote's second regime ("Obote II") in 1985 and Museveni's coming to power in 1986 ended fifteen years of unrest. Since then, Museveni has remained in power, with Christian leaders only rarely prominent in either support or opposition.

The undemanding cooperation with independent African

28. Paul Gifford, *African Christianity: Its Public Role* (Bloomington: Indiana University Press, 1998), 117.

29. Ludwig, *Church and State in Tanzania*, 198.

countries' new governments was typical for African church leaders from the 1960s to the 1980s. In the early 1990s, however, much of Africa underwent what has been sometimes called its "second era of liberation," with a number of repressive regimes overthrown. This often occurred with the help of Christian leaders who published public statements in favor of rights to associate, educated voters about their civil rights, and provided havens for political gatherings of those opposed to regimes. In eastern Africa, only Kenya participated in this trend, and somewhat belatedly, with a change of regime through election in 2001. This followed a decade of unrest in which Christian leaders figured prominently, especially in response to land clashes that pitted ethnic groups against one another, and which many suggested the government may have instigated.[30] Leading up to the 2001 election, Muslim and Christian religious leaders connected to the so-called Ufungamano (KiSwahili for "getting together") initiative, mobilized after the Moi regime attacked them in 1998, and came together to protest against a corrupt regime. Since then, Muslim-Christian unity has been less evident in Kenya, as some Christians have resisted efforts to institutionalize *kadhi* courts for Muslims, and Muslims have resented their marginalization in national politics.[31]

In Uganda, as noted, formal Christian opposition to the government has been rare over the past several decades. That said, prominent Christian leaders have resisted perceived government overreach at times. Beginning in the 1990s, some began to advocate genuine multi-party democracy against government efforts to maintain a single "movement." Some church leaders accused this position, taken ostensibly for national unity in light of the risk of ethnic or regional divisiveness, of undoing any legitimate political opposition. Then in 2007 Christian leaders questioned the government again. This came when Museveni agreed to allow other parties, but at the same time also convinced Parliament to amend the Constitution to remove presi-

30. Jacqueline Klopp, "The NCCK and the Struggle against 'Ethnic Clashes' in Kenya," in *Religion and Politics in Kenya: Essays in Honor of a Meddlesome Priest*, ed. Ben Knighton (New York: Palgrave Macmillan, 2009).

31. Kuhn, *Prophetic Christianity in Western Kenya*, 132–60; Chesworth, "Fundamentalism."

dential term limits, allowing him to continue in power indefinitely. These efforts were attacked publicly then by the Catholic leader Cardinal Wamala of Kampala, and since then both Anglican and Catholic leaders have questioned such changes. In addition, they have criticized violations of free speech by the government.[32] Given questions about the political future of the country in light of Museveni's willingness to cling to power through nearly any means, Uganda might well be awaiting a "new era of liberation."

In Tanzania, unlike Kenya and Uganda, formal political transitions have been more peaceful. Nyerere's decision to step down in 1985 led to an election for his successor, and he retired a revered national hero, so that no "second era of liberation" was seen to be needed. Among political leaders in Africa, Nyerere's guiding ideas have been among the most significant, and their roots in his Catholic faith quite obvious. That said, he faced considerable criticism from Catholic leaders in Tanzania while president for alleged sympathy with socialism. At the same time, Nyerere found Catholic bishops lacking in prophetic courage, which he felt explained their reluctance to support his attempts at social change.[33] His successors have been Muslim and Christian in more or less alternating order, reflective of Tanzania's religious makeup.

In eastern Africa there have been heroic church leaders who resisted government violations of human rights and blatant corruption. In Kenya they include Timothy Njoya, Henry Okullu, Alexander Muge, and David Gitari, all Protestants, as well as the Catholic bishop Raphael Ndingi.[34] As this suggests, mainline Protestant churches were more critical of the single-party regime than the Catholic Church. In Uganda, the Catholics Father Clement Kiggundu and Judge Benedict Kiwanuka, as well as Anglican bishop Janani Luwum,[35] paid with their lives

32. Robert A. Dowd, *Christianity, Islam, and Liberal Democracy in Africa* (Oxford: Oxford University Press, 2015), 112–13.

33. Ludwig, *Church and State in Tanzania*, 101–24.

34. Ben Knighton, ed., *Religion and Politics in Kenya: Essays in Honor of a Meddlesome Priest* (New York: Palgrave Macmillan, 2009), 1–53; Galia Sabar, *Church, State and Society in Kenya: From Mediation to Opposition, 1963–1993* (London: Frank Cass, 2002).

35. Kevin Ward, "Archbishop Janani Luwum: The Dilemmas of Loyalty, Oppo-

in the Amin years, but most churches were co-opted. The most extreme example of a church in uncritical support of the governing regime was perhaps the Africa Inland Church in Kenya, which became a mouthpiece for Kenyan dictator Daniel Arap Moi, yet it was not alone.[36] And it was not a new pattern, for nearly all churches were silent in Kenya in the wake of the mysterious murders of Tom Mboya, J. M. Kariuki, and Robert Ouko, political rivals to Kenyatta and then Moi, and in the curbing of press and other freedoms in the 1980s and 1990s.

Recently, churches have had difficulty knowing how to engage the political realm in a united and effective way, feeling both dependent on governments and yet frustrated by widespread corruption and consequent demoralization of the populace. In 2010 the Kenyan government sponsored a bill to implement a new constitution, some elements of which—allowance of Muslim law, openness to contraceptive rights that allegedly legalized abortion—were unpopular with certain major Christian leaders. Despite church pressure, the bill passed, showing a populace arguably less amenable to suggestions from religious officials' guidance. To many, this signaled a definite loss in formal Christian political influence since the 1990s, when the churches were seen as supporters of democracy. This waning is likely due to perceptions that churches in Kenya are too divided over ethnicity, a common complaint in the wake of the 2007–2008 violence.

In much of eastern Africa, ethnicity serves as the most reliable basis for political mobilization, with Tanzania a partial exception. Yet even its Christian leaders also struggle to know how to address political issues in a sophisticated way[37]—a common phenomenon across the globe, of course. Galia Sabar describes Kenya's Anglican leaders, for example, adopting a stance of

sition and Witness in Amin's Uganda," in *Christianity and the African Imagination: Essays in Honour of Adrian Hastings*, ed. David Maxwell with Ingrid Lawrie (Leiden: Brill, 2002).

36. Robert Calderisi, *Earthly Mission: The Catholic Church and World Development* (New Haven: Yale University Press, 2013), 111.

37. Ludwig, *Church and State in Tanzania*, 194–207; Kuhn, *Prophetic Christianity*, 119–64. Paul Gifford (for example, see *Christianity, Politics, and Public Life in Kenya*) has been a consistent critic of African Christian leaders' failures with regard to politics.

"mediative ambiguity" during the Kenyatta regime of 1963–1978, followed by a slowly developing theology for political activism under Daniel Arap Moi.[38] Most African-initiated churches and many Pentecostal churches operate from an official "dogma of non-interference,"[39] yet they at times have supported dictators, as many did with Kenya's Daniel Arap Moi in the 1990s.

Despite strong accusations that all Christian churches are co-opted by their national leaders, Christian religious leaders' efforts to engage politics continue. For example, Tanzania's Catholic bishops still try to shape national conversations through public documents like their 2013 *Manifesto: Proposal of National Priorities*, which pushes Catholic principles without dictating voting preferences in elections.[40]

Churches have also spearheaded efforts at political education to encourage responsible Christian citizenship. These had begun before independence, with various groups' bishops writing to guide their adherents as they moved toward citizenship, but political struggles intensified such efforts beginning in the 1980s. Instrumental in such education have been the founding of centers that work to teach people their rights and responsibilities as citizens, like the Catholic Church's John Paul II Justice and Peace Center in Kampala.[41] In addition, Christian journals oriented for believers have also addressed political education. The Baganda had long had Christian periodicals, Protestant and Catholic, but with independence the older journals like the Catholic *Munno*, which was published in Luganda, and the Protestant *Uganda Journal* were supplemented by national periodicals like *Leadership* and *New Day*, both Catholic. In Kenya, *Target* and *Lengo*, English and Swahili respectively, linked to Protestants and building on an earlier periodical called *Rock*,

38. Sabar, *Church, State and Society in Kenya*; Galia Sabar, "'Was There No Naboth to Say No?' Using the Pulpit in the Struggle for Democracy: The Anglican Church, Bishop Gitari, and Kenyan Politics," in *Religion and Politics in Kenya: Essays in Honor of a Meddlesome Priest*, ed. Ben Knighton (New York: Palgrave Macmillan, 2009).

39. Kuhn, *Prophetic Christianity*, 119–22.

40. Calderisi, *Earthly Mission*, 114.

41. See John Paul II Justice and Peace Centre, www.jp2jpc.org/.

have also educated Christians in politics.[42] *Kiongozi* in Tanzania, which is Catholic, has done the same.

To this day, many of the mainline churches seek to influence political deliberations around poverty alleviation, medical relief, and conflict resolution, sometimes directly through political advocacy, other times through voter education. As Harri Englund puts it, given the history of the relation between Christianity and politics in Africa and the current confusing situation, it can be easier to think critically about how Christianity constitutes certain kinds of "publics"—that is, bodies of citizens who can be addressed—than to try to analyze the churches' direct political roles.[43]

Besides the dynamics within each of the three countries, regional unrest in neighboring states has at times spilled over into eastern Africa itself. Like several other African countries, for example, Tanzania offered itself as a safe-haven to South Africa's ANC during the apartheid regime, a so-called "front-line state" with camps for training to fight the white-dominated government. Other kinds of fighting have led to refugees who were assisted directly by churches as well as by Christian relief organizations in the region. Sudan's civil war, which ran episodically for decades, eventuated in the founding of South Sudan in 2011, but meanwhile led to thousands of refugees in Kenya and Uganda. As of this writing, South Sudan stands mired in ongoing internal conflicts, with refugees again fleeing into eastern Africa.

The intermittent post-independence political violence of Rwanda and Burundi also led to refugees in all three countries, with local Christian churches aiding in providing food and shelter. Uganda, for example, served as the main base for the Rwandan Patriotic Front, which in 1994 removed the Hutu-dominated leadership of Rwanda and took power, allegedly ending genocidal violence against Tutsis and moderate Hutus in the country, and Christian churches in eastern Africa were little involved. Refugees from the fighting that ended the genocide in Rwanda and others from Burundi have fled to northwest-

42. Ward, *History of Global Anglicanism*, 183–84.
43. Englund, *Christianity and Public Culture*, 8–9.

ern Tanzania, however, where churches offered relief. Uganda, too, was involved in the wake of the Rwandan genocide, sending soldiers into the Democratic Republic of the Congo, again with little formal Christian reaction. The international Christian community has also been questioned about its absence in the violence and humanitarian crises of Rwanda and Burundi, something addressed by Ugandan Catholic theologian Emmanuel Katongole.[44]

CHRISTIANITY'S ROLES IN SOCIAL TRANSFORMATION

As historical methods have advanced, deeper appreciation has grown for the ways that European contact and colonial overrule, along with Christian missionization and the adoption of Christianity, created more than only formal political transformations. Political domination and occupation of land led to immense social change and often profound suffering certainly, yet such historical processes also prompted changes in longstanding patterns within languages, social reproduction, gender relations, religious systems, and local political economies of less formal types.[45] In addition, considerable scholarship has also studied the environmental impact of the coming of Europeans to the region, which also changed social realities in complex ways.[46]

The most obvious consequences of Christianization in eastern

44. Emmanuel Katongole, *The Sacrifice of Africa: A Political Theology for Africa* (Grand Rapids: Eerdmans, 2010); Emmanuel Katongole, *Born from Lament: The Theology of Politics and Hope in Africa* (Grand Rapids: Eerdmans, 2017).

45. Recent studies that focus on hitherto ignored aspects of social transformation include Pawelczak, *State and the Stateless*, and Stephens, *History of African Motherhood*.

46. Important environmental studies of eastern Africa include Helge Kjekshus, *Ecology Control and Economic Development in East African History* (Berkeley: University of California Press, 1977); Philip W. Porter, *Challenging Nature: Local Knowledge, Agroscience, and Food Security in Tanga Region, Tanzania* (Chicago: University of Chicago Press, 2006); Jan Bender Shetler, *Imagining Serengeti: A History of Landscape Memory in Tanzania from the Earliest Times to the Present* (Athens: Ohio University Press, 2007); Michael McInneshin, "Collaborative Landscape: Missions, States, and Their Subjects in the Making of Northeastern Tanzania's Terrain, 1870–1914," in *Missions, States, and European Expansion in Africa*, ed. Chima J. Korieh and Raphael Chijioke Njoku (New York: Routledge, 2007); and Thaddeus Sunseri, *Wielding the*

Africa concern new forms of education and healthcare. After looking at transformations in these areas due to Christianity's presence, we will turn to changes that have been subtler and also profoundly transformative in ethnicity and language, then in gender relations.

EDUCATION

Nearly all missionary groups in eastern Africa focused on schools from the beginning of their work. Rudimentary education in Zanzibar was a priority for both Catholics and Anglicans who worked mostly with ransomed and escaped slaves. Anglicans focused on literacy, emphasizing the need for an African elite and the priority of understanding the word of God. For the Catholics, education became a way to create the church, composed of agricultural and more skilled workers, young African women trained to assist in the clinic, parents, and a small elite potentially to become assistants to the missionaries themselves.[47]

The earliest intense efforts at education among a settled people took place in Uganda, linked to the rapid growth of Christianity there. Already in 1879, CMS leader Alexander Mackay carved wooden letters to teach reading, and in November of that year he had a rudimentary printing press working. Catholics soon followed suit, anxious that the young pages assisting the kings not find the Anglicans more attractive due to what one dubious Anglican missionary called "the disease of alphabetarianism."[48] These "reading schools" opened the way to a system in which Catholic and Anglican missions created formalized "central schools" at the main station, with "bush schools" near the village chapels—a system that continues to this day in many places. In 1895, the CMS founded a central school for girls at Namirembe, with a boys' school following in 1898, soon with 140 students.[49]

Both Catholics and Anglicans founded secondary schools for the sons of chiefs and other elites by the early twentieth cen-

Ax: State Forestry and Social Conflict in Tanzania, 1820–2000 (Athens: Ohio University Press, 2009).

47. Kollman, *Evangelization of Slaves*, 2005.

48. Wandira, *Early Missionary Education in Uganda*, 115.

49. Wandira, *Early Missionary Education in Uganda*, 123.

tury.[50] The first Anglican effort, Mengo School, began in 1904 on Namirembe hill in Kampala and officially opened in 1907 with Winston Churchill as the chief guest.[51] The future British Prime Minister wrote that missionary societies formed "an island of hope and progress in the very heart of the Dark Continent."[52] King's College in Budo, soon to become the Anglican flagship, was founded in 1906 on the road to Masaka to the west, and it welcomed girls, an unprecedented move toward coeducation, in 1933. Most Christian secondary schools remained single gender for decades.

The Catholic Mill Hill missionaries founded the first Catholic higher school at Namilyango east of Kampala in 1902, organized to train catechists and chiefs' sons. In 1909, its band played for the visiting Theodore Roosevelt.[53] Anglican visitors there were inspired to found King's College at Budo. In 1904, the White Fathers founded St. Mary's College in Kampala after an appeal by the Catholic chiefs through lay leader Stanislaus Mugwanya. It moved to Kisubi, south of the capital, in 1924, then was handed over to the French Brothers of Christian Instruction in 1926. Both the CMS and the Catholics also established technical schools in Uganda.

A famous post–World War I visitation by a group of American educational reformers, inspired by a Ghanaian, James Aggrey, sought to expand their previous focus on African Americans and Native Americans to Africa in order to improve and standardize education across the continent. The subsequent Phelps-Stokes Report of 1923–24, jointly sponsored by the colonial authorities and Christian missionaries, only deepened missionary commitments to school-building. The report recognized the need for widespread training to a certain minimal level as well as the need for elite schools to train leaders for the colonial territories. In 1928, the English Catholic archbishop Arthur Hinsley, later cardinal archbishop of Westminster (the Catholic designation of the diocese that includes London), visited eastern Africa on the Vatican's behalf. He famously told

50. Wandira, *Early Missionary Education in Uganda*, 119–27.

51. Wandira, *Early Missionary Education in Uganda*, 141.

52. Wandira, *Early Missionary Education in Uganda*, 142.

53. Wandira, *Early Missionary Education in Uganda*, 153–54.

Catholic missionaries that "where it is impossible for you to carry on both the immediate task of evangelization and your educational work, neglect your churches in order to perfect your schools."[54] This encouragement, accompanied by similar exhortations from Protestant leaders, led to expansions in education at every level. Rivalries developed among denominations, and educational systems emerged in all three colonies that had very large numbers in elementary schools, with swiftly narrowing possibilities moving upward. In Uganda, for example, 1950 saw 159,000 students in elementary education and 700 in secondary schools. By 1959, these numbers were 993,000 and 3,728 respectively.[55]

Elsewhere in eastern Africa, education also grew. Where mission Christianity was strongest in what became Kenya and Tanzania—around Mount Kilimanjaro and in Bukoba in northern Tanganyika, and near Peramiho in the south, as well as in central and western Kenya—there schools developed most impressively. At Peramiho, hundreds of German Benedictine monks eventually built a huge complex, including an imposing monastic residence for the men, soon joined by a smaller residence for the Missionary Benedictine Sisters of Tutzing who had their own schools for girls. Eventually there arose a huge brick church, workshops and schools, hospitals and clinics mostly led by the sisters, all surrounded by extensive agricultural developments, with education a focus of the famous mission.

Lutheran efforts in Tanganyika in the colonial period educated an African and expatriate colonial elite, including many leaders of the independence movement. Besides impressive institutions around Mount Kilimanjaro, the Leipzig Mission also worked among the Maasai through education.[56] In central Kenya, Alliance High School for Protestants and Kabaa for Catholics developed great reputations. Tanganyika's Catholics had St. Mary's in Tabora, while Anglicans founded St. Andrew's in Minaki, near Dar es Salaam, and St. Philip's in Kongwa, near Dodoma. There were certainly schools not linked to mis-

54. Sundkler and Steed, *History of the Church in Africa*, 641.

55. Sundkler and Steed, *History of the Church in Africa*, 642.

56. Kim Groop, *With the Gospel to Maasailand: Lutheran Missionary Work among the Arusha and Maasai in Northern Tanzania, 1904–1973* (Åbo, Finland: Åbo Akademi University Press, 2006), 235–44.

sions—some excellent ones led by colonial officials or private expatriates, a very small number Muslim, and a few others independent and run by Africans, arising usually in the aftermath of disputes with missionaries such as in the wake of the Kenyan controversy over female circumcision. The vast majority of schools were founded and led by missionaries, however, even if they were formally "government schools." Some scholars have called the type of Christianity that arose "*kusoma* Christianity," from the Swahili verb "to read," and certainly literacy marked the Christian elites—and many ordinary Christians, too—across the region.

Post-secondary education also grew in eastern Africa after World War I. Its origins lay in missionary foundations. Small attempts at advanced schooling, usually seminary education, had begun in Zanzibar and Tanganyika already in the nineteenth century under Catholic and Anglican auspices, as well as by Anglicans near the Kenyan coast at Freretown. The seminary in Freretown later became St. Paul's in Limuru, not far from Nairobi. In Uganda, Catholics established Katigondo Seminary near Masaka in 1911 and Anglicans their own Bishop Tucker Theological College near Mukono in 1913. In Tanganyika, the White Fathers later founded a seminary in 1923 at Kipalapala, which became St. Paul's Senior Seminary in 1925. Lutherans established their own theological college, Makumira, near Arusha in 1947.

From the 1920s, Britain started formulating educational policies for its African colonies, partly in response to African agitation for improvements. The colonizers also needed an educated populace to help run things and believed in schooling's power to civilize and improve Africans. Missionaries certainly agreed. By the mid-twentieth century, many Africans themselves viewed education as the single most important investment for social and political advancement.

Though nationalization of schools in Uganda and Tanzania after independence removed formal control from church bodies of their schools, many of the most respected retained their Christian identity. New church-linked schools founded since independence have proliferated in all three countries, and national governments no longer seek the same level of oversight. These new schools vary in quality, yet Christian schools continue the tradition of comparative educational excellence long a hallmark of Christian education in the region, especially compared to the numerous other private schools that have arisen, where standards can be very poor. Education remains linked to Christianity across eastern Africa, with the best primary and secondary schools usually linked to churches. Indeed, education unites governments and the churches in complex ways as each pursues legitimacy among citizens. As Amy Stambach argues in a recent study, schools can become vehicles through which religion can strive to encompass the state, and also through which states work to contain religion.[57]

Secular higher education began with a technical school at Makerere in Kampala in 1922 and, though not directly run by missionaries, it depended on missionary teachers for decades. In 1935, it became a higher education center for all of British East Africa, and in 1949 an affiliate college of University College, London. Makerere represented the flagship of the University of East Africa, which developed branches in Nairobi and Dar es Salaam that continued after independence.[58]

The newly independent nations naturally applied themselves to establishing their systems of higher education, initially building on the networked University of East Africa. When the union dissolved during the Amin regime, each nation reinforced its flagship. Kenya, more economically successful than Tanzania and not plagued by Uganda's political turmoil, made the quickest advances in expanding higher education, with numerous universities founded after independence: the flagship University of Nairobi (begun as a technical college for subjects not taught at Makerere in 1954), followed by Kenyatta University (beginning as a teachers' training college linked to the University of Nairobi in 1970), Moi University in Eldoret (1984), Egerton

57. Amy Stambach, *Faith in Schools: Religion, Education, and American Evangelicals in East Africa* (Stanford: Stanford University Press, 2010), 5.

58. British efforts in eastern Africa lagged behind their support of higher education elsewhere in the empire. See Arthur T. Porter, "University Development in English-Speaking Africa: Problems and Prospects," *African Affairs* 71, no. 282 (1972): 78–79.

University (1987), and the Jomo Kenyatta University of Agriculture and Technology (1994). Uganda and Tanzania followed suit and today also have secular universities outside the original flagships.

Christian higher education outside of seminary and other ministerial formation meanwhile has had explosive growth across the continent, including eastern Africa, beginning in the 1980s. Forty-six new Christian universities were established in Africa between 1990 and 2010.[59] Part of this has to do with growth in theological education, to be discussed in a later chapter, but most students in Christian higher education do not pursue degrees in theology but secular subjects. Degrees directed to employment in education, healthcare, and business are especially prominent. Africans pursue such degrees at Christian schools for the same reasons they seek higher education in the first place. As populations have soared, primary and secondary schools have proliferated, and fees supporting public education have fallen, thus the demand for higher education has grown enormously. In many places, Christian institutions are perceived as trustworthy.

Many denominations in eastern Africa have their own schools, so that Christian universities in eastern Africa in Nairobi alone include: Daystar (nondenominational evangelical), Africa Nazarene University, Hope Africa University (Methodist), and the Catholic University of East Africa. Meanwhile Kenya Methodist University is in Meru, and Limuru is the site for the multi-denominational St. Paul's University. In Uganda, the Anglican seminary at Mukono became Uganda Christian University in 1997, and Catholics founded Uganda Martyrs' University near Masaka in 1994. In Tanzania, Lutherans founded Tumaini University out of a seminary in Makumira and Catholics have St. Augustine's University in Mwanza.

HEALTHCARE

The earliest missionaries at the Indian Ocean coast, both Catholic and Anglican, founded medical clinics. A bit later,

59. Joel Carpenter, Perry L. Glanzer, and Nicholas S. Lantinga, eds., *Christian Higher Education: A Global Renaissance* (Grand Rapids: Eerdmans, 2014), 16.

Cardinal Lavigerie, founder of the Missionaries of Africa, had pushed his missionaries to develop medical skills, both to provide care and to attract converts, and he trained a number of "doctor-catechists" from former slaves. One such ex-slave, Adrian Atiman, offered great service for years in southwestern Tanganyika until his death in 1956, becoming a revered national hero.

Protestant and Catholic clinics and a few hospitals, on the Catholic side usually led by nuns, developed everywhere. Over the objections of some missionaries that providing medical care interfered with their evangelical mission,[60] the CMS in Uganda welcomed the physician Albert Cook in 1896. Cook always insisted conversion was his first priority, yet his medical skills were in high demand. Clinics he oversaw treated 16,000 outpatients in 1897 and 90,000 in 1903. He helped develop the colonial medical system, including Mengo Hospital, with his wife (who took a keen interest in training midwives), brother (also a physician), and an X-ray technician nephew also assisting. He later founded the predecessor to Mulago Hospital, which began as a clinic for sleeping sickness and venereal diseases. Cook and his colleagues oversaw efforts to combat devastating waves of sleeping sickness in Uganda in the late nineteenth and early twentieth centuries, which led to large depopulation, especially near Lake Victoria and others of the Great Lakes. Over half of the population of Busoga, east of Kampala, died, and Cook himself estimated that between 200,000 and 300,000 people died on shores of Lake Victoria between 1900 and 1905.[61]

Stories of Ugandans amazed by Cook's surgeries—removing cataracts, for example, so that the blind could see—were many. Cook remained active until 1937, dying in Uganda in 1951. Meanwhile each of the local kings in the Ugandan protectorate tried to erect his own hospital, with Kabarole in what is now Fort Portal one of the earliest.

Kenya's missions had small clinics early on, and a more substantial one led by Presbyterian missionaries from 1912 at

60. Wandira, *Early Missionary Education in Uganda*, 98; Megan Vaughan, *Curing Their Ills: Colonial Power and African Illness* (Stanford: Stanford University Press, 1991), 58–59.

61. Grace Bantebya Kyomuhendo and Marjorie Keniston McIntosh, *Women, Work and Domestic Virtue in Uganda, 1900–2003* (Oxford: James Currey, 2006), 49.

Tumutumu near Nyeri. Its African assistants surprised colonial officials with their skills during the Spanish influenza epidemic starting in 1919, which hit eastern Africa hard. The Africa Inland Church founded a hospital at Kijabe northwest of Nairobi in 1915. Other Protestant and Catholic mission stations also established smaller medical facilities.

In Tanganyika, missionaries had small clinics near many missions and more substantial facilities under missionary control in Zanzibar and in places of a larger missionary presence, such as around Moshi near Mount Kilimanjaro. In 1921, Swiss Catholic Capuchin sisters began the Ifakara Medical Institute near Iringa, which became a hospital in 1951. A female physician and Capuchin sister, Dr. Ingrid Schuster, overcame Catholic resistance to nuns serving as doctors and served there, as well as later at Peramiho from 1936, and then from 1943 to 1956 in Mahenge. UMCA-linked Anglicans at Masasi opened a hospital in 1936 with an elaborate religious ceremony.[62] One famous Anglican missionary physician in Tanganyika was Leader Dominic Stirling (1906–2003), who worked for the UMCA for fourteen years before converting to Catholicism and joining a Benedictine mission at Mnero. He later served the Catholic hospital in Kibosho, near Kilimanjaro, and was elected to the first Parliament of Tanzania. A friend of Julius Nyerere, he served five years as national Health Minister.

Critical analysis of European medical care in colonial Africa details how it helped construct the image of Africans as unhealthy and unfit for self-rule.[63] One historian isolates three trends in British medical descriptions of sub-Saharan Africa in the early twentieth century: the heroism of white doctors, the dangers of the African environment for Europeans, and the moral culpability of Africans in their illnesses. Each trend persisted even when the proper disease vectors like insects were recognized.[64] The discourse of the primitive, superstitious African in need of intervention was a powerful one, legitimating

62. Vaughan, *Curing Their Ills*, 55.

63. Vaughan, *Curing Their Ills*.

64. Anna Crozier, "Sensationalizing Africa: British Medical Impressions of Sub-Saharan Africa, 1890–1939," *Journal of Imperial and Commonwealth History* 35, no. 3 (2007): 393–415.

political intervention by European Christians in the name of saving lives.

At independence, the new African governments sought control over healthcare, sometimes seeking to assume responsibility for Christian hospitals.[65] As with schools, such attempts have eased over time, and Christian institutions providing healthcare have continued to the present day, serving the needs of thousands of eastern Africans daily. Large Christian hospitals exist in all three countries, many with strong reputations. Two large Catholic hospitals exist in Mwanza, Tanzania, and the Kilimanjaro Christian Medical Centre in Moshi, a cooperative work of Protestants spearheaded by Lutherans, has achieved regional renown. In addition, numerous local churches—especially those linked to the Catholic Church and larger Protestant denominations—staff local clinics that extend into rural areas.

The epidemic of HIV/AIDS, which has ravaged eastern Africa since the 1980s, has generated a great deal of Christian institutional response, both in direct care to the afflicted and with educational efforts to counteract the spread of the disease. Hospice care and orphanages for children left behind by the deaths of family members have appeared.[66] Many Christian hospitals, clinics, and churches have shifted resources toward public health in response.[67]

Historian Shane Doyle has produced a longer-term study of fertility and sexuality in eastern Africa, focusing on three large people-groups living in Uganda and Tanzania: the Haya in Tanzania, and the Baganda and people of Ankole in Uganda.[68] Doyle argues that social mores surrounding sexual behavior changed in the region in the mid-twentieth century due to new economic and political realities, which undid earlier cultural expectations. The rapid spread of HIV/AIDS in that region arose partly because of such trends with their late-colonial roots.

65. Ludwig, *Church and State in Tanzania*, 137–40.

66. Sundkler and Steed, *History of the Church in Africa*, 914–16.

67. Linda Hogan, ed., *Applied Ethics in a World Church: The Padua Conference* (Maryknoll, NY: Orbis, 2008); Edwina Ward and Gary Leonard, eds., *A Theology of HIV and AIDS on Africa's East Coast* (Uppsala: Swedish Institute of Mission Research, 2008).

68. Shane Doyle, *Before HIV: Sexuality, Fertility and Mortality in East Africa, 1900–1980* (Oxford: British Academy, 2013).

Interestingly, he also argues that the dramatic lowering of infection rates in the 1990s through better education and other social pressures depended upon the same learned social realities, since the population was open to healthcare information from governmental and other sources.

As healthcare in eastern Africa evolves in step with advances in global health elsewhere, partnerships that produce innovative community-based healthcare emerge in the region. Some initiatives, such as those organized by US-based Christian Connections for International Health, focus efforts on community resource pooling and advancing local community efforts through resource and knowledge sharing in Uganda and Kenya. Other networks, such as the Christian Health Association of Kenya, have formed to promote access to quality healthcare by assisting health facilities to deliver accessible, comprehensive, quality health services to the people of Kenya in accordance with Christian values, professional ethics, and national health sector policies. These associations and organizations demonstrate congregational- and community-driven means to fuel health advances. Many draw upon intentional mission statements and policies signaling local leadership and long-term investment, a far cry from the visiting or missionary doctor patterns of the past.

Such efforts also can be notably marked by faith-based social agendas in delivering healthcare. For example, abstinence joins more common forms of family planning when addressing infectious venereal disease control. Messages from healthcare and religious leaders find biblical support for healthy timing and spacing of pregnancies. Thus, one Kenyan pastor refers to 1 Timothy 5:8 ("Whoever does not provide for relatives and especially family members has denied the faith") and Genesis 1:28 ("Be fertile and multiply; fill the earth and subdue it") to explain how Christians ought to follow God's call to be responsible parents and stewards of creation by planning their families.[69]

In addition, Christians pursuing healthcare advances in eastern Africa also join other practitioners to overcome the onetime divide between traditional and modern approaches to healthcare.

69. See the video at "Voices from the Global South," Christian Connections for International Health, https://tinyurl.com/y7nag64l.

In particular, medical professionals seeking to address issues of mental health, for example in the wake of social trauma suffered by refugees in the region, draw upon both bio-medical insights and cultural forms of social healing. Christian providers have participated in such efforts, for example in northern Uganda and northern Kenya.

Healthcare in eastern Africa remains dynamic, with new hospitals and clinics opening all the time. Governments strive to keep up while facing challenges of expanding populations, while private institutions of varying quality also appear, some ostensibly Christian. Certain areas have pioneered innovative community-based healthcare—again, at times Christian—but these are too few to meet the burgeoning health needs of today's eastern Africans.

CHANGES IN SOCIAL RELATIONS

Nearly always, the first African Christians at the earliest missions came from elsewhere, whether partners with the missionaries in the building of the station—often onetime slaves trained at the coastal Protestant and Catholic missions—or refugees for whom the mission became a welcome safe-haven. First-person accounts of Christian conversion testify to a new subjective sense of personal value that some believers experienced, along with growing social awareness.[70] Such experiences reflect the reversals felt, since many of those earliest Christians came from the margins of surrounding societies, while at the mission their proximity to the missionaries gave them new social power.[71]

Of course, such testimonies, often extolling the education and literacy that came with Christianity in colonial times, reflect

70. See for example the testimonies in J. Gaume, *Suéma: Or the Little African Slave Who Was Buried Alive*, trans. Mary Elizabeth Herbert (London: Burns, Oates, 1870); A. C. Madan, *Kiungani, or Story and History from Central Africa* (Zanzibar, 1886); and Marcia Wright, "Mama Adolphina Unda (c. 1880–1931): The Salvation of a Dynastic Family and the Foundation of Fipa Catholicism, 1898–1914," in *The Human Tradition in Modern Africa*, ed. Dennis D. Cordell (Lanham, MD: Rowman & Littlefield, 2012).

71. Justin Willis, "The Nature of a Mission Community: The Universities' Mission to Central Africa in Bonde," in *Missionary Encounters: Sources and Issues*, ed. Robert A. Bickers and Rosemary Seton (Richmond, UK: Curzon, 1996), 143.

European and missionary desires for appreciation of their roles in "civilizing" Africans. They thus must be interpreted cautiously, for those reporting may not have been free to express all they wanted. Moreover, those who suffered corresponding losses of social power and diminished personal authority in colonial processes had much less recourse to personal expression that has been recorded for posterity in writing. The novels of Ngugi wa Thiong'o set in the colonial period skillfully depict such tensions, as Christianity's coming at once empowers and disempowers the Kenyans who encounter it, depending in varying ways on both involuntary social locations and voluntary responses of different people.[72]

Individual transformations were only part of the story, of course. In addition, the coming of Christianity shaped local environments, for missions bringing new religious ideas also often brought coffee, tea, mangoes, papayas, and citrus, as well as new forms of animal husbandry. They also trained people with skills like bricklaying, carpentry, and forms of metalwork not before seen, leading to construction and other physical transformation at the mission station and beyond.[73] Because of these changes, eastern Africa has been one of the places where environmental historians have investigated the impact of colonialism and Christianity.

Earlier studies presented such processes as undoing a supposedly bucolic precolonial environment.[74] Later work has stressed that Africans had adapted and manipulated their locales in transformative ways before European contact.[75] Still, the spread of colonial-era plantations of coffee, sisal, and cotton had unprecedented environmental effects on soil, as well as local flora and fauna, devastating some rural populations reliant on a previously

72. Nicholas Kamau-Goro, "Rejection or Reappropriation? Christian Allegory and the Critique of Postcolonial Public Culture in the Early Novels of Ngũgĩ wa Thiongo'o," in *Christianity and Public Culture in Africa*, ed. Harri Englund (Cambridge: Cambridge University Press, 2011).

73. Oliver, *Missionary Factor in East Africa*; Calderisi, *Earthly Mission*, 101.

74. Kjekshus, *Ecology Control and Economic Development*.

75. Gregory Maddox, James Giblin, and Isaria N. Kimambo, eds., *Custodians of the Land: Ecology and Culture in the History of Tanzania* (London: James Currey, 1996); Spear, *Mountain Farmers*.

existing set of productive relations.[76] Catholic missionaries in northern Tanzania, historian Robert Munson argues, pursued what he calls "botanical proselytization." As they sought to make Catholics, he explains, "the spread of religion assisted and was supported by the landscape and botanical transformation."[77]

Collectively these Christianity-linked changes in self-awareness and environment could have profound social consequences, upending previous power structures by transforming relations based on age, gender, and possession of religious and political authority that governed many social processes.[78] The introduction of a cash economy, the growing value of literacy and numeracy, Christian resistance to cultural practices like polygamy, and links to missionaries all allowed some Africans to grow in social power in new ways. The young could use school-learning or money to unsettle existing gerontocracies, for example, and the new faith could erode older local religious specialists whose capacity for healing and divination looked feebler in the new circumstances.

In eastern Africa, particularly important changes in ethnicity and gender relations have been linked to Christianity.

Ethnicity

Aspects of identity once thought abiding and central to personal selfhood underwent transformation with the coming of the faith. These include ethnicity or, to use an older term, the links to "tribe." Indeed, missionary linguistic and cultural efforts that shaped ethnicity have likely had even more far-reaching effects

76. Sunseri, *Wielding the Ax*, xviii–xix.

77. Robert B. Munson, *The Nature of Christianity in Northern Tanzania: Environmental and Social Change, 1890–1916* (Lanham, MD: Lexington, 2013), 252.

78. Willis, "Nature of a Mission Community"; Birgitta Larsson, *Conversion to Greater Freedom? Women, Church and Social Change in North-Western Tanzania under Colonial Rule* (Uppsala: Acta Universitatis Upsaliensis, 1991); Dorothy L. Hodgson, *The Church of Women: Gendered Encounters between Maasai and Missionaries* (Bloomington: Indiana University Press, 2005); Mika Vähäkangas, "Ghambageu Encounters Jesus in Sonjo Mythology: Syncretism as African Ritual Action," *Journal of the American Academy of Religion* 76, no. 1 (2008): 111–37.

for eastern Africans' self-identification than European territorial occupation in the colonial period.

A great deal of recent research has investigated the complex histories of ethnic identities in eastern Africa, often emphasizing the role of Christianity. The process in which new Christian realities and then Christian growth led to changes in ethnic self-understanding were many. In quite a few settings, soon-naturalized ethnic identities found a causal beginning—or at least significant impetus—in biblical and other Christian translations initiated by Europeans and their earliest converts. The process in each place was unique, and nowhere did missionaries create an African people *ex nihilo.* After all, linguistic and cultural similarities united people already. Yet generally the codification and streamlining of various dialects over time—with biblical translation often a crucial watershed—eventuated in the systematization of what came to be seen as "the" native language. Missionary strategy depended on linguistic mastery, which required discovering (or helping to create) a language. Large missionary bodies like the Anglicans and Catholics did this for many peoples, as did smaller groups like the Quakers in western Kenya. In certain places in eastern Africa, this process has continued to the present day, yet the larger groups across the region saw it initiated by the early twentieth century.[79]

Western Kenya is an especially instructive region for appreciating these processes of ethnogenesis. Today, a great number of Kenyans from this region self-identify as Luyia (sometimes spelled Luhya), Luo, or Kalenjin—among other ethnic designations. Julie MacArthur shows, however, that the Luyia *per se* were nonexistent before 1935, with various groups of missionaries describing the group among which they worked and their language by terms that have now become linked to contemporary sub-ethnicities of "the Luyia": the Catholic Mill Hill missionaries were linked to the Wanga, the Quakers worked among the Maragoli, the CMS served the Hanga, the Church of God used the language Lunyore. A linguistic committee in 1941 led to the choice of the word "Luyia" for all of them and for

79. For insights into some of the contingencies in Kenyan history, see Peterson, *Ethnic Patriotism.*

the consolidated language; the term meant a gathering site for elders.[80] The word "Kalenjin" had equally contingent origins, emerging from radio broadcasts starting in the 1940s in what had been called "Nandi" in which the phrase "Kalenjin," meaning "I say (to you)," introduced the programming.[81] The radio broadcasts' linguistic terminology gave rise to the ethnic designation. Similarly contingent and retrospectively determinative processes led to "the Luo," Maasai, and the Acholi.[82]

From this perspective, the kingdoms of Uganda look to be the exceptions, since their comparatively secure political consolidation easily became so-called tribal identity. Yet even so supposedly secure an identity as that of those within the Buganda kingdom was, as Nakanyike Musisi shows, much more contested than later certainties suggest. Various other ethnicized and class-based terms that identified people operated for social differentiation prior to colonialism. Over time, however, they gradually lost their importance as centralization linked to Christianization and a church-sanctioned monarch advanced through the twentieth century and "the Baganda" emerged.[83]

Even abolitionism encouraged by missionaries could lead to concretizing of previously more dynamic ethnic identities. This was especially the case at the Swahili coast where "Africans" were distinguished from "Arabs" by Europeans, some of them anxious to protect the former from the depredations of the latter. This overrode longstanding fluidity in racialized notions of personhood and social belonging.[84] Even categories that seem self-evident like "Arab" and "African" underwent transformation through historical processes.

Ethnicity continues to be a crucial factor in politics and soci-

80. MacArthur, "Making and Unmaking of African Languages," 151–72.

81. Lynch, *I Say to You.*

82. Heike Behrend, *Alice Lakwena and the Holy Spirits: War in Northern Uganda, 1986–1997* (Kampala: Fountain Publishers, 1999), 14–19; John R. Campbell, "Who Are the Luo? Oral Tradition and Disciplinary Practices in Anthropology and History," *Journal of African Cultural Studies* 18, no. 1 (2006): 73–87.

83. Nakanyike B. Musisi, "Morality as Identity: The Missionary Moral Agenda in Buganda, 1877–1945," *Journal of Religious History* 23, no. 1 (1999): 51–74.

84. Jonathon Glassman, "Racial Violence, Universal History, and Echoes of Abolition in Twentieth-Century Zanzibar," in *Abolitionism and Imperialism in Britain, Africa, and the Atlantic*, ed. Derek R. Peterson (Athens: Ohio University Press, 2010).

ety in eastern Africa, especially in Kenya and Uganda, where the long-term viability of pan-ethnic national identity remains a live question. Mainline Christian churches were the earliest multi-ethnic voluntary organizations in the region, but it is unclear if they contributed thereby to a reduction in inter-ethnic tensions and to the formation of a broader sense of national identity, since they also reinforced ethnic identities. To this day, churches continue efforts at political education that challenge the too-often default ethnicization of politics, yet ethnic and religious identities can also overlap and reinforce each other, reinforcing political tribalism.

Gender

Christianity has also fostered complex transformations in gender relations in eastern Africa. Such changes took different forms, depending on cultural expectations, missionary strategies, and other historical circumstances. Events like the controversy over so-called "female circumcision" in Kenya in the late 1920s and early 1930s, prompted by missionary intervention ostensibly to protect women, show that practices linked to gender could have explosive political implications—in this case, inadvertently galvanizing proto-independence sentiments.

At times, the coming of missionaries allowed local males to draw upon Christian social expectations to reinforce an existing patriarchy, or even to create a supposed timeless system of gender relations that buttressed male privileges.[85] Along with that, however, the missionary-brought faith occasioned new possibilities for social prestige accruing to women—increasing respect for widows, for instance, who were often very vulnerable and subject to "widow inheritance" by their late husband's relatives,[86] and for women who became educated or gained income by employment at missions or schools. The chance to become a Catholic nun represented another source of power and authority

85. Stephens, *History of African Motherhood*, 145–46.

86. Ruth Prince, "Public Debates about Luo Widow Inheritance: Christianity, Tradition, and AIDS in Western Kenya," in *Christianity and Public Culture in Africa*, ed. Harri Englund (Cambridge: Cambridge University Press, 2011).

for some African women, as they gained education and leadership, and the activities of nuns could also empower other African women. Finally, if the new religion at times undid older religious bonds uniting women,[87] it also allowed new ties to form through boarding schools, revival meetings, and laywomen's devotional groups.[88]

In the early twentieth century, CMS missionary wives in Uganda had founded the Mothers' Union of the (Anglican) Church of Uganda, institutionalizing what historian Elizabeth Prevost calls "maternal Christianity," that is, the expectations that mature women faced in the new system. The Mothers' Union, which became very popular with Anglican Ugandan women who joined missionary wives in the organization, founded a Maternity Training School for midwifery to lower infant mortality. The Union idealized monogamy while also defending women who were impoverished by supposedly "traditional" inheritance practices.[89] Ugandan men, as well as some missionaries, found the Mothers' Union too independent and pushed back against it at times. The Union also, however, exposed contradictions between the interests of missionaries and male Ugandans: "the Mothers' Union's emphasis on monogamy undermined men's attempts to circumvent the church's marriage requirements and to maintain their social and economic leverage simultaneously through polygamy and Christianity."[90]

The Mothers' Union was part of what Grace Kyomuhendo and Marjorie McIntosh call the Christianity-linked "Domestic Virtue" model for women, which idealized females as keepers of the home and providers of childcare. There was also the "Service Career" version for some, to become nurses or teachers, yet the demands of the home did not thereby cease. Catholic expectations were similar, embodied in the Catholic Women's Guild.[91] At times, missionaries could draw upon the Domestic Virtue model to defend women against the behavior of men—against

87. Hodgson, *Church of Women*.

88. Shetler, *Imagining Serengeti*.

89. Prevost, *Communion of Women*, 157–87.

90. Prevost, *Communion of Women*, 187–88.

91. Kyomuhendo and McIntosh, *Women, Work and Domestic Virtue in Uganda*, 96–97.

polygyny, drunkenness, or financial impropriety. At other times missionaries used it to restrict women's freedoms—in mandating male demands for sexual access, for instance.[92]

Birgitta Larsson identifies four stages through which Haya women in northwestern Tanzania engaged Christianity. First, the earliest Catholic mission served as a welcome refuge from slavery or abusive marriages. In a second stage, missionary encouragement of coffee cultivation and support for bridewealth undid women's self-determination, undermining subsistence agriculture and restricting marital freedom. As women gathered authority from Christianity—either through the East African Revival or, for Catholics, in lay groups like Catholic Action or the Children of Mary—they pushed back, asserting themselves, and in a fourth phase, late twentieth-century educational initiatives spearheaded by Lutherans have created female professionals.[93]

The biographies of certain eastern African women shaped by Christianity reveal the diverse experiences they faced as gender expectations changed. Powerful Kenyan women like Nobel Peace Prize–winner Wangari Maathai (d. 2011) and women's rights campaigner Wambui Otieno Mbugua[94] (d. 2011) received missionary-sponsored educations that opened doors to their leadership even if they did not continue to practice their faith.

Influential women in the colonial period also usually were shaped by Christianity. Marcia Wright has detailed the life-story of Mama Adolphina Unda (d. 1931), an elite Fipa woman who helped bring about the conversion of her people in southwestern Tanzania to Catholicism. After serving as a catechist, she entered the convent, then left to marry. In a political conflict over the kingship, she sided with her brother against her husband, eventually serving as regent. In this capacity she cooperated with the

92. Kyomuhendo and McIntosh, *Women, Work and Domestic Virtue in Uganda*, 13–19, 52–56, 66–73.

93. Larsson, *Conversion to Greater Freedom?*

94. Cora Ann Presley, "Wambui Waiyaki Otieno Mbugua (b. 1928): Gender Politics in Kenya from the Mau Mau Rebellion to the Pro-Democracy Movement," in *The Human Tradition in Modern Africa*, ed. Dennis D. Cordell (Lanham, MD: Rowman & Littlefield, 2012).

White Father missionaries as they pursued the conversion of the Fipa.[95]

Christianity also empowered Anna Inondi (d. 1992), a woman studied by Cynthia Hoehler-Fatton. Like many others, Inondi became a prophet in a Roho church in western Kenya early in the twentieth century.[96] Resembling female Pentecostal leaders in Kenya today, Inondi and other AIC female leaders embody how Christianity serves to support their authority, overcoming traditional obstacles for women that gender expectations otherwise create. That said, certain messages can empower those who speak them even when their content repeats constrictive social expectations facing women.[97]

Christianity is no panacea for the challenges facing women in Africa. Nyambura Njoroge, a Kenyan Presbyterian theologian and onetime pastor with a doctorate from Princeton, faced obstacles in her pastoral work due to her gender. Denied a role at a funeral due to cultural expectations that disqualified her as a woman, she acquiesced in the moment. Such impediments, however, help explain her willingness to leave Kenya to serve in Geneva as Program Executive of the HIV/AIDS Initiative of the World Council of Churches.[98]

Other historians show how missionary Christianity changed local conceptions of divinity rooted in gender. At times, earlier high gods designated as female in local, pre-Christian symbolism became sidelined as Christianity took hold.[99] Yet Christianity could also create leadership opportunities for women. This could be in missionary Christianity, for instance for Catholic nuns and Christian laywomen in schools and hospitals, or in contemporary Pentecostal churches, where women can wield leadership

95. Wright, "Mama Adolphina Unda."

96. Hoehler-Fatton, *Women of Fire and Spirit.*

97. Parsitau, "'Arise, Oh Ye Daughters of Faith.'"

98. Frances S. Adeney, *Women and Christian Mission: Ways of Knowing and Doing Theology* (Eugene, OR: Pickwick, 2015), 149, 112–13.

99. Hodgson, *Church of Women*; Bilinda Straight, *Miracles and Extraordinary Experience in Northern Kenya* (Philadelphia: University of Pennsylvania Press, 2007), 48–52; Musa Dube, "Christianity and Translation in the Colonial Context," in *The Routledge Companion to Christianity in Africa*, ed. Elias Kifon Bongmba (New York: Routledge, 2016).

quite decisively.[100] Such leadership is not always obviously salutary. The Catholic Marian Movement was founded by a Ugandan woman, Credonia Mwerinde, in the 1990s. Facing obstacles to expansion of the movement, possibly due to her gender, she enlisted the help of layman Joseph Kibweteere and Father Dominic Kataribabo, who served as official leaders in attempts to garner official Catholic support. It was not forthcoming, and the movement ended in a violent loss of life at Kanungu in western Uganda, with around 900 dead, either through murder or collective suicide.[101]

Gender has also played a role in attempts to control sexual behavior through legislation sponsored by some of Uganda's Christians. One notable effort was linked to so-called "Domestic Relations" bills that sought to make polygamy illegal, beginning in the late 1980s. A concerted campaign by some Christian leaders for a new law in 2003 led to large demonstrations by Muslims, who saw it outlawing what they viewed as a religious right. It eventually was rejected by Parliament in 2008 despite President Museveni's support.[102]

Soon new efforts at social legislation against homosexuality sponsored by Ugandan Christians brought more concerted global attention. In 2009, after preaching tours by evangelical missionaries from the US, a bill was brought to the Parliament making homosexual behavior punishable by death. Worldwide campaigns called for restrictions on foreign aid in response, and the legislation was softened, then sidelined. It returned a few years later, however, and was passed in 2014 and signed into law. A constitutional review has subsequently set aside the law, and its future is unknown. Most Ugandan Christians, however, see

100. Mwaura, "Gender and Power in African Christianity."

101. Narcisio Bagumisiriza, *The Kanungu Tragedy: 17th March 2000 and Details of Related Discoveries about "The Movement for the Restoration of the Ten Commandments of God"* (Kabale, Uganda: Kabale Diocese, n.d.); Emmanuel K. Twesigye, *Religion, Politics and Cults in East Africa: God's Warriors and Mary's Saints* (New York: Peter Lang, 2010); Richard Vokes, *Ghosts of Kanungu: Fertility, Secrecy, and Exchange in the Great Lakes Region of East Africa* (Woodbridge, UK: James Currey, 2009).

102. Abasi Kiyamba, "'The Domestic Relations Bill' and Inter-Religious Conflict in Uganda: A Muslim Reading of Personal Law and Religious Pluralism in a Postcolonial Society," in *Displacing the State: Religion and Conflict in Neoliberal Africa*, ed. James Howard Smith and Rosalind I. J. Hackett (Notre Dame: University of Notre Dame Press, 2012).

homosexual behavior as both un-African and un-Christian, and were likely in favor of the legislation.[103]

Global trends connected to gender expectations of course have their effects in eastern Africa. In response, governments and local communities at times seek to enforce traditional values in the face of perceptions of their erosion. Christians can find themselves on both sides of contested issues. For example, a recent government campaign in Uganda calls for decent dress among civil servants. This includes specifications about skirt lengths and the outlawing of visible cleavage for women, while men must keep their hair short and wear closed-toe shoes. Clearly many Christians sympathize with such efforts to reinforce so-called traditional values, yet many of those who see restrictions in such values also draw upon their Christian faith and linked efforts to advance social justice, including gender equality. One anthropologist detects in such measures a return to colonial-era civilizing efforts, some linked to Christianity, that also focused on dress and deportment.[104]

EASTERN AFRICA AND GLOBAL CHRISTIANITY: DISCOURSES AND PRACTICES OF DEVELOPMENT

As is clear, the era of independence has seen an expansion of Christianity's forms and diversification of its impacts in eastern Africa, even as the direct role of Christian bodies in formal governing processes in all three nation-states is less than in the colonial period. The number of registered churches continues to grow, and numerous unregistered Christian bodies also operate. Schools, linked formally or informally to Christianity, proliferate, as do healthcare providers. Christian groups run insurance agencies, banks, as well as a variety of other sorts of service-providers. Some churches have been accused of corruption in national media campaigns.

103. For further discussion, see "Roundtable on LGBTIQ Persons in Africa" in the December 2015 issue of the *Journal of the American Academy of Religion* (83, no. 4: 887–997), which has articles that discuss Uganda and Kenya directly.

104. See Anneeth Kaur Hundle, "Uganda's Colonial-Style Dress Code," Al Jazeera, August 14, 2017, https://tinyurl.com/yczavt3g.

A number of international nongovernmental organizations (NGOs) operate in eastern Africa, with the capital cities, smaller cities, and areas that were subjected to long-term unrest like Gulu in northern Uganda housing hundreds of different groups. Kibera, a slum in Nairobi, is estimated to have over one thousand NGOs providing service to its perhaps one million inhabitants. Many NGOs are linked to Christianity, and this kind of provision has raised questions not unlike those raised about earlier Christian missionary efforts that were linked to European colonialism.

If one were to examine a stereotypical international Christian charity website or brochure produced by a group serving in eastern Africa, its iconography would replicate older patterns. Pictures of suffering children would be placed alongside alternating photos of post-intervention, happy children. Nineteenth-century Christian missionaries, Catholic and Protestant, raised money for the ransoming of slave children with similar rhetoric and images in eastern Africa.[105] Today's NGO might offer programs for Christian leadership alongside education and opportunities for eastern African participants to become fully developed agents of change in their nation. The providentialist promises of Livingstone-era missionaries, seeking to civilize and Christianize, prefigure such promises. It is easy to see that today's NGOs, many of them Christian, often replicate tropes and strategies of the past.

The power wielded by NGOs has received searing criticisms lately from across the ideological spectrum, from western academics and economists, as well as from intellectuals in countries that receive them like Uganda, Kenya, and Tanzania. Many see such bodies as neither neutral nor innocent bystanders in the great developmentalist drama unfolding in Africa; rather, they are integral to the neocolonial and neoliberal project of western imperialism that has done so much to disempower African populations. Such critics see NGOs as a continued imperialism, the latest vehicle for upward mobility for the ambitious educated classes: academics, journalists, and professionals. Such organiza-

105. Kollman, *Evangelization of Slaves*, 2005.

tions have also been implicated in the rampant corruption linked to aid delivery in developing communities.

Official governments in eastern Africa have also criticized NGOs, including Christian ones. In June 2016, Kenya's Ministry of Devolution and Planning, in conjunction with the country's NGO Board, released a circular claiming that foreign NGO workers on average earned four times as much as their Kenyan peers, and that they failed to transfer jobs to local workers over time, instead staying on too often in Kenya as lifelong "career expats."[106] The pressure on NGOs has occurred elsewhere, too, often motivated by understandable desires to promote local sustainability and to develop skills among citizens. Others, however, see in such pressures another sign of larger crackdowns on independent civil society more generally.

Eastern Africa's Christians, however, also present cases for optimism about the faith's potential to advance the common good and local well-being. Urban poverty, homelessness, and drug abuse have led to various Christian responses, both local and international in origin, including new church structures and a variety of local centers. Many Christian churches have begun to serve children in communities modeled after SOS Children's Villages, which house orphans in family-style living to raise and educate them. Dar es Salaam saw the rise of the Msimbazi Centre among Catholics, which addressed a number of social problems, as did the Undugu ("brotherhood" in Swahili) Society of Kenya, founded by Missionary of Africa Father Arnold Groll. God's House of Miracles in Lugazi, Uganda, provides similar care, as does Faith's Children's Home, both under Protestant direction.

Another response to changes since independence such as intensified urbanization has been the development of small Christian communities to create more intimate connections among believers in parishes. These novel forms of social outreach and Christian community have prioritized addressing the cultural disorientation and other problems many face in growing cities like Nairobi, Dar es Salaam, and Kampala. Promoted and studied by American Maryknoll Catholic priest Joseph

106. See the discussion at Lily Kuo, "Kenya Is Pressuring Thousands of Expat NGO Workers and Volunteers to Go Home," Quartz, July 19, 2016, https://tinyurl.com/yd7edvmj.

Healey, small Christian communities have appeared across eastern African Catholic parishes, with many experiments in efforts to mobilize Christian discipleship.[107]

Finally, local Christian efforts can sometimes address African concerns better than global attempts to redress lack of development. Anthropologist China Scherz's book *Having People, Having Heart* compares the reception accorded two kinds of development efforts in central Uganda. She shows that the non-professionalized yet caring work of a group of African Catholic sisters achieves more than the sophisticated development attempts undertaken by international NGOs. The reason lies in the discrepancy between their approaches to development. The sisters, on the one hand, act naturally out of cultural assumptions they share with the people they serve. The NGO that Scherz studies, on the other hand, unwittingly undermines those same assumptions with its well-intentioned yet foreign-feeling attempts to foster development without creating dependence.[108]

Theological reflection in eastern Africa, the subject of the next chapter, has never ignored social and political issues like those discussed here. Today, however, theologians are increasingly direct in addressing the social, economic, and political challenges facing the region.

107. Healey and Hinton, *Small Christian Communities Today*.

108. China Scherz, *Having People, Having Heart: Charity, Sustainable Development, and Problems of Dependency in Central Uganda* (Chicago: University of Chicago Press, 2014).

5.

Theological

The Shape of Christian Theology in Eastern Africa

Christian theology in eastern Africa, like theology elsewhere, has always reflected the lived experiences of those who carry it out. In eastern Africa this means that theology has engaged other religious perspectives—those of expatriate missionaries or Muslims, for example. And, almost invariably, when Africans have produced theology it has reflected existing African religiosities linked to sociocultural identity, or what is known as "African traditional religion" (ATR) or "African religion" (AR). The extent to which Christianity was felt to cohere with, or clash against, such preexisting religious beliefs has varied widely, yet many features of those traditional beliefs have shaped how Christianity has evolved in eastern Africa. Thus, what some have called the "primal religion" is a constant background in relationship to which theology has taken place.

Theology has been defined many ways. In light of the comparatively short history of Christianity in eastern Africa, it is best to consider theology broadly, as any type of reflection on faith and other religious experiences, and thus begin by distinguishing between two types of theology. First, there is the formal reflection on faith that is usually written. Second, there is the natural, rarely written reflection on faith-as-lived that many adherents undertake as rational believers. In eastern Africa, the practice of formal, academic theology is relatively young—though some of it has important implications and promise for world Christianity. Informal theology, however, has long gone on, carried out by missionaries, their African coworkers, and the many Africans who have responded affirmatively to the Christian message within the richness of their cultural heritage. Much informal theology, therefore, has been transmitted orally. Such an informal and often oral theology, in its myriad forms, has unique value for understandings of Christianity, not only in eastern Africa but also elsewhere. Here we will consider both forms of theological reflection, shaped by a world-Christianity perspective that seeks to appreciate the diversity and richness of the varieties of Christian experience.

Challenges arise in understanding both formal theology and informal theology—though of different sorts. Grasping informal theology always remains a partial, unfinished business, for countless processes of theological reflection have unfolded and continue to proceed with no one recording them. Or, if they are recorded, they are done so unselfconsciously, often in formats that require concerted historical interpretation, including at times oral history methods. In addition, many who study theology, whether in eastern Africa or elsewhere, are inclined to overlook informal theology. Some are resigned to its irretrievability; others consider it unimportant. Appreciating informal Christian theology, past and present, is vital for capturing the scope of theological activity in eastern Africa. The benefits are not restricted to those interested in Christianity in Africa. In addition, informal theology represents indigenous African intellectual creativity, sometimes undertaken in difficult circumstances, easily overlooked.

At face value, written theology by academic professionals seems easily accessible. Yet what constitutes "eastern African Christian theology" is not obvious and raises at least three questions. First, must theology for eastern Africa come from there, and be carried out by eastern Africans? After all, theology emerging from many other places has affected eastern Africa, non-eastern Africans have written important theology in eastern Africa, and some people born in eastern Africa have pursued theological careers mostly elsewhere. Meanwhile, considerable theology has been produced in eastern Africa and by eastern Africans. While emphasizing this last form of written theology, one cannot ignore the others, for theological movements from around the world have certainly shaped eastern Africa. These include theological currents linked, for example, to the modern missionary movement, to the rise of cultural anthropology and its place in making cultural appreciation important for missionary practice, to implicit ecclesiological assumptions that have shaped how evangelization has proceeded and thus been received, to changes in theology due to global Christian trends—the rise of ecumenism or, for Catholics, new ideas linked to Vatican II and its aftermath.

At the same time, eastern Africa itself has been home to important theological innovations—for instance, in types of missionary practice, in embodying evangelical impulses with roots in Keswick spirituality that blossomed in the East African Revival, in African-initiated churches (AICs), in the development of women as theologians, and in the particular writings of noted eastern African theologians like the Kenyans John Mbiti and Esther Mombo, Ugandans like the late John Waliggo, and Tanzanians like Charles Nyamiti. In considering persons whose theological efforts concern eastern Africa, moreover, important work has been written with reference to the region by scholars from elsewhere: from the United Kingdom, the late John V. Taylor, for example, and Aylward Shorter; from continental Europe, Mika Vähäkangas; from the United States, Joseph Healey; from Nigeria, A. E. Orobator; and from Canada, Diane Stinton.

A second question arises because of the difficulty of isolating eastern African theology from other African theology, since formal theology in Africa over the past half-century has usually addressed Africa as a whole instead of taking a regional focus—South African theology's focus on apartheid being a notable exception. The larger distinctions in the African theological enterprise have been linguistic instead of regional—with Francophone and Anglophone theologians often working apart from one another. The fact that theologians from, or working in, eastern Africa—unlike western or central Africa—have almost entirely written in English has meant two things. First, they are particularly prone to appreciate English theological work from elsewhere in the continent, and, second, they are less inclined to know theology from Africa written in French. At the same time, like most other African theologians, they usually do not think of their work as specific to eastern Africa but link it to African theology more generally.

The third question arises when supposed "eastern African Christian theology" addresses or derives from the particular experiences of certain eastern African Christians, but perhaps not others. A great deal of the most distinctive theology arising in the region has been self-conscious about cultural identity and historical particularity—for the Kamba of Kenya, in Mbiti's case, before and during initial evangelization; or arising due to missionary efforts to evangelize the Chagga of then-Tanganyika by the German Lutheran missionary Bruno Gutmann; in connection to women-founded African Independent churches in Kenya by Philomena Mwaura; or with particular reference to experiences of violence, for example, in Rwanda and by the Acholi in northern Uganda over the past few decades by Emmanuel Katongole. Since the theological projects in such cases derive from the specific cultural and historical circumstances that gave rise to them, their applicability to and relevance for other cultural and historical settings, even in eastern Africa, can seem elusive. The commendable effort to have theology address the concerns of real Africans with precise social and historical experiences has meant that its bearing on other Africans with a different set of experiences has not always been obvious.

THEOLOGY IN AN INFORMAL MODE

INFORMAL THEOLOGY IN MISSIONARY EVANGELIZATION

The few Portuguese who sought intermittently to evangelize in eastern Africa from the sixteenth to early eighteenth century left little theological material in their wake. The later European missionaries who arrived starting in the mid-nineteenth century and presaged colonial overrule, however, were another story. Accounts of the earliest responses by eastern Africans to these representatives of the nineteenth-century missionary renewal consisted mostly of bemused rejection of strange visitors who preached a very foreign religion. Around missions there were often a few converts among the formerly enslaved, for example, or vulnerable women. Such marginalized people no doubt carried out informal theological reasoning, making sense of the Christian message using tools available, and seeing it as a source of social power and protection. There were exceptions to this small-scale theological work, the most significant being the Baganda in the late 1880s and early 1890s, who soon after missionary contact responded vigorously to Christianity in written reflection and pastoral engagement. As colonial control became more solidified, discernible collective responses grew more numerous among eastern African peoples.

One ubiquitous form of informal theology took place through the translation work initiated by missionaries, beginning in coastal Kenya with KiSwahili by pioneers in the nineteenth-century return of Christianity, CMS missionaries Krapf and Rebmann. Such efforts always relied as well on eastern Africans, though such assistance was not always acknowledged. In seeking to render the Bible—or in Catholic cases, usually some form of a catechism—into African languages, translators implicitly carried out a theological task as they chose local idioms to express Christian ideas. Such efforts often represent serious theological work with profound effects on local peoples. Notable examples include the dictionary of KiSwahili and subsequent religious texts assembled beginning in the 1870s by Bishop Edward Steere of the UMCA in Zanzibar, and later efforts by Catholic Joseph Crazzolara, an Italian Comboni priest who prepared grammars and dictionaries in a number of languages of northern Uganda and Kenya, as well as southern Sudan, in the twentieth century.

Early missionaries in eastern Africa also advanced anthropological scholarship about African peoples. For example, Alexandre LeRoy, a French Spiritan priest, drew upon his missionary work in late nineteenth-century Tanganyika and Kenya to write an early landmark study of so-called "primitive religion." In so doing, LeRoy depicted the religious beliefs and practices he discerned using theological categories, even though he did not think of his work as formally theological. Though this book has long been superseded and is marked by the racism of its time, it was widely admired. LeRoy was also the first chair-holder in the History of Religions at the *Institut Catholique* in Paris.

Missionary-produced scholarship on African worldviews also shaped early theology emerging from eastern Africa. One influential discussion of the so-called "primal worldview" that supposedly lies at the foundation of African religiosity was produced by CMS missionary in Uganda John V. Taylor, later bishop and then head of the CMS in London. Taylor's engaging 1963 *The Primal Vision: Western Christendom and the African View of Life*, with each chapter introduced by an African proverb, remains an admired and sensitive discussion of how Christianity in Africa might move beyond being "the white man's religion." Taylor draws insights from across Africa, discussing how monotheism and the person of Christ can be presented in such a way that the church is not restricted to meeting Africans, as he puts it devastatingly, "only in their best clothes"—that is, in the formal settings of church or school. Instead, through skillfully recounted anecdotes and with reference to African intellectuals and anthropologists who study African peoples, he argues that Christianity must respond to "that sense of cosmic oneness which is an essential feature of primal religion."[1] Taylor's work thus blurs the line between the informal theology he observed and the formal act of writing theology.

Early missionaries also engaged in practical theology as they carried out their evangelization. Preaching, undertaken even when linguistic barriers made understanding very unlikely, required theological reflection on the Scriptures in light of the circumstances in which it was carried out.[2] Missionaries also undertook practical theology due to obstacles they faced, includ-

1. John V. Taylor, *The Primal Vision: Western Christendom and the African View of Life* (Philadelphia: Fortress Press, 1963), 20, 72.

2. Few have studied early missionary preaching, one reason being the lack of sources. See the thoughtful discussion in Sundkler and Steed, *History of the Church in Africa*, 665–69.

ing Islamic overrule at the coast, which required careful inter-religious sensitivity at times, as well as the slave trade. Most of the early Protestant missionaries were abolitionists while their Catholic counterparts, mostly French, linked anti-slavery movements with the French Revolution and thus were more reticent to condemn the practice. Cardinal Lavigerie, founder of the Missionaries of Africa, however, was an ardent abolitionist who spearheaded a Catholic anti-slavery campaign starting in the 1880s that included arming men linked to his missionary society who would defend Africans and his missionaries.

Though not supporting slavery, both Catholics and Protestants long purchased and gathered slaves to start their missions. Throughout the nineteenth century, missionaries also argued over the best ways to educate as part of the evangelizing process, including the education given former slaves. Catholics tended to favor industrial or practical training for all but those possibly heading toward ordination or other formal ministerial service, while Protestants encouraged literacy for all believers. Both approaches depended on theological assumptions about proper Christian belonging—for the Catholics, prioritizing obedient participation in a hierarchized church; for the Protestants, self-reflective voluntary discipleship.

Finally, missionaries carried out theological reflection when they encountered cultural practices that offended them—polygyny, infanticide, female circumcision (or genital mutilation)—and sought to stop some and adapt to others. One Spiritan at an early inland mission in Tanganyika gathered chiefs in an 1883 effort to end the killing of children whose teeth came in irregularly, reasoning with them that neighboring peoples let such infants live with no ill effects. Later, a mostly evangelical Protestant attempt to counter female genital mutilation and clitoridectomy in the late 1920s among the Kikuyu led to violent resistance and the polarization of Kikuyu Christians. It also generated new churches and schools that considered themselves independent (that is, not linked with missionaries), reactions that helped to galvanize Kikuyu ethnic consciousness. This process, depicted in Ngugi wa Thiong'o's classic novel *The River Between*, also helped prompt the first ethnography written by an eastern African, Jomo Kenyatta's *Facing Mount Kenya*, and arguably fostered the Mau Mau uprising in the 1950s, which facilitated Kenyan independence.

No doubt their work in translation and related forms of anthropological understanding represent the most important missionary contributions to eastern African Christian theology. Missionaries were usually the first to write a language down and they organized efforts that systematized various dialects into a shared language moving forward—an ambiguous achievement since it meant the loss of linguistic-cultural diversity even as it allowed the formation of a shared identity. Yet language was only part of the missionary task, which also included cultural understanding. Anglican missionary John Roscoe's ethnographic descriptions of the Baganda, for instance, both drew upon and laid the groundwork for Anglican leader Apolo Kagwa's deeply influential historical and anthropological studies of his people, which helped forge Baganda identity in the early twentieth century.

In addition, certain practical choices made by missionaries can also be deemed theologically innovative. The work of the Missionaries of Africa in Uganda saw a number of such achievements, including the restoration of the ancient church's multi-year catechumenate for would-be Catholics, which had repercussions for the worldwide church culminating in the establishment of formal processes for joining the Catholic Church now operative across the globe in the Rite of Christian Initiation for Adults. Other aspects of the White Fathers' strategy showed their attention to local culture, such as their early efforts—inspired by perceptions of the importance of healing for Africans—to implement medical training for catechists. This was famously enacted in Adrian Atiman, a onetime slave who served as a catechist-doctor for over half a century near Karema, Tanganyika, beginning in the 1890s. Perhaps most interestingly, the White Fathers also instituted the practice in the 1880s of placing a Marian shrine—usually a small church-like building—at the entrance to all their missions, as a site for women's devotions. This began in recognition of the important political and ritual role of the Queen Mother, the mother of the Baganda kabaka.

The missionaries saw the shrine's placement and location as a way to build on an existing cultural reference point to develop Catholic piety connected to the Virgin Mary. This architectural feature, reflective of an early attempt at inculturation—the interrelating of Christian faith and local culture—was replicated across eastern Africa, even where peoples had no traditions like the Queen Mother whatsoever.

Even more ambitious early attempts at missionary-led inculturation arose in Tanganyika before independence. At Masasi, an early mission station founded by the UMCA from Zanzibar and located inland from Lindi to the south, the local people along with their Anglican priest, later bishop, Vincent Lucas, developed a Christianized version of male circumcision, or *jando* in the Yao language. Beginning in 1913, cultural features of Yao male initiation—sequestration of the young men to be initiated, teaching by elders, the surgical operation itself, and subsequent rites of reincorporation—all underwent Christian transformation, with even the symbolic ritual tree replaced by the cross. This allowed Christians to belong more fully to their Yao culture without renouncing their faith, and it lasted until independence.[3]

A still more comprehensive effort to engage a local eastern African culture was undertaken by the German Lutheran missionary Bruno Gutmann among the Chagga at Old Moshi mission near Mount Kilimanjaro, where he served from the early twentieth century until 1938. Of the three main groups of German missionaries who entered German East Africa, his, the Leipzig Lutherans, was most inclined to close cultural attention. Gutmann embodied this like no one else, publishing over 500 works on Chagga culture and language, including many large monographs. He was convinced of the malignity of European modernity for Africans and sought to build the church only on indigenous Chagga assumptions, focusing on clan belonging. His

3. William Vincent Lucas, *Christianity and Native Rites* (London: Parrett & Neves, 1948); T. O. Ranger, "Missionary Adaptation of African Religious Institutions: The Masasi Case," in *The Historical Study of African Religion*, ed. T. O. Ranger and Isaria Kimambo (London: Heinemann, 1972); Anne Marie Stoner-Eby, "African Clergy, Bishop Lucas and the Christianizing of Local Initiation Rites: Revisiting 'the Masasi Case,'" *Journal of Religion in Africa* 38, no. 2 (2008): 171–208.

anthropological work remains unrivaled as a work of retrieval even if his cultural romanticism undermined its practical impact. Not only was Gutmann resisted by his fellow missionaries, but younger Chagga Lutherans also resented his warnings about the loss and disorientation they would suffer by learning KiSwahili, much less German and then English.[4]

One celebrated story of later missionary activity in eastern Africa that shows creative theology at work is Vincent Donovan's *Christianity Rediscovered*, first published in 1971 and reissued many times. Donovan, an American Catholic Spiritan priest, worked among the Maasai in Tanganyika, later Tanzania, starting in the late 1950s. Shaped by the cultural sensitivity of his fellow American Spiritan, theologian Eugene Hillman, who authored an important study that reconsidered Catholic condemnations of polygyny, Donovan in the 1960s decided to eschew the missionary strategy that had long operated in eastern Africa. He argued that this older approach, stressing the mission-station and focusing on education of the young, created a shallow faith. Moreover, designed for more settled peoples such as the Baganda, in the case of nomads like the Maasai it yielded no permanent converts. Instead Donovan opted to go to the Maasai settlements himself and preach, village by village, seeking collective conversion after carefully building cultural connections between the abiding religious convictions of the Maasai and the Christian message embodied in Christ himself. The book is a moving study of a missionary at work and his own personal conversion. It probes profound theological questions that primary evangelization raises about the person of Christ, the nature of God, the role of the Bible, the shape of pastoral leadership, and the place of rituals like the Catholic sacraments.[5] More recent research by anthropologist Dorothy Hodgson focused on Maasai women and the Catholic Church revisits those communities and questions some of Donovan's assumptions.[6] Yet his work con-

4. Jaeschke, *Bruno Gutmann*; Fiedler, *Christianity and African Culture*, 28–130.

5. For further insight into Donovan's life and work, see the edition of his letters in John P. Bowen, ed., *The Missionary Letters of Vincent Donovan, 1957–1973* (Eugene, OR: Pickwick, 2011).

6. Hodgson, *Church of Women*.

tinues to appeal to those preparing for or engaged in missionary activity across the globe, especially evangelical Christians.

The work of inculturation goes on in countless ways across eastern Africa, as those preaching and teaching Christianity seek to render its message in ways comprehensible and acceptable to local people. In northern Kenya, a Catholic priest among the Gabbra has adapted the celebration of the Eucharist with a new ritual practice responsive to local culture. Those attending who are unable to receive Eucharist—whether due to being unbaptized, or because they are in situations that disallow it, which usually means living in partnership with someone to whom they are not yet married in the church's eyes—instead of receiving Eucharist do something else. They come forward and simply touch the Eucharistic chalice. Such a gesture draws on Gabbra cultural practices associated with ritual sacrifices of unblemished lambs, in which those present for the sacrifice touch the lamb prior to its being bled to death.[7]

Likely the missionary himself did not inaugurate this practice, but followed the example of the Gabbra themselves, especially those who early on were drawn to Christianity, seeing in its symbols and practices analogies to what they had long known and believed. One surmises that a Gabbra hand reached to the proffered chalice before any missionary suggested that those unable to receive communion touch it. After all, informal theology has also long been undertaken not only by missionaries but by eastern Africans themselves.

RESPONSES TO MISSIONARY EVANGELIZATION: EASTERN AFRICANS AS INFORMAL THEOLOGIANS

Eastern African responses to missionary evangelization ranged widely and certainly had abiding effects on the kinds of Christians they became. Widespread and early conversions occurred, for example, among the Baganda remarkably, less dramatically

7. Felix Nzioka Ngao, "Christian Presence among Marginalized Groups in Northern Kenya," in *Exploring the Future of Mission in Africa: In Celebration of Maryknoll's 100 Years in Mission*, ed. Laurenti Magesa and Michael C. Kirwen (Nairobi: Maryknoll Institute of African Studies, 2012), 84.

but still quite thoroughly among the Fipa in southern Tanganyika, but they were rare. Where they happened, they invariably reflected intellectual work by local people and not merely instrumentalized self-interest pursuing conversion for practical benefits. Donovan's Maasai, for instance, evince both acceptance and rejection of his message, while the Maasai women depicted by Hodgson see in the Catholic Church a chance to recover their gender-based spiritual power, which had been eroded by historical circumstances linked to colonialism and political changes since independence. Wherever Africans encountered Christianity, they did so with an existing spirituality that had particular features, some of which likely were widely shared despite local differences.[8]

At times, missionary decisions had unforeseen consequences in prompting local informal theologizing. The White Fathers among the Fipa, for example, unwittingly forged connections between Christian identity and local assumptions about developing personhood by founding boarding schools. This was because Fipa culture saw changing residences—from mother to grandparents to father's hut (for boys; girls returned to their mothers), then to shared residence with like-gendered young people and on to newly married independent hut—as the normal trajectory toward adulthood. The boarding school experience was adapted to this trajectory by the Fipa, partially explaining how 75 percent of their population was baptized by 1920, and their kingdom became nearly completely Catholic by the mid-twentieth century.[9]

The many lay catechists, Catholic and Anglican, who spread Christianity from Buganda from the 1890s across eastern Africa, exercised creative pastoral theology in countless ways as they met new cultures and circumstances. The later preaching efforts connected with the East African Revival beginning in the late 1920s show similar creativity and the fruit of informal theologizing. They reveal the specific effects of Keswick Evangelicalism on local believers, first encountered in Rwanda, then coming to Uganda. In Revival gatherings, inspired by the

8. For the best discussion so far of this shared spirituality, see Magesa, *What Is Not Sacred?*

9. Smythe, *Fipa Families.*

missionary Joseph Church, Simon Nsibambi, and those newly reborn, believers became newly enthused, challenging the perceived spiritual lethargy and traditionalist backsliding of the Anglican Church in Uganda. The *Balokole*, or "saved ones," upset the training regime at the flagship CMS theological college in Mukono, detecting there a pernicious modernism that undermined the work of the Spirit. In 1941, thirty *Balokole* were expelled from Mukono. Meanwhile, revivalists spread throughout eastern Africa, carrying with them the famous Luganda hymn "*Tukutendereza Yezu*" ("We praise you Jesus"), and challenging listeners, "Are you saved?" Public confessions of personal sinfulness and testimonies of lives redeemed featured at large rallies, and many so-called fetishes were burned. Nearly all Protestant churches in eastern Africa were affected, with the message moving along the railways. Many prominent Protestant church leaders in the post-independence period—Festo Kivengere, Janani Luwum, David Gitari—were shaped by the Revival.[10]

African-initiated churches (AICs) also show the fruit of informal theological reflection. One older typology distinguishes AICs called "Ethiopian" from those designated "Zionist." Ethiopian AICs resemble the missionary churches from which their members came, yet take on African leadership after some type of schism. These have been rare in eastern Africa, compared to western or southern Africa. Instead, not a few eastern Africans have been notable in linking themselves to Orthodox Christian

10. Even rejections of the missionary message often reflected theological reasoning, with organized resistance to colonialism and to Christianity usually taking religious forms, sometimes drawing on aspects of Christianity in doing so. The Maji Maji uprising against the Germans starting in 1905 drew upon southern Tanganyikan beliefs in spirit possession linked to lakes and rivers. One such spirit seized group leader Kinjikitile Ngwale, whose followers believed that drinking a special water made them immune to bullets. (*Maji* in KiSwahili means "water," and duplicating the word marks it as especially potent.) Mumboism, a millennial possession movement in western Kenya starting in 1913, also linked water with its founding prophet, who claimed to have been swallowed and spit out by a serpent in Lake Victoria. The Bamalaki movement around the same time in Uganda was led by Malaki Musajjakawa, who prepared for baptism as an Anglican but was twice refused. He then founded "The Society of the One Almighty God," which combined Christianity and Judaism while rejecting modern medicine as violating Scripture's promises of a healing God.

bodies overseas when dissatisfied with the mission churches from which they depart, as occurred in Uganda under the leadership of Semei Kakungulu and in central Kenya.

Zionist churches, that is, those with quite distinctive features compared to missionary-founded churches, have been more common, especially in western Kenya. There a number of so-called "Roho" churches—from the Swahili word for "spirit"—emerged beginning in the 1920s, usually led by local leaders trained at missionary churches and inspired by Pentecostal currents in the region. The fissiparous nature of these churches makes keeping track of them difficult, yet theological reasoning—whether an appeal to the Spirit's vitality or to cultural values—usually appears to explain the secession or innovation. Many of the earlier AICs ran into trouble with colonial authorities, who saw threats to order and perceived violent resistance to colonial overrule, often with specious evidence. Usually the protests were directed more at social renewal rather than formal political structures.

The historical origins of these churches in a place like western Kenya, where many of eastern Africa's AICs began, reflect certain theological commonalities. These include a tendency to attack traditional African religion as pagan, a belief in the immediacy of God's spirit active in the founding prophet, a willingness to draw upon the Bible to defend practices like polygyny that missionaries had condemned, and narrated stories of persecution by missionary leaders, colonial officials, or both. In the past few decades, global Pentecostalism has shaped many of these churches, so that speaking in tongues, healing rallies, and prosperity preaching are becoming more common. In addition, these churches have assumed a prominence in countries like Kenya as indicated by numerical growth and elite participation that has forced them to reconsider their political roles in light of a previous sectarianism and strategy of withdrawal from public life.[11] Now they struggle to determine how to engage the nation-state—whether to join other churches in ecumenical political engagement, hew their own path in their relations with their governments, or continue in sectarianism.

11. Kuhn, *Prophetic Christianity in Western Kenya.*

When divisions arose, such new churches often stood accused by missionaries and some African Christians as promoting schism. As noted in an important work by Cynthia Hoehler-Fatton, the model of schism that has often governed descriptions of these churches is problematic for two reasons. First, it is often misleading historically since these churches at times emerged among those expelled instead of those who wanted to split. Second, the label "schism" asserts the theological normativity of mission-led Christianity at the expense of the Roho churches. As Hoehler-Fatton also shows, such churches from western Kenya have evinced theological creativity yet remained obviously Christian. They have also been notable in the strong women leaders they have featured from their early days.[12]

Many of these churches show the effects of the East African Revival. For instance, Anna Inondi, a member of one of the Roho AICs of western Kenya, drew upon the Revival's enthusiasm to narrate her own spiritual journey in a way that fed other women's faith.[13] Another AIC from western Kenya, Maria Legio, founded in 1963 by Gaudencia Aoko and Simeon Ondeto, is one of the few AICs to self-consciously draw its identity from prior belonging to the Catholic Church. It too reflects the lay empowerment and public witnessing typical of the East African Revival. Ondeto, adherents claim, was conceived like Jesus, without his mother's encounter with a man, and later assumed the Messiah-like role. Like the Roho churches, Maria Legio explicitly attacks beliefs and practices linked to pre-Christian religiosity, yet many observers detect lingering aspects of the traditional religion.

Theological reflection linked to Christianity has also played a role in tragic religio-political movements in more recent years. Though certainly most eastern African Christians would deny the validity of their Christian motivations, both Alice Lakwena and later Joseph Kony in northern Uganda drew upon their faith-based upbringing among the Acholi as they led violent anti-government uprisings. In Lakwena's case, the Holy Spirit Movement arose against the Ugandan government in 1986, and

12. Hoehler-Fatton, *Women of Fire and Spirit*; Kuhn, *Prophetic Christianity*.
13. Hoehler-Fatton, *Women of Fire and Spirit*.

in Kony's, the even deadlier Lord's Resistance Army ravaged northern Uganda in the 1990s and first decade of the twentieth century. Another tragic turn of events was linked to the Movement for the Restoration of the Ten Commandments, a breakaway cult from the Catholic Church in Uganda, which featured a prominent priest as well as former priests and nuns. After tensions with the local churches, with distraught families anxious about family members who joined, it ended in an explosion and ensuing fire in Kanungu, and over 700 bodies were found, many strangled.[14] Such movements have not been the only source of accusations that Christianity has led to tragedy. Critics also question the moralizing tone of some Christian responses to HIV/AIDS, linked to international groups at times, for undermining more systematic and effective approaches to public health.[15] Religious convictions and resulting theological reflection are demonstrably not always perceived as salutary.

Many forms of theological reasoning that proceeded as eastern Africans have made Christianity their own elude scholarly understanding. Eastern Africans adapted to colonialism and embraced (and adapted) missionary Christianity, endured the tumult of world wars, underwent missionary education (including in seminaries), welcomed independence and sought to reconcile their national citizenship with their ethnic identity and their faith commitments, and brought faith to bear in their daily lives, personal prayer, common worship, and in small Christian communities. And today informal theology continues in countless settings, small and large, as Christians in eastern Africa bring their experiences into conversation with new forms of Christianity, notably those linked to global Pentecostalism. The vast majority of these human, Christian, and African achievements are difficult to understand much less analyze. Yet in a world-Christian perspective, these many examples of theology at work in eastern Africa as Africans have appropriated the faith in hidden ways ought at least to be acknowledged as genuinely theological activity.

14. See Bagumisiriza, *Kanungu Tragedy*, for a description and analysis by a Ugandan Catholic bishop whose diocese was deeply involved.

15. See James Kassaga Arinaitwe "How US Evangelicals Are Shaping Development in Uganda," Al Jazeera, July 25, 2014, https://tinyurl.com/y7scr7v7.

FORMAL THEOLOGY IN EASTERN AFRICA

THEOLOGICAL PIONEERS IN EASTERN AFRICA

Most historical accounts of African Christian theology emphasize its formal origins in the groundbreaking work of French-speaking Catholic priests from western and central Africa educated in Europe. Beginning in the 1950s, these pioneers asked themselves and the church questions about the distinctive theological needs and possibilities arising from their particular cultural and historical experiences. They were shaped by broad discussions of distinctive African culture and personality sometimes called *négritude.* Not long after, theologians in southern Africa also raised novel questions linked to the racial history of the region and the gradual imposition of more restrictive racialized laws, instantiated in formal *apartheid* in 1948 and violently amplified in the decades following. Compared to these other parts of Africa, eastern Africa produced few self-identified early theologians of note prior to independence. Even more recently the region is less represented than other parts of the continent in texts on African theology.[16]

Yet there has been notable formal theological work in eastern Africa for over half a century. In 1959, Uganda's Catholic Katigondo Seminary began to publish the *African Ecclesiastical Review* (AFER), which continues to this day as a leading Anglophone Catholic theological journal on the continent.[17] In 1969, Pope Paul VI became the first pope to visit sub-Saharan Africa, and besides honoring the Uganda martyrs who were canonized in 1964, he told the assembled Catholic bishops of Africa and

16. For example, see Bénézet Bujo and Juvénal Ilunga Muya, eds., *African Theology: The Contribution of the Pioneers*, vol. 1 (Nairobi: Paulines Publications, 2003); Bénézet Bujo and Juvénal Ilunga Muya, eds., *African Theology: The Contribution of the Pioneers*, vol. 2 (Nairobi: Paulines Publications, 2008); Bénézet Bujo, ed., *African Theology: The Contribution of the Pioneers*, vol. 3 (Nairobi: Paulines Publications, 2012). Of the twenty-eight theologians who receive chapter-length studies in those three volumes, five are eastern Africans. Eastern African theologians similarly are mostly overlooked in Paulinus Ikechukwu Odozor, *Morality Truly Christian, Truly African* (Notre Dame: University of Notre Dame Press, 2014).

17. Hastings, *Church in Africa*, 567.

Madagascar that they must have a Christianity and a theology that was African: "The expression, i.e., the language, the fashion that manifests the unique faith can be varied and therefore original, according to the tongue, style, temperament, genius and culture of the one who professes this unique faith. . . . In this sense, you can and ought to have an African Christianity."[18] Two notable eastern African theologians had recently begun their careers, anticipating and responding to Paul VI's invitation. In the 1960s, Kenyan John Mbiti, an Anglican priest, and Tanzanian Charles Nyamiti, a Catholic priest from Bukoba diocese, received doctorates in theology in Europe and began teaching and writing.

Nyamiti, whose Christology will be discussed more fully below, in his many works seeks to integrate African cultural insights into a theological framework shaped by Thomas Aquinas, and he followed up a doctorate in theology from Louvain in Belgium with one in anthropology from the University of Vienna. Nyamiti's methodological rigor, which has led some to accuse him of a narrow neo-scholasticism, nonetheless allows him to explore many theological topics from an African perspective—indeed, almost every Catholic doctrinal issue.

John Mbiti has had a more formidable global impact on Christian theological reflection than Nyamiti and remains perhaps the most well-known eastern African Christian theologian. In his influential 1969 *African Religions and Philosophy*, Mbiti theologically interrogated the Akamba culture in which he was raised, finding in it and other African cultures evidence of a vibrant religiosity that was monotheistic and thus superb preparation for Christianity. Mbiti thereby countered negative missionary assessments of traditional African beliefs. He also argued that rejection of those foundational beliefs undermined any genuine conversion to Christianity by Africans formed by them. Mbiti wrote,

> Since traditional religions occupy the whole person and the whole of his life, conversion to new religions like Christianity and Islam

18. Paulin Poucouta, "Meinrad Pierre Hebga: Theologian and Healer," in *African Theology: The Contribution of the Pioneers*, vol. 2, ed. Bénézet Bujo and Juvénal Ilunga Muya (Nairobi: Paulines Publications, 2008), 73.

> must embrace his language, thought patterns, fears, social relationships, attitudes and philosophical disposition, if that conversion is to make lasting impact upon the individual and his community.[19]

In other important works, Mbiti compared notions of time in the New Testament and in African traditional religions (ATRs) and analyzed traditional African proverbs for their philosophical and theological congruence with Christianity.

Mbiti's work has prompted diverse theological reactions. The majority have appreciated his thoughtful reflections on traditional African religions and applauded his theological insights. Not all, however. In the early 1970s, Okot p'Bitek, a famous Acholi poet from Uganda, gave a biting response to Mbiti's assertions that ATR was monotheistic and thus predisposed Africans to Christianity. P'Bitek famously accused him and other like-minded African theologians—as well as western scholars before them like Edwin Smith and John V. Taylor—of allowing their theological presuppositions to override countervailing evidence regarding African religious beliefs. An atheist, p'Bitek argued that many African peoples were not well captured in ATR as it had been presented but instead had a variety of worldviews, many incompatible with Christianity.

THEOLOGY INSTITUTIONALIZED

Early theologians in eastern Africa depended on institutions that supported their work. Formal academic theology has also thus implied the existence of Christian institutions where such activity has taken place, especially seminaries, universities, and pastoral centers. Both Catholics and Protestants have long had centers that support academic theology, and AICs have recently founded centers of their own. This began naturally first in seminaries and catechist-training centers designed to create ministerial assistants to missionaries. Those who established and taught at such places did not think of themselves as producers of theology but as its transmitters.

Anglicans and Catholics had founded small-scale institutions

19. John S. Mbiti, *African Religions and Philosophy* (New York: Praeger, 1969), 3.

for ministerial formation in Zanzibar and coastal Tanganyika already in the late nineteenth century, but none lasted very long. Institutions with more staying power included the Bishop Tucker School of Divinity and Theology at Mukono in Uganda, founded in 1913 by the Anglican CMS, what is now Uganda Christian University. The Catholic White Fathers had two years earlier initiated a seminary at Katigondo near Masaka, and after World War I, founded another at Kipalapala in Tanganyika. Theology has also been carried out in the post-independence period at St. Paul's United Theological College (now St. Paul's University), which in 1955 moved from coastal Kenya to Limuru near Nairobi while it expanded from an Anglican to an ecumenical Protestant theological institute. For Catholics, similar innovation in theology took place at the Gaba Pastoral Institute founded in 1967 near Entebbe in Uganda, which in 1976 moved to Eldoret, Kenya. Gaba was founded by the regional conference of Catholic bishops, AMECEA (the Association of Member Episcopal Conferences of Eastern Africa). AMECEA, established in 1960, includes the bishops of Kenya, Uganda, and Tanzania as well as Sudan, Ethiopia, Zambia, Malawi, Eritrea, and South Sudan. Besides offering training for Catholic religious workers from these countries, Gaba also in 1968 began an influential series of publications called Spearhead Monographs, and over 150 studies on pastoral and theological topics have been published.

Today faculties in religious studies and theology exist at a variety of seminaries across the region, as well as at secular and Christian universities. Christian institutes of higher education with a global theological reputation include Uganda Christian University and St. Paul's University and several in Nairobi, now an international center for Christian higher education. Important Christian universities in the Kenyan capital include the Catholic University of Eastern Africa, founded as the Catholic Higher Institute of Eastern Africa in 1984; the African International University, formerly the Nairobi Evangelical Graduate School of Theology; and Daystar University, a nondenominational evangelical school chartered in Kenya in 1994 as part of a larger network begun in the 1970s in what is now Zimbabwe. Mention should also be made of Tumaini University Makumira, formerly Lutheran Theological College-Makumira, founded in 1997 and located in northern Tanzania.

Another aspect of the institutionalization of formal theology in eastern Africa concerns the efforts of the region's theological institutions and theologians to join international theological associations and to form their own organizations. In 1960, leaders of some of the major Protestant theological institutions of the region formed a network called the Association of Theological Institutions of Eastern Africa (ATIEA), which sought to standardize theological accreditation and received funding from international mission support agencies in the later 1960s. The founding members of the association included the Bishop Tucker Memorial College in Mukono, Uganda; Lutheran Theological College, in Makumira, Tanzania; St. Paul's United Theological College, Limuru, Kenya; and several smaller schools. ATIEA later developed a three-year diploma in theology at Makerere University in Kampala, while adding partner institutions from Ethiopia, Sudan, and Zambia, as well as Catholic seminaries. Its theological courses reflected developments in African theology and assisted in the creation of curricula that tried to respond to the changing realities of the church in eastern Africa. Starting in the 1970s, ATIEA was hampered by political unrest in Uganda, moving to Nairobi in 1978. Over the next decades, most institutions sought accreditation within their own countries, and ATIEA declined in importance. In a joint 2010 meeting with the All African Conference of Churches, however, ATIEA founders reported on their efforts to coordinate library and internet-based resources among the region's theological institutions, among other topics. The extent to which the ATIEA has served as an effective accrediting agency and resource for partner institutes has varied over time.

Many individual theologians from eastern Africa have joined and taken leadership in theological associations, including the Ecumenical Association of Third World Theologians (or EATWOT), formally inaugurated in Dar es Salaam, Tanzania, in 1976, and the Circle of Concerned African Women Theologians, to be discussed below. They also formed their own organizations, beginning in 1989, when theologians in eastern Africa formed the Ecumenical Symposium of Eastern African Theologians (ESEAT), at the urging of Maryknoll missionary Fr. Carroll Houle. Houle contacted Jesse Mugambi of the University of Nairobi who subsequently formed a nucleus of senior theologians in eastern Africa, most of whom were based in Nairobi. These included Bénézet Bujo of the Democratic Republic of the Congo (DRC) and John Mary Waliggo of Uganda, both of whom were teaching at the Catholic Higher Institute of Eastern Africa (now Catholic University of Eastern Africa). Others included Douglas Waruta and Hannah Kinoti of the University of Nairobi, and the late Anne Nasimiyu-Wasike of Kenyatta University.

ESEAT, in the words of Mugambi, aimed at "cultivating an ecumenical profile in which scholars from all brands of Christianity would be accommodated and their diverse theological perspectives would interact and challenge each other." He contended that "African Christian theology ought to be an ecumenical and Pan-African endeavor, rather than a denominational, sectarian and parochial one."[20] Theologians involved in the initiative were therefore drawn from Catholic and Protestant traditions, ordained and lay, men and women. They meet every year a week before Palm Sunday, a process that continues to the present.

In addition, since 1993 there has been a Kenya chapter of EATWOT, founded under the leadership of Mary Getui, who was succeeded in 1998 by Philomena Mwaura. Some of the issues addressed at meetings have included gender-based violence, globalization, interfaith dialogue, poverty, conflicts, and peace-building. Both ESEAT and Kenya's EATWOT chapter have organized meetings and subsequently published a number of edited volumes of theological essays.

20. J. N. K. Mugambi, "Ecumenical Contextual Theological Reflection in Eastern Africa 1989–1999," in *Challenges and Prospects for the Church in Africa: Theological Reflections for the 21st Century*, ed. Nahashon W. Ndung'u and Philomena Mwaura (Nairobi: Paulines Publications, 2005), 19.

PATTERNS AND TRENDS IN EASTERN AFRICAN CHRISTIAN THEOLOGY

Work in these institutional settings has taken a variety of forms, and theologians linked to eastern Africa have also worked elsewhere around the world as they have pursued academic theology. Much theology in the region has been preoccupied by the question of culture, so much so that African Christian theology that does not address African culture almost seems a misnomer. American Maryknoll missionary Michael Kirwen established in Nairobi's Catholic Tangaza College an Institute of African Studies that seeks to develop a cultural understanding of Africa for those seeking to serve in the church there. Out of his work with hundreds of students he published a textbook for teaching cultural understanding of Africa, *African Cultural Knowledge*, which organizes its subject into fifteen themes such as the Creator God, the diviner, ancestors, and polygyny.[21]

The emphasis on culture has raised two different kinds of challenges. First, given the diversity of cultural realities in Africa, any serious effort to address culture usually means specifying which African culture is being considered. Since African theologians often seek to respond to continent-wide issues, the particularity of cultural attention can make a pan-African theological approach difficult. Certain theologians, in response, have discerned a generalizable "African religion" that captures a sufficiently common singularity in ATRs, something to which John Mbiti expressed an openness in a 1990 introduction to a new edition of *African Religions and Philosophy*. Laurenti Magesa, to be more fully discussed below, has developed this perspective most fully,[22] arguing the spirituality of Africans has a coherence rooted in shared worldviews and cultural practices. Others resist such efforts to generalize, detecting a homogenization—usually around an African monotheism and a continent-wide affirma-

21. Michael C. Kirwen, ed., *African Cultural Knowledge: Themes and Embedded Beliefs* (Nairobi: MIAS Books, 2005).

22. Laurenti Magesa, *African Religion: The Moral Traditions of Abundant Life* (Maryknoll, NY: Orbis, 1997).

tion of the value of life—that is problematic since it is so long on oversimplifications as to be vacuous.

Yet the focus on culture has also been challenged in a second way, as making theology irrelevant. Certain African theologians, in light of pressing social problems facing the continent over the past half-century such as political violence, corruption, diseases like HIV/AIDS, and grinding poverty, have urged theology to address such problems more directly. They have felt that focusing on culture can too blithely ignore the needs of Africans in their daily lives. In addition, efforts to engage African culture by theologians have tended to treat the cultural realm as unchanging, coherent, and easily bounded—something linked to the structural-functional approach that shaped cultural anthropology through most of the twentieth century but that is increasingly contested.

In light of these difficulties, critics of the unilateral focus on culture emphasize the need for African theologies of liberation that, like famous similar efforts arising from Latin America and South Africa, take as their starting point the lived experiences of Christian believers and communities, especially experiences of suffering. Others have countered that, without denying its pervasiveness, suffering is not the only reality for most African Christians, and thus is itself a limiting perspective through which to pursue African theology rooted in African experiences.

These two emphases—on culture, and on Africa's social problems, especially suffering—have meant that overviews often stress that academic theology on the continent falls into two types: theologies of inculturation and theologies of liberation. Inculturation refers to theological efforts that seek to link Christian faith and culture, while liberation refers to the efforts at political and social betterment that theology pursues. That binary, however, overlooks much other theological work.

Here, in an effort to lend some order to the diverse trajectories of theological methods and orientations in eastern African, the discussion of formal theology will be organized around six themes: (a) inculturation, (b) liberation, (c) reconstruction, (d) theology addressing particular sociopolitical concerns, (e) theological efforts by women, and (f) finally, theologies linked to AICs, Pentecostalism, and other independent Christian groups.

These topics are, of course, not all of the same sort, nor are they exclusive of each other. Theological efforts by women in eastern Africa, for example, have pursued inculturation and liberation, and indeed fit into all the other categories. Meanwhile social and political concerns have motivated AIC and Pentecostal theologians, and those who embrace the notion of reconstruction. These six headings instead represent one way to present necessarily selective heuristic categories for organizing disparate intellectual activity reflective of formal theology in eastern Africa over the past few decades.

Inculturation

The most developed efforts at theologies of inculturation in Africa, including eastern Africa, have revolved around the person of Christ. Inculturation refers to theological work that seeks to connect Christianity and culture, and, in its efforts to link the person of Christ to African cultures, African theology today thus replicates the practice of the church's first centuries. Then, too, Christological reflection stood at the center of theological concern in the formation of creedal affirmations.[23]

There are a number of theologians linked to eastern Africa who have contributed to African Christology in important ways. Charles Nyamiti's ancestral Christology represents perhaps the most ambitious systematic approach to a theological topic coming from an eastern African theologian. He develops his approach in a series of smaller publications as well as a larger 1984 manuscript, *Christ as Our Ancestor: Christology from an African Perspective*. Nyamiti's analogical theological method, mentioned briefly above, is displayed very clearly in his development of an ancestral Christology. As in the rest of his theology, he brings a traditional theological topic—in this case, Christ—into dialogue with an aspect of African culture that seems to resemble it—the African notion of ancestorhood. He

23. Victor I. Ezigbo, "Jesus as God's Communicative and Hermeneutical Act: African Christians on the Person and Significance of Jesus Christ," in *Jesus without Borders*, ed. Gene L. Green, Stephen T. Pardue, and K. K. Yeo (Grand Rapids: Eerdmans, 2014).

then considers what insights each might give the other, in a back-and-forth process of mutual illumination. Throughout, Nyamiti deliberately acknowledges and highlights the ways Christianity challenges cultural assumptions, questioning their validity. His focus on the integrity of doctrinal truths in the face of challenges from cultural particularity seeks to guarantee that Christian revelation is preserved intact. He does, however, appreciate when hitherto underappreciated aspects of that revelation can be more fully disclosed by comparison with African cultural values.

In the midst of his exposition, Nyamiti discusses five common characteristics of ancestors in African traditional beliefs: (1) they have a natural relationship with earthly family or tribal members; (2) they potentially achieve a supernatural status at death; (3) they serve as mediators between the divine and human realm; (4) they led morally exemplary lives; and (5) they live in regular contact with earthly family members.[24] Jesus can be seen to fulfill each of these roles, depending on one's interpretation of Scripture and the Christian tradition, yet Nyamiti is keen to identify the differences between Christ and African ancestors.

First, through Jesus all people are connected to each other, not only those of same tribe or clan. The connection to him thus allows each person to have by adoption the nearness of God that Jesus himself embodied by his nature. Second, Jesus is more than an example, since through the activity of his Spirit he can be both the object and subject of human actions, as he acts in persons and they do so in him. Third, contact with Jesus through the sacraments of baptism and communion is intended to change lives, not simply benefit believers—they serve as an invitation to ongoing conversion. Fourth, the link with Jesus is by human choice, not by birth. Finally, people connect to him not through natural shrines or particular local settings linked to sacred ancestral history, but through sacraments and the church.

Given these similarities and differences, Nyamiti wants Jesus to be considered the brother-ancestor *par excellence* for Christians. This, he believes, allows one to avoid the watering down

24. Martien E. Brinkman, *The Non-Western Jesus: Jesus as* Bodhisattva, Avatara, Guru, *Prophet, Ancestor or Healer?* (London: Equinox, 2009), 226.

of Christ's distinctiveness, while allowing for African insights to enrich our appreciation for Christ's potential roles in Africa and elsewhere. Nyamiti thus effects what others call a "double transformation" through this act of inculturation—both ancestorhood and the notion of Christ are reconsidered and supplemented by being brought into relation with each other through theological reflection.

Though widely admired for its cultural insights, faithfulness to the Catholic Church's teaching, formal theological rigor, and clarity, Nyamiti's Christology has also been criticized. In particular, he has been accused of inattentiveness to the specific historical and social situations in which African believers live. This lack of contextualization means that, for some critics, Nyamiti fails to address the sociocultural challenges facing African Christians.

Another theologian linked to eastern Africa who has pursued an inculturationist Christology is Aylward Shorter, a British Missionary of Africa (White Father) priest whose anthropological fieldwork for his doctorate took place in Tanzania, and who has for many years taught and carried out pastoral work in eastern Africa. In the 1960s and 1970s, Shorter carried out a number of visits across the region, assessing the pastoral challenges facing the Catholic Church on behalf of the region's bishops. Shorter most recently has published several volumes of history on the White Fathers' work in Africa, and he is a generous contributor to the Dictionary of African Christian Biography (www.dacb.org), an online, open-source website where thousands of African Christians' lives are memorialized.

Shorter in 1985 published *Jesus and the Witchdoctor: An Approach to Healing and Wholeness*, the provocative title of which suggests the inculturation that he attempts.[25] As Shorter makes clear, the common Bantu term *nganga* (or *mganga*), though commonly translated as "witchdoctor," usually instead means "healer," and he seeks to recover the term from missionary and colonial opprobrium. And it is the role of Jesus as healer—and as someone who existed within the healing traditions of his time,

25. For a discussion and development of the Christology of Shorter, see Fernando Domingues, *Christ Our Healer: A Theological Dialogue with Aylward Shorter* (Nairobi: Paulines Publications, 2000).

place, and culture—that Shorter adduces in linking Jesus with African approaches to securing health and well-being. "Jesus," Shorter writes, "shared the integrated approach to healing which characterizes the so-called witchdoctor, but he carried it infinitely further in every dimension."[26]

Inculturation is not only a method for theologians in eastern Africa, but also a pastoral practice carried out by the churches, with varying degrees of self-consciousness and success. The most comprehensive study of the pastoral practices of inculturation in eastern Africa is Laurenti Magesa's 2004 *Anatomy of Inculturation: Transforming the Church in Africa*. Magesa, a Catholic priest from Musoma diocese in Tanzania, has had a long career as a theologian, teaching mostly in Nairobi in Catholic universities and seminaries. He has been attentive to pastoral realities in his extensive theological writing, and *Anatomy of Inculturation* typifies this tendency, beginning as it does with data from interviews with and observations of Christians from a variety of churches in Kenya, Tanzania, and Uganda. Magesa finds much writing on inculturation "pedantic" and "static," and he sees inculturation instead as "a prism through which the whole personal and communal life can be understood, including one's relationship to church laws and practice."[27]

Noting that in most places efforts at liturgical inculturation have been undertaken, he detects limits to other aspects of inculturation nearly everywhere, some from official church pronouncements, others due to believers' resistance. He then explores the types of inculturation evident in Scripture and throughout subsequent Christian history. Drawing on this often-overlooked legacy, he makes recommendations for overcoming what he calls the "dual religious consciousness"[28] that afflicts many African Christians, whose faith and cultural values conflict. Arguing that both the gospel and individual cultures enjoy divine origins, he pushes a "mature, non-alienating

26. Aylward Shorter, *Jesus and the Witchdoctor: An Approach to Healing and Wholeness* (London: Geoffrey Chapman, 1985), 12–13.

27. Laurenti Magesa, *Anatomy of Inculturation: Transforming the Church in Africa* (Maryknoll, NY: Orbis, 2004), 7–8, 61.

28. Magesa, *Anatomy of Inculturation*, 79.

encounter" between them.[29] African gifts to Christianity include a capacity for ritual celebration, Magesa argues, insufficiently tapped by the churches. Borrowing an image from Nigerian Catholic theologian Eugene Elochukwu Uzukwu, Magesa argues for a "listening church," one that, like a stream gathers silt from surrounding regions, draws upon cultures for growth.[30]

Magesa has not only studied inculturation closely; he also is the most distinguished practitioner of liberationist theology in eastern Africa.

Liberation

In eastern Africa, liberation theology has not had the numerous strong voices found elsewhere in the continent, for example, southern Africa, which faced South Africa's *apartheid* and Zimbabwe's war for independence. Eastern Africa thus has few figures in African liberation theology with the global reputations of South Africa's Allan Boesak or Cameroon's Jean-Marc Éla.

Laurenti Magesa, however, does enjoy a distinguished status in the international theological community and embraces liberation theology as especially pertinent in Africa.[31] Trained as a moral theologian and shaped by the social justice orientation of Tanzania's first president, Julius Nyerere, Magesa has taken liberation as a basic motif for theological work, arguing that the church's practice and reflection ought to respond to the practical challenges facing Africans such as poverty, corruption, disease, and warfare. Reflecting on his career as a theologian, he has emphasized the "liberation context" of his scholarship in theological ethics, mindful of the assaults on their dignity that Africans have suffered in the past and present. This has been nourished by study of the South African experience, liberation theology elsewhere especially in Latin America, and

29. Magesa, *Anatomy of Inculturation*, 142.

30. Eugene Elochukwu Uzukwu, *A Listening Church: Autonomy and Communion in African Churches* (Maryknoll, NY: Orbis, 1996); Magesa, *Anatomy of Inculturation*, 262–70.

31. Richard Rwiza, "Laurenti Magesa: An African Liberation Theologian," in *African Theology: The Contribution of the Pioneers*, vol. 2, ed. Bénézet Bujo and Juvénal Ilunga Muya (Nairobi: Paulines Publications, 2008).

an embrace of social analysis as central to legitimate theology. Magesa calls the churches, especially the Catholic Church to which he belongs, to recognize their vital role in political life in Africa, and he draws upon the Catholic social tradition to guide church-based efforts to advance human dignity, political self-determination, and the common good in the face of historical and contemporary obstacles to human flourishing in Africa.

Another theologian in eastern Africa who takes liberation seriously is Peter Kanyandago, a Catholic priest from Uganda.[32] Kanyandago was shaped by his youth in a newly independent Uganda and his country's acute sufferings in the 1970s and 1980s, when he was a seminarian and doctoral student. Like Magesa, he brings a liberationist perspective to a number of problems facing Africa, including violence and warfare, widespread poverty, HIV/AIDS, the inequalities arising from global economic structures, and endemic corruption. He has also drawn upon social anthropology and historical scholarship to trace these violations of human dignity to notions of European arrogance manifested in the slave trade and colonialism, both of which led to immense African suffering. In response, he has called African theologians and church leaders to work at social reconciliation and the rehabilitation of African cultures, as well as reforms in the global economic system.

Reconstruction

Many theologians have sought to break out of the inculturation/liberation dichotomy, including Magesa and Kanyandago. They and others find it a straitjacket that unhelpfully separates abiding cultural values and traditional symbolic practices from specific historical experiences in theological reflection. One notable effort in this direction has come from Kenyan Anglican theologian Jesse Mugambi, already discussed for his pivotal role in organizing and institutionalizing theological activity in eastern Africa. Beginning in the early 1990s, Mugambi began to ques-

32. Odomaro Ndyabahika, "The Theology of Peter Kanyandago," in *African Theology: The Contribution of the Pioneers,* vol. 3, ed. Bénézet Bujo (Nairobi: Paulines Publications, 2012).

tion the priority of the liberation motif, grounded in the biblical story of Exodus, since Africa had been freed from the bondage of colonial overrule.[33] He also found limits in the approach of inculturation, which was not always responsive to African problems. Instead, he posited the value for Africa of the metaphor of *reconstruction*. In so doing, Mugambi drew on other biblical roots, namely from the Old Testament postexilic period. The Scriptures of that period—books like Ezra and Nehemiah—derive from the sixth and fifth centuries BCE, when the Jewish people rebuilt their nation and their religion after the Babylonian exile. This metaphor and scriptural background seemed to Mugambi more pertinent for Africa's problems. Instead of needing liberation from oppression by others, for Mugambi, the end of apartheid and the Cold War meant that reconstruction best identified the challenges, including theological challenges, facing Africa. Mugambi's theology of reconstruction has been quite influential, generating a great deal of commentary and discussion.[34]

Theological Responses to Changing Social and Political Rrealities

As noted already, African theology tends to be self-consciously contextual—that is, a response to lived experience. At times, that experience has been construed through the lens of culture, as in much of the inculturationist Christological reflection just recounted. At other times, however, the context shaping theological reflection has been of a more complex political or social sort, and historically and geographically specific. Some theological

33. J. N. K. Mugambi, *From Liberation to Reconstruction: African Christian Theology after the Cold War* (Nairobi: East African Educational Publishers, 1995); J. N. K. Mugambi, *Christian Theology and Social Reconstruction* (Nairobi: Acton, 2003).

34. Diane B. Stinton, "Africa's Contribution to Christology," in *African Theology Comes of Age: Revisiting Twenty Years of the Theology of the Ecumenical Symposium of Eastern African Theologians (ESEAT)*, ed. Laurenti Magesa (Nairobi: Paulines Publications, 2010); Isaac T. Mwase and Eunice K. Kamaara, eds., *Theologies of Liberation and Reconstruction: Essays in Honor of Professor Jesse N. K. Mugambi* (Nairobi: Acton, 2012).

responses are deliberately liberationist in orientation, as noted above, yet others eschew that label.

Of course, informal theology—whether undertaken by missionaries or African Christians—equally responded to distinct social and political realities on the ground. Thus, Bishop Alfred Tucker, early in the twentieth century, sought to create a church constitution for the growing Anglican community among the Baganda. He was motivated by the longstanding CMS push toward "three-self" missionary strategy—that is, that the goal of missionary work was to establish local churches that were self-governing, self-supporting, and self-propagating. He was also inspired by Baganda Christian leaders. Despite pressure from his fellow missionaries who wanted firmer paternalistic control over their burgeoning church, Tucker succeeded in 1913, thus creating the Church of Uganda as a constituent body in the Anglican Communion. Similarly, AIC movements in central and western Kenya and elsewhere arose as theological responses to particular contextual factors. These included perceptions of restrictive missionary control over African pastoral instincts and leadership opportunities, colonial-era seizures of African land, and new theological currents like Pentecostalism to which Africans wanted to respond positively against missionary reluctance.

The coming of independence led to formal theological reflection on the role of Christians and their churches in their new nations. The first leaders of all three countries—Milton Obote in Uganda, Julius Nyerere in Tanzania, and Jomo Kenyatta in Kenya—were educated in mission schools and, formally at least, were Christians. Only Uganda had something like a national church in the Anglican-linked Church of Uganda, but everywhere Protestant and Catholic leaders sought to educate their adherents to take responsibility as citizens of their new nations.

Among Catholics, the pastoral writings of Joseph Kiwanuka, first bishop of Masaka and then archbishop of Rubaga (Kampala), stand out for their forthright encouragement to engaged citizenship, and a refusal of divisive partisan politics based on religious or ethnic identity. His 1961 pastoral letter tried to stem the potential discord of the upcoming first national election. Later Ugandan church leaders have also sought theological responses to political problems. The post-independence political turmoil of Uganda has led to many calls from church leaders, Catholic and Protestant, for peace and justice. These protested against the predatory policies of Milton Obote, Uganda's first president; against the violent repressions of Idi Amin, his successor; and against the civil wars plaguing Obote's second presidency that culminated in the coming of Yoweri Museveni as Uganda's leader in 1986. Bishops like the Anglican Janani Luwum of northern Uganda and the Catholic priest Clement Kiggundu, editor of the periodical *Munno*, paid for their prophetic roles with their lives during the Amin years.[35] The unrest in northern Uganda that has persisted during Museveni's regime also led to pastoral-theological reflection as Christian leaders like Catholic archbishop John Odama of Gulu have pursued peace.

In Kenya and Tanzania, national politics have been less tumultuous, yet Christian leaders have also addressed political realities connected to violence, citizenship, justice, and political participation. In Kenya, the suspicious murders of political rivals to Kenyatta and his successor, Daniel Arap Moi, led to calls from church leaders for investigations. During the Moi regime, Kenya's Christian leaders particularly responded to issues of land disenfranchisement and local violence during the so-called "land clashes" in the Rift Valley in the early 1990s, and many also worked to move toward multi-party democracy, which is now in place after struggles in the 1980s and 1990s. American Catholic Mill Hill missionary priest John Kaiser collected reports of government-linked fomenting of those land clashes, as well as other human rights abuses. In 2000, as the days of the Moi regime wound down, Kaiser was murdered. The post-election violence in 2007 and 2008 also has engaged Christian leaders.[36]

A number of Christian leaders have offered practical theological responses to Kenyan political realities in the post-independence period.[37] These include the late Henry Okullu, an Anglican bishop from western Kenya who protested against injustice in the Kenyatta and Moi regimes; Presbyterian Timothy Njoya, who has criticized government brutality and pushed

35. Dowd, *Christianity, Islam*, 190.
36. Klopp, "The NCCK."
37. Knighton, *Religion and Politics in Kenya*.

for gender equality; Catholic Rafael Ndingi Mwana'a Nzeki, who was bishop in Machakos, then Nakuru, and finally archbishop of Nairobi; and Anglican archbishop of Eldoret Alexander Muge, who was killed in mysterious circumstances in 1990 after criticizing the Moi regime. Perhaps the most prominent critic of the Kenyan government in recent times among Christian leaders has been Anglican bishop David Gitari (d. 2013), whose resolve grew after the 1975 murder of the up-and-coming politician J. M. Kariuki in mysterious circumstances late in Kenyatta's rule.

In Tanzania, the fervent Catholic faith of the nation's first president, Julius Nyerere, clearly was a theological motivation for his most famous policies. These include his declaration of nonalignment in the midst of Cold War polarization; the famous 1967 Arusha Declaration, which pushed democracy and socialism as the best approaches in pursuit of social justice and liberation of oppressed peoples everywhere; and the policy of *ujamaa*, or "familyhood" in KiSwahili, which tried to create national unity through universal education, the promotion of KiSwahili as a common language, and a widespread and centralized program of national service.

Notable among attempts to create a more comprehensive theological response to eastern Africa's current problems is Emmanuel Katongole's highly regarded *The Sacrifice of Africa*. Katongole, a Ugandan Catholic priest trained in theological ethics, previously taught at various universities in the US including Duke, and now holds a faculty position in theology and peace studies at Notre Dame. In *The Sacrifice of Africa*, Katongole argues that Christian social ethics in Africa needs to offer better historical and social analysis before presenting solutions to current problems. Through a series of historical episodes highlighting disappointments and heroic exceptions, he draws lessons for Christian leaders and theologians alike, using stories to encourage a more prophetic social imagination for the churches. Lamenting a destructive legacy of church-state relations, Katongole urges an end to "this Western heritage" and a "move beyond the narrow spiritual and pastoral areas to which [the church] is consigned [so that it can] claim full competence in the social, material, and political realities of life in Africa."[38]

Some theologians have combined formal scholarship and actual engagement in addressing African political and social concerns, perhaps the most notable being the late John Mary Waliggo (1942–2008). A Catholic priest of the diocese of Masaka in Uganda, Waliggo was trained as a historian at Cambridge University and wrote an important 1976 dissertation on the history of his diocese, relying on invaluable and irreplaceable interviews with elderly Baganda witnesses to the early Catholic efforts in the region. In numerous other works, he took seriously both inculturation and liberation as theological themes, all the while training seminarians and scholars in institutions in Uganda and Kenya.[39]

Waliggo's contribution to eastern Africa, however, far exceeded his formal theological work. From 1989 to 1995 he served as secretary to the Constitutional Commission of Uganda, becoming one of the major writers of the eventual constitution. Besides continuing to serve the church—in the Ugandan bishops' Justice and Peace Commission, for example—and remaining a leading active theologian, he also served as secretary of the Uganda Human Rights Commission and cofounded the Uganda chapter of the international anti-corruption organization Transparency International.

Contributions from Women Theologians in Eastern Africa

There is a danger in presenting a separate section on women theologians, since it suggests that their gender is what is most important about their work, and that their theological scholarship has been produced apart from other trends in theological activity. Yet two reasons suggest the value of such a section.

38. Katongole, *Sacrifice of Africa*, 19.

39. Peter Kanyandago, "John Mary Waliggo: The Theology of John Mary Waliggo," in *African Theology: The Contribution of the Pioneers*, vol. 2, ed. Bénézet Bujo and Juvénal Ilunga Muya (Nairobi: Paulines Publications, 2008).

First, women who have pursued theological training and sought to have their work published—in eastern Africa as elsewhere—face obstacles that male theologians have not faced, thus their achievements merit special consideration. Second, one of the most promising aspects of Christian theological activity in eastern Africa has been the important work of women theologians in and from the region. In addition, acknowledging the importance of their gender for the theology produced does not thereby reduce the significance of women's theological efforts in the region.

Several eastern African women were founding members of the Circle of Concerned African Women Theologians (CCAWT), an ecumenical and interfaith group that has over the past few decades been very active.[40] Yet many other woman theologians also write and study, seeking to do the church's work of faith seeking understanding, often under difficult circumstances. Their efforts have addressed issues like inculturation and liberation, sometimes expressing the same concerns as male theologians, at times striking a different tone.

Bringing distinct tones to their experiences, women theologians such as Kenyan Lutheran feminist theologian Musimbi Kanyoro have reacted against uncritical efforts at inculturation. While acknowledging the importance of culture in theological reflection, Kanyoro emphasizes the need for a hermeneutics of culture when it is invoked in African theology. She argues that many aspects of culture depicted as "traditional" are morally problematic, for example, those that reinforce the marginalization of women. Kanyoro has questioned polygamy, for instance, calling it a "thorn in the flesh" of African Christianity.[41] A scholar of the Hebrew Bible and contextual theology, Kanyoro possesses doctorates in both linguistics and feminist theology.

40. Nyambura J. Njoroge, "A New Way of Facilitating Leadership: Lessons from African Women Theologians," in *African Christianity: An African Story*, ed. Ogbu Kalu (Trenton, NJ: Africa World, 2007); R. N. Fiedler and J. W. Hofmeyr, "The Conception of the Circle of Concerned African Women Theologians: Is It African or Western?" *Acta Theologica* 31, no. 1 (2011): 39–57; Esther Mombo, "Women in African Christianities," in *The Routledge Companion to Christianity in Africa*, ed. Elias Kifon Bongmba (New York: Routledge, 2016).

41. Diane B. Stinton, *Jesus of Africa: Voices of Contemporary African Christology* (Maryknoll, NY: Orbis, 2004), 146–47.

Like John Waliggo, she has also been active in Christian and other global networks in addressing social issues that cause suffering in Africa and elsewhere. She serves as president and CEO of the Global Fund for Women and has been active in other international organizations addressing global health.

Perhaps the most widely known single work by a female theologian connected to eastern Africa is the 2004 book *Jesus of Africa: Voices of Contemporary African Christology* by Canadian Diane Stinton, a Protestant theologian. Stinton presents a broad overview of African Christology from an ecumenical perspective. She draws on both Francophone and Anglophone scholarship, addressing both the formal work of theologians and the operative, informal Christology that ordinary African believers manifest. Since 2011, Stinton has been teaching in Vancouver at Regent College, yet she long lived in Kenya, carrying out fieldwork for her doctorate there and elsewhere in eastern Africa. Later she taught both at Daystar University and the Nairobi Evangelical Graduate School of Theology (or NEGST, now part of the African International University).

Kenyan Catholic theologian Anne Nasimiyu-Wasike is among those whose Christology is featured in Stinton's volume. Like Kanyoro, Nasimiyu-Wasike questions the uncritical acceptance of African cultural values that normalize dehumanizing practices that victimize women. Distinctively, Nasimiyu-Wasike also explores Christ through the image of an African mother. She emphasizes the similarities between the care of an African mother and Christ's way of being among us and for us. Both embody "one who nurtures all life without discrimination, favouritism, or nepotism."[42] In his solidarity with Africa, Christ "is said to be reliving his passion in the people of Africa, as a mother giving birth to a new Africa."[43] Though not herself a mother, Nasimiyu-Wasike served as the mother superior of the Little Sisters of St. Francis, a Catholic religious order working in eastern Africa, "mothering" 520 of her fellow sisters. This only heightened her connection between the role of mother and Christ's witness, for her leadership "has made me experience

42. Stinton, *Jesus of Africa*, 156–57.
43. Stinton, *Jesus of Africa*, 157.

what I'm talking about, in reality . . . so that I am really washing my sisters' feet. I am their mother."[44]

Philomena Mwaura, another Kenyan Catholic theologian and a laywoman, has been among the most prolific academic theologians from eastern Africa in recent years. A professor at Kenyatta University near Nairobi, she has written extensively about many different topics, and in venues around the world. Her most influential work has explored the theologies and practices of women leaders in contemporary African-initiated and Pentecostal churches, among whom she discerns distinct insights and achievements for the global church, including an attention to social justice and the voicing of concerns important to women.

Other eastern African woman theologians also have produced important work, both as formal academics and by bringing their theological training to bear in practical action. Teresia Mbari Hinga is a Kenyan Catholic currently teaching at Santa Clara University in California. Hinga has addressed a wide range of topics, including globalization and environmental ethics, often seeking to highlight the contribution of women to Christianity in Africa and elsewhere. Anna Elisha Mghwira, a Tanzanian Lutheran, belongs to the CCAWT, has worked in her national church offices, and in 2015 ran for president of Tanzania, representing the ACT-Wazalendo party, of which she is national chair. Fellow Tanzanian Canon Hilda Kabia, an Anglican, served as dean and in 2015 became the first woman principal of a theological college in her country when she took over at Msalato Theological College of St. John's University in Dodoma.

Esther Mombo, a Kenyan Anglican theologian, has addressed issues of interreligious dialogue in eastern Africa and served as an administrator at St. Paul's University in Limuru. Fellow Kenyan Njoroge Nyambura, an ordained Presbyterian minister, was among the first African women to receive a doctorate in theology when she graduated from Princeton Theological Seminary in 1992.[45] She worked on global theological education for the Reformed churches, then moved into ecumenical theologi-

44. Stinton, *Jesus of Africa*, 156.

45. See Toya Richards Hill and Michelle E. Melton, "Nyambura Njoroge Is a 2009 Distinguished Alum," Louisville Seminary, March 20, 2009, https://tinyurl.com/y6uccgml.

cal education, and now serves at the World Council of Churches in the office addressing HIV/AIDS.

Though women continue to face challenges in achieving equality in Uganda, Kenya, and Tanzania, more receive education and training that equips them to provide leadership in nearly every field in each country. In light of this, women theologians in eastern Africa will continue to generate theological insights into how the Christian faith addresses issues faced by African believers.

Theological Efforts from African-Initiated Churches, Independent Evangelicals, and Pentecostals

Formal theological writing, accessible to outsiders, has been comparatively rare from AICs and some evangelical and Pentecostal Christian groups in eastern Africa. For many leaders among such Christian communities, theological training has taken place outside of traditional academic settings like seminaries and universities. Gleaning the results of theological efforts from AICs and other independent Christian groups in eastern Africa thus faces special challenges, since it circulates in different communicative channels than typical academic production.

Much theological reflection among the region's evangelical and Pentecostal churches occurs through preaching. The preaching of most resembles that of similar groups elsewhere within Africa and across the world, and is transmitted in tapes, videos, and websites. Standard themes from these Christian traditions appear in eastern Africa: for example, calls to salvation by personal commitment to Christ, the invitation to spread the gospel with zeal, the promise of healing, and also messages linked to the so-called Prosperity Gospel that urges believers to trust material advancement as they grow in faithfulness. Such messages, even the Prosperity Gospel, respond to political and social needs in a manifestly appealing theological way.

Many churches in eastern Africa typify this trend. Robert Kayanja, for example, founded the Miracle Centre Cathedral, a Kampala-based megachurch with a growing media presence. Similar messages come from the Victory Christian Centre, also of Kampala, founded and led by Joseph Serwadda and his wife Freda. Similar messages can be found in numerous churches in Nairobi, notably Nairobi Pentecostal Church, Nairobi Lighthouse Church, and Jesus Is Alive Ministries, which was founded by a Kenyan woman, Margaret Wanjiru; and in the United Pentecostal Church of Tanzania, which has branches across the country.

Harnessing the energy of fast-growing Pentecostal churches for formal theological work remains difficult. At times, the rhetoric and practices of such churches flirt with a worldview that by denying the value of bio-medicine and modern education is arguably ill-suited for the contemporary world. Even historical denominations find their members—and sometimes their leaders—mired in a strident anti-intellectualism as their own churches become Pentecostalized—that is, shaped by Pentecostal discourse and practice. In addition, some of these pastors—for example, Robert Kayanja of Uganda—have drawn close to the current political regime in their countries, raising questions about their credibility.

One need not accept entirely the gloomy outlook of critics of Pentecostalism like Paul Gifford[46] to recognize that the theological approach of some churches does little for either Africa or world Christianity. Fortunately, a good number of Pentecostal churches, as well as AICs, now make theological education a priority through the formalization of ministerial training, opening their pastors to broader perspectives and giving them tools to answer African needs without abandoning the virtues of a scientific worldview. Pursuing theological research that reflects Pentecostal and AIC experiences in future efforts in ministerial education—some of which are increasingly ecumenical—will be a priority for Christianity in eastern Africa.

46. Gifford, *Christianity, Development and Modernity.*

Study of theological efforts by African-initiated churches—many of them also increasingly shaped by Pentecostal influences—have also begun to emerge. One early effort was the study of the theology of Matthew Ajuoga, founder of the Kenyan Church of Christ in Africa, also known as the Johera, carried out in cooperation with American theologian George Pickens. In 1993, Ajuoga shared his "Johera narrative" that described the 1957 founding of his church with Pickens, an ordained Church of the Brethren minister who teaches at Messiah College in Pennsylvania. This narrative recounts Ajuoga's memories of prior AIC activity in western Kenya and his view of the primal religious landscape of African believers, as well as the particular colonial-era experiences that prompted the appearance of the new church. Though published by an American theologian, this effort prominently highlighted theological work in an important AIC in eastern Africa, making it rare and thus quite valuable.[47] More such studies are needed.

THE FUTURE OF THEOLOGY IN EASTERN AFRICA

Traditional theological topics studied elsewhere have not been ignored by theologians in eastern Africa. The Nigerian Jesuit A. E. Orobator, besides convening important theological meetings in eastern Africa, has written an introduction to African theology, reflecting both his background in Nigeria as well as his experiences in Nairobi, where he has lived and served as a teacher and priest.[48] Ugandan Catholic priest John Lukwata has explored liturgical history and theology in several works.[49] More speculative work has also occurred, for example Kenyan Anglican theologian James Kombo's study of the Trinity, which draws upon African approaches to personhood that, Kombo argues, can deepen Trinitarian reflection by building on the

47. Pickens, *African Christian God-Talk*.

48. Agbonkhianmeghe E. Orobator, *Theology Brewed in an African Pot* (Maryknoll, NY: Orbis, 2008).

49. John Lukwata, *The First Hundred Years of the Buganda Church and Her Worship* (Rome: San Anselmo, 1991); John Lukwata, *Integrated African Liturgy* (Eldoret, Kenya: Gaba Publications, 2003).

ancient anthropological assumptions that forged classical doctrine.[50]

The energy in theology in eastern Africa, however, continues to surround practical issues facing the region and its churches. Recent years have seen publication of a number of essays, monographs, and edited volumes that concern contemporary problems facing eastern Africa. These have addressed issues like the following: pastoral and theological responses to HIV/AIDS;[51]

50. James Henry Owino Kombo, *The Doctrine of God in African Christian Thought: The Holy Trinity, Theological Hermeneutics and the African Intellectual Culture* (Leiden: Brill, 2007). For other contributions in systematic theology from eastern African theologians, see Ezigbo, "Jesus as God's Communicative and Hermeneutical Act"; Andrew M. Mbuvi, "Christology and *Cultus* in 1 Peter: An African (Kenyan) Appraisal," in *Jesus without Borders*, ed. Gene L. Green, Stephen T. Pardue, and K. K. Yeo (Grand Rapids: Eerdmans, 2014) on Christology; and Samuel Waje Kunhiyop, "The Trinity in Africa: Trends and Trajectories," in *The Trinity among the Nations: The Doctrine of God in the Majority World*, ed. Gene L. Green, Stephen T. Pardue, and K. K. Yeo (Grand Rapids: Eerdmans, 2015) on Trinitarian theology.

51. For a sample, see Peter Kanyandago, "Is God African? Theological Reflections on the AIDS Scourge," in *Challenges and Prospects for the Church in Africa: Theological Reflections for the 21st Century*, ed. Nahashon W. Ndung'u and Philomena Mwaura (Nairobi: Paulines Publications, 2005); Emmanuel Katongole, "AIDS, Africa, and the 'Age of Miraculous Medicine': Naming the Silences," in *Applied Ethics in a World Church: The Padua Conference*, ed. Linda Hogan (Maryknoll, NY: Orbis, 2008); Agbonkhianmeghe E. Orobator, "Ethics of HIV/AIDS Prevention: Paradigms of a New Discourse from an African Perspective," in *Applied Ethics in a World Church: The Padua Conference*, ed. Linda Hogan (Maryknoll, NY: Orbis, 2008); Paul Chummar, "HIV/AIDS in Africa: An Urgent Task for an Inculturated Theological Ethics," in *Applied Ethics in a World Church*, ed. Linda Hogan (Maryknoll, NY: Orbis, 2008); and Teresia Hinga, "Teaching to Transform: Theological Education, Global Consciousness, and the Making of Global Citizens," in *Teaching Global Theologies: Power and Praxis*, ed. Kwok Pui-lan, Cecilia González-Andrieu, and Dwight N. Hopkins (Waco, TX: Baylor University Press, 2015). See also the edited collections: Ward and Leonard, *Theology of HIV and AIDS*; and Jacquineau Azetsop, ed., *HIV and AIDS in Africa: Christian Reflection, Public Health, Social Transformation* (Maryknoll, NY: Orbis, 2016).

environmental degradation;[52] Christian-Muslim relations;[53] and violence and reconciliation.[54]

Informal theology will continue in eastern Africa, and it will remain a challenge for scholars to understand and interpret. The growth of small Christian communities, for example, has no doubt increased the amount of focused, congregationally based reflection on faith that believers enact. Considerable work has evaluated that pastoral strategy, while gathering its accumulating wisdom as theological insights for all believers remains unexplored. In addition, new social problems arise in eastern Africa all the time—recently, Islamist violence and ongoing concerns about political stability in all three countries. Theological activity will proceed as Christians interpret and respond to the world around them in light of their faith.

Theologians in eastern Africa, though trying to respond to African concerns, can at times find themselves far from the concerns of believers. As Diane Stinton notes in her overview of

52. C. M. Mwikamba, "Shifts in Mission: An Ecological Theology in Africa," in *Mission in African Christianity: Critical Essays in Missiology*, ed. A. Nasimiyu-Wasike and D. W. Waruta (Nairobi: Uzima Press, 2000); Nahashon W. Ndung'u, "Environmental Management: Constraints and Prospects in Africa in the 21st Century," in *Challenges and Prospects for the Church in Africa: Theological Reflections for the 21st Century*, ed. Nahashon W. Ndung'u and Philomena Mwaura (Nairobi: Paulines Publications, 2005); Peter Kanyandago, "'Let Us Feed the Children First' (Mark 7:27): The Church's Response to the Inequitable Extraction of Resources and Related Violence," in *Reconciliation, Justice, and Peace: The Second African Synod*, ed. Agbonkhianmeghe E. Orobator (Nairobi: Acton, 2011); Frederick Kisekka Ntale, "Being Wealthy Must Not Be a Burden," in *Africa Is Not Destined to Die: Signs of Hope and Renewal*, ed. Ambrose John Bwangatto (Nairobi: Paulines Publications, 2012); Cornelius Ssempala, "Back to the Future in Africa; Relocating Water and Food Sovereignty among Local Communities," in *Africa Is Not Destined to Die: Signs of Hope and Renewal*, ed. Ambrose John Bwangatto (Nairobi: Paulines Publications, 2012).

53. Alexander Lucie-Smith, ed., *Mission Ad Gentes: The Challenge for the Church in Kenya* (Nairobi: Paulines Publications, 2007); Fritz Stenger, Joseph Wandera, and Paul Hannon, eds., *Christian-Muslim Co-Existence in Eastern Africa* (Nairobi: Paulines Publications, 2008).

54. Peter Kanyandago, "Towards Reconciliation and Healing in Africa," in *African Theology Comes of Age: Revisiting Twenty Years of the Theology of the Ecumenical Symposium of Eastern African Theologians (ESEAT)*, ed. Laurenti Magesa (Nairobi: Paulines Publications, 2010); Nehemiah Nyaundi, "The Phenomenon of Violence in Eastern Africa," in *African Theology Comes of Age: Revisiting Twenty Years of the Theology of the Ecumenical Symposium of Eastern African Theologians (ESEAT)*, ed. Laurenti Magesa (Nairobi: Paulines Publications, 2010).

African Christology, ordinary African Christians can resist theological innovations by professional theologians about the person of Christ. These include notions of Jesus depicted as ancestor or *nganga*, the former because it is unfamiliar, the latter because the term itself has been linked through common usage with non-Christian religious practices. Nasimiyu-Wasike's positing of Jesus as mother, too, faces criticism, for it seems transgressive of gendered understandings of Christ's humanity. Other Christians, though, naturally appreciate these metaphors, some of which have already shaped their faith. Christ's healing role in particular has a large place in the faith-practices of many Christians in eastern Africa. The theological balancing act of simultaneously responding to the faith experiences of Christian communities, on the one hand, and, on the other, challenging those communities with the fruit of theological research and reflection remains difficult.

Growing concerns for theologians in their writing, that is, in formal theology, will be many. They will likely include theological reflection on environmental challenges connected to global warming. With much of eastern Africa dependent on annual rainfall for food production, changes in long-term weather patterns could present unprecedented challenges to human well-being and political stability. Some work has been done on this issue, but little that is systematic in its scope.

Another area likely to generate theological reflection will be Muslim-Christian relations. For much of the region's history, the two religions have coexisted in relative amity, yet global Islamic currents have led to terror attacks in all three countries, while perceptions of corrupt Christian political hegemonies fuel Muslim resentments, especially in Kenya and Tanzania. New forms of interreligious dialogue and comparative theology represent ways forward that theologians in the region are only beginning to try. They face challenges since both Muslims and Christians in the region are divided among themselves, so that finding a unified voice for either is difficult. Such disunity makes concerted action with broad appeal elusive.

As it faces these and other issues deserving of theological reflection, the Christian movement in eastern Africa brings certain strengths to the task. Fortunately, networks and institutions—and entrepreneurial theological innovators and organizers like the Nigerian-born Jesuit A. E. Orobator in Kenya—exist to advance the theological enterprise in the region. In addition, the growth of Christian higher education and the strong institutions that support theological education in particular mean that Christians have resources—schools, libraries, books, money, and especially scholars—to support formal theological work. Nairobi in particular has become a continental and even global hub for theology, helped by universities with international connections, some of them linked to churches like the Catholic University of Eastern Africa and Hekima University, which is run by the Jesuits, and St. Paul's in Limuru, linked to several Protestant churches, as well as the national universities. At Hekima, the Jesuits have established an archival center for their records in Africa. Other cities in the region—Kampala, Arusha, Dar es Salaam—could also serve a similar convening role.

As theological work—informal and formal—continues in eastern Africa, it will reflect the experiences of African believers who live their faith amid the complex challenges of a changing world. In this task, eastern African Christians can draw upon the examples of their forebears, some of whom will be profiled in the next chapter.

6.

Biographical

Important Figures in Eastern African Christianity

Many people have played prominent roles in the history of Christianity in eastern Africa. After describing the earliest Christian martyrs in the region, this chapter will proceed with portraits in three groups: expatriates who entered eastern Africa and shaped its Christian history, mostly missionaries; eastern Africans who responded to the early missionary message and built various forms of Christianity in the region; and figures from the latter twentieth century to the present day, both from inside and outside eastern Africa, who have helped constitute the current state of Christianity in the region.[1]

1. Much of the information in these sections comes from the relevant entries in the Dictionary of African Christian Biography (DACB), an online, open-access source found at www.dacb.org. Where we have been able to locate dates of birth and death, we have provided them. Another outstanding resource is Louise Pirouet's work on Ugandan biographies, *Historical Dictionary of Uganda* (Metuchen, NJ: Scarecrow, 1995).

THE MOMBASA MARTYRS

The witness of the so-called Mombasa Martyrs of 1631 continues to interest Christians today in eastern Africa.[2] The background to the story lies in the intermittent conflicts between local Muslims and the Portuguese, who had coastal forts at the Indian Ocean beginning in the early sixteenth century. Yusuf al-Hasan, orphaned son of a local sultan who died at Portuguese hands, was taken to Goa, the Portuguese capital for its Asian empire located in western India, for his education. He returned and was appointed by the Portuguese to serve as Sultan of Mombasa, having become Catholic under missionary tutelage and baptized Jerónimo. Not unnaturally, however, his loyalties were divided, for he knew of his father's death and also always felt his loyalty suspected by the Portuguese.

In August 1631, fed up with his Portuguese sponsors, Jerónimo entered Mombasa's Fort Jesus, only completed shortly before, ostensibly to pray at the fort's chapel. Instead, having secretly returned to Islam, he and coconspirators attacked the fort, eventually killing all who refused to become Muslim, a total of 288 men, women, and children, both African and Portuguese. The dead included Portuguese sailors and soldiers, African converts, the children of the partnerships between Iberians and local women, and Augustinian friars who served the local Catholic community. Others were enslaved and sold. The Portuguese subsequently retook the fort and Jerónimo became a pirate in the Red Sea.

The deaths led to formal processes toward the canonization of the three Augustinians and around 150 of the Portuguese victims, begun in Goa shortly after their deaths. The similar or greater number of African and mixed-race people, many of whom also clearly chose death instead of committing apostasy, were ignored at the time, a revealing omission that suggests Portuguese indifference to evangelization in eastern Africa. Though approved in a preliminary way by Rome, the process of beatification stalled for over three centuries, probably because the Por-

2. On the martyrs and the Portuguese history in eastern Africa, see Alonso, *History of the Augustinians*, and the DACB.

tuguese themselves lost interest. The martyrs' cause, however, has recently been reinitiated by the Augustinians in Rome with the support of the Catholic Church in Kenya.

The official number of Christians killed lies at 288, yet some believe up to 400 people lost their lives for their faith. The first martyr after the killing of the fort's garrison was an Augustinian hermit, Brother Diego de la Madre de Dios. A few days later nearly all who had sought refuge were killed, including the three Augustinian priests who staffed the church where refuge was taken: Anthony of the Nativity, Anthony of the Passion, and Dominic of the Birth of Christ. Antonio de Melinde, cousin of the self-declared king Jerónimo, was one of those killed, along with hundreds of others, African and European, slave and free, men, women, and children. Ironically, a letter from Pope Urban VIII, sent, of course, without knowledge of his apostasy and ensuing violence, arrived a year later, praising Jerónimo for his faithfulness and urging him to continue advancing the Catholic religion in Mombasa and its environs.

EXPATRIATES WHO HELPED FOUND CHRISTIANITY IN EASTERN AFRICA

JOHANN KRAPF (1810–1882) AND JOHANNES REBMANN (1820–1876)

Krapf and Rebmann are remembered as the first two Christian European missionaries to return to eastern Africa after the Portuguese expulsion. Both German, they were sent in the 1840s by the Church of England's Church Mission Society (CMS), an evangelical Anglican voluntary missionary-sponsoring organization founded in 1799.

Johann Ludwig Krapf was born to a rural Lutheran family in Germany. While studying for missionary service at the Basel Missionary Institute in Switzerland, one of the earliest institutions of its kind, Krapf met compatriot Johannes Rebmann. Coming to doubt his missionary call, however, Krapf continued his theological study to be a pastor and was ordained in 1834.

Another missionary, however, prompted Krapf to offer his service to the CMS, which he did. After acquiring Ge'ez and Amharic, the ancient church language and the modern language of Ethiopia, respectively, he went to Ethiopia, where he worked from 1837 to 1842. In Ethiopia, Krapf translated the gospels of John and Matthew into Oromo, the language of the so-called Galla and the main tongue of central and southern Ethiopia.

Political machinations in Ethiopia forced Krapf to head to Mombasa in 1844, and eventually to Rabai, inland a bit from Mombasa. There Krapf was joined by Johannes Rebmann in 1846, where they led a small group of servants and former slaves at the mission. Krapf's reports upon his return to England in 1850 excited many about the prospects of growth in the faith in eastern Africa. He returned to Kenya in 1852, but ill health forced his return to Germany in 1853. Still, he continued his involvement in missionary activity, both in Kenya and in Ethiopia, advising others and visiting the region several times. In 1862, he helped the Methodist Thomas Wakefield found a mission at Ribe in Kenya. Krapf also continued to publish important works on the languages of eastern Africa and Ethiopia.

Rebmann, also a German Lutheran, is credited as the first European to enter Africa in the modern period via the Indian Ocean. In 1848, he became the first European to see Kilimanjaro and, drawing upon his travels, created a rough map of eastern Africa. His writings and explorations affected the future expeditions of Sir Richard Burton, John Hanning Speke, and David Livingstone.

Krapf and Rebmann's lofty goal was to establish a chain of mission stations to connect eastern Africa with western Africa at fifty-mile intervals, and eventually a similar chain from Jerusalem to Abyssinia, continuing to the south of Africa. Their diaries and journals reveal their idealism and the hopes and frustrations they faced. Both suffered from frequent illness and lost family members to early deaths. Though in their day few African converts joined them, they are today revered as founders of the Anglican Church in Kenya and groundbreaking pioneers of the modern missionary movement's entry into eastern Africa.

ANTOINE HORNER, CSSP (1827–1880), EDOUARD BAUR, CSSP (1835–1913), ALEXANDRE LEROY, CSSP (1854–1938), AND RAOUL DE COURMONT, CSSP (1841–1925)

The first Catholic missionaries into eastern Africa in the modern period were diocesan clergy and nuns of the Daughters of Mary from the Indian Ocean island of Réunion, who came to Zanzibar in 1860.[3] The bishop of Réunion, Armand René Maupoint of St. Denis, was named prefect apostolic of Zanzibar in 1862. In 1863, however, responsibility for the Zanzibar mission was given to the Congregation of the Holy Ghost, who also served on Réunion. Horner, Baur, LeRoy, and de Courmont are four of the most prominent missionaries to eastern Africa of that congregation, also known as Spiritans.

Horner, an Alsatian, was the first Spiritan superior, assuming control in 1863 of the existing mission on Zanzibar, with its chapel, schools, workshops, and small clinic run by the sisters. Like the priests before him, he and his confreres—who included two Spiritan brothers as well as fellow priest, the younger Edouard Baur—welcomed fleeing slaves, gathered the dying, and purchased slaves at the open market of Zanzibar. Unable to preach publicly in the Islamic milieu, they made the formation and education of those slaves their chief work, eyes always on the mainland where they foresaw more success. They founded a mission at Bagamoyo in 1868. From there they hoped to establish Christian villages with the former slaves, who would then evangelize other Africans nearby. Horner left eastern Africa in 1877, dying not long afterward. Baur, however, remained until his death in 1913, by then the longest-serving missionary in eastern Africa.

LeRoy joined the Spiritan mission in eastern Africa in 1881, soon making his presence known by a keen observational instinct about local people and customs and writing much-appreciated travel accounts that were published in France. In 1883, he promoted a shift in missionary strategy away from

3. On the nineteenth-century Spiritan work in Zanzibar and its environs, see Kollman, *Evangelization of Slaves.*

reliance on former slaves. Later he left eastern Africa, first to serve as apostolic prefect in the Spiritan mission in Gabon, then serving as a professor of the history of religions in Paris, and finally as the Spiritan superior general from 1896 to 1928.

Raoul de Courmont was named vicar apostolic in Zanzibar, thus the first Catholic bishop in eastern Africa, assuming his post in 1883 and serving until 1896. During his ministry he oversaw the expansion of Catholic missions into northern Tanganyika and Kenya, while other parts of the Spiritan territory in southern Tanganyika were taken over by German Benedictines.

EDWARD STEERE (1828–1882)

Edward Steere was a British UMCA missionary and then bishop who helped found the Anglican presence in Zanzibar. He worked with David Livingstone and Sir Bartle Frere to abolish the slave trade there, and later placed the foundation stone of Christ Church, establishing the Anglican cathedral on the site of the former slave market. Steere's greatest legacy is due to his linguistic prowess. His careful study of KiSwahili, the predominant language of the Indian Ocean coast, and Yao, a common language in southern Tanzania, helped move both toward developed written form.

After a few years in Zanzibar starting in the 1860s, Steere returned to England in the early 1870s, where he pursued Swahili translations for the Bible Society. An ardent abolitionist, he delivered an important address at an 1871 church congress at Nottingham on the duty of the country as regards the slave trade. When news came in 1872 of Bishop Tozer's ill-health in Zanzibar, he volunteered to return, and soon was back. The slave trade was ended with British naval help, and the Zanzibar slave market closed soon thereafter.

In 1879, Steere issued his complete translation of the New Testament and prayer book in Swahili, while on Christmas day of the same year he presided at the opening of the cathedral church at Zanzibar. He also wrote numerous books on his travels in eastern Africa, besides writing a handbook on Swahili grammar and preparing a book of Swahili folktales.

THOMAS WAKEFIELD (1836–1901)

Wakefield was a United Methodist Free Church missionary in Kenya. Born in Derby, England, he became a full-time preacher at twenty-two and in 1861 accepted a new mission to go with Johann Krapf to the Oromo people. They reached Zanzibar in 1862 and chose Ribe in Kenya as the site for the first Methodist station. When others withdrew, Wakefield carried on the mission himself, and for the next decades he was considered the backbone of the mission and often its sole representative. Wakefield had excellent relationships with other Protestant missions in eastern Africa, including the CMS and the UMCA in Zanzibar. Bishops Tozer of the UMCA and the CMS's Hannington were considered friends.

ALEXANDER MURDOCH MACKAY (1849–1890)

Mackay was an accomplished Scottish engineer who applied to be a CMS missionary in 1875 and arrived with the first CMS missionary team to Uganda in 1877. His skills at tasks like gun repair won him favor with Kabaka (King) Mutesa, and he also pioneered the printing press in Uganda, helping to translate the Bible first into Swahili and then into Luganda, and printing versions of each.

Mackay had a complex relationship with Mutesa, whom he admired but whose cruelties—human sacrifices and brutal raids on neighboring peoples—he condemned. Mackay also held strong anti-Catholic views, which helped deepen a rivalry with Father Simon Lourdel, the early leader of the Catholic Missionaries of Africa, or White Fathers. Both Catholics and Anglicans also struggled with Muslims, who felt the Christians threatened their influence with the king.

The Catholic-Anglican rivalry was of particular historical importance. First, the royal court in Buganda was intrigued by the vigor of their debates, and numerous pages joined both groups as inquirers, then as early members. Some of these young men became the Uganda Martyrs, and those who survived became leaders in the young and fast-growing Anglican and

Catholic churches in Uganda. Once the Muslims were sidelined after a complex series of armed conflicts, the Anglican-Catholic enmity fueled the furthering of both faiths in Uganda, as they competed with each other to grow in numbers and the quality of their lay and ordained leaders.

When Mutesa's son and successor Mwanga killed the Uganda Martyrs in the mid-1880s, Mackay was the only missionary who stayed through this ordeal. Mackay died suddenly in 1890 of malaria in Tanganyika, where he had fled during a Muslim coup.

FATHER SIMEON LOURDEL, M.AFR. (1853–1890)

Lourdel was a French White Father who, after his ordination, joined the first group of White Fathers to arrive in sub-Saharan Africa, disembarking at Zanzibar in 1878. After planning extensively for their caravan across Tanganyika with the help of the Spiritans already present there, they left with a caravan of missionaries and hundreds of porters. They arrived after a harrowing trek across Tanzania, in which one of their number died at the south shore of Lake Victoria. Leaving behind most of the group, Lourdel and a religious brother, Amans, crossed Lake Victoria, arriving near Entebbe and proceeding to the court of Kabaka Mutesa in 1879.

At court, the missionaries worked to establish good relations with Mutesa but were hampered by denominational differences and polemic attitudes between themselves and the British Anglicans led by Alexander Mackay. In 1879, Mutesa allowed the Catholics to move near the capital and several young men from the court came to hear about Christianity. The missionaries' lives continued to revolve around the royal court, audiences with the king, and presentations of gifts. Both groups of Christian missionaries faced opposition from Muslim leaders who were also attempting to influence the king. Regardless, they continued their work there, much of which included teaching inquirers, some of whom formally became catechumens, those seeking baptism. Lourdel came to be called "Mapera," a corruption of the French *mon père*, "my father."

In 1882, mounting violence and hostility toward missionaries caused the Catholics to leave the Buganda mission, keeping in touch through regular letters to their followers. Anglicans faced similar scrutiny. After three years away, both groups returned in 1885 to an initially warm royal welcome. There was now a strong Christian nucleus in the court, both Catholic and Anglican, that had developed in the absence of missionaries, and these believers supported them in their return.

A few years later, however, with Mwanga having succeeded his father Mutesa upon the latter's death, the tide turned, and some of Lourdel's converts became martyrs and the Catholic mission was pillaged. In the years of unrest that followed, Lourdel remained leader of the Catholics, who cooperated with the Anglicans and Muslims to overthrow Mwanga, then with the Anglicans to resist the Muslims. He died in 1890, the same year as Mackay, his longtime rival for the kabakas' affections.

BISHOP ALFRED ROBERT TUCKER (1849–1914)

Tucker was born in the Lake District and went to Oxford to become ordained. In 1890, he was sent out by the Church Mission Society to become the bishop of Eastern Equatorial Africa. Arriving in the chaotic aftermath of the political upheavals following the Uganda Martyrs' deaths and subsequent civil wars, he led the Anglicans as they advanced their interests in cooperation and competition with Muslims, Catholics, and eventually in close cooperation with the Imperial British East African Company. This process culminated in colonial control by Great Britain over Uganda. In 1899, he became bishop of Uganda.

Tucker's approach was considered moderate at the time; he preferred to work with the culture rather than replace it with European attitudes. Consequently, his paradigm was reflected in a constitution he helped to write for the Native Anglican Church, which allowed Ugandans a significant measure of participation in decision-making, particularly through the Synod. Tucker was also keen to foster a "native clergy," and the first ordinations took place in 1893.

Tucker wrote a two-volume account of his work, *Eighteen*

Years in Uganda and East Africa, which primarily focused on his time as Anglican bishop of Eastern Equatorial Africa in 1890–99 and as the first bishop of Uganda from 1899 until 1908. Tucker was instrumental in encouraging the British to remain in Uganda and to establish in 1894 a British protectorate. He believed in building a strong African church and wrote that CMS missionaries did not want "to denationalise the Baganda . . . turn them into black Englishmen (if such a thing were possible) but rather to strengthen their own national characteristics."[4]

To make this happen, Tucker committed himself to strong training of Uganda church leaders so that they could assume responsibility. The year before Tucker died, Uganda's first theological college was formed. On his death, it was named Bishop Tucker Theological College. Uganda Christian University was founded in 1997 by the Anglican Church of Uganda and incorporates Bishop Tucker Theological College. In 2004, the University's theology faculty was named "The Bishop Tucker School of Divinity and Theology."

DANIEL COMBONI (1831–1881) AND THE COMBONI MISSIONARIES

The Comboni Missionaries, long known as the Verona Fathers, were founded by Comboni, a Catholic missionary to Africa and canonized saint. Born in Italy, Comboni's interest in becoming a priest led him to an institute founded by Father Nicola Mazza that was training missionaries for central Africa. In 1854, he was ordained a priest and three years later he left for Africa along with five other missionaries from the Mazza Institute. After four months, Comboni reached Khartoum, capital of the Sudan. His first face-to-face encounters with the climate, sickness, the deaths of several of his young fellow-missionaries, and the poverty and dereliction of the population, served to drive him to a deeper commitment to the mission in the Sudan and eventually northern Uganda.

Famously, Comboni worked out a fresh missionary strategy

4. Alfred R. Tucker, *Eighteen Years in Uganda and East Africa* (Westport, CT: Negro Universities Press, 1970), 366.

in 1864 in Italy. While praying at the Tomb of Saint Peter in Rome, he was struck by an inspiration that led to the drawing up of his "Plan for the Rebirth of Africa." This missionary project can be summed up in an expression that indicates his boundless trust in the human and religious capacities of the African peoples: "Save Africa through Africa." Despite his homegrown strategy, he appealed to the Catholic Church throughout Europe for both spiritual and material aid for the African missions from royalty, bishops, and nobles, as well as from laypeople. As part of these efforts, Comboni also launched the first Italian missionary magazine and, as the theologian of the bishop of Verona, took part in the First Vatican Council, where he convinced seventy bishops to sign a petition for the evangelization of Central Africa: *Postulatum pro Nigris Africae Centralis*.

In 1877, Comboni was named Vicar Apostolic of Central Africa, and ordained bishop, a confirmation that his ideas and his activities, which some considered foolhardy, were recognized by the official church as an effective means for the proclamation of the gospel. His work culminated in the establishment of a men's missionary institute in 1867 and one for women in 1872. Those two congregations exist to this day. Notably, Comboni was the first to bring women into missionary work in central Africa. In 1880, Bishop Comboni traveled to Africa for the eighth and final time, to stand alongside his missionaries and fight the slave trade. In October 1881, Comboni died of illness in Khartoum. His final words were reported to be, "I am dying, but my work will not die." A few decades later Comboni priests and brothers entered northern Uganda where they established the Catholic Church. They moved to Tanzania in the mid-twentieth century, and later to Kenya.

Priests, brothers, and sisters belonging to the Comboni religious family continue to work in all three countries. They comprise the largest single Catholic missionary body in Uganda, most of them in the north of the country.

DR. ALBERT COOK (1870–1951)

Sir Albert Ruskin Cook was a British-born medical missionary in Uganda, and founder of Mulago Hospital and Mengo Hospital. Cook first went to Uganda with a Church Missionary Society mission in 1896. Together with his wife Katharine Cook, he established a maternity training school in Uganda. Mengo Hospital, the oldest hospital in eastern Africa, was established one year later. In 1899, his brother, Dr. John Cook, joined them.

Cook is outstanding among medical missionaries for his efforts to train Africans to become skilled medical workers. He established a treatment center for venereal diseases and sleeping sickness in 1913, which later became Mulago Hospital. He also helped prepare a manual in Luganda for midwifery training. He was knighted by the British king in 1932.

BISHOP HENRY HANLON, MHM (1862–1937)

Henry Hanlon was an English Roman Catholic bishop of the Mill Hill missionary society who served in eastern Africa from 1895 to 1911. Before arriving in Kampala in 1895, Hanlon served in northern India, from where he was appointed as the vicar apostolic of Upper Nile District. The Upper Nile was part of the original territory assigned to the Missionaries of Africa, or White Fathers, who invited the Mill Hill missionaries to take over in 1895. Hanlon served as bishop of the Upper Nile District until 1911, overseeing the expansion of the Catholic Church in eastern Uganda and western Kenya.

The background to the invitation extended to Mill Hill lay in the conflicts between the Catholics and the Anglicans that led to war in the early 1890s. These conflicts convinced Catholic leaders to invite an English-speaking Catholic missionary group to Uganda in recognition of British colonial control. The White Fathers welcomed Hanlon and his confreres, who not only assumed responsibility for eastern Uganda, but also for what is now western Kenya, then part of the Uganda Protectorate.

The Mill Hill cathedral in Kampala was on Nsambya Hill, while the White Fathers' was on Rubaga. Hanlon and his confreres founded new parishes throughout his territory. He also invited the Franciscan Sisters of St. Joseph to come from England, who in turn began schools and clinics. Their most famous member was Mother Kevin, who founded the Little Sisters of St. Francis for Ugandan women wanting to be nuns.

GEORGE PILKINGTON (1865–1897)

Pilkington was a Church Missionary Society (CMS) lay missionary. A graduate of the University of Cambridge and strongly influenced by the Keswick movement, he arrived in Buganda (now Uganda) with Bishop Alfred Tucker's party in 1891. There he found a militarized society rent by religious factionalism and the conflicts of the colonial scramble. Pilkington's remarkable linguistic ability enabled him quickly to get alongside the Baganda soldiers and to recognize their spiritual hunger and desire for literacy.

In 1893, troubled by the confusion of Christianity and politics, he went on retreat to Kome Island in Lake Victoria. During prayer, Pilkington was overwhelmed by an experience of the Holy Spirit that led him to a deeper embrace of personal holiness and a desire to testify to God's power. This sparked a religious revival that profoundly affected the life of the Ugandan church. His experiences later inspired the *Balokole* revival of the 1930s, which looked back to Pilkington as a role model. Pilkington's other great contribution was his translation of the Bible into Luganda.

Despite Pilkington's desire for a purely spiritual understanding of Christianity, he was a firm believer in the benefits of British colonialism. In 1897 he accompanied his beloved Baganda soldiers as they went to quell the mutiny of Sudanese troops in eastern Uganda. Pilkington's death in battle was universally mourned.

BISHOP HENRI STREICHER, M.AFR. (1863–1952)

Streicher was the most important Catholic missionary bishop in eastern Africa. He was instrumental in obtaining the first African

Catholic priests and the first African Catholic bishop of modern times, and served as leader in eastern Africa's largest diocese for over three decades.

Streicher was born in Alsace, joined the Missionaries of Africa (White Fathers), and was ordained priest in 1887. After teaching in seminaries in Jerusalem and Carthage, he was appointed to the Victoria Nyanza mission in 1890. He arrived in 1891 and was sent to Buddu county in southern Uganda, soon to become a Catholic stronghold in the wake of the civil war that culminated in the 1892 British annexation of Uganda. Amid an uneasy peace, Streicher, who was called "Stensera" by the Baganda, founded the mission station of Villa Maria.

In 1894 the Victoria Nyanza Catholic mission was divided into three. After the death of the vicar apostolic of Northern Nyanza in 1896, Streicher became bishop in 1897. Streicher's diocese covered the whole southern and western portion of modern Uganda. He was bishop for thirty-six years and made Villa Maria his headquarters. When he took over the diocese, there were 30,000 baptized Catholic Christians. When he retired in 1933, there were 303,000. There were, moreover, forty-six African priests and 280 African religious sisters.

Since the royal family of Buganda was tied to the Anglican Church of Uganda, Streicher became in many ways a "royal" focus for Ganda Catholics, a veritable prince-bishop. Yet Streicher's overriding aim was pastoral, to help his people become convinced and exemplary Christians. The running of schools was a major part of his strategy, since experience proved that educated Christians were more persevering. To that end, Streicher insisted that there be a school in every parish center and every village outstation. In 1902, he started a training college for teacher-catechists. His French missionaries, on the whole, knew no English, and, in any case, Streicher banned the teaching of English in his schools so that Christians would not be tempted by the secularizing influence of urban living and government employment. One result of this policy was that Uganda developed a mostly Protestant elite and a larger Catholic peasantry.

Streicher was determined to advance seminary education and the training of indigenous priests, a declared priority on the day of his episcopal ordination. "To get one indigenous priest is for me more important than to convert ten thousand people," he declared in 1929. In 1911, after starting at smaller schools, the senior seminarians crossed to Katigondo, which has trained nearly one thousand priests. From this seminary in 1913 came the first two African priests of modern times, Bazilio Lumu and Victoro Mukasa Womeraka, both ordained by Streicher.

The beatification of the Uganda Martyrs in Rome in 1920 was another important achievement, with the necessary documentation for the process prepared by Streicher and the ceremony in Rome attended by him in person, together with two confessors of the faith who had narrowly escaped martyrdom in 1885–1886. For the rest of his reign, Streicher occupied himself preparing his missionaries and the diocese for African autonomy. This was already accepted in principle when he retired in 1933.

For six years after his retirement, an African Vicar General administered Masaka, where Catholics were initially confined at the beginnings of the colonial period by the British, and which became the largest Catholic diocese in Uganda. In 1939, Joseph Nakabaale Kiwanuka, a Baganda Missionary of Africa from Masaka, was appointed its first African bishop. Streicher assisted Pope Pius XII on October 29, 1939, at the consecration in Rome of Kiwanuka as vicar apostolic of Masaka and first African Catholic bishop of modern times. Retiring to Ibanda in his former diocese, Henri Streicher died on June 4, 1952, after receiving the last rites from Bishop Kiwanuka. He is buried in the church he built at Villa Maria.

PETER CAMERON SCOTT (1867–1896)

Peter Cameron Scott, a naturalized American citizen, was born in Scotland in 1867. After his conversion in 1889, Scott was convinced that God had called him to be a missionary to Africa. In November 1890, he set out for the Belgian Congo as a missionary of the Christian and Missionary Alliance. After two years, he went to Kenya and formed the Africa Inland Mission (AIM) in 1895. With his associates he established a mission near Mombasa, at Nzawi, a location with both endemic malaria and local tensions. Scott died in 1896 soon after arriving in Kenya, leading to the disruption of the mission. The AIM returned, however, and since has made a large impact on Christianity in eastern Africa and beyond, becoming the Africa Inland Church in 1943.

BISHOP FRANK WESTON (1871–1924)

London-born and Oxford-educated, Weston was a UMCA missionary who came to Zanzibar in 1898. While there he decided to pursue ordination, eventually becoming diocesan chancellor as well as chaplain and principal of St. Andrew's College in Zanzibar. He became the bishop of Zanzibar from 1907 until his death, which at the time included much of Kenya and Tanganyika.

In World War I, Weston served with distinction and was awarded an OBE (Order of the British Empire) for his role as a major commanding the Zanzibar Carrier Corps. In the postwar years, he became increasingly influential as a result of his advocacy against labor impressment by colonial officials, writing "The Serfs of Great Britain" to protest the poor treatment of Africans by the British.

Before the war, Weston was at the center of one of the deepest disputes within the Anglican Communion, the Kikuyu controversy of 1913. In that episode Weston, in his role as leading Anglican bishop of eastern Africa, denounced fellow Anglicans Bishop Peel of Mombasa and Bishop Willis of Uganda as heretics for their participation in an ecumenical communion during an interdenominational missionary conference at the Church of Scotland's parish in Kikuyu. Weston appealed to the archbishop of Canterbury for support in his accusations. Ultimately, the two bishops were not tried for heresy, yet the union the conference had supported was delayed. Later it returned as an "alliance," which led to important ecumenical cooperation in Kenya.

MOTHER KEVIN (SISTER TERESA KEARNEY, 1875–1957)

Mother Kevin, born Teresa Kearney in County Wicklow, Ireland, came to Uganda as a Franciscan sister working with the Mill Hill Fathers in 1903. Later she founded the Franciscan Missionary Sisters for Africa, also known as the Little Sisters of St. Francis in Uganda.

Upon entering the Franciscan convent, she took the name "Sister Kevin." She volunteered to go to Uganda and was soon struck by the inadequacy of the church's response to sickness and disease there, especially leprosy, along with the absence of maternity and childcare services. In response, Sister Kevin founded the Congregation of the Little Sisters of St. Francis in 1923, a community of African nuns for teaching and nursing. She became the superior and took the title "Mother Kevin." As needs persisted, both Mother Kevin and the bishop agreed that the major obstacle to a meaningful Catholic medical apostolate was the church's refusal to allow priests and nuns to practice maternity nursing, medicine, and surgery. Consequently, she founded several novitiates in England and Ireland in order to serve her growing number of convents in Uganda. To this day, the Little Sisters of St. Francis are sometimes called "the Mother Kevin Sisters."

FILIPPO PERLO (1873–1948)

Perlo, ordained a Catholic priest in Italy in 1895, joined the Consolata congregation and was one of the first Consolata missionaries to arrive in Kenya in 1902. Helping to establish and direct a number of missions in central Kenya, he became superior of the Consolata missions in Kenya in 1905, then in 1909 became vicar apostolic, or acting bishop, of Nyeri, later called the Vicariate of Kenya. In that role he oversaw the expansion of the Catholic Church throughout Nyeri and neighboring Meru. In 1924, he returned to Italy to become Superior General of the Consolatas, serving until 1930.

EDEL QUINN (1907–1944)

Born in Ireland, Edel Quinn was a Catholic lay missionary and traveling evangelist who helped to spread the Legion of Mary, a Catholic association, in eastern Africa. As a young girl, she felt a call to religious life but was prevented due to advanced tuberculosis. At age twenty, after spending a year and a half in a sanatorium with little improvement, she decided to actively join the Legion of Mary. She gave herself completely to its work in the form of helping the poor in the slums of Dublin for almost a decade. Then in 1936, though very sick with tuberculosis, Quinn became a Legion of Mary Envoy to East and Central Africa. She settled in Nairobi, which served as a base for her work across Kenya and into Sudan, Mauritius, Tanzania, Uganda, and Malawi. In 1941, she was admitted to a sanatorium near Johannesburg where she later died.

All the while fighting illness, Quinn established hundreds of Legion branches and councils. She was also helpful in spreading the act of praying the rosary as a significant spiritual practice. Quinn's cause for beatification was introduced in 1956, and she was declared venerable by Pope John Paul II in 1994. The campaign for her beatification continues.

BISHOP JOHN V. TAYLOR (1914–2001)

John V. Taylor was an Anglican missionary in Uganda and general secretary of the Church Missionary Society (CMS). He was a learned scholar, studying English literature and history at Cambridge and theology at Oxford. After serving in two parishes in England he became a CMS missionary in Uganda, serving as warden of Bishop Tucker Memorial College, the theological seminary, from 1944 to 1954. During his time there he encouraged his students in the creative arts, including the writing and performance of African passion plays. Among his most influential literary works is a pioneering study on the immanence of God in Africa, titled *The Primal Vision: Christian Presence amid African Religion* (1963). In the early 1970s, he published *The Go Between God*, which has become a spiritual classic republished many times. Taylor later served as the bishop of Winchester and chaired the influential doctrine commission of the Church of England, which produced *Believing in the Church: The Corporate Nature of Faith*, in 1981.

BISHOP VINCENT JOSEPH MCCAULEY, CSC (1906–1982)

McCauley was an American priest of the Congregation of Holy Cross who became the first bishop of Fort Portal, Uganda, in 1961. Later, he served as executive director of the Association of Member Episcopal Conferences in Eastern Africa (AMECEA) from 1972 to 1979. A Servant of God, his cause for canonization was introduced in the Congregation for the Causes of Saints in August 2006.

McCauley began as a missionary in 1936 in what is today Bangladesh. Illness forced him home in the early 1940s, serving at his congregation's seminary for training missionaries in Washington, DC. In the late 1950s, he undertook a journey of potential mission territories that the Vatican was offering to Holy Cross, and found himself drawn to western Uganda, where he led a group of other Holy Cross priests in 1958.

McCauley organized his new diocese according to principles that would be promoted at the Second Vatican Council, where he helped organize the bishops of eastern Africa to contribute as a united group. These principles included inculturation and promotion of the local church and local clergy. McCauley also led and supported the development of religious congregations of women and promoted their movement into new areas of ministry, all the while pursuing ecumenism and the expansion of education in his diocese.[5]

WALTER EDWIN OWEN (1878–1945)

Owen, born in Birmingham, England, served as an Anglican missionary and archdeacon in both Kenya and Uganda. He

5. On McCauley, see Gribble, *Vincent McCauley*.

worked in several parts of the British East Africa protectorate from 1904 to 1918. In 1918, Owen was appointed Anglican archdeacon of Kavirondo, then a part of the Ugandan diocese, though located in western Kenya. The region had linguistic and cultural complexity, with ethnic identities now identified as Luo, Luyia, Kalenjin, and Kisii all extant and emerging.

As Archdeacon, Owen famously created the Kavirondo Taxpayer's Welfare Association in 1920 in an effort to encourage development and give Africans a say in their own affairs. The Association taught Africans tools for self-governance and economic development, as well as practical skills to produce watermills, farm new crops, and in bookkeeping. Though never seriously questioning the colonial system, Owen also fought for the rights of Africans under the colonization and advocated for the rights of missionaries to be involved in local politics. This earned him the sobriquet "Archdemon Owen" from some strident colonialists. One of Owen's final accomplishments was his work revising the Anglican Book of Common Prayer, in Luo, before his death in 1945.

JOHN ARTHUR (1881–1952)

Arthur served as a missionary in Kenya with the Church of Scotland from 1907 to 1937. During much of his career he was the leading missionary in the colony, yet he is most famous for his effort to end Kikuyu female initiation practices like excision and clitoridectomy, which led to a strong reaction by the Kikuyu people, including the creation of independent churches and schools free from missionary control in the 1930s. The reaction against Arthur's campaign to end so-called "female circumcision" helped galvanize Kenya's independence movement.

Arthur received a degree in medicine from the University of Glasgow, and began service in Kenya, opening an early hospital. Five years later, in 1912, Arthur was appointed as the head of the mission, which he led through a period of exceptional growth. He was ordained in 1916, at which point he officially moved his mission work focus from medicine to ministerial. There he remained until his retirement in 1937.

While serving as a leader, Arthur successfully advocated for inter-mission cooperation, eventually bringing Protestant agencies and denominations together in 1913 in the town of Kikuyu for a unity meeting. The full hopes of the group were undone when Anglican bishop Frank Weston heard that two of his fellow Anglican bishops had received communion at the gathering. Weston accused them of heresy, which undid the concord established, though the two bishops were not prosecuted by the archbishop of Canterbury. Despite the setback, Arthur's ecumenical efforts bore fruit. Eventually an Alliance of missions was established, which cooperated in numerous educational and healthcare initiatives.

Arthur worked with the colonial government to address injustices suffered by Kenyans, joining the Legislative Council of the colony in 1924 to represent African interests. The so-called "Female Circumcision Controversy" of the late 1920s and early 1930s, which was discussed in London's Parliament, undermined the confidence of his Kenyan supporters, and he retired in 1937, returning to Scotland.

BRUNO GUTMANN (1876–1966)

Gutmann was a German Lutheran missionary who served among the Chagga people around Mount Kilimanjaro in German East Africa, later Tanganyika, in the early twentieth century. Despite his removal after World War I for a number of years by the British, he had a remarkable impact on Lutheran missionary strategy, and his efforts at inculturating the faith continue to be much admired.

Arriving first in 1902, Gutmann returned to Germany in 1908 and upon reentering German East Africa took over the Old Moshi mission. He served there, except for the brief period of his expulsion beginning in 1920, until he departed in 1938. Gutmann's orientation toward close cultural attention, particularly in linguistics, shaped a theological and missionary commitment to build a church in close alignment with Chagga culture. He was deeply committed to understanding and protecting traditional Chagga culture, so much so that he never learned KiSwahili or English well but knew KiChagga as well as any native. Wary of modernity, he saw Chagga culture threatened by changes connected with colonialism and European contact more generally. This kind of protectionism was resisted by many Chagga converts, who sought to advance themselves in the colonial order. His most enduring contribution lies in the large volume of more than 500 written works on the Chagga, more than twenty of which are hundreds of pages long, an almost unprecedented written record on a single African people by a European. His writings have had broad influence in the fields of anthropology and missiology.[6]

BISHOP WILLIAM VINCENT LUCAS (1883–1945)

Lucas was an Anglican missionary priest and bishop who worked in southern Tanganyika in the early twentieth century. Today he is best known for efforts at Christianizing male initiation rites of circumcision called *jando* among the Yao people.

Lucas started near Masasi with the UMCA, eventually becoming bishop of what would become southern Tanzania. Recognizing the central role of initiation rites, Lucas wanted new converts to experience Christian transformation without losing allegiance to their native Yao culture. With the support of local Yao Christian leaders—some say led by them—he sought to adapt the male and female rites, the former with more success than the latter.[7]

Although his early work flourished for more than a decade, World War II brought such hardship to the region that much of the progress was lost. Lucas resigned in 1944 and returned to England, dying shortly thereafter.

VINCENT DONOVAN, CSSP (1926–2000)

Donovan was an American Catholic missionary among the Maasai of Tanzania during the 1950s and 1960s, later returning

6. On Gutmann, see Jaeschke, *Bruno Gutmann*.

7. See Ranger, "Missionary Adaptation"; and Stoner-Eby, "African Clergy," 171–208.

to teach in the US. He is most renowned as the author of *Christianity Rediscovered* (1978), a missiological classic, both for its stirring prose and its missiological insights.

Working with his fellow American Holy Ghost missionary priests, Donovan sought a new missionary strategy to adapt to the nomadic Maasai people. His efforts to travel with the Maasai to their bomas, or places of cattle-keeping, led to encounters that are vividly described in *Christianity Rediscovered*, which captures both the challenges and joys of missionary work. The book celebrates missionary creativity and contributes insights for the application of Jesus's parables in the Maasai context, as well as the memorable phrase, "the lion is God," symbolic of the inner workings of grace.

One year after Donovan's death, Orbis Books published a twenty-fifth anniversary edition, and the book remains commonly taught in missiological curricula.

JOHN KAISER, MHM (1932–2000)

Kaiser was a Catholic American Mill Hill priest who was allegedly murdered in Morendat, Kenya by unknown assailants in 2000. Many believe that his criticisms of the government amid land clashes led to his death. Kaiser's missionary work in the Kisii Diocese exposed him to extreme poverty and refugee experiences. In 1994, the forceful closing of a refugee camp led to Kaiser's public protest, arrest, beating, and eventual release.

Kaiser's fight against government violence, however, had just begun. He later testified before the Akiwumi Commission, which investigated the causes of violence and the closing of the camps, accusing then President Daniel Arap Moi and prominent cabinet ministers of complicity. His testimony was dismissed, but his threat to the government was obvious. After the government attempted to deport Kaiser in 1999, he went into hiding in Kisii and was later found dead with a gun wound to the head. After dubious claims of Kaiser's suicide, the Law Society of Kenya renamed its annual award the Fr. Kaiser Human Rights Award. The Kenyan National Human Rights Commission also posthumously honored Fr. Kaiser with its 2006 *Milele*

(KiSwahili for "lifetime") Achievement Award. Both houses of the United States Congress passed a joint resolution calling Fr. Kaiser's death "an assassination," and calling for the US State Department to investigate. A 2007 inquest declared that Kaiser was murdered and that the allegation of suicide was false.

DAVID BARRETT (1927–2011)

Barrett, one of most important scholars of the spread of Christianity in the latter twentieth century, began his career as an Anglican missionary in western Kenya in the late 1950s. Frustrated by the divisions among the Christians he met and disappointed by tensions between missionaries and increasingly restive independent Christian movements, he took a leave and studied at Union Theological Seminary and Columbia University in the US from 1961 to 1965.

Barrett's research revolutionized the study of Christianity in Africa, and he quickly became an expert in new religious movements. His skills and ability to form effective research teams eventually led to the groundbreaking *World Christian Handbook* and *World Christian Encyclopedia.* Attentive to indigenous religious innovations, denominational variations, and historical trends, Barrett helped lay the basis for the field of world Christianity.

NOTABLE EARLY EASTERN AFRICAN CHRISTIANS

MRINGE (D. 1850?)

Mringe was the first Anglican convert from Kenya, thus CMS missionary Johann Krapf's first convert and companion. Suffering from physical disabilities, he came to the mission at Rabai near Mombasa, likely drawn there due to the social ostracism he faced. Krapf drew inspiration from him and movingly described some of their conversations. When Krapf returned to Rabai in the early 1850s, he learned that Mringe had died, but not before being baptized by his colleague Rebmann.

HILARION MARUAMMAKOMA

The first notable Catholic lay catechist in eastern Africa was a former slave named Hilarion Maruammakoma, who assumed his duties in 1877 at Mhonda, in what is today Tanzania. Mhonda was the first Catholic mission founded inland from the coast, and Hilarion and his wife traveled there with other married couples shortly after their weddings at the main mission at coastal Bagamoyo. Comprising the first Catholic families in eastern Africa inland from the coast, they were seen by the Holy Ghost missionaries as the kernel of the future church.

The missionaries depended on Hilarion especially and, at first, their relations were mutually cordial with their African assistant. Over time, however, tensions developed. This first occurred when Hilarion's ambitions drew him into conflict with neighboring villages, later when he took more wives, then later when he purchased slaves of his own. He ended his life as a Muslim, working closely with the Germans. Despite his separation from the mission, power and resources stemming from his various endeavors allowed him to become a cultural and political broker in the complex relations among the colonial authorities, the mission, and surrounding peoples.

Hilarion's life demonstrates how social realities like poverty, racialized identity, and social influence impacted young converts in eastern Africa. His life course, moving from slave to Catholic Christian to catechist, then to village leader and eventually Muslim, reveals the ways that changing political realities in eastern Africa shaped Christian experiences before and then during the early colonial period.[8]

JAMES JUMA MBOTELA

Mbotela was an early UMCA convert who wrote *The Freeing of the Slaves in East Africa*,[9] based on memories of his father, a slave freed at sea by the British who became an interpreter for

8. Kollman, *Evangelization of Slaves*, 256–60.

9. James Juma Mbotela, *The Freeing of the Slaves in East Africa* (London: Evans Brothers, 1956).

Europeans before dying during a caravan safari. Mbotela's work describes slave caravans and British anti-slavery activities from the perspective of African captives set free by British patrols. Many were brought to Freretown and other freed slave settlements at coastal Kenya. Mbotela later became the official historian of Freretown. His son, also a Christian, was killed during the Mau Mau revolt, accused by anti-colonialists of collaboration with the colonial regime.[10]

CECIL MAJALIWA

Majaliwa, a freed slave educated by the Anglican UMCA missionaries at Zanzibar in their school at Kiungani, became the first native priest of eastern Africa, ordained at Christ Church, which was built on the old slave market closed in 1873.

Before leaving for Great Britain for theological training, Majaliwa taught at Zanzibar beginning in 1878, and in 1879 he married a fellow ex-slave teacher, Lucy Magombeani. After his ordination as a deacon in 1886, Majaliwa helped start a new mission among the Yao—Majaliwa's own people—at Chitangali in 1888 and served there until 1894. According to early accounts, he soon relearned the language of the people into whom he was born. Local conflicts made life difficult, yet he worked there effectively, gathering believers in ways that inspired visitors. Majaliwa's letters from Chitangali, where he lived with his wife and four children, tell of the complex politics of the time—with differing peoples contesting with each other for superiority. They also describe his suffering: fleeing into the bush for safety and enduring loneliness after two English fellow missionaries died.

After serving in Chitangali, Majaliwa returned to Zanzibar. There he continued to serve, often in conflict with the UMCA missionaries in authority. He was even suspended from his orders. Still, in 1914, just after German shelling of Zanzibar after the Great War broke out, he is recorded as having a Communion service at Mbweni. Though Majaliwa never became a

10. For a study of Mbotela, mostly in his own words, see Joseph E. Harris, *Recollections of James Juma Mbotela* (Nairobi: East African Publishing, 1977).

bishop, blocked perhaps by the racism of his time, his grandson, John Ramadhani, was bishop in Zanzibar and primate of the Anglican Church in Tanzania in the 1980s.[11]

THE BOMBAY AFRICANS

The history of the "Bombay Africans" or "Bombayans"[12] encompasses the processes of the Indian Ocean slave trade and its abolition, as well as efforts to found the Anglican Church in eastern Africa. Originally the Bombay Africans were slaves freed at sea near the coast of the Indian Ocean by the British. Then taken to India, they were educated and trained at a CMS mission near Bombay called Nasik, returning later to eastern Africa. Chuma and Sisi, assistants to David Livingstone, were Bombay Africans.

Later, after the Parliament-sponsored 1873 visit of Sir Bartle Frere that led to the end of the slave trade at Zanzibar, the British government assisted Anglican missionaries from the CMS and UMCA to found freed slave settlements at the coast of eastern Africa. To assist the effort, they brought large numbers of the Bombay Africans back to live in the newly established Freretown and the older mission at Rabai. The first batch brought 150 to the mission at Rabai in 1875. Due to their training, the Bombay Africans served in the freed slave settlements as teachers, catechists, and skilled craftsmen.

The Bombay Africans lived a complex social reality. First, though Africans, the returnees originated from different parts of the region and were conversant neither with the Swahili language nor the customs of the coast. At the same time, the Bombay Africans were accustomed to the same standard of living as other missionaries, preferring to dress as the English, but such standards were not provided in the new setting. Resentments

11. A. E. M. Anderson-Morshead, *The History of the Universities' Mission to Central Africa, 1859–1909* (London: Butler & Tanner, 1909); Iliffe, *Modern History of Tanganyika*, 229–30; Daniel O'Connor, *Three Centuries of Mission: The United Society for the Propagation of the Gospel 1701–2000* (London: Continuum, 2000), 335–41; James Tengatenga, *The UMCA in Malawi: A History of the Anglican Church, 1861–2010* (Zomba, Malawi: Kachere Press, 2010), 188.

12. Harris, *Recollections of James Juma Mbotela*, 52.

and conflicts thus naturally arose, both with other Africans recently freed from slavery and with the missionaries. Tensions increased when inexperienced missionaries like John Streeter assumed control at Rabai and Freretown in the late 1870s. By the early 1880s, there was serious discord, with the Bombay Africans openly defying Streeter's authority. They eventually appealed to the mission headquarters in Zanzibar, and Streeter was removed.[13]

Trained as a blacksmith at Nasik after his arrival in India in 1850, one of the most prominent Bombay Africans was William Jones (ca. 1840–1904) who had returned with a few others to eastern Africa in 1864 to assist Rebmann at Rabai. He became a leader among the Bombay Africans at the freed slave settlements, with other major figures including George David, Jacob Wainwright, Ishmael Semler, James Deimler, and Matthew Wellington.

The founding of Freretown led to more Bombay Africans coming to eastern Africa, while some of those already present moved into prominent roles. Jones was eventually ordained a deacon in 1885 and assumed leadership at Rabai. Due to his open welcome to freed slaves in the area, local landowners resented him and the mission-founded Christian villages. This led to armed conflicts in the late 1880s and early 1890s. Jones was ordained a priest in 1895, and over the next decades tensions grew between him and the missionaries, whom he felt discriminated against him unfairly—which looks to be the case from the historical record. By the time of his death in 1904, Freretown and Rabai had become incorporated into colonial Kenya and the Bombay Africans were a less distinctive social grouping in the growing Christian communities of eastern Africa.

The story of the Bombay Africans sheds light on the early Protestant experience in Kenya, as well as the challenges connected with slavery in the early colonial period. In 2007, the National Museums of Kenya hosted an exhibition about the Bombay Africans in Nairobi, updating contemporary Kenyans on this important chapter in their history.

13. Colin Reed, *Pastors, Partners, and Paternalists: African Church Leaders and Western Missionaries in the Anglican Church in Kenya, 1850–1900* (Leiden: Brill, 1997), 89–90.

THE UGANDA MARTYRS

The "Uganda Martyrs" refers primarily to a group of twenty-three Anglican and twenty-two Catholic converts to Christianity who were executed between 1885 and 1887 by the order of Kabaka Mwanga II as part of the struggle for political influence in the royal court. Most were pages in the court who had been attracted by the missionaries' preaching over the previous years. Their deaths helped Uganda's two Christian bodies grow enormously in the decades following.

The largest group of martyrs, around thirty, were captured and taken to Namugongo in May 1886. On arrival, they were kept in confinement for a week. Preparations for the execution pyre were not completed until June 2. During that time the martyrs prayed and sang together, while the missionaries, Catholic and Anglican, conferred among themselves and paid fruitless visits to the king to appeal for their young neophytes. Most of those killed were burnt alive, while others died after excruciating tortures.

In Great Britain, the martyrs' fate served to support the imposition of colonial overrule, which was in place by the early 1890s after several years of complex political turmoil. Both churches revered their martyrs, but the Catholic Church in particular emphasized their role as the faith spread, developing local shrines in many places where the martyrs came from or where they were killed. They were beatified in 1920 and canonized in 1964. Five years later Pope Paul VI came to Uganda and consecrated the Martyrs' shrine at Namugongo, a place of pilgrimage and site of a huge celebration annually on Martyrs' Day, June 3, which is a national holiday.

The phenomenon of the martyrs has not been free of controversy. Nationalist historians, for instance, have seen in the Christian commemorations a pretext for imperialism. Another issue has been the link between the martyrs and homosexuality. Early accounts suggest that the kabaka's wrath against his pages, leading to their martyrdom, was inflamed because they refused his sexual advances. Some have seen this as "evidence" of so-called Arab or Muslim influences on Mwanga, a point adduced in recent bills in the Ugandan Parliament that stiffen penalties for homosexual activity. Some advocates of such laws stress the anti-African and anti-Christian nature of homosexuality and use the martyrs in support. Others question the veracity of the historical accounts about the king's sexual frustration as a cause. They emphasize instead the political threats he faced—Christian missionaries and Muslims at the court, with linked threats from both Europeans and Arabs to the kingdom. This climate thus made any insubordination very worrisome to him, explaining his death-dealing. The extent to which the deaths reflected the cultural practice of ritual murders that often accompanied royal transfers of power has also been considered.

Less controversial is the role of the Uganda Martyrs in helping to grow Christianity, especially the Catholic Church, in eastern Africa. Drawing on Catholic traditions of hagiography and linking them with Uganda's cultural geography, the White Fathers and their converts soon linked certain martyrs to particular groups or activities, and to different parts of the emerging colony. The pages came to the kabaka's court from many parts of the country, and their particular histories were often recounted. Soon, therefore, there were martyrs who became patrons for schoolchildren, musicians, and soldiers, and many districts in the southern and western parts of the country soon had their own martyr (or martyrs).

When Pope John Paul II named two new Uganda martyrs from northern Uganda in 2002, this replicated the pattern of linking the martyrs to regions in the country. These two, Daudi Okello and Jildo Irwa, were killed in 1916 shortly after their conversions, three decades after the others and in very different circumstances. Their recognition, however, allows the commemoration of the Martyrs to include more fully the many Catholics of northern Uganda.

Several of the Catholic martyrs deserve special mention due to their importance in the martyrs' history and the special way in which they are remembered today. For example, Joseph Mukasa Balikuddembe came to the kabaka's court from a neighboring kingdom in 1874, shortly before the Anglican and Catholic missionaries arrived. An effective worker, before long he served in Mutesa's private apartments. Initially drawn by the Christian message of the Anglicans, in 1879, one year after the White Fathers came, Mukasa enrolled as catechumen with the Catholics and was baptized by Lourdel in April 1882 along with Andrew Kaggwa, another future martyr. Taking the name Joseph, a few months later the expulsion of the Catholic missionaries from the capital led him to become the leader of the Catholic pages. He continued as a favorite of Mutesa until the kabaka's death in 1884.

When Mwanga became king, Joseph Mukasa was reappointed to the royal service and remained the kabaka's personal attendant. He was also made majordomo of the royal household with permission from the king to administer reproof to him, if Mukasa thought the king guilty of unbecoming conduct. In this capacity, he was able to intercede successfully with Mwanga on behalf of Sarah Nalwanga, an Anglican convert who had been condemned to death. In addition, he helped Mwanga thwart a plot against the king's life in early 1885. He also, however, began to alienate Mwanga by urging him to put away his charms, openly organizing catechism classes at court, and protecting the pages in his care from the king's advances.

In late October 1885, after the return of the missionaries, it became known that the Anglican Bishop Hannington was making his way from the Indian Ocean coast overland to Uganda, instead of traveling across Lake Victoria from the south, which was the customary route. This news, coupled with rumors of British and German activity at the coast, and the growing influence of Christian missionaries at court, made Mwanga determined to murder Hannington en route. On October 28, Mwanga sent for Joseph Mukasa, who urged him not to put the bishop to death, adding that his father, Mutesa, had never killed a European. Mwanga ignored him and five days later the news of Hannington's murder reached Kampala.

In November, Mwanga used the side effects of medicine administered by Lourdel as an excuse to accuse the Catholics of a plot against his life. In a memorable nightlong interview with Joseph Mukasa, he poured out all his resentment against the majordomo, for his insult over the death of Hannington and his obstruction of the king's vices. The next morning, Joseph assisted at the Holy Eucharist and received Communion from

Lourdel. Summoned again by the king, the latter condemned him to death, making it clear that he was to die for his religion. Joseph was taken to a spot near the Nakivubo River, between Mengo and Nakasero hills. Here he forgave the king and his other enemies, before being knifed and his body burned to ashes on a pyre.

Fellow Catholic page Charles Lwanga stepped into Mukasa's role as their leader, having been his immediate subordinate until Mukasa's death. Lwanga had been drawn to the Catholic message in 1880 and later entered the service in the royal household of Mwanga. The day Mukasa was killed, Lwanga sought baptism as a Catholic by a missionary priest. On May 25, 1886, Mwanga ordered a general assembly of the court, where he condemned two of the pages to death. The following morning, Lwanga secretly baptized those of his charges who were still only catechumens and later the same day, the king called a court assembly in which he interrogated all present to see if any would renounce Christianity. Led by Lwanga, the royal pages declared their fidelity to their religions, upon which the king ordered them bound and condemned them to death, directing that they be marched to the traditional place of execution. Two of the prisoners were executed on the march there.

On June 3, 1885, just before killing the main body of prisoners, the executioners put Charles Lwanga to death on a small pyre on the hill above the execution place. He was wrapped in a reed mat, with a slave yoke on his neck, but he was allowed to arrange the pyre himself. To make him suffer the more, the fire was first lit under his feet and legs. These were burnt to charred bones before the flames were allowed to reach the rest of his body. Taunted by the executioner, Charles replied, "You are burning me, but it is as if you are pouring water over my body." He then remained quietly praying. Just before the end, he cried out in a loud voice "*Katonda*"—in Luganda, "My God."

MARIA MATILDA MUNAKU (1858–1934)

Munaku was the sister of the Catholic Ugandan martyr Noah Mawaggali. After becoming Catholic, she pledged lifelong virginity and served at Catholic seminaries in Uganda beginning in 1903, becoming known as the "Mother of the Seminary."

Seized by Kabaka Mwanga's messenger when her brother was taken and killed in May 1886, Munaku then endured beatings as her captor sought to make her his wife. After her repeated refusals and claims to desire martyrdom herself, she was ransomed to the leader of the Catholic mission, Fr. Simon Lourdel. Lourdel baptized her soon thereafter and during political unrest of the late 1880s she spent time at the Catholic mission in Tanganyika at Bukumbi. There she founded an orphanage for young girls before returning to Uganda in the early 1890s.

In her role as manager of the kitchen and banana plantations at Bukalasa seminary from 1903 and then Katigondo Seminary in 1911, Munaku gathered about her other unmarried women to assist at these Ugandan Catholic sites for the formation of clergy. They served in these capacities until 1924, when they were replaced by the new Catholic women's religious order composed of Ugandans, the *Bannabikira* or "daughters of the Virgin."

HENRY WRIGHT DUTA (D. 1913?)

Duta, one of the earliest Anglican converts among the Baganda, was expelled from the country for showing an interest in Christianity. Taken to Zanzibar by missionaries for education, he later returned to Buganda, where he assisted the CMS missionaries in their ministry during the period of the martyrs.

Duta was a key figure in translating the Bible into Swahili in the late 1890s, following in the footsteps of the earlier efforts by the CMS figures Krapf and Rebmann in Kenya, and the UMCA bishop Edward Steere in Zanzibar. Serving as the chief assistant to George Pilkington, Duta finalized the New Testament translation and then revised the whole translation and later carried it to press in England. He was later ordained a deacon by Bishop Tucker of Eastern Equatorial Africa and took an interest in recording the history of the kingdom of Buganda in the early twentieth century.

APOLO KIVEBULAYA (1864–1933)

Apolo Kivebulaya was a CMS Anglican catechist from Uganda best known as the "Apostle to the Pygmies" in eastern Congo. Formerly a Muslim jihadist against Christians, he eventually fled military service, inspired by the CMS missionary leader Alexander Mackay. He was baptized in 1895 and enrolled in classes to become a catechist later that same year in Kampala. His first mission in the Toro region was a marked success. After a few unsuccessful months in Nyawaki, he was sent to Boga in the Congo (today the Democratic Republic of the Congo), where he traveled the entire way on foot, over the Rwenzori Mountains. He brought only a hoe in order to work and feed himself, and his Bible.

In Boga, many were offended by Kivebulaya's preaching as it countered cultural practices such as alcohol-drinking and polygamy. The chief, Tabaro, forbade the building of a church for the few converts and tried to drive the catechist away by denying him any food. Yet he fended for himself and continued to preach in Boga. In an unfortunate turn of events, he became a scapegoat for the accidental death of the chief's sister and was arrested, beaten, and sent to Uganda for trial in 1898. In prison, Kivebulaya had a spiritual dream that encouraged him in his faith. He reported, "I saw Jesus shining like the sun. He said to me, 'Take heart, for I am with you.' Since that year whenever I preach, people leave their old customs and repent." Upon his release, the catechist did the unthinkable. He returned to Chief Tabaro, who was converted, and the two became close friends. Kivebulaya was ordained deacon in Toro in 1900 and in 1903 became a priest.

In 1921, Kivebulaya had another spiritual experience in which he witnessed Christ sending him to the forest. He declared it to be "the year of the Gospel" and preached to many inhabitants in the wilderness such as the Walese, the Wanyali, and the Wambuti. In 1932, he first baptized so-called pygmies.

In 1933, Kivebulaya died in Boga and was buried, counter to tradition, with his head facing toward the west to indicate the need for the gospel to spread in that direction. The influence and prominence of the Anglican Church in the DRC today is still attributed to his work.[14]

YOHANA KITAGANA (1858–1939)

Kitagana was a lay catechist who became the first Catholic missionary to Ankole and southwest Uganda. A late convert, Kitagana had already amassed a small fortune and five wives before converting to Catholic Christianity in Buganda. As he became a Catholic he learned to read and write, and, after baptism in 1896, he decided to live as a single person in order to devote himself to evangelization.

Full of charisma, Kitagana first worked in eastern Uganda among the Basoga and Teso, then was sent by Bishop Streicher to Bunyoro. After formal training at the catechist center in Rubaga, Kampala, he went to Ankole, where he joined the work of catechism with service as a healer who relied on both western and traditional medicines. After the White Father missionaries arrived in Ankole in 1910, Kitagana was sent to Kigezi to begin the Catholic presence there, again preparing for the eventual missionary arrival in 1923. Then he was sent to Bufumbira, working in a difficult area to establish the Catholic Church.

Kitagana epitomized the energetic Ugandan lay evangelist—both Anglican and Catholic. The growth of the Catholic Church in the regions of his evangelization has been credited to his piety and hard work.[15]

VICTORO MUKASA WOMERAKA (1882–1979) AND BAZILIO LUMU (1875–1946)

These two Ugandans were ordained together in 1913 as the first two indigenous African Catholic priests in eastern Africa. Entering the seminary in 1903, they were ordained at Villa Maria mission near Masaka by Bishop Henri Streicher. Thousands of

14. The DACB has several articles about Kivebulaya. See also Hastings, *Church in Africa*, 470, and Emma Wild-Wood, "A Biography of Apolo Kivebulaya," *International Bulletin of Missionary Research* 38, no. 3 (2014): 145–48.

15. See DACB entry, also Hastings, *Church in Africa*, 470.

Ugandans attended the ceremony in what was a day of triumph for the Catholic Church in Uganda—some say those attending constituted the largest crowd ever assembled in Buganda, perhaps 15,000.

Lumu, who lived with a lifelong disability, was an industrious scholar, learning new languages. He is remembered for his orderly, stately conduct as well as his acts of charity, and he died with honor. He is buried in Villa Maria Cathedral.

Womeraka had a long career as a seminary professor and parish priest, serving as a beloved leader among the Baganda clergy through the turmoil of the end of missionary control over the diocese of Masaka and the ordination of Bishop Joseph Kiwanuka, and into the postcolonial period. His death at ninety-seven marked the end of a long life of service as a priest.

SEMEI KAKUNGULU (1868–1928)

Kakungulu was a native of Buganda who converted to Anglican Christianity in the 1880s. Already a leader among his people, he assisted British colonial leaders in subjugating Bunyoro and northern groups of the Ugandan territory in the 1890s. Soon he was cooperating with the British in their efforts to extend their colonial control over eastern Uganda, especially among the Bukedi and Busoga. He assumed a formal leadership role there and thought he might even be appointed the king of those people by the British, but he was disappointed.

After 1900, Kakungulu grew more frustrated with the British. In 1913, he joined the Malakite religious movement, a mixture of traditional and Christian elements that the British condemned. Then in 1917 he founded the Abayudaya, a group of Jewish believers among Ugandans that exists to this day, centered near Mbale, where they gather for holidays on Kakungulu Hill. They number about 6,000.[16]

16. Michael Twaddle, *Kakungulu and the Creation of Uganda* (London: James Currey, 1993).

JOSEPH ADRIAN ATIMAN (1866–1956)

Atiman served for nearly seven decades as a catechist and doctor in western Tanzania, near Karema. Enslaved as a boy in Mali, he was ransomed from slavery by the White Fathers and trained in Malta to be a catechist-doctor, part of White Father founder Cardinal Lavigerie's plan to evangelize Africa through healing and teaching.

Atiman drew upon western medical training and indigenous knowledge in his healing efforts. His ministry was widely admired and earned him numerous accolades, including the papal medal *Pro ecclesia et Pontifice*, the French Legion of Honor, and the British Wellcome Medal, which he was the first African to receive.

APOLO KAGWA (1865–1927)

Apolo Kagwa was an administrative apprentice at the royal palace of Buganda when the first Christian missionaries arrived in the 1870s and became one of the earliest converts to the Anglican faith. He was spared from becoming a martyr possibly due to his skills as an adept treasury administrator. Kagwa later worked with British missionaries to establish boarding schools, notably King's College Budo, and his manuscripts and personal papers are in the Africana collection of the Makerere University library in Kampala.

A noted authority on his people's culture and history, Kagwa authored many books on Buganda. These include a general history, a treatise on laws and customs, and a collection of folklore. His history of Buganda included brief histories of the neighboring kingdoms of Bunyoro and Ankole. Kagwa was appointed prime minister (*katikkiro*) of the kingdom of Buganda by King Mwanga II and became the first African to receive the honor of knighthood as an honorary member of the Order of the British Empire.

HAM MUKASA (CA. 1868 [1871?]–1956)

Ham Mukasa, once a Ugandan page in the court of Mutesa I of Buganda, became an Anglican and later served as secretary to Apolo Kagwa. Known as a scholar though he never had formal schooling, Mukasa acquired his education through extensive reading, becoming fluent in both English and Swahili. Close contact with the early European missionaries as they visited Kabaka Mutesa established him as a learned man.

Mukasa wrote one of the first glossaries of Luganda, the language of the Baganda. He also wrote *Sir Apolo Kagwa Discovers Britain* and *Uganda's Katikiro in England*, the latter narrating his visit to England with Apolo Kagwa for the coronation of Edward VII in 1902. In the late 1930s and 1940s, he wrote a three-volume work, *Simuda Nyuma*, Luganda for "Do not turn back," recounting the story of Christianity and colonialism coming to Uganda. Grateful for his faith, Mukasa nonetheless was very proud of his Baganda culture and heritage, and his writings have helped preserve that legacy.

MUSAJJAKAWA MALAKI (1875–1929)

Although Malaki was a product of Anglican missionaries, he was refused baptism twice. Influenced by Joswe Kate Mugema, an early convert and later a protester against the Europeans, Malaki eventually formed a separatist revival movement and church, the "The Society of the One Almighty God," or the Malakite Church, in 1914. This church was the first independent church in Uganda. It famously denounced European medical techniques and advocated for land redistribution, sowing the seeds of anti-colonial dissent. It grew to more than 90,000 members by the early 1920s.

The Malakite Church was suppressed during colonial rule as a result of its public stance against vaccination programs during a medical emergency. The movement declined swiftly from its peak in 1921 until it disappeared around 1930. Malaki died in a hunger strike in 1929.

DAMARI VIGOWA SAGATWA (1875–1960)

Damari was a famous Bible Woman, that is, a female catechist and evangelist with the CMS in Ugogo and Ukaguru in central Tanganyika. She began her work while married, and after her husband's death in 1927 went to a series of missions in northern and western Tanganyika as a missionary. The East African Revival inspired her work beginning in the 1930s.

JOHN (JOE) CHURCH (1899–1989), WILLIAM NAGENDA (1912–1973), AND SIMEONI NSIBAMBI (1897–1978)

Nagenda and Nsibambi were well-educated Baganda Anglicans who became among the most prominent African leaders of the East African Revival, working closely with missionary Dr. Joe Church and others in the 1930s and 1940s to spread the revival message throughout central and eastern Africa. Nsibambi's spiritual meeting with Church in 1929 has often been seen as the original event of the Revival, while Nagenda became its most prominent public preacher.

Church was an open-minded CMS Anglican missionary doctor who, with the educated Muganda convert and fellow medical professional Nsibambi, sought deeper holiness through a close study of the Bible. Transformed by their friendship, soon they were preaching a deeper life in Christ through confession and a strict Christian morality. Nagenda, a relative of Nsibambi through marriage, also joined the evangelical campaign. The Revival's rallies featured personal testimonies of conversion, and both Church and Nsibambi spoke passionately of the power of their interracial friendship.

Tensions arose both within the Revival and with other established churches. One of the most serious conflicts appeared at Mukono, site of the Anglican seminary, where in the early 1940s the seminarians, among whom was Nagenda, resisted so-called "liberal" biblical scholarship that they felt undermined Christian faith. Nagenda and others were eventually expelled, but his preaching continued, even becoming international in the 1940s and 1950s in campaigns with Church and others. Despite such conflicts, both Nagenda and Nsibambi took seriously their links to the Anglican Church and resisted calls to start independent churches.

BISHOP STEFANO REUBEN MOSHI (1906–1976)

A native of Moshi in northern Tanzania, Moshi became the first African bishop of the Lutheran Church in Tanzania in 1958 and later headed up the unified Evangelical Lutheran Church of Tanzania, beginning in 1963.

Moshi's father was a convert of the Leipzig Mission and a teacher who ensured a good education for his son. Becoming first a teacher, Moshi later entered the seminary, eventually studying in the US in the early 1950s. While leader of the Lutherans in newly independent Tanzania, he also dedicated himself to ecumenical unity among Tanzania's Christian groups, global Lutheran concerns, and pan-African Christian cooperation, all the while calling for justice both in the country and throughout the continent. He especially focused on southern Africa, where racist regimes persisted in Rhodesia (today Zimbabwe), Mozambique, and South Africa.

JAMES CAMISASSA (CA. 1899–1979)

Camisassa was the first Kenyan Catholic priest. He began as a priest of what would become the diocese of Nyeri, and later joined the Consolata fathers, who named him after one of the earliest Consolata cofounders, Giacomo Camisassa, who died in 1923.

When he was four, the young boy, then a slave, was handed over by the Italian governor of Somalia and the Italian consul of Zanzibar to the third group of Consolata missionaries when they arrived in Mombasa on May 10, 1903. At the time, his name was Marzuk.

He was later ordained in 1927 and, in 1950, after being a priest for twenty-three years, he joined the Consolata fathers, attending novitiate in Rome. He returned to Kenya in 1951 and served in central Kenya until his death. Camisassa performed heroic work during World War II, when the Italian Consolata missionaries were detained by the British, as well as during the Mau Mau unrest of the 1950s. As a result of his efforts, there were many conversions to Catholicism.

STANISLAUS MUGWANYA (1849–1938)

Mugwanya was a Catholic leader among the Baganda beginning in the late nineteenth century until his death. He is also considered the father of formal education in Uganda since he successfully urged Catholic missionaries to start a school that eventually became the Catholic flagship secondary school St. Mary's College at Kisubi.

Baptized in Nalukolongo in Rubaga in 1886, Mugwanya soon helped negotiate on behalf of Catholics in the conflicts with the Anglicans as the British assumed colonial control over Uganda. For a brief period he was Catholic prime minister, or *katikkiro*, while Apolo Kagwa was his Protestant counterpart, but later he became head of the justice ministry in Ganda kingdom, or *omulamuzi*, a position he held between 1900 and 1921. He also served as one of the regents during the first years of the reign of Kabaka Daudi Chwa, who assumed the throne with British support when he was one year old, ruling from 1897 to 1939. Mugwanya's father-like role is credited with developing a strong character in one who became a popular monarch among the Baganda. A noted leader in education, Mugwanya supported women's education especially, and paid school fees for many Baganda. His compound in Bukeerere, near Masaka, has a museum-like exhibit in his memory.

IMPORTANT FIGURES FOR LATTER TWENTIETH- AND TWENTY-FIRST-CENTURIES EASTERN AFRICA

BISHOP OBADIAH KARIUKI (1902–1978)

Kariuki was born in central Kenya to a family that would be drawn into the CMS-founded Anglican Church. Eventually he attended a local school in Kabete, mentored by the famous anthropologist and missionary, Canon Harry Leakey.

After his baptism in 1922, Kariuki began to demonstrate a passion for education. Eventually Leakey secured his education at the CMS Buxton School in Mombasa, after which he taught at a CMS school in Kiambaa. Later he went for further training at Alliance High School and then St. Paul's Seminary in Limuru, after which he left teaching and assumed leadership in the church.

In the 1930s, Kariuki learned about the East African Revival and became a strong supporter, which caused some tensions with other church leaders. These were overcome, however, by his steadfast orthodoxy and generous leadership. Ordained in 1940, he served the church in Kiambaa, eventually serving as dean in the area around Fort Hall (today Murang'a).

Starting in the 1950s, the Mau Mau movement began to unsettle the area, often targeting local Kenyan Christians who were seen as collaborators with the British colonizers. In the face of this, Kariuki courageously withstood calls for oathing, part of the Mau Mau indoctrination, even though he came to accept the justice of the anti-colonial cause. He saw the Mau Mau practice of oathing, however, as contrary to Christian beliefs.

In 1961, Kariuki was enthroned as diocesan bishop of Fort Hall in the Church of the Province of East Africa at the same ceremony where Festo Olang' was also ordained bishop. He served in that post until 1976, presiding over great growth in the Anglican Church in the area. He was admired for his humility and his forthright faithfulness. In 1985, seven years after his death, Kariuki's autobiography was published, titled *A Bishop Facing Mount Kenya.*

ARCHBISHOP FESTO OLANG' (1914–2004)

Festo Olang' was the first African Anglican archbishop of Kenya, a post he served in from 1970 to 1980. Growing up in western Kenya, he was exposed to both Luo and Luyia tongues and later chaired Bible translation committees for both languages.

After Christian schooling in western Kenya, Olang' eventually was sent to Alliance High School in Kikuyu, proceeding into teacher training after finishing secondary school. After teaching at several schools, he attended St. Paul's Divinity School in Limuru and was ordained a deacon in 1945. Three years later he was chosen to attend Wycliffe Hall at Oxford for further training, returning to Kenya in 1950. Ordained an assistant bishop in 1955 at Namirembe Cathedral in Kampala, he became bishop of Maseno—covering much of western Kenya—in 1961.

When in 1970 the Anglican province of East Africa split into two, one province in Kenya and one in Tanzania, Olang' became the first archbishop of Kenya as well as bishop of Nairobi. In his ten years in that role he gathered African Anglicans for meetings, led ecumenical efforts with other Christians, and presided over growth in the Anglican Church in Kenya. At his death in 2004, he was widely admired for his leadership and his humility.

BISHOP ABERI K. BALYA (1877–1979)

Balya was a leader in the Anglican Church of Uganda for much of the first half of the twentieth century, becoming the first Anglican eastern African bishop in 1947. At that time, he assumed leadership of the Anglican Church in almost all of southwestern Uganda—Bunyoro, Toro, Ankole, and Kigezi.

Balya was born in Toro in western Uganda and after time at the court of Kabarega, king of Bunyoro, returned to his home after the king's defeats at the hand of the British. He then joined the court of Kasagama, king of Toro, eventually becoming an Anglican and a teacher. Ordained a priest in 1922, he served in a number of capacities in the church, serving as a missionary among several people-groups before becoming a bishop. He retired in 1960, having earned a reputation as a founder of schools and a man of prayer. He was awarded the Order of the British Empire in 1952.

BISHOP YOKANA MUKASA BALIKUDEMBE (1917–2005)

Balikudembe served as a leader in the Anglican Church of Uganda, first as dean at Namirembe Cathedral in Kampala during the politically fraught 1960s and 1970s, later as first bishop in Mityana beginning in 1977, when the regime of Idi Amin persecuted many Christians. Balikudembe's leadership mixed political savvy, ecumenical efforts with other Christians, and organizing for social development. The author of a number of books in Luganda on spiritual topics, he retired in 1989.

BISHOP JOSIAH KIBIRA (1925–1988)

Kibira was a bishop in the Lutheran Church in Tanzania, and also held the post of president of the Lutheran World Federation from 1977 to 1984. Born in Bukoba district, Kibira was four years old when his father died, and subsequently he was raised by his mother, who taught him to follow God and to live out faith. German Lutherans baptized him as young boy and confirmed him at fifteen. A leader at school, Kibira underwent a conversion experience after preaching by visiting Anglican missionaries linked to the East African Revival. Eventually he attended Tabora Government School to become a teacher. He married Martha Yeremiah, with whom he would have nine children. His leadership in schools helped him advance eventually into the role of secondary school headmaster.

In 1957, Lutheran missionaries offered him the chance to study theology in Germany in order to become a pastor. He returned to Africa in 1960 and was ordained, but his own strong temperament made ordinary pastoral work difficult. Instead, he began to agitate for the independence of the Lutheran Church among the Haya, his people. Assisted by the then bishop, Bengt

Sundkler, Kibira then went to Boston University for a master's in theology from 1962 to 1964. Upon his return he was elected assistant bishop over the fears of many missionaries who regarded him as headstrong. He served as bishop—eventually of the Northwestern Diocese of the Evangelical Church in Tanzania—for the next twenty years.

Kibira had a number of Africa-wide and international roles. He delivered the keynote address at the All Africa Conference of Churches' 1965 meeting in Addis Ababa, then led worship at the World Council of Churches meeting in Uppsala in 1968. Then in 1977 at the Lutheran World Federation General Assembly at Dar es Salaam he was elected the first African president of the Lutheran World Federation. In 1996, the All Africa Conference of Churches named the main building of its headquarters in Nairobi after Kibira.

REUBEN MUKASA SPARTAS (1895–1982)

Bishop Christopher, born Reuben Mukasa Mugimba Sobanja but referred to as Reuben Mukasa Spartas, was a twentieth-century Christian reformer in Uganda. Born into an Anglican family, he became a leader of the Orthodox Church in Africa. This move was linked to his conviction that colonial rule in Africa had to end, and that a key step would be religious movements, especially Christian churches independent of missionaries yet tied to venerable Christian bodies.

Spartas developed an admiration for the ancient Greeks while a student, eventually attending the Anglican flagship secondary school, King's College, Budo. He joined the King's African Rifles, then left and grew fascinated with the African Orthodox Church (AOC), which began in the US among African Americans. Learning that South Africa had a bishop in this church, Daniel William Alexander, he requested that the bishop visit Uganda in the late 1920s, and Alexander came in 1931–32, training Spartas and his brother-in-law. Eventually, however, Spartas began to doubt the validity of the AOC as an independent church. He instead sought formal communion with the Patriarchate of Alexandria, which had a Greek Orthodox priest in Moshi, Tanganyika in the early 1930s who served the local Greeks in that area. Eventually, an Orthodox bishop visited Uganda in 1942, initiating a process by which the AOC joined the Patriarchate of Alexandria in 1946. Spartas himself became Bishop Christopher.

Spartas's efforts to teach English in schools he founded in the 1950s clashed with British colonial officials who legally forbade such teaching outside government schools. Spartas spent five years in prison, but after independence he became the recognized leader of the Orthodox Church in Uganda.

ARCHBISHOP JOSEPH KIWANUKA (1899–1966)

Joseph Nakabaale Kiwanuka was the first native African to become a Roman Catholic bishop in modern times, assuming the post of vicar apostolic in Masaka, Uganda, in 1939. In 1960, he became archbishop of Rubaga, the Catholic archdiocese under the White Fathers' control in Kampala.

Kiwanuka was born to a devout Catholic family and joined the junior seminary at Bukalasa, then proceeded to study philosophy and theology at the Catholic major seminary at Katigondo. Ordained a priest in 1929, he overcame missionary opposition to join the Society of Missionaries of Africa (known as the White Fathers) three years later, at the conclusion of graduate study in canon law in Rome, undertaken at Archbishop Streicher's urging. As a priest he did pastoral work in parishes near Masaka and taught at Katigondo. His 1939 ordination as a bishop was conferred by Pope Pius XII in St. Peter's Basilica in Rome, with Streicher also assisting. Kiwanuka then oversaw the Africanization of the entire diocese.

In the early 1960s, Kiwanuka played a prominent role in the celebrations accompanying the attainment of political independence in Uganda. He attended the Second Vatican Council in Rome between 1962 and 1965, assisting Pope Paul VI at the canonization of the Uganda Martyrs in 1964. In 1965, the government of the first president of Uganda, Milton Obote, started to become unpopular, and Kiwanuka published a landmark pastoral letter urging responsible citizenship and the development of democratic maturity. Soon afterward, Kiwanuka died unexpectedly. He is buried in Rubaga Cathedral, Kampala.

JANANI JAKALIYA LUWUM (1922–1977)

Luwum, revered as one of the later martyrs of Uganda, was archbishop of the Church of Uganda from 1974 to 1977. He is regarded as one of the most influential leaders of the modern church in Africa. Archbishop Luwum was a leading voice in criticizing the excesses of the Idi Amin regime, which assumed power in 1971. In 1977, Luwum delivered a note of protest to Amin against his policies of arbitrary killings and unexplained disappearances. Shortly afterward, he and other leading churchmen were accused of treason. Later, Luwum and two of his cabinet members were arrested for planning a coup against Amin.

Luwum and the two arrested with him were murdered in 1977 either by Idi Amin or at his orders. Original news reports claimed that the three had been killed when the car transporting them to an interrogation center had collided with another vehicle. Yet according to later testimonies, Luwum and his companions had been taken to an army barracks, where they were beaten and murdered. The Church of England and the Anglican Communion recognize Luwum as a martyr, and his statue is among the Twentieth-Century Martyrs on the front of Westminster Abbey in London. Since 2015, Uganda holds a public holiday on February 16 to celebrate his life.

FESTO KIVENGERE (1919–1988)

Festo Kivengere was a Ugandan Anglican evangelical leader, sometimes known as the "Billy Graham of Africa" for his eloquent public speaking. While he was serving as bishop of Kigezi in southwestern Uganda, he fled the country to escape persecution by Idi Amin after the suspicious death of Archbishop Janani Luwum. After Amin fell, Kivengere returned and remained active in evangelization until his death.

Kivengere was born into a leading non-Christian family in southwestern Uganda. After schooling, he converted at a revival meeting, and soon joined the seminary to prepare himself for ministry in the (Anglican) Church of Uganda. Due to his reputation, Kivengere came to know Billy Graham, joining him at revivals and translating many of Graham's sermons into African languages. He founded his own African Evangelic Enterprise in 1971 and it exists to this day as the African Evangelistic Enterprise.

Kivengere's opposition to Amin's conduct as Uganda's president galvanized when he witnessed the execution of political prisoners. He visited in order to convert them before their deaths, yet their faith impressed him with its calm joy. Eventually he came to protest the abuses of the regime, which endangered him along with other church leaders. Kivengere was one of the last people to see Archbishop Luwum alive and waited outside the building where Luwum was interrogated until guards forced him to leave at gunpoint. Expecting arrest, Kivengere escaped Uganda on foot. Within the year he published a controversial book titled *I Love Idi Amin* that emphasized how a living church cannot be destroyed by fire or by guns, and that Christians must pray for those who persecute them.

JULIUS NYERERE (1922–1999)

Julius Kambarage Nyerere, referred to as the father of Tanzania, was the first of President of Tanganyika (modern-day Tanzania), a proponent of African socialism, and a strong Roman Catholic. Today he is seen as one of the most admirable African leaders of the twentieth century, and he is also revered in the Catholic Church.

Born in the northwestern part of Tanganyika and educated at Makerere University in Uganda, Nyerere began his career as a teacher at St. Mary's School in Tabora, and this vocation gave him the title by which he was known—Mwalimu, or "Teacher"—once he became Tanganyika's leader. His gifts were recognized by colonial leaders and he was called to Edinburgh University to study history, politics, and economics, as well as Greek and Latin. He earned his master's degree in 1952, the first

Tanzanian to do so. He then returned to teach at St. Francis School in Pugu.

Meanwhile Nyerere became active in local politics, leaving teaching in 1954 and organizing the Tanganyika African National Union to work for independence. Peaceful yet persistent, Nyerere became Chief Minister when Tanganyika was granted responsible government in 1960. He led Tanganyika to independence a year later and became the new country's first Prime Minister. The country became a republic in 1962, with Nyerere as the country's first president.

During the first years, Nyerere created a single-party system and used controversial "preventive detention" to eliminate trade unions and other opposition. In 1964, Tanganyika became politically united with Zanzibar and was renamed Tanzania, with Nyerere as president of the unified country. In 1965, he was the sole candidate for president in the unified country's first election. By 1967, influenced by the ideas of African socialism and drawing upon principles of Catholic social teaching, Nyerere issued the Arusha Declaration, which outlined his vision of *ujamaa*, which means "familyhood" and translated into a form of socialism. *Ujamaa* was a concept that came to dominate Nyerere's policies and has inspired Africans and others pursuing social justice and unity throughout the world.

For a variety of reasons—among them corruption, high-handed and violent tactics, war with Uganda in the late 1970s, inability to control international commodity prices, and misplaced idealism—Nyerere's policies led to economic decline and unavailability of goods. Despite these conditions, Nyerere was reelected unopposed every five years for two decades until his retirement in 1985. At that time, he relinquished power to his handpicked successor, Ali Hassan Mwinyi. He remained the chairman of the Chama Cha Mapinduzi, or Revolutionary Party, for another five years until 1990.

Determining Nyerere's legacy in a univocal way is not easy. On the one hand, Tanzanians have an unusually strong sense of their national identity and considerable national unity—indeed, more than nearly anywhere else in Africa—and Nyerere is the single person most responsible. His support for national education in KiSwahili and his own personal integrity helped cement Tanzania's sense of itself. At the same time, Tanzania has lagged behind both Kenya and at times Uganda in economic development. Regardless, Nyerere is a national hero whose personal integrity has rarely been questioned, and his voluntary relinquishing of power was almost unique among Africa's independence leaders. In addition, his Catholic faith was famously strong, linked to both his personal integrity and aspects of his governing philosophy. In light of his achievements and virtues, the Catholic Church has initiated the process moving toward his canonization, in acknowledgment of which Nyerere has been named a "Servant of God."[17]

SAMUEL JOHN CHEGE (1927–1995)

Chege served as a leader of the various churches called the Wakorino (or Akurinu) in Kenya, and as bishop for one of them, the African Christian Holy Ghost Church, from 1968 until his death.

Born in Murang'a, central Kenya, early on Chege belonged to the Africa Inland Church, but he joined the Wakorino in the early 1950s. He suffered imprisonment from 1953 to 1956, accused of spying for Mau Mau rebels, and in the post-independence period helped to integrate the competing Wakorino churches. He eventually succeeded in gaining for the churches governmental approval and also worked to standardize requirements for ordained ministry for those seeking to serve in his church.

SIMEO ONDETO (1926–1992), GAUDENCIA AOKO (1943–1988), AND REGINA OWITCH (CA. 1876–1966)

These three are prominent figures in the history of Legio Maria or Maria Legio, an independent church that emerged from the Catholic Church in western Kenya. Ondeto and Aoko are

17. See James Jay Carney and Krystina Kwizera-Masabo, "The Social Legacy of (Saint?) Julius Nyerere," Catholics and Cultures, last updated November 8, 2016, https://tinyurl.com/y6wakfu6.

revered as cofounders, and some believe that their falling out led Ondeto to lift up Owitch as fellow cofounder in an effort to sideline Aoko.

Born to Luo parents, Ondeto was baptized as Simeo after years of studying catechism. After his parents' attempts to marry him off, he opted for a life of solitude and meditation. According to the lore of his church, he moved to Sagegi to live with a Catholic catechist and while there is said to have died for three days and come back to life. After rising from death, Ondeto began to call himself the "Black Son of God." Ondeto then preached that he had gone to confer with God the Father, chat with saints and angels, and that he was freed to begin his mission which included the baptism of polygamists and Catholic converts without going through catechism training, as well as beginning the church he called Legio Maria.

Aoko like Ondeto grew up a Luo Catholic, and also claimed visions that authorized her for church leadership. By 1964, she was seen as second to Ondeto. Later, however, she was pushed out of leadership, possibly part of Ondeto's efforts before his death to cement his own authority in the later 1960s when he felt threatened by Aoko. Her appeal now appears to abide only in certain regions, while others disregard her role.

As a female founder revered by most present-day Legio Maria adherents, Aoko has been supplanted in esteem for most by Mama Maria, Regina Owitch. Owitch participated in public leadership in small ways and also drew close to Simon Ondeto. Her preeminence in the official narrative of the church, however, grew in the later 1960s after her death, likely due to Ondeto's efforts to undermine Aoko's role.

FATHER CLEMENT KIGGUNDU (D. 1973)

Father Clement Kiggundu, a graduate in journalism from Duquesne University in Pittsburgh, was editor of the Catholic newspaper *Munno* ("friend" in Luganda) in Kampala in the early 1970s. Engaged in analyzing and critiquing Ugandan politics, Kiggundu had criticized the regime of Milton Obote, Uganda's first president, and been praised by Idi Amin after the dictator's

1971 coup. Soon, however, *Munno* also began criticizing the Amin regime's violence and extrajudicial behavior, including the expulsion of the country's Asian population and detention and murder of alleged political opponents. In January 1973, Kiggundu's body was found burned inside his car. An autopsy revealed that had been strangled and shot to death.

FATHER JOSEPH KURUPPAMPARAMBIL (1928–2008)

Better known as Fr. Bill, Kuruppamparambil first came to Uganda in 1992 at the invitation of a local Ugandan Catholic priest after years of preaching the values of the Catholic Charismatic Renewal in the US, India, and around the world. Over the next decade and a half, he preached to thousands of eastern Africans, first in Uganda and then throughout the region, raising the profile of the Catholic Charismatic movement throughout eastern Africa.

Born in Kerala, India, Fr. Bill joined the local Vincentian congregation, linked to the larger Congregation of the Mission, also known as the Vincentians (the international men's Catholic religious congregation that in the US founded DePaul and St. John's University). Ordained a priest in 1958, Fr. Bill suffered a series of heart attacks in 1976 and was bedridden. He then heard about the Charismatic Renewal and felt healed after attending a retreat. Inspired, Fr. Bill headed to Duquesne University in Pittsburgh to be trained in charismatic preaching, and later in Boston encountered a paralyzed man who experienced healing after Fr. Bill prayed over him. Soon he was preaching around the world. His move to Uganda focused his ministry over the final years of his life primarily in eastern Africa.

By the time of his death, Fr. Bill had led thousands of Catholics and others in eastern Africa into charismatic prayer practices. His humility, evident faith, and joyful spirit inspired them. The Vincentian Prayer House in Nairobi and Emmaus Centre in Katikamu, Uganda, are thriving Catholic institutions whose growth over the past decade can in part be credited to his popularity.

ARCHBISHOP DAVID GITARI (1937–2013)

Gitari served as the primate of the Anglican Church of Kenya and archbishop of Nairobi from 1997 to 2002. Through his career as a priest and bishop, beginning in the 1970s to his death, he was a critic of government corruption and injustice. At times he was attacked for his outspoken views, and in the late 1980s was nearly killed by thugs suspected to have been sent by the government.

A native of central Kenya, Gitari became the first bishop of Mount Kenya East diocese in 1975, overseeing expansion and founding new parishes and schools until he left the post in 1990. After that he served in Kirinyaga as bishop until 1996, where again growth occurred. Wherever he went, Gitari chastised government-sanctioned land seizures, rigged voting schemes, and other forms of injustice. In his retirement he served as a member of the Constitution of Kenya Review Commission. A volume of essays in his honor was published in 2009 titled *Religion and Politics in Kenya: Essays in Honor of a Meddlesome Priest*.[18]

BENA KANYENDAKI (1903–1992)

Kanyendaki was prominent among the *Balokole* ("saved") Christians in Hoima, western Uganda, beginning from her conversion in 1966. Later she lost her sight after illness, yet her capacity to gather and inspire believers only increased, as her house near St. Peter's cathedral in Hoima town became a fertile site of evangelization.

She epitomizes countless other lay evangelists of the *Balokole* movement in eastern Africa who spread the gospel by their kindness, witness, and courageous preaching. She was famous for providing Bible verses to those who came to visit her, chosen in light of their own needs as she perceived them.

18. Knighton, *Religion and Politics in Kenya.*

JOSEPH KAYO (1936–)

Kayo founded the Deliverance Church in Kenya in 1970, focusing on urban youth. Soon he had branched out to Uganda and Zambia, forging ties and helping to expand the Evangelical Fellowship of Kenya. In the late 1970s, he faced charges of misconduct and resigned from Deliverance Church, but he then founded the Christian Family Church and Joe Kayo Ministries International, which today has a global reach.

Born in western Kenya, Kayo underwent conversion during illness in 1957 and soon after entered the ministry as a Pentecostal preacher. Ever since he has been one of the most prominent Pentecostals in eastern Africa, holding large exuberant rallies with dynamic healing and fervent testimonies.

SPETUME FLORENCE NJANGALI (1908–1984)

Njangali was a leader in the Anglican Church of Uganda, advancing the ministry of women while also pushing for women's ordination. Ordained the first deaconess in eastern Africa in 1973, she lived to see women ordained priests in the Anglican Church in Uganda.

Originally from Hoima in western Uganda, Njangali trained as a schoolteacher, eventually becoming a headmistress, but in 1938 she was touched by the East African Revival and decided to enter the Anglican seminary at Mukono. She was the only female student among a class of thirty, and afterward returned to being a headmistress. In the 1950s, however, the national church recognized her leadership and appointed her to its Native Synod. She pushed for fuller participation of women in church leadership over the next decade, eventually enrolling again at Mukono and graduating in 1960, after which she was appointed to church service in Ankole-Kigezi diocese. Though consistently serving at the highest level, she was denied ordination until 1973, but never succumbed to bitterness.

PAULO KAJIRU MASHAMBO (1889–1980) AND ELIZAPHAN BWIRIMA WANJARA (1924–2005)

Mashambo and Wanjara are two of the most prominent leaders of the Seventh-Day Adventist (SDA) Church in Tanzania in the twentieth century. Mashambo, a native of Upare and the Usambara Mountains, joined the church in 1913, soon becoming a teacher and church leader. He came to particular prominence when he led a protest against a colonial tax change in the mid-1940s, overseeing a peaceful demonstration with thousands of participants. Scholars have described this campaign and his leadership in a 1987 booklet titled *A Peasant and Political Leader in Upare: Paulo Mashambo.*[19]

After a conversion experience in 1940 when he escaped a deadly crocodile, Wanjara became a teacher before joining the seminary in the 1950s. Over the next several decades, he oversaw a number of different SDA constituencies, bringing about growth wherever he served and overcoming what had been a very localized or folk identity of the SDA church, thus bringing about a national profile. Many admired his integrity and moral uprightness, and in the years prior to independence he successfully defended SDA principles that forbade political engagement, resisting complaints of pro-independence leaders who wanted adherents to participate and threatened the church with violence for its stance.

FATHER JOHN MARY WALIGGO (1942–2008)

John Waliggo was a Ugandan Catholic priest of the diocese of Masaka. A professor and scholar, after the end of Uganda's tumultuous years of violence between 1972 and 1985, he served his country as commissioner of the Uganda Constitutional Commission beginning in 1989, overseeing the writing of the document approved by the Constitutional Assembly in 1993.

After studies in Ugandan and Roman seminaries, Waliggo

19. Isaria N. Kimambo, Eliud Lushino Abdallah Lukwaro, and Paulo Mashambo, *A Peasant and Political Leader in Upare: Paulo Mashambo* (Dar es Salaam: Historical Association of Tanzania, 1987).

was ordained a priest and then sent to Cambridge University for a doctorate in history. His dissertation has become the definitive work on the origins of the Catholic Church among the Baganda, relying on hundreds of interviews with elderly Baganda who witnessed the earliest years. His academic career in Uganda was interrupted in the 1980s when his criticisms of human rights abuses forced his exile to Kenya, where he continued teaching.

Waliggo's service in preparing the Ugandan Constitution made him a prominent national figure and a strong proponent of human rights and corruption-free government. He was also a respected leader among the Catholic clergy of Uganda and a distinguished international theologian.

SARAH MUGANZI LUCHETU (1947–2012)

Luchetu was among the founders of the Kenyan Assemblies of God. She and her husband were one of the four couples who helped build a church with over a million members and 4000 congregations in Kenya.

Born in western Kenya, Luchetu first became a Quaker before encountering the Assemblies of God (AoG) in 1972 in Mwanza, Tanzania, where she and her husband were living. She assisted missionaries in Bible translation and local evangelization before she and her husband returned to Kenya, where they began to form the first Kenyan AoG church in Bahati, a neighborhood of Nairobi. She first taught small children and then founded several church-linked nursery schools, all the while providing leadership in the growing AoG church in Kenya. After her diagnosis, her faith-filled and courageous battle with cancer inspired many fellow believers, and their grief at her early death deepened their commitments to Christ.

MARY AKATSA (B. 1964)

Mary Sinaida Akatsa,[20] a prophetess originally from western Kenya, established the Jerusalem Church of Christ (JCC), a prominent African-initiated church in Kenya, in 1983. Her congregation, which gathers prominently in Kawangware, a poorer neighborhood of Nairobi, draws people from all over Kenya for healing services and Akatsa's forceful preaching. There are also branches of the church in western Kenya in Vihiga and Kakamega districts, composed mostly of people in Akatsa's ethnic group, the Luhya.

Akatsa's account of her early years includes a harrowing rescue from death shortly after her birth, when a vigilant grandmother, a pious Pentecostal believer, saved her from the murderous attempts of her father. She claims to have begun having clairvoyant powers at age five, and by eight she was fully able to heal, read people's minds, tell if a woman was pregnant and the sex of the unborn child. She also received a vision that she would found a church to be called "Jerusalem Church of Christ." After turmoil with her in-laws following a young marriage to Francis Akatsa, she experienced a vision of dying and being reborn in 1983. She then went to Nairobi and soon began to preach and heal. Eventually she moved to Kawangware in 1985 and became involved with the Church of Bethlehem East Africa (COBEA) starting in 1987, with whom her own church was connected. A split in 1989 with COBEA led to the JCC's official registration in 1990.

A prominent figure in Nairobi, "Mama" Akatsa and the Jerusalem Church of Christ drew attention in 1988 when she prophesied that the Messiah would drop by her church on June 11. That day a tall, barefoot, bearded man dressed in white robes came to the church, and thousands joined "Jesus" in an enthusiastic prayer service. He turned out to be an Indian named Maitreya, a professional Jesus imitator. She later drew attention

20. O. M. Jacob Nandi, "The Jerusalem Church of Christ: A Prophet-Healing Independent Church in Kenya" (MA thesis, University of Nairobi, 1993); Philomena Njeri Mwaura, "A Theological and Cultural Analysis of Healing in Jerusalem Church of Christ and Nabii Christian Church of Kenya" (PhD diss., Kenyatta University, 2001).

by presiding at a wedding between a man and his deceased wife in 1998 in western Kenya. The theological and pastoral message of the JCC has been studied and praised by scholars, who see the church meeting the needs of Kenyan believers.

CARDINAL MAURICE OTUNGA (1923–2003)

Maurice Michael Otunga was the first Kenyan to become archbishop and cardinal in the Catholic Church. First a bishop in 1956, he became archbishop of Nairobi in 1971, then cardinal in 1973. He retired in 1997. Soon after his death, local church leaders began the process leading to beatification and canonization, so that Otunga was deemed a "Servant of God" by the Catholic Church in 2009.

The son of a western Kenyan chief who had dozens of wives, Otunga converted to Catholicism in 1935 and eventually entered seminary, studying both in Kenya and Uganda. Later studies took him to Rome and he returned as a seminary teacher, then became secretary to the British apostolic delegate, the leading Catholic official in the colony, in the mid-1950s. He attended the five sessions of the Second Vatican Council between 1962 and 1965. His grave in Resurrection Gardens outside Nairobi is a destination for pilgrims.

Otunga's leadership occurred during moments of great political and social transformation in Kenya, from the colonial period to the rise of multi-party democracy. Disinclined to direct criticism of political leaders, his attacks on corruption and calls for justice were nonetheless forthright and clear. He also supported traditional Catholic teachings, prominently assisting in 1996 at a Nairobi event that featured the burning of condoms, which he deemed contrary to both African and Christian morality.

REVEREND TIMOTHY MURERE NJOYA (B. 1941)

Timothy Njoya is a retired minister of the Presbyterian Church of East Africa (PCEA) and a well-known advocate of justice and democratization in Kenya. Physically attacked several times in the 1990s, he continues to call for justice in Kenya, focusing especially on equality for women.

Born in Nyeri district, central Kenya, Njoya was ordained in the PCEA in 1967 and received a PhD from Princeton Theological Seminary in 1976. By the mid-1980s, he was preaching at St. Andrews church in downtown Nairobi in support of multi-party democracy and an end to rampant corruption. He was arrested several times, warned to leave politics out of the church. Eventually he was removed from St. Andrews by the PCEA. He accepted the disciplining but returned to other smaller Nairobi churches and his public preaching continued with the same message, by which time many Kenyans agreed with him. The first multi-party elections took place in 1992. By the late 1990s, Njoya was among the leaders of the political opposition and was twice beaten by government-hired security forces.

BISHOP HENRY OKULLU (1929–1999)

Henry Okullu served as bishop in the Anglican Church of Kenya from 1971 to 1994. A prominent leader among Kenyan Christians, he criticized Kenya's government, especially the regime of Daniel Arap Moi, over corruption, violations of human rights, and the blocking of multi-party democracy.

Okullu was born to a Luo family in western Kenya, and after initial education entered seminary. He spent the late 1950s and much of the 1960s serving Luo speakers at Namirembe Cathedral in Kampala, Uganda, and serving as editor of the Ugandan Christian newspaper *New Day*. He studied at Virginia Theological Seminary from 1963 to 1965. Upon assuming the role of provost at Nairobi's All Saints Cathedral in 1971, he worked with Christian publications in Kenya such as *Target* and *Lengo*. His 1974 book, *Church and Politics in East Africa*, was a call for pluralistic democracy and, with other leaders like David Gitari and Timothy Njoya he fought for justice, the investigation of murders of political opponents like Robert Ouko, and transparent governance in Kenya, criticizing the one-party state until the first multi-party elections in 1992. He retired from his role as bishop of Maseno South, his official bishop's see in western Kenya, in 1994.

BISHOP CHRISTOPHER MWOLEKA (1927–2002)

Bishop Mwoleka was consecrated and installed the Catholic bishop of Rulenge Diocese, Tanzania in 1969. He served as bishop for thirty years and was known as friend of President Julius Nyerere and supporter of Nyerere's political agenda.

Mwoleka was ordained a priest in 1962 and worked in the Ministry of Education before becoming bishop, and he retired as bishop in 1996. Noted for his simple lifestyle and humility, Mwoleka's motto as bishop was "May they all be one" from John 17:21. This motto shaped two well-known aspects of his leadership. First, it explains his support for Nyerere's philosophy of *ujamaa* (Swahili for "familyhood"), a political program of collectivization that was linked to promotion of African values and also drew upon Catholic social teaching. Eventually known as the "*ujamaa* bishop," Mwoleka saw the process of villagization connected to *ujamaa* as a way beyond the competitiveness of traditional village life toward a lifestyle of cooperation drawing on the best of African traditions and also compatible with Christianity exemplified in the unity of the Trinity. Mwoleka thus sought to challenge criticisms of *ujamaa* that saw it simply as a socialist program.

Besides his connection to Nyerere, Mwoleka was also known for his support of small Christian communities (or SCCs)—in Swahili, *jumuiya ndogo ndogo*—as a pastoral strategy for the churches of eastern Africa. This began in 1976, and Mwoleka participated in an SCC the rest of his career, often introducing himself as a member of his SCC.

JOSEPH KIBWETEERE (1932–2000[?]) AND CREDONIA MWERINDE (1952–2000[?])

Kibweteere and Mwerinde were leaders of the Movement for the Restoration of the Ten Commandments of God, a splinter group from the Catholic Church that appeared in western Uganda in the late 1980s and 1990s. Mostly obscure, the death of nearly 800 of its members in March 2000 brought the Movement international notoriety. The circumstances surrounding that event remain mysterious, since it bore marks of mass suicide as well as mass murder. The consensus now is that long patterns of manipulation led to cooperation in a murderous plot to remove dissenters, real and imagined. Many of the bodies were subsequently burnt in what has become known as the "Kanungu massacre."

Kibweteere was raised a pious Catholic and served as a lay leader in Catholic education in western Uganda in the 1980s. In 1989 he met Credonia Mwerinde, a Catholic woman who claimed to have received visions of the Virgin Mary, something Kibweteere himself also began to claim. Soon they were traveling together, preaching about the apocalypse and organizing the Movement, which they led together along with several others, including Catholic priest Dominic Kataribabo, who studied theology in the US, as well as other clergy and members of religious orders. The group never formally left the Catholic Church, though eventually some members were excommunicated, including priests and nuns. Meanwhile, participation numbers in their prayer services and vigils grew. As the year 2000 approached, the group developed heightened apocalyptic expectation. Some see the failure of the end-times after January 1, 2000 as leading to the March 2000 calamity due to internal dissension that threatened the group's leadership. The deaths at Kanungu led to investigations at other Movement properties, where hundreds of other bodies were also discovered.

Kibweteere's own fate remains unknown, as does Mwerinde's. Once assumed to have perished in the March 2000 event, a 2014 report suggested the Uganda police heard that he was hiding abroad, and an international warrant exists for the arrest of both of them.

JOHN GATU (1925–2017)

Gatu, a Kenyan from the central part of the country, became a Presbyterian minister in 1956 and later the General Secretary of the Presbyterian Church of East Africa (PCEA) in 1964. In 1971, motivated by a conviction that dependence on international support created weakness in the African church, Gatu issued a famous moratorium on foreign missionaries and funds to Africa. He reiterated this call in 1974. Gatu's call for a missionary moratorium provoked contradictory responses, both in Africa and in the global Christian community. Some saw it as an overdue invitation to self-reliance; others discerned an arrogance that undermined missionary zeal. From 1979 to 1985 he served as Moderator of the Presbyterian Church in Kenya. Besides his pastoral work, Gatu also published poems in Kikuyu, his first language.

A 2016 autobiography[21] reveals that Gatu fought as a soldier in Ethiopia with the King's African Rifles on behalf of the British in World War II. He returned to join the Mau Mau movement, which he felt did not contradict his Christian faith, eventually becoming a leader in the movement. Involvement with the East African Revival led to training for ministry at St. Paul's United Theological Seminary and eventually grew into church leadership. In the late 1950s he also studied briefly in Scotland. While serving as PCEA General Secretary, he was also in charge at St. Andrew's in Nairobi. He later served on a number of national ecumenical bodies in Kenya and across eastern Africa, becoming a confidante of Kenya's national leaders Jomo Kenyatta, Daniel Arap Moi, and Mwai Kibaki.

ELDER BLASIOUS M. RUGURI

Ruguri, a Kenyan, was elected president of the East-Central Africa Division of the Seventh-Day Adventists in 2010, thus overseeing the church's work in eleven countries. He has graduate degrees from Andrews University in Michigan. Ruguri began his ministry in 1982 and was ordained in 1986, assuming

21. John G. Gatu, *Fan into Flame* (Nairobi: Moran, 2016).

leadership in youth ministry for the church. In 2012, he became a controversial figure due to his alleged support of proposed legislation before the Ugandan Parliament that included incarcerating and even executing people for same-sex relations.

DAVID ZAKAYO KIVULI (1896–1974)

Kivuli is the founder of the African Israel Church Nineveh (AICN), one of the largest AICs in eastern Africa. At the time of his death his church, founded in Kenya but spread throughout the region, numbered over 100,000 and the AICN became a member of the World Council of Churches in 1975.

Kivuli was born in western Kenya, where he grew up to be a member of Pentecostal Assemblies of Canada, eventually serving as a preacher and school supervisor. In 1932, after an illness, he began to experience gifts of the Holy Spirit, including healing and speaking in tongues. These gifts drew him into the East African Revival, and tensions with his missionary roots led to a split in 1942, and the subsequent founding of the AICN. Most members of the AICN are, like Kivuli, connected to western Kenya, thus Luo and Luhya, but there are branches all over the region, as well as overseas.

ELIJAH MASINDE (1910–1987)

Elijah Masinde was the founder and leader of Dini ya Msambwa ("Religion of the Ancestor" or "Faith through the Spirit of Our Ancestors"), an anti-colonial African traditional religion practiced among the Luhya people of western Kenya. Detained during the colonial period for urging his followers to refuse to cooperate with the regime, he also suffered imprisonment after independence due to anti-government agitation against the Kenyatta and Moi regimes.

Masinde began to gather people in 1942 and soon started the Dini ya Msambwa, mostly members of his own Bukusu branch of the Luhya who were attracted by his preaching. He had a reputation for prophetic insights and the capacity to curse effectively those who crossed him. Never a nationally recognized political figure, he nonetheless gained renown among a variety of anti-colonial and anti-government groups.

Masinde's reputation has continued in Kenya decades after his death. Several of his alleged prophecies have been seized upon by Kenyan politicians to justify their own decisions about alliances and the formation of new parties. In addition, his detention during the colonial and postcolonial eras often featured questions about his mental health, and his case has been cited by those who seek a more comprehensive and Africa-centered approach to mental health in the country.

ARCHBISHOP MATTHEW AJUOGA (1925–)

Ajuoga is the founder of the Church of Christ in Africa, a large AIC that arose in western Kenya beginning in 1957. Also known as the *Johera*, Ajuoga's church arose after a schism from the Anglican Church and was registered in 1958. By 1990 it was estimated to have 200,000 members.

Ajuoga received his early education among Anglicans and was baptized in 1943. Ordained in 1954, he worked among Luos in western Kenya and advocated for unity in response to the *Balokole* movement connected to the East African Revival. He sought to appease those who wanted more freedom from missionary control, but eventually left the Anglican Church himself, along with a large number of clergy and others. In the mid-1960s, Ajuoga spent time studying at Union Theological Seminary in New York.

The personal story of Ajuoga has been captured in a remarkable study by George Pickens, in which the archbishop tells the "Johera narrative" about his religious experiences, his struggles for church unity, the resistance of missionary leaders, and the eventual decision to begin a new church.[22]

22. Pickens, *African Christian God-Talk*.

ARCHBISHOP JOHN SEPEKU AND JOHN EDMUND (D. 1975)

These two brothers were leaders in the Anglican Church of Tanzania. Sepeku was the first Anglican archbishop of Tanzania, named to the position after the formation of the separate national Anglican Church following the formal end of the Anglican Province of East Africa in 1970. He served until 1978. After a 1967 vision, his brother Edmund started an Anglican congregation in Dar es Salaam that served as the beginning of the House to House Fellowship, an ecumenical revival-like healing ministry centered on visiting the sick in their homes.

Born in Tanga, Sepeku and Edmund were two of five children. Prior to being named Tanzania's first Anglican archbishop, Sepeku served as assistant bishop in Zanzibar in 1963 before moving to be bishop of Dar es Salaam in 1965. His wife was the first head of Tanzania's branch of the Mothers' Union, a worldwide Anglican fellowship, beginning in 1970.

Before his vision, Edmund had a career in the civil service, then with Radio Tanzania. His healing ministry, however, grew into a full-time responsibility that drew many others with its revival-style spirituality, spreading far beyond its origins in Dar es Salaam. When he died, there were branches of the Fellowship across Tanzania and they have persisted to this day.

TEOFILO KISANJI (1915–1982), ANETH TUSANYE MBAPA KABISA (1915–1998), AND YOHANA LUCAS WAVENZA (1934–1999)

These are three prominent leaders among Moravians in Tanzania in the twentieth century. Kisanji was the first African to serve as bishop of the Moravian Church in Tanzania and an ecumenical leader among Tanzanian Christians in the 1960s and 1970s. Kabisa was a prominent leader among Moravian women, beginning by heading up women's organizations and then becoming the first woman elected to the Provincial Board of the Moravian Church in Southern Tanzania. Wavenza began his ministry in the church in the early 1960s, and in 1982 became the first bishop of the newly formed Southwest Province of the Moravian Church of Tanzania.

Kisanji's father was a Moravian evangelist. In the 1930s and 1940s, Kisanji served as a teacher in western Tanganyika, then in the 1950s studied theology in Europe before returning to duties as a pastor. A natural leader, he was elected superintendent of the Moravians of western Tanzania in 1962, then bishop three years later. He helped start a Moravian theological college in the late 1960s, which after a series of changes was named Teofilo Kisanji University, located in Mbeya. In the 1960s and 1970s he joined Lutheran bishop Stefano Moshi and Anglican John Sepeku in providing leadership to the Christian Council of Tanzania, which sought to build Christian unity in the new country. His own pastoral style was warm and wise, and he was admired by his fellow Moravians and other Tanzanians.

GRESFORD CHITEMO (1927–2009)

Chitemo served as an Anglican minister in Morogoro in Tanzania, eventually becoming its bishop in 1965. Eight years later he encountered the healing ministry of Edmund John, brother of CMS archbishop John Sepeku, and he himself became a leader in an evangelical and Pentecostal healing ministry, all the while continuing his episcopal leadership until his retirement in 1987. He then assumed leadership of African Evangelistic Enterprise for East Africa following the death of Festo Kivengere, holding the post until retiring in 1995.

Besides his much-appreciated formal ministry, Chitemo also served on an ecumenical team of translators that rendered the Bible in his native Kagulu language.

PASTOR ROBERT KAYANJA

Robert Kayanja is the founder and pastor of Miracle Centre Cathedral, also called the Rubaga Miracle Centre, a large Pentecostal Church in Kampala, Uganda. It is one of the largest churches in eastern Africa, holding 10,000 people, and its lively worship sessions are live-streamed each week on his television station. He has two older brothers who are also prominent Ugandan Christian leaders: John Sentamu, Anglican archbishop of York since 2005, and David Makumbi, a bishop in another independent church in Uganda.

Kayanja's ministry has brought him into contact with powerful Ugandan and international leaders, including the wife of Uganda's president, and famous preachers from around the world. His efforts to relieve hunger in South Sudan have received praise both within Uganda and outside. At the same time, he is a controversial figure, and both he and his ministry have been the subject of investigations into financial and sexual impropriety.

PASTOR JOSEPH SERWADDA

Serwadda and his wife Freda are the pastors of Victory Christian Centre (VCC), a large Pentecostal church in Kampala, Uganda. The ministry of the VCC includes television and radio broadcasts, as well as books and pamphlets.

Serwadda started preaching in the 1970s, when Idi Amin had outlawed preaching by independent churches in Uganda. After Amin's fall, Serwadda sought to reverse the slow growth of evangelical and Pentecostal churches in Uganda, which he blamed on the political refusal to allow such churches to register separately from the Anglican and Catholic churches. His preaching has been successful. Well known for large Passover Festival rallies at the Mandela National Stadium outside Kampala, with attendees numbering over 100,000, he has also become one of the foremost advocates against homosexuality in Uganda.

BENEDICTO KAGIMU MUGUMBA KIWANUKA (1922–1972)

One of a handful of eastern Africans who had studied at the university level in Europe in the colonial period, Benedict Kiwanuka was the first prime minister of Uganda and Democratic Party (DP) leader through Uganda's transition between colonial British rule and independence from 1961 to 1962. A fervent Catholic, he drew upon his faith to help found the DP, a party that appealed to Ugandan Catholics and drew in others who sought to move beyond ethnicity as a basis for political representation. The DP lost the first election for the presidency in 1962 to Milton Obote and his Uganda People's Congress despite having the largest single number of votes in the run-up election to independence.

In 1969, Kiwanuka was imprisoned by the Obote regime. Released by Amin after Obote was overthrown, he became Chief Justice of the Ugandan High Court in 1971. The next year, however, Amin turned on him, allegedly due to Kiwanuka's refusal to acquiesce in wanton disregard for law, something Kiwanuka decried with reference to his religious convictions. He was brutally murdered in 1972 and is revered by many as an honorable figure from the age of Uganda's coming to independence.

MARGARET WANJIRU (1961–)

Wanjiru leads the Jesus Is Alive Ministries, an independent church in Kenya. Founded in 1996 with only thirty members, Jesus Is Alive Ministries (JIAM) is now part of the larger Redeemed Gospel Church. Part of Wanjiru's message includes applications that Christ's nailed feet and hands were for the blessing of our hands and feet and that the holes punctured into Christ's hands are the assurance that "there can be no holes in our pockets or bank accounts (sic) because Christ has borne it on our behalf."[23]

Wanjiru was elected to the National Assembly of Kenya in 2007 and she served as Assistant Minister of Housing in 2008. Since entering politics, she has appeared in Kenyan papers accused of attempted bigamy in 2007, financial scandal linked to

23. Damaris Parsitau and Philomena Njeri Mwaura, "God in the City: Pentecostalism as an Urban Phenomenon in Kenya," *Studia Historiae Ecclesiasticae* 36, no. 2 (2010): 101.

property allegedly obtained by her church dishonestly in 2012, and electoral fraud in 2017.

PHILOMENA NJERI MWAURA (B. 1957)

Mwaura, a married Kenyan Catholic laywoman, is a distinguished scholar of African Christianity teaching at Kenyatta University in Nairobi. She has written extensively on many issues in African Christianity, especially women's leadership in African independent churches.

Mwaura is a former President of the International Association for Mission Studies, a member of the Circle of Concerned African Women Theologians, and the African region coordinator of the Theology Commission of the Ecumenical Association of Third World Theologians (EATWOT). Mwaura is a much sought-after speaker in international theological meetings.

ERASTUS OTIENO (1935–2000)

Erastus Otieno was an influential figure during the 1960s transition from missionary leadership to local leadership in the Pentecostal churches of Kenya. Otieno was born in Sare, in southwestern Kenya, and after schooling became a local teacher. During one of his teaching positions he encountered a Pentecostal church and joined it. Soon he moved into full-time ministry, eventually studying in the US between 1963 and 1966. Beginning in 1966, Otieno served as president of the Pentecostal Evangelistic Fellowship of Africa (PEFA), which began in 1962 with the merger of two Pentecostal churches, the Elim Missionary Assemblies Mission and the International Pentecostal Assemblies Mission. He provided leadership during a time of immense growth among Pentecostals in eastern Africa.

ANNA MARIA NAMUTEBI, OR MOTHER ANTOINETTA (1910–2006)

Mother Antoinetta served from 1949 to 1967 as superior general of the *Bannabikira* (Luganda for "Daughters of the Virgin") Sisters of Uganda, founded in central Uganda in 1910 as the first Roman Catholic religious order of women in sub-Saharan Africa. A visionary leader, she also served as a consultant to the Vatican's Congregation on the Evangelization of Peoples after Vatican II.

Anna Maria was born in central Uganda to pious parents, afterward joining the formation program of the *Bannabikira* Sisters. For several decades she served as a teacher and in the formation of younger sisters before moving to leadership of her congregation. A strong leader, she pushed for the professional formation of members of her congregation, the training of women and girls for social and political leadership, and the generation of income for self-support. In 1958, during her time as superior general, the *Bannabikira* Sisters gained the status of a Pontifical order, meaning that it was no longer under the direction of the Catholic bishops in Uganda.

SAMUEL KOBIA (B. 1947)

Kobia is a Kenyan Methodist clergyman and the first African to be elected General Secretary of the World Council of Churches (WCC), a position he held from 2004 to 2009.

Kobia was born in Meru, central Kenya, and eventually attended seminary at St. Paul's in Limuru. Soon after he went to Chicago to study urban ministry at McCormick Theological Seminary, proceeding from there to the Massachusetts Institute of Technology for a master's in City Planning, awarded in 1978. His thesis studied squatters' communities in Kenya, which prepared him to take the WCC post in charge of Urban Rural Mission that same year.

In 1984, Kobia returned to Kenya to oversee Church Development for the National Council of Churches of Kenya

(NCCK) and in 1987 he became NCCK General Secretary, serving until 1993. He then returned to the WCC, serving in several posts before becoming General Secretary in 2004. Kobia's retirement in 2009 came as a surprise, possibly related to a scandal over the validity of his claimed doctoral degree the previous year. He later earned a doctorate from the Christian Theological Seminary in Indianapolis.

Since leaving the WCC, Kobia has worked for the All Africa Conference of Churches on ecumenism and in pursuit of peace in South Sudan. He also has served on the Judicial Services Commission of the Kenyan government, appointed by President Uhuru Kenyatta, until he left in 2015.

Conclusion

Eastern Africa and World Christianity

In a journal entry from November 29, 1848, Johannes Krapf, the first missionary in eastern Africa in the modern period, wrote about his first convert:

> Mringe was with me during the night. We discoursed towards midnight about the world to come and the City of God; about the occupations of the blessed, and the incorruptible body of our future state, and many other things. My poor cripple devoured the words as they fell from my lips; and I saw that they made an impression on him, and felt happy indeed, for it is at moments like these that one feels the importance of a missionary's calling. A missionary who feels the working of the Spirit within him, and is upheld in its manifestation to others, is the happiest being upon earth. In his sight what are royal and imperial honours compared with the office of a preacher in the bush or lonely hut? And sure it is, that unless a missionary feels ennobled by his calling, he will forsake his post, or become an unprofitable labourer in the vineyard.[1]

Within a few years, Mringe was dead, having been baptized by Krapf's colleague Johannes Rebmann. Millions of eastern Africans have taken his place, as Christianity in the region has grown enormously since the mid-nineteenth century. The efforts of Krapf, Rebmann, and other "labourer[s] in the

1. This excerpt appears in an 1882 sketch of Krapf compiled from the *Church Mission Intelligencer*. It was drawn from "The Missionary Career of Dr. Krapf" (London: Gilbert and Rivington, 1882) as found on Project Canterbury, https://tinyurl.com/y94mwg3y.

vineyard" after them—most of them themselves eastern Africans—have grown and consolidated the Christian faith, transmitting it to generations afterward, proving themselves anything but unprofitable.

Many years later, with Christianity taking multiple and varying shapes in eastern Africa that Krapf and Rebmann never could have foreseen, one can admire the hopefulness and idealism in Krapf's musing, even as we cringe at his paternalistic tone. Kenya, Tanzania, and Uganda now house vital Christian communities of many sorts. Such bodies follow the aspirations of their adherents, which are at once very personal and yet also collectively create observable social trends. Believers' aspirations vary, but they usually consist of some combination of a desire for a hope-giving faith in a powerful God as revealed in Jesus in the Gospels and the Holy Spirit's ongoing dynamism, practical guidance in everyday life, supportive social networks, authentic rootedness in perceived cultural values, global connections, and a felt contribution to world Christianity.

In some ways, Christianity in eastern Africa epitomizes trends in contemporary Christianity elsewhere, resembling Christianity in other parts of Africa and around the globe. In other ways, however, it is distinctive, if not unique, embodying unusual features in its Christian profile. This book will conclude with brief reflections on Christianity in eastern Africa in relationship to Christianity elsewhere, and consider its likely shape in the future.

CHRISTIANITY IN EASTERN AFRICA IN LIGHT OF GLOBAL TRENDS

It is easy to recognize global trends among Christian churches and believers in eastern Africa. Like their coreligionists elsewhere, Christians in the region grow increasingly Pentecostal in their style of religious practice. Second, they expand the practices of their faith in ways that draw on religious forms at odds with their self-professed religious identity. A third commonality with many Christians elsewhere lies in the greater contact with other religious discourses and communities, especially, for eastern Africa, Islam. Fourth, Christianity finds its way into political life in new and complex ways. Amid these resemblances with Christianity elsewhere, however, there are certain distinctions within the larger trends.

PENTECOSTALIZATION IN EASTERN AFRICA

Pentecostalism in eastern Africa, while burgeoning, has not generated the large churches that have emerged elsewhere, such as in western Africa, southern Africa, or Brazil. Eastern Africans have joined Pentecostal churches founded in those regions —large ones with a global reach—but have not founded similar bodies of their own.

Attempts to explain the absence of this large institutional Pentecostal presence raise methodological problems, yet one might consider the formidable success of the East African Revival, beginning in the 1930s. Occurring mostly within existing mission-founded Protestant churches in Rwanda and Uganda, then in Kenya and Tanzania and beyond, it created patterns of revivalist Christianity that anticipated certain contemporary globalized Pentecostal patterns: for example, the public confession of sins, reliance on the gifts of the Holy Spirit, and the prominence of healing. One reason for the absence of large Pentecostal (or neo-Pentecostal) churches emerging from eastern Africa, therefore, might be that the earlier Revival satisfied religious desires that went unmet elsewhere in equally compelling ways. Admittedly, this represents an intuitive guess and further research would be required to make a stronger case.

CHRISTIAN IDENTITIES AND DIVERSE PRACTICES

With regard to a second global Christian trend—the tendency for believers to engage faith practices outside their formal denominational identities—eastern Africa follows suit, despite ongoing ties to particular denominations. In certain places, the identity of Christians in a region has remained the same for decades, with long-term bodies of various sorts continuing intact: for example, Catholics and Lutherans on the slopes of

Mount Kilimanjaro in Tanzania, Anglicans in much of central Uganda, Presbyterians in parts of central Kenya. Yet even places of relative Christian homogeneity undergo transformation, as believers in eastern Africa draw upon the diversity and availability of other denominational influences, shaping their faith-lives with aspects of religious practice and belief that come from outside previously conceived orthodoxies. Protestants have recourse to Catholic approaches to Mary, mother of Jesus, while Catholics pray in a Pentecostal fashion. Lutheran congregations, which might have been quite staid in their liturgical style into the 1960s, now at times pray in tongues and celebrate personal healing cults. Advances in video and social media draw the previously exotic onto anyone's screen and speakers, and videos and cassettes can be easily shared.

Within this larger trend of eclectic styles with Christian religious practice, eastern Africa has notably seen the emergence of forms of religion with roots in Christianity that stretch and challenge easy attempts to define Christianity in the first place. Already in the early twentieth century, for example, the religious movement linked to Musajjakawa Malaki in Uganda combined elements of traditional African religion and supposed Judaism with the ascendant Anglicanism of the new British territory. One of his early followers, Semei Kakungulu, later founded one of the few new Jewish communities to emerge in sub-Saharan Africa. Contemporary preachers on television at times transgress perceived Christian orthodoxies, with some very critical of prosperity preaching. The Holy Quaternity, a quasi-Christian group formed in western Uganda in the 1980s under the leadership of a former Catholic catechist, questions normative Christian beliefs about the triune God.

Global Christianity evinces a great deal of eclecticism in practice, but few regions have produced such notoriously para-Christian phenomena, especially recently, as eastern Africa. Groups with Christian origins in the region have not just been diverse but have even been linked to tragedy. Some have led to movements of armed resistance, for instance those appearing in northern Uganda beginning in the mid-1980s—first the Holy Spirit Movement under the direction of Alice Lakwena, later the Lord's Resistance Army under Joseph Kony. Both combined political organizing, Christian symbols, and traditional religious practices linked to local ethno-linguistic identity. Even more notoriously, the Movement for the Restoration of the Ten Commandments of God, founded and organized by onetime Catholic clergy and lay leaders, ended in the death of 900 adherents in western Uganda at Kanungu in 2000.

RELATIONS WITH ISLAM

Christians everywhere interact more than in the past with other believers in an increasingly interconnected world shaped by the flood of media and other forms of globalization, and eastern Africa is no exception. All three countries contain sizeable Muslim populations, with Tanzania's the largest in absolute and relative terms. In the region there remain areas that are largely Muslim, such as the coasts of Kenya and Tanzania, as well as the islands of the Indian Ocean like Zanzibar and Pemba. In other places, Christians predominate. Yet all major cities have sizeable populations of both Christians and Muslims, and relationships linked to commerce, education, leisure, and governance generate more regular interactions between Muslims and Christians than previously.

Compared to other parts of Africa, such as Nigeria and Sudan, eastern Africa has seen relatively little Muslim-Christian controversy, and open conflict along interreligious lines has been rare. Islam united some of the anti-colonial resistance in Kenya and Tanzania, but most such movements had dissipated by the mid-twentieth century. The national identities of the three countries each were constructed without religious essentialism; unlike Zambia, none has declared itself a Christian nation, and Uganda's brief declaration as an Islamic state under Idi Amin was rendered null soon after. Amin's regime in Uganda, ostensibly Muslim, sought ties with Islamic nations, and leaders from Saudi Arabia, Sudan, and Libya visited the country. Still, Amin never generated abiding pan-Muslim antagonisms against Christians in Uganda, and in the end his support was more regional and ethnic than religious.

Tanzania's origins, despite the violence by which the Omani-linked regime in Zanzibar was vanquished in 1964 leading to the federation of Zanzibar and what was then Tanganyika, allowed sufficient representation to Zanzibaris to allay suspicions of Christian hegemony, at least until recently. The pattern whereby Muslims and Christians have more or less alternated as head of state has generated ongoing control by the founding national party, the CCM (*Chama cha Mapinduzi*, KiSwahili for "Party of Revolution"), usually with majorities of the citizenry from both religions in support.

Like Uganda, Kenya's Muslim population is relatively small and relations with Christians have been mostly peaceful.[2] In Kenya, Muslims centered at the coast have never held national power, and rarely has there been significant tension with Kenya's Christians or the national government—at least from Muslims who are Kenya-born.

In the past few years, however, Islamic militant-inspired violence has erupted in all three countries, though its origins lie as much if not more in countries at the borders as from within Kenya, Tanzania, or Uganda. In Uganda, the liberalized religious climate of the post-Amin years has brought new forms of Islam into the country, often linked to Saudi Arabia, Libya, and Iran. In addition, the Allied Defense Force (ADF) claims Muslim identity and has been an intermittent anti-government military movement operating mostly in western Uganda and eastern Congo. Terrorist attacks linked to the ADF and to Al-Shabaab in Somalia—where Ugandan troops have been part of the African Union force—have also taken place over the past decade.

Violence traceable to Somalia's unrest has also led to deaths in Kenya, whose troops also fight in Somalia. Notoriously, Al-Shabaab militants attacked the Westgate Mall in Nairobi in September 2013, leading to the deaths of sixty-seven, and later in 2015 attacked Garissa University in the country's northeast, killing 148. In both cases, a few Kenyan Muslims were involved but the motivation lay outside of Kenya itself. As in the wake of

2. There were, however, reprisals against Muslims seen as allied to Amin after his fall in 1979, including some allegedly brutal massacres. See Abdulhakim A. Nsobya, "Uganda's Militant Islamic Movement ADF: A Historical Analysis," *Annual Review of Islam in Africa* 12/13 (2015–16): 32.

less deadly, yet still destructive, events in Uganda, local Muslims condemned the incidents. Such incidents have not unraveled generally peaceful relations between Christians and Muslims in the region.

Tanzania, which has the largest number of Muslims in the region, has also seen an uptick of violence linked to Muslim extremists, though less spectacularly than in Kenya. Most have occurred against minority Christians in heavily Muslim Zanzibar. Local Zanzibari Muslim authorities have decried such actions, which included a 2012 attack on a Catholic priest. At the same time, longstanding tensions with the national government rooted in Zanzibar's supposed historical sidelining can easily become anti-Christian in their tone.

Eastern Africa remains a place with relatively amicable relations between Muslims and Christians in all three countries. That said, historical tensions exist over perceptions of Muslim marginalization, and they might easily be stoked by Islamic insurgencies and political unrest in neighboring regions of abiding turmoil: Somalia, Sudan and South Sudan, and the eastern Congo.[3]

CHRISTIANITY AND POLITICS IN EASTERN AFRICA

Over the past several decades, observers of political life in Africa have noted the growing presence of religious language in political discourse, and eastern Africa in some ways follows that trend, especially Kenya.[4] At the same time, there remain significant structural supports for the official secular status of all three countries, so that each nation-state remains a substantial supporter of religious freedom, at least officially.

Elections in Uganda and Tanzania, though not without their problems, rarely occasion religiously motivated controversy. One reason might be the substantial strength of mainline Christian denominations like Roman Catholics, Lutherans, and Angli-

3. Abdisaid M. Ali, "Islamic Extremism in East Africa," *Africa Security Brief* 32 (August 2016): https://tinyurl.com/yashbcva.

4. Jon Abbink, "Religion and Politics in Africa: The Future of the 'Secular,'" *Africa Spectrum* 49, no. 3 (2014): 83–106.

cans, whose denominational global stances vis-à-vis politics support secular governance. From the late 1950s into the 1970s, Uganda's Catholics and Anglicans were linked to the two largest parties, leading to disunity and unrest, but those parties and denominationally linked affiliations play small roles today. In Tanzania, where Muslims and Christians are nearly equal in number, there exist several Muslim-linked parties, but none has successfully represented a majority of the country's Muslims. Though Christians make up a majority of the ruling party's voters, the CCM, it is not seen as simply representative of Christian interests.

In Kenya, too, larger global Christian communities remain strong, and parties rarely become tied to religious adherence. One difference with its eastern African neighbors, however, lies in the more overtly Christian tone of Kenya's political discourse. In particular, the political violence linked to the election in 2007 seems to have heightened the distinctly evangelical Christian tone in national political conversations, a tone that was present in the 2013 and 2017 elections, where the personal righteousness of candidates was publicly debated.[5] Neo-Pentecostal preachers refer often to chapter 13 of Paul's letter to the Romans and its injunctions to support legitimate authorities. Certain observers have become concerned about the shape of that discourse, which can alienate not only non-Christians, but also Christians who resist born-again language.[6] References to Christian symbolism and supernatural beliefs had shaped Kenyan politics earlier, too, with the Parliament even investigating alleged Satanism in the 1990s,[7] but the current salience of Christian language seems linked to concerns about more recent political violence.

Still, even in Kenya many prominent religious leaders, especially among the larger religious groups, express hopes that

5. Gregory Deacon, "Driving the Devil Out: Kenya's Born-Again Election," *Journal of Religion in Africa* 45, no. 2 (2015): 200–220.

6. Gifford, *Christianity, Politics, and Public Life*; Gifford, *Christianity, Development and Modernity*.

7. Rosalind Hackett, "Is Satan Local or Global? Reflections on a Nigerian Deliverance Movement," in *Who Is Afraid of the Holy Ghost? Pentecostalism and Globalization in Africa and Beyond*, ed. Afe Adogame (Trenton, NJ: Africa World, 2011), 114. The resulting report, issued in 1999, was mocked by journalists and its results faced scrutiny from the US State Department.

greater political stability will allow churches to avoid formal politics as political parties become more responsive to the needs of the electorate. Most Christian leaders seek to avoid formal political engagement. Acknowledging his fellow bishops' role in the 1990s efforts to move toward multi-party democracy, one Kenyan Catholic bishop said that it was different now: "'We don't need to be involved as we once were,' since it was now 'the role of political parties to mobilize people.'"[8] They had been willing to challenge an unjust political system but have no desire for an abiding political role.

THE FUTURE OF CHRISTIANITY IN EASTERN AFRICA

It seems likely that the vitality, variety, and volatility of Christianity in eastern Africa highlighted in the introduction will only grow. Numerous Christian bodies thrive, new ways of being Christian appear, and Christianity continues to generate controversy—sometimes through tragedies like the deaths in Kanungu, Uganda, in 2001, and also when Christian tropes enter electioneering cycles in polarizing ways. And sometimes almost as farce, as when a retired Lutheran pastor in northern Tanzania began a healing ministry in 2011, inviting suffering people to drink a concoction guaranteed for healing. Protected by the national Lutheran church as well as government security figures, his popular movement evaporated after several people with HIV/AIDS stopped taking their anti-retroviral drugs and died quickly.[9]

Meanwhile, Christianity in the region faces new circumstances and its adherents respond using the resources within their faith. Emmanuel Katongole has highlighted Christian responses to needs for social reconciliation after violent trauma, and eastern Africa not only serves as a setting for many of the processes he describes, but hosts meetings that address such issues

8. Mark Juergensmeyer, Dinah Griego, and John Soboslai, *God in the Tumult of the Global Square: Religion in Global Civil Society* (Berkeley: University of California Press, 2015), 25.

9. Mika Vähäkangas, "Babu wa Loliondo—Healing the Tensions between Tanzanian Worlds," *Journal of Religion in Africa* 45, no. 1 (2015): 3–36.

in neighboring countries and regions.[10] The presence of Chinese settlers in eastern Africa has led some mission-minded congregations to consider how to evangelize the newcomers.[11] Contemporary Pentecostal Christians have tried to Christianize female initiation rites in Kenya that in the past featured so-called genital mutilation, returning in a new way to a missionary goal of the colonial period that eventuated in the so-called "Female Circumcision Crisis" of the late 1920s.[12] No doubt the future will create more novelty, as well as new approaches to older issues.

One thing seems likely: unlike parts of Europe and the US, whose future might signal a post-Christian society, the role of Christianity in eastern Africa within the world Christian movement seems likely to increase. Uganda, Kenya, and Tanzania all possess institutional structures poised to support the globalization of Christian discourses and practices. These include widespread facility in English, comparative political stability, an attractive climate, universities interested in religion and possessing resources, as well as relatively livable cities where African elites, expatriates, the urban poor, and different forms of vibrant Christianity exist. The same features make the region a frequent beneficiary of development efforts, some linked to Christianity, efforts that lately have drawn scrutiny from wary national governments. As the world Christian movement moves ahead, its embodiment in eastern Africa promises to remain an important setting for whatever unfolds.

10. Katongole, *Sacrifice of Africa*; Katongole, *Born from Lament*.

11. Wenhui Gong and Kenneth Nehrbass, "Reaching Out to Diaspora Chinese in East Africa: Barriers and Bridges," *Missiology* 45, no. 3 (2017): 236–51.

12. Yvan Droz, "Jeunesse et âge adulte en pays kikuyu: Des éthos précoloniaux aux nouveaux mouvements politico-religieux," *Cahier d'études africaines* 55, no. 218 (2015): 213–30.

Bibliography

Abbink, Jon. "Religion and Politics in Africa: The Future of the 'Secular.'" *Africa Spectrum* 49, no. 3 (2014): 83–106.

Adeney, Frances S. *Women and Christian Mission: Ways of Knowing and Doing Theology*. Eugene, OR: Pickwick, 2015.

Adogame, Afe, ed. *Who Is Afraid of the Holy Ghost? Pentecostalism and Globalization in Africa and Beyond*. Trenton, NJ: Africa World, 2011.

Adogame, Afe, Roswith Gerloff, and Klaus Hock, eds. *Christianity in Africa and the African Diaspora: The Appropriation of a Scattered Heritage*. London: Continuum, 2008.

Adogame, Afe, and Lazio Jafta. "Zionists, Aladura and Roho: African Instituted Churches." In *African Christianity: An African Story*, edited by Ogbu Kalu, 270–87. Trenton, NJ: Africa World, 2007.

Akiri, Raphael Mwita. "The Growth of Christianity in Ugogo and Ukaguru (Central Tanzania): A Socio-Historical Analysis of the Role of Indigenous Agents, 1876–1933." PhD thesis, University of Edinburgh, 1999.

Ali, Abdisaid M. "Islamic Extremism in East Africa." *Africa Security Brief* 32 (August 2016): https://tinyurl.com/yashbcva.

Allen, Richard B. *European Slave Trading in the Indian Ocean, 1500–1850*. Athens: Ohio University Press, 2014.

Alonso, Carlos. *A History of the Augustinians and the Martyrs of Mombasa (1568–1698)*. Nairobi: Paulines Publications, 2007.

Anderson, David M., and Douglas H. Johnson, eds. *Revealing Prophets: Prophecy in Eastern African History*. London: James Currey, 1995.

Anderson, William B. "Africa." In *A History of Presbyterian Missions, 1944–2007*, edited by Scott W. Sunquist and Caroline N. Becker, 234–55. Louisville: Geneva, 2008.

———. *The Church in East Africa: 1840–1974*. Translated by Maureen Eyles. Dodoma, Tanzania: Central Tanganyika Press, 1977.

Anderson-Morshead, A. E. M. *The History of the Universities' Mission to Central Africa, 1859–1909*. London: Butler & Tanner, 1909.

Azetsop, Jacquineau, ed. *HIV and AIDS in Africa: Christian Reflection, Public Health, Social Transformation*. Maryknoll, NY: Orbis, 2016.

Bagumisiriza, Narcisio. *The Kanungu Tragedy: 17th March 2000 and Details of Related Discoveries about "The Movement for the Restoration of the Ten Commandments of God."* Kabale, Uganda: Kabale Diocese, n.d.

Baur, John. *2000 Years of Christianity in Africa: An African Church History*. 2nd ed. Nairobi: Daughters of St. Paul, 1998.

Behrend, Heike. *Alice Lakwena and the Holy Spirits: War in Northern Uganda, 1986–1997*. Kampala: Fountain Publishers, 1999.

Bellagamba, Alice, Sandra E. Greene, and Martin Klein, eds. *African Voices on Slavery and the Slave Trade*. Cambridge: Cambridge University Press, 2013.

Bennett, Norman R. *Arab versus European: Diplomacy and War in Nineteenth-Century East Central Africa*. New York: Africana Publishing, 1986.

———. *Studies in East African History*. Boston: Boston University Press, 1963.

Benson, John S. *Missionary Families Find a Sense of Place and Identity: Two Generations on Two Continents*. London: Lexington, 2015.

Bongmba, Elias Kifon, ed. *The Routledge Companion to Christianity in Africa*. New York: Routledge, 2016.

Bowen, John P., ed. *The Missionary Letters of Vincent Donovan, 1957–1973*. Eugene, OR: Pickwick, 2011.

Brennan, James R. *TAIFA: Making Nation and Race in Urban Tanzania*. Athens: Ohio University Press, 2012.

Bridges, Roy. "The Christian Vision and Secular Imperialism: Missionaries, Geography, and the Approach to East Africa, c. 1844–1890." In *Converting Colonialism: Visions and Realities in Mission History, 1706–1914*, edited by Dana Robert, 43–59. Grand Rapids: Eerdmans, 2008.

Brinkman, Martien E. *The Non-Western Jesus: Jesus as* Bodhisattva, Avatara, Guru, *Prophet, Ancestor or Healer?* London: Equinox, 2009.

Bujo, Bénézet, ed. *African Theology: The Contribution of the Pioneers.* Vol. 3. Nairobi: Paulines Publications, 2012.

Bujo, Bénézet, and Juvénal Ilunga Muya, eds. *African Theology: The Contribution of the Pioneers.* Vol. 1. Nairobi: Paulines Publications, 2003.

———, eds. *African Theology: The Contribution of the Pioneers.* Vol. 2. Nairobi: Paulines Publications, 2008.

Bunker, Stephen G. *Peasants against the State: The Politics of Market Control in Bugisu, Uganda, 1900–1983.* Chicago: University of Chicago Press, 1987.

Burgman, Hans. *The Way the Catholic Church Started in Western Kenya.* Nairobi: Mission Book Service, 1990.

Burlacioiu, Ciprian. "Expansion without Western Missionary Agency and Constructing Confessional Identities: The African Orthodox Church Between the United States, South Africa, and East Africa (1921–1940)." *Journal of World Christianity* 6, no. 1 (2016): 82–98.

Bwangatto, Ambrose John, ed. *Africa Is Not Destined to Die: Signs of Hope and Renewal.* Nairobi: Paulines Publications, 2012.

Calderisi, Robert. *Earthly Mission: The Catholic Church and World Development.* New Haven: Yale University Press, 2013.

Campbell, Gwyn, and Alessandro Stanziani, eds. *Bonded Labour and Debt in the Indian Ocean World.* London: Pickering & Chatto, 2013.

Campbell, John R. "Who Are the Luo? Oral Tradition and Disciplinary Practices in Anthropology and History." *Journal of African Cultural Studies* 18, no. 1 (2006): 73–87.

Carpenter, Joel. "New Evangelical Universities: Cogs in a World System or Players in a New Game?" In *Interpreting Contemporary Christianity: Global Processes and Local Identities*, edited by Ogbu U. Kalu and Alaine Low, 151–86. Grand Rapids: Eerdmans, 2008.

Carpenter, Joel, Perry L. Glanzer, and Nicholas S. Lantinga, eds. 2014. *Christian Higher Education: A Global Renaissance*. Grand Rapids: Eerdmans, 2014.

Ceillier, Jean-Claude. *History of the Missionaries of Africa (White Fathers)*. Nairobi: Paulines Publications, 2011.

Chesworth, John A. "Fundamentalism and Outreach Strategies in East Africa: Christian Evangelism and Muslim *Da'wa*." In *Muslim-Christian Encounters in Africa*, edited by Benjamin F. Soares, 159–86. Leiden: Brill, 2006.

Chrétien, Jean-Pierre. *The Great Lakes of Africa: Two Thousand Years of History*. Translated by Scott Straus. New York: Zone Books, 2003.

Chummar, Paul. "HIV/AIDS in Africa: An Urgent Task for an Inculturated Theological Ethics." In *Applied Ethics in a World Church: The Padua Conference*, edited by Linda Hogan, 155–62. Maryknoll, NY: Orbis, 2008.

Cisternino, Mario. *Passion for Africa: Missionary and Imperial Papers on the Evangelisation of Uganda and Sudan, 1848–1923*. Kampala: Fountain, 2004.

Cohen, David William, and E. S. Atieno Odhiambo. *Siaya: The Historical Anthropology of an African Landscape*. London: James Currey, 1989.

Collins, Robert O. *Eastern African History*. Vol. 2 of *African History: Text and Readings*. New York: Markus Wiener, 1990.

Cooper, Frederick. *Plantation Slavery on the East Coast of Africa*. New Haven: Yale University Press, 1977.

———. *From Slaves to Squatters: Plantation Labor and Agriculture in Zanzibar and Coastal Kenya, 1890–1925*. New Haven: Yale University Press, 1980.

Cronk, Lee. *From Mukogodo to Maasai: Ethnicity and Cultural Change in Kenya*. Cambridge: Westview, 2004.

Crozier, Anna. "Sensationalizing Africa: British Medical Impressions of Sub-Saharan Africa, 1890–1939." *Journal of Imperial and Commonwealth History* 35, no. 3 (2007): 393–415.

Darch, John H. *Missionary Imperialists? Missionaries, Government and the Growth of the British Empire in the Tropics, 1860–1885*. Milton Keynes, UK: Paternoster, 2009.

Daughrity, Dyron B. *Bishop Stephen Neill: From Edinburgh to South India*. New York: Peter Lang, 2008.

Deacon, Gregory. "Driving the Devil Out: Kenya's Born-Again Election." *Journal of Religion in Africa* 45, no. 2 (2015): 200–220.

De Jong, Albert. *The Challenge of Vatican II in East Africa: The Contribution of Dutch Missionaries to the Implementation of Vatican II in Tanzania, Kenya, Uganda, and Malawi, 1965–1975*. Nairobi: Paulines Publications, 2004.

———. *Father Michael Witte of Kabaa High School, Missionary and Educationist: A Study in Mission Strategy*. Nairobi: Paulines Publications, 2011.

———. *Mission and Politics in Eastern Africa: Dutch Missionaries and African Nationalism in Kenya, Tanzania and Malawi, 1945–1965*. Nairobi: Paulines Publications, 2000.

Doerr, Lambert. *Peramiho, 1898–1998: In the Service of the Missionary Church*. 3 vols. Ndanda-Peramiho, Tanzania: Benedictine Publications, 1998.

Domingues, Fernando. *Christ Our Healer: A Theological Dialogue with Aylward Shorter*. Nairobi: Paulines Publications, 2000.

Donovan, Vincent. *Christianity Rediscovered*. Chicago: Fides/Claretian, 1978.

Dowd, Robert A. *Christianity, Islam, and Liberal Democracy in Africa*. Oxford: Oxford University Press, 2015.

Doyle, Shane. *Before HIV: Sexuality, Fertility and Mortality in East Africa, 1900–1980*. Oxford: British Academy, 2013. (Available only electronically via Oxford University Press.)

———. *Crisis and Decline in Bunyoro: Population and Environment in Western Uganda, 1860–1955*. Athens: Ohio University Press, 2006.

Droz, Yvan. "Jeunesse et âge adulte en pays kikuyu: Des éthos précoloniaux aux nouveaux mouvements politico-religieux." *Cahier d'études africaines* 55, no. 218 (2015): 213–30.

Dube, Musa. "Christianity and Translation in the Colonial Context." In *The Routledge Companion to Christianity in Africa*, edited by Elias Kifon Bongmba, 156–72. New York: Routledge, 2016.

Englund, Harri, ed. *Christianity and Public Culture in Africa*. Cambridge: Cambridge University Press, 2011.

Ezigbo, Victor I. "Jesus as God's Communicative and Hermeneutical Act: African Christians on the Person and Significance of Jesus Christ." In *Jesus without Borders*, edited by Gene L. Green, Stephen T. Pardue, and K. K. Yeo, 37–58. Grand Rapids: Eerdmans, 2014.

Faupel, J. F. *African Holocaust: The Story of the Uganda Martyrs*. New York: P. J. Kenedy, 1962.

Feierman, Steven. *Peasant Intellectuals: Anthropology and History in Tanzania*. Madison: University of Wisconsin Press, 1990.

Fiedler, Klaus. *Christianity and African Culture: Conservative Protestant Missionaries in Tanzania, 1900–1940*. Leiden: Brill, 1996.

Fiedler, R. N., and J. W. Hofmeyr. "The Conception of the Circle of Concerned African Women Theologians: Is It African or Western?" *Acta Theologica* 31, no. 1 (2011): 39–57.

Frere, Sir Bartle. 1873. Correspondence concerning the mission of Sir Bartle Frere. Archives of the Congregation of the Holy Ghost, Chevilly-Larue, France. Box 196bi, #3.

Gale, H. P. *Uganda and the Mill Hill Fathers*. London: Macmillan, 1959.

Gatu, John G. *Fan into Flame*. Nairobi: Moran, 2016.

Gaume, J. *Suéma: Or the Little African Slave Who Was Buried Alive*. Translated by Mary Elizabeth Herbert. London: Burns, Oates, 1870.

Getui, Mary N., ed. *Theological Method and Aspects of Worship in African Christianity*. Nairobi: Acton, 1998.

Getui, Mary N., and Peter Kanyandago, eds. *From Violence to Peace: A Challenge for African Christianity*. Nairobi: Acton, 1999.

Gibellini, Rosino, ed. *Paths of African Theology*. Maryknoll, NY: Orbis, 1994.

Giblin, James L. *The Politics of Environmental Control in Northeastern Tanzania, 1840–1940*. Philadelphia: University of Pennsylvania Press, 1992.

Gifford, Paul. *African Christianity: Its Public Role*. Bloomington: Indiana University Press, 1998.

———. *Christianity, Development and Modernity in Africa*. London: Hurst, 2015.

———. *Christianity, Politics, and Public Life in Kenya*. New York: Columbia University Press, 2009.

Githieya, Francis Kimani. "The Church of the Holy Spirit: Biblical Beliefs and Practices of the Arathi of Kenya, 1926–1950." In *East African Expressions of Christianity*, edited by Thomas Spear and Isaria N. Kimambo, 231–43. Oxford: James Currey, 1999.

Glanzer, Perry L., and Joel Carpenter. "Evaluating the Health of Christian Higher Education around the Globe." In *Christian Higher Education: A Global Renaissance*, edited by Joel Carpenter, Perry L. Glanzer, and Nicholas S. Lantinga, 277–305. Grand Rapids: Eerdmans, 2014.

Glassman, Jonathon. *Feasts and Riot: Revelry, Rebellion, and Popular Consciousness on the Swahili Coast, 1856–1888*. Portsmouth, NH: Heinemann, 1995.

———. "Racial Violence, Universal History, and Echoes of Abolition in Twentieth-Century Zanzibar." In *Abolitionism and Imperialism in Britain, Africa, and the Atlantic*, edited by Derek R. Peterson, 174–206. Athens: Ohio University Press, 2010.

Gogan, Cothrai. *History of the Holy Ghost Mission in Kenya*. Nairobi: Paulines Publications, 2005.

Gong, Wenhui, and Kenneth Nehrbass. "Reaching Out to Diaspora Chinese in East Africa: Barriers and Bridges." *Missiology* 45, no. 3 (2017): 236–51.

Green, Gene L., Stephen T. Pardue, and K. K. Yeo, eds. *Jesus without Borders*. Grand Rapids: Eerdmans, 2014.

———, eds. *The Trinity among the Nations: The Doctrine of God in the Majority World*. Grand Rapids: Eerdmans, 2015.

Green, Maia. *Priests, Witches and Power: Popular Christianity after Mission in Southern Tanzania*. Cambridge: Cambridge University Press, 2003.

Gribble, Richard. *Vincent McCauley, C.S.C.: Bishop of the Poor, Apostle of East Africa*. Notre Dame, IN: Ave Maria, 2008.

Groop, Kim. *With the Gospel to Maasailand: Lutheran Missionary Work among the Arusha and Maasai in Northern Tanzania, 1904–1973*. Åbo, Finland: Åbo Akademi University Press, 2006.

Hackett, Rosalind. "Is Satan Local or Global? Reflections on a Nigerian Deliverance Movement." In *Who Is Afraid of the Holy Ghost? Pentecostalism and Globalization in Africa and Beyond*, edited by Afe Adogame, 111–27. Trenton, NJ: Africa World, 2011.

Hansen, Holger Bernt. *Mission, Church and State in a Colonial Setting: Uganda, 1890–1925*. New York: St. Martin's, 1984.

Hansen, Holger Bernt, and Michael Twaddle, eds. *Changing Uganda: The Dilemmas of Structural Adjustment and Revolutionary Change*. London: James Currey, 1991.

———, eds. *Religion and Politics in East Africa*. Athens: Ohio University Press, 1995.

———, eds. *Uganda Now: Between Decay and Development*. London: James Currey, 1988.

Harris, Joseph E. *Recollections of James Juma Mbotela*. Nairobi: East African Publishing, 1977.

Hastings, Adrian. *The Church in Africa: 1450–1950*. Oxford: Oxford University Press, 1994.

———. *A History of African Christianity, 1950–1975*. Cambridge: Cambridge University Press, 1979.

Hayes, Stephen. "Orthodox Mission in Tropical Africa." *Missionalia* 24 (1996): 383–98.

Haynes, Jeff. *Religion and Politics in Africa*. Nairobi: East African Educational Publishers, 1996.

Healey, Joseph G. *Building the Church as the Family of God: Evaluation of Small Christian Communities in Eastern Africa*. Limuru, Kenya: Catholic University of Eastern Africa, 2012.

Healey, Joseph G., and Jeanne Hinton, eds. *Small Christian Communities Today: Capturing the New Moment*. Maryknoll, NY: Orbis, 2005.

Healey, Joseph G., and Donald Sybertz. *Towards an African Narrative Theology*. Maryknoll, NY: Orbis, 1996.

Hellberg, Carl J. *Missions on a Colonial Frontier West of Lake of Victoria: Evangelical Missions in North-West Tanganyika to 1932*. Translated by Eric Sharpe. Uppsala, Sweden: Gleerups, 1965.

Hertlein, Siegfried. *Ndanda Abbey*. Part 1, *Beginning and Development up to 1932*. St. Ottilien, Germany: EOS, 2008.

———. *Ndanda Abbey*. Part 2, *The Church Takes Root in Difficult Times, 1932–1952*. St. Ottilien, Germany: EOS, 2011.

Hildebrandt, Jonathan. *History of the Church in Africa: A Survey*. Achimota, Ghana: Africa Christian Press, 1987.

Hinga, Teresia. "Teaching to Transform: Theological Education, Global Consciousness, and the Making of Global Citizens." In *Teaching Global Theologies: Power and Praxis*, edited by Kwok Pui-lan, Cecilia González-Andrieu, and Dwight N. Hopkins, 125–42. Waco, TX: Baylor University Press, 2015.

Hodgson, Dorothy L. *The Church of Women: Gendered Encounters between Maasai and Missionaries*. Bloomington: Indiana University Press, 2005.

Hoehler-Fatton, Cynthia. *Women of Fire and Spirit: History, Faith, and Gender in Roho Religion in Western Kenya*. Oxford: Oxford University Press, 1996.

Hofmeyr, J. W. "Mainline Churches in the Public Space, 1975–2000." In *African Christianity: An African Story*, edited by Ogbu Kalu, 314–37. Trenton, NJ: Africa World, 2007.

Hogan, Linda, ed. *Applied Ethics in a World Church: The Padua Conference*. Maryknoll, NY: Orbis, 2008.

Höschele, Stefan. *Christian Remnant—African Folk Church: Seventh-Day Adventism in Tanzania, 1903–1980*. Leiden: Brill, 2007.

Iliffe, John. *A Modern History of Tanganyika*. Cambridge: Cambridge University Press, 1979.

Isabirye, Bukyanagandi Anthony. *Challenges to Traditional Methods of Catholic Evangelization in Busoga Region (1889–2004)*. Kisubi, Uganda: Marianum, 2007.

Isichei, Elizabeth. *A History of African Societies to 1870*. Cambridge: Cambridge University Press, 1997.

———. *A History of Christianity in Africa: From Antiquity to the Present*. Grand Rapids: Eerdmans, 1995.

Jaeschke, Ernst. *Bruno Gutmann: His Life, His Thoughts, and His Work*. Arusha, Tanzania: Makumira, 1985.

Jones, Ben. "Pentecostalism and Development in Sub-Saharan Africa: In the Office and in the Village." In *Pentecostalism in Africa: Presence and Impact of Pneumatic Christianity in Postcolonial Societies*, edited by Martin Lindhardt, 248–69. Leiden: Brill, 2015.

Juergensmeyer, Mark, Dinah Griego, and John Soboslai. *God in the Tumult of the Global Square: Religion in Global Civil Society*. Berkeley: University of California Press, 2015.

Kabazzi-Kisirnya, S., Nkurunziza R. K. Deusdedit, and Banura Gerard, eds. *The Kanungu Cult-Saga: Suicide, Murder or Salvation?* Kampala: Marianum, 2000.

Kalu, Ogbu, ed. *African Christianity: An African Story*. Trenton, NJ: Africa World, 2007.

———. *African Pentecostalism: An Introduction*. Oxford: Oxford University Press, 2008.

———, ed. *Interpreting Contemporary Christianity: Global Processes and Local Identities*. Grand Rapids: Eerdmans, 2008.

Kamau-Goro, Nicholas. "Rejection or Reappropriation? Christian Allegory and the Critique of Postcolonial Public Culture in the Early Novels of Ngũgĩ wa Thiongo'o." In *Christianity and Public Culture in Africa*, edited by Harri Englund, 67–85. Cambridge: Cambridge University Press, 2011.

Kanyandago, Peter, ed. *Cries of the Poor in Africa: An International Perspective*. Kisubi: Marianum Publishing, 2002.

———. "Is God African? Theological Reflections on the AIDS Scourge." In *Challenges and Prospects for the Church in Africa: Theological Reflections for the 21st Century*, edited by Nahashon W. Ndung'u and Philomena Mwaura, 145–59. Nairobi: Paulines Publications, 2005.

———. "John Mary Waliggo: The Theology of John Mary Waliggo." In *African Theology: The Contribution of the Pioneers*, vol. 2, edited by Bénézet Bujo and Juvénal Ilunga Muya, 215–30. Nairobi: Paulines Publications, 2008.

———. "'Let Us Feed the Children First' (Mark 7:27): The Church's Response to the Inequitable Extraction of Resources and Related Violence." In *Reconciliation, Justice, and Peace: The Second African Synod*, edited by Agbonkhianmeghe E. Orobator, 159–70. Nairobi: Acton, 2011.

———, ed. *Marginalised Africa: An International Perspective*. Nairobi: Paulines Publications, 2002.

———. "Towards Reconciliation and Healing in Africa." In *African Theology Comes of Age: Revisiting Twenty Years of the Theology of the Ecumenical Symposium of Eastern African Theologians (ESEAT)*, edited by Laurenti Magesa, 107–22. Nairobi: Paulines Publications, 2010.

Karanja, John. "The Role of Kikuyu Christians in Developing a Self-Consciously African Anglicanism." In *The Church Mission Society and World Christianity, 1799–1999*, edited by Kevin Ward and Brian Stanley. Grand Rapids: Eerdmans, 2000.

Katongole, Emmanuel. "AIDS, Africa, and the 'Age of Miraculous Medicine': Naming the Silences." In *Applied Ethics in a World Church: The Padua Conference*, edited by Linda Hogan, 137–46. Maryknoll, NY: Orbis, 2008.

———. *Born from Lament: The Theology of Politics and Hope in Africa.* Grand Rapids: Eerdmans, 2017.

———. *The Sacrifice of Africa: A Political Theology for Africa.* Grand Rapids: Eerdmans, 2010.

Kenyatta, Jomo. *Facing Mount Kenya: The Tribal Life of the Gikuyu.* London: Secker & Warburg, 1938.

Kimambo, Isaria N. "The Impact of Christianity among the Zaramo: A Case Study of Maneromango Lutheran Parish." In *East African Expressions of Christianity*, edited by Thomas Spear and Isaria N. Kimambo, 63–82. Oxford: James Currey, 1999.

———. *Penetration and Protest in Tanzania: The Impact of the World Economy on the Pare, 1860–1960.* London: James Currey, 1991.

Kimambo, Isaria N., Eliud Lushino Abdallah Lukwaro, and Paulo Mashambo. *A Peasant and Political Leader in Upare: Paulo Mashambo.* Dar es Salaam: Historical Association of Tanzania, 1987.

Kimball, Herbert, and Beatrice Kimball. *Go into All the World: A Centennial Celebration of Friends in East Africa.* Richmond, IN: Friends United, 2002.

Kinoti, H. W., and J. M. Waliggo, eds. *The Bible in African Christianity: Essays in Biblical Theology*. Nairobi: Acton, 1997.

Kirwen, Michael C., ed. *African Cultural Knowledge: Themes and Embedded Beliefs.* Nairobi: MIAS Books, 2005.

———. "Africans in Global Mission." In *Exploring the Future of Mission in Africa: In Celebration of Maryknoll's 100 Years in Mission*, edited by Laurenti Magesa and Michael C. Kirwen, 9–14. Nairobi: Maryknoll Institute of African Studies, 2012.

Kiwanuka, Joseph. *Church and State.* Pastoral Letter. Kampala, 1961.

Kiyamba, Abasi. "'The Domestic Relations Bill' and Inter-Religious Conflict in Uganda: A Muslim Reading of Personal Law and Religious Pluralism in a Postcolonial Society." In *Displacing the State: Religion and Conflict in Neoliberal Africa*, edited by James Howard Smith and Rosalind I. J. Hackett, 240–80. Notre Dame: University of Notre Dame Press, 2012.

Kjekshus, Helge. *Ecology Control and Economic Development in East African History*. Berkeley: University of California Press, 1977.

Klobuchar, Jim. *The Cross under the Acacia Tree: The Story of David and Eunice Simonson's Epic Mission Africa*. Minneapolis: Kirk House, 1998.

Klopp, Jacqueline. "The NCCK and the Struggle against 'Ethnic Clashes' in Kenya." In *Religion and Politics in Kenya: Essays in Honor of a Meddlesome Priest*, edited by Ben Knighton, 183–99. New York: Palgrave Macmillan, 2009.

Knighton, Ben, ed. *Religion and Politics in Kenya: Essays in Honor of a Meddlesome Priest*. New York: Palgrave Macmillan, 2009.

Kollman, Paul V. "Classifying African Religions Past, Present, and Future: Part One. Ogbu Kalu and the Appropriation of Pentecostalism." *Journal of Religion in Africa* 40, no. 1 (2010): 3–32.

———. *The Evangelization of Slaves and Catholic Origins in Eastern Africa*. Maryknoll, NY: Orbis, 2005.

Kombo, James Henry Owino. *The Doctrine of God in African Christian Thought: The Holy Trinity, Theological Hermeneutics and the African Intellectual Culture*. Leiden: Brill, 2007.

Koponen, Juhani. *Development for Exploitation: German Colonial Policies in Mainland Tanzania, 1884–1914*. Helsinki: Finnish Historical Society, 1994.

Koren, Henry J. *The Evolution of the Church in Africa since the Beginning of the Nineteenth Century*. Bethel Park, PA. Unpublished manuscript, N.d.

Kuhn, Marko. *Prophetic Christianity in Western Kenya: Political, Cultural and Theological Aspects of African Independent Churches*. Frankfurt am Main: Peter Lang, 2008.

Kunhiyop, Samuel Waje. "The Trinity in Africa: Trends and Trajectories." In *The Trinity among the Nations: The Doctrine of God in the Majority World*, edited by Gene L. Green, Stephen T. Pardue, and K. K. Yeo, 55–68. Grand Rapids: Eerdmans, 2015.

Kustenbauder, Matthew. "Believing in the Black Messiah: The Legio Maria Church in an African Landscape." *Novo Religio* 13, no. 1 (2009): 11–40.

Kyomuhendo, Grace Bantebya, and Marjorie Keniston McIntosh. *Women, Work and Domestic Virtue in Uganda, 1900–2003*. Oxford: James Currey, 2006.

Lambert, C. A., and S. A. Tishkoff. "Genetic Structure in African Populations: Implications for Human Demographic History." *Cold Spring Harbor Symposia on Quantitative Biology* 74 (2009): 395–402.

Lambourn, R. G. P. "Zanzibar to Masasi in 1876: The Founding of the Masasi Mission." *Tanganyika Notes and Records* 31 (1951): 42–46.

Larsson, Birgitta. *Conversion to Greater Freedom? Women, Church and Social Change in North-Western Tanzania under Colonial Rule*. Uppsala, Sweden: Acta Universitatis Upsaliensis, 1991.

Lema, Anza A. "Chaga Religion and Missionary Christianity on Kilimanjaro: The Initial Phase, 1893–1916." In *East African Expressions of Christianity*, edited by Thomas Spear and Isaria N. Kimambo, 39–62. Oxford: James Currey, 1999.

Lindhardt, Martin. "Continuity, Change or Coevalness? Charismatic Christianity and Tradition in Contemporary Tanzania." In *Pentecostalism in Africa: Presence and Impact of Pneumatic Christianity in Postcolonial Societies*, edited by Martin Lindhardt, 162–90. Leiden: Brill, 2015.

———, ed. *Pentecostalism in Africa: Presence and Impact of Pneumatic Christianity in Postcolonial Societies*. Leiden: Brill, 2015.

Lonsdale, John. "Kikuyu Christianities: A History of Intimate Diversity." In *Christianity and the African Imagination: Essays in Honour of Adrian Hastings*, edited by David Maxwell with Ingrid Lawrie, 157–97. Leiden: Brill, 2002.

Low, D. A. *Fabrication of Empire: The British and the Uganda Kingdoms, 1890–1902*. Cambridge: Cambridge University Press, 2009.

Lucas, William Vincent. *Christianity and Native Rites*. London: Parrett & Neves, 1948.

Lucie-Smith, Alexander, ed. *Mission Ad Gentes: The Challenge for the Church in Kenya*. Nairobi: Paulines Publications, 2007.

Ludwig, Frieder. *Church and State in Tanzania: Aspects of a Changing Relationship, 1961–1994*. Leiden: Brill, 1999.

Lukwata, John. *The First Hundred Years of the Buganda Church and Her Worship*. Rome: San Anselmo, 1991.

———. *Integrated African Liturgy*. Eldoret, Kenya: Gaba Publications, 2003.

Lynch, Gabrielle. *I Say to You: Ethnic Politics and the Kalenjin in Kenya*. Chicago: University of Chicago Press, 2011.

MacArthur, Julie. "The Making and Unmaking of African Languages: Oral Communities and Competitive Linguistic Work in Western Kenya." *Journal of African History* 53, no. 2 (2012): 151–72.

Madan, A. C. *Kiungani, or Story and History from Central Africa*. Zanzibar: 1886.

Maddox, Gregory, James Giblin, and Isaria N. Kimambo, eds. *Custodians of the Land: Ecology and Culture in the History of Tanzania*. London: James Currey, 1996.

Magesa, Laurenti. *African Religion: The Moral Traditions of Abundant Life*. Maryknoll, NY: Orbis, 1997.

———, ed. *African Theology Comes of Age: Revisiting Twenty Years of the Theology of the Ecumenical Symposium of Eastern African Theologians (ESEAT)*. Nairobi: Paulines Publications, 2010.

———. *Anatomy of Inculturation: Transforming the Church in Africa*. Maryknoll, NY: Orbis, 2004.

———. "Challenging Models of Governance for Development in Africa." *Tangaza Journal of Theology and Mission* 1 (2011): 70–90.

———. "The Political Axis of African Liberation Theology." In *Liberation Theologies on Shifting Grounds: A Clash of Socio-Economic and Cultural Paradigms*, edited by G. De Schrijver, 130–52. Leuven: Leuven University Press, 1998.

———. *Rethinking Mission: Evangelization in Africa in a New Era*. Eldoret, Kenya: Gaba Publications, 2006.

———. "A Theological Journey." *Exchange* 32, no. 1 (2003): 43–53.

———. *What Is Not Sacred? African Spirituality*. Maryknoll, NY: Orbis, 2013.

Magesa, Laurenti, and Michael C. Kirwen, eds. *Exploring the Future of Mission in Africa: In Celebration of Maryknoll's 100 Years in Mission*. Nairobi: Maryknoll Institute of African Studies, 2012.

Magesa, Laurenti, and Zablon Nthamburi, eds. *Democracy and Reconciliation: A Challenge for African Christianity*. Nairobi: Acton Publishers, 2003.

Mamdani, Mahmood. *Citizen and Subject: Contemporary Africa and the Legacy of Late Colonialism*. Princeton: Princeton University Press, 1996.

Maseno, Loreen. "Christianity in East Africa." In *The Routledge Companion to Christianity in Africa*, edited by Elias Kifon Bongmba, 108–21. New York: Routledge, 2016.

Maxwell, David, with Ingrid Lawrie, eds. *Christianity and the African Imagination: Essays in Honour of Adrian Hastings*. Leiden: Brill, 2002.

Mbiti, John S. *African Religions and Philosophy*. New York: Praeger, 1969.

Mbotela, James Juma. *The Freeing of the Slaves in East Africa*. London: Evans Brothers, 1956.

Mbuvi, Andrew M. "Christology and *Cultus* in 1 Peter: An African (Kenyan) Appraisal." In *Jesus without Borders*, edited by Gene L. Green, Stephen T. Pardue, and K. K. Yeo, 141–61. Grand Rapids: Eerdmans, 2014.

McInneshin, Michael. "Collaborative Landscape: Missions, States, and Their Subjects in the Making of Northeastern Tanzania's Terrain, 1870–1914." In *Missions, States, and European Expansion in Africa*, edited by Chima J. Korieh and Raphael Chijioke Njoku, 187–202. New York: Routledge, 2007.

McMahon, Elizabeth. *Slavery and Emancipation in Islamic East Africa*. Cambridge: Cambridge University Press, 2013.

Médard, Henri, and Shane Doyle, eds. *Slavery in the Great Lakes Region of East Africa*. Oxford: James Currey, 2007.

Middleton, John. *The World of the Swahili: An African Mercantile Civilization*. New Haven: Yale University Press, 1992.

Mndolwa, Maimbo W., and Fergus J. King. "In Two Minds? African Experience and Preferment in UMCA and the Journey to Independence in Tanganyika." *Mission Studies* 33, no. 3 (2016): 327–51.

Mombo, Esther. "Women in African Christianities." In *The Routledge Companion to Christianity in Africa*, edited by Elias Kifon Bongmba, 173–85. New York: Routledge, 2016.

Morton, Fred. *Children of Ham: Freed Slaves and Fugitive Slaves on the Kenyan Coast, 1873–1907.* Boulder, CO: Westview, 1990.

Mugambi, J. N. K. *Christian Theology and Social Reconstruction.* Nairobi: Acton, 2003.

———. "Ecumenical Contextual Theological Reflection in Eastern Africa 1989–1999." In *Challenges and Prospects for the Church in Africa: Theological Reflections for the 21st Century*, edited by Nahashon W. Ndung'u and Philomena Mwaura, 17–29. Nairobi: Paulines Publications, 2005.

———. *From Liberation to Reconstruction: African Christian Theology after the Cold War*. Nairobi: East African Educational Publishers, 1995.

Mugambi, J. N. K., and Laurenti Magesa, eds. *Jesus in African Christianity: Experimentation and Diversity in African Christology*. Nairobi: Initiatives Publishers, 1989.

Mugambi, J. N. K., and A. Nasimiyu-Wasike, eds. *Moral and Ethical Issues in African Christianity*. Nairobi: Initiatives Publishers, 1992.

Munson, Robert B. *The Nature of Christianity in Northern Tanzania: Environmental and Social Change, 1890–1916.* Lanham, MD: Lexington, 2013.

Muoria-Sal, Wangari, Bodil Folke Frederiksen, John Lonsdale, and Derek Peterson, eds. *Writing for Kenya: The Life and Works of Henry Muoria.* Leiden: Brill, 2009.

Musisi, Nakanyike B. "Morality as Identity: The Missionary Moral Agenda in Buganda, 1877–1945." *Journal of Religious History* 23, no. 1 (1999): 51–74.

Mutongi, Kenda. *Worries of the Heart: Widows, Family, and Community in Kenya*. Chicago: University of Chicago Press, 2007.

Mwase, Isaac T., and Eunice K. Kamaara, eds. *Theologies of Liberation and Reconstruction: Essays in Honor of Professor Jesse N. K. Mugambi.* Nairobi: Acton, 2012.

Mwaura, Philomena Njeri. "Concept of Basic Human Rights in African Independent Pentecostal Church of Africa and Jesus Is Alive Ministries." *Journal of World Christianity* 5, no. 1 (2012): 9–42.

———. "Gender and Power in African Christianity: African Instituted Churches and Pentecostal Churches." In *African Christianity: An African Story*, edited by Ogbu Kalu, 359–88. Trenton, NJ: Africa World, 2007.

———. "Gendered Appropriation of Mass Media in Kenyan Christianities: A Comparison of Two Women-Led African Instituted Churches in Kenya." In *Interpreting Contemporary Christianity: Global Processes and Local Identities*, edited by Ogbu U. Kalu and Alaine Low, 274–95. Grand Rapids: Eerdmans, 2008.

———. "The Role of Charismatic Christianity in Reshaping the Religious Scene in Africa: The Case of Kenya." In *Christianity in Africa and the African Diaspora: The Appropriation of a Scattered Heritage*, edited by Afe Adogame, Roswith Gerloff, and Klaus Hock, 180–92. London: Continuum, 2008.

———. "A Theological and Cultural Analysis of Healing in Jerusalem Church of Christ and Nabii Christian Church of Kenya." PhD diss., Kenyatta University, 2001.

Mwikamba, C. M. "Shifts in Mission: An Ecological Theology in Africa." In *Mission in African Christianity: Critical Essays in Missiology*, edited by A. Nasimiyu-Wasike and D. W. Waruta, 11–39. Nairobi: Uzima, 2000.

Nandi, O. M. Jacob. "The Jerusalem Church of Christ: A Prophet-Healing Independent Church in Kenya." MA thesis, University of Nairobi, 1993.

Napachihi, Sebastian Wolfgang. *The Relationship between the German Missionaries of the Congregation of St. Benedict from St. Ottilien and the German Colonial Authorities in Tanzania, 1887–1907*. Ndanda, Tanzania: Benedictine Publications, 1998.

Nasimiyu-Wasike, Anne. "Prophetic Mission of the Church: The Voices of African Women." In *Mission in African Christianity: Critical Essays in Missiology*, edited by Anne Nasimiyu-Wasike and D. W. Waruta, 179–99. Nairobi: Uzima, 2000.

Nasimiyu-Wasike, Anne, and D. W. Waruta, eds. *Mission in African Christianity: Critical Essays in Missiology*. Nairobi: Uzima, 2000.

Ndung'u, Nahashon W. "Environmental Management: Constraints and Prospects in Africa in the 21st Century." In *Challenges and Prospects for the Church in Africa: Theological Reflections for the 21st Century*, edited by Nahashon W. Ndung'u and Philomena Mwaura, 54–70. Nairobi: Paulines Publications, 2005.

Ndung'u, Nahashon W., and Philomena Mwaura, eds. *Challenges and Prospects for the Church in Africa: Theological Reflections for the 21st Century*. Nairobi: Paulines Publications, 2005.

Ndyabahika, Odomaro. "The Theology of Peter Kanyandago." In *African Theology: The Contribution of the Pioneers*, vol. 3, edited by Bénézet Bujo, 134–48. Nairobi: Paulines Publications, 2012.

Ngao, Felix Nzioka. "Christian Presence among Marginalized Groups in Northern Kenya." In *Exploring the Future of Mission in Africa: In Celebration of Maryknoll's 100 Years in Mission*, edited by Laurenti Magesa and Michael C. Kirwen, 81–92. Nairobi: Maryknoll Institute of African Studies, 2012.

Ngugi, Wa Thiong'o (James). *The River Between*. Nairobi: Heinemann, 1965.

Nguru, Faith W. "Development in Christian Higher Education in Kenya: An Overview." In *Christian Higher Education: A Global Renaissance*, edited by Joel Carpenter, Perry L. Glanzer, and Nicholas S. Lantinga, 43–67. Grand Rapids: Eerdmans, 2014.

Njoroge, Lawrence M. *A Century of Catholic Endeavor: Holy Ghost and Consolata Missions in Kenya*. Nairobi: Paulines Publications, 1999.

Njoroge, Nyambura J. "A New Way of Facilitating Leadership: Lessons from African Women Theologians." In *African Christianity: An African Story*, edited by Ogbu Kalu, 389–408. Trenton, NJ: Africa World, 2007.

Nolan, Francis. *Mission to the Great Lakes: The White Fathers in Western Tanzania, 1878–1978*. Tabora, Tanzania: TMP, 1978.

———. *The White Fathers in Colonial Africa, 1919–1939*. Nairobi: Paulines Publications, 2012.

Noll, Mark A. *The New Shape of World Christianity: How American Experience Reflects Global Faith*. Downers Grove, IL: InterVarsity, 2009.

Nsobya, A. Tarcis. *The Uganda Martyrs Are Our Light*. Kisubi, Uganda: Marianum, 2006.

Nsobya, Abdulhakim A. "Uganda's Militant Islamic Movement ADF: A Historical Analysis." *Annual Review of Islam in Africa* 12/13 (2015–16): 30–39.

Ntale, Frederick Kisekka. "Being Wealthy Must Not Be a Burden." In *Africa Is Not Destined to Die: Signs of Hope and Renewal*, edited by Ambrose John Bwangatto, 162–84. Nairobi: Paulines Publications, 2012.

Nyaundi, Nehemiah. "The Phenomenon of Violence in Eastern Africa." In *African Theology Comes of Age: Revisiting Twenty Years of the Theology of the Ecumenical Symposium of Eastern African Theologians (ESEAT)*, edited by Laurenti Magesa, 123–31. Nairobi: Paulines Publications, 2010.

O'Connor, Daniel. *Three Centuries of Mission: The United Society for the Propagation of the Gospel 1701–2000.* London: Continuum, 2000.

Odozor, Paulinus Ikechukwu. *Morality Truly Christian, Truly African.* Notre Dame: University of Notre Dame Press, 2014.

Oliver, Roland. *The Missionary Factor in East Africa.* London: Longman, Green, 1952.

O'Neil, Robert. *Mission to the Upper Nile: The Story of St. Joseph's Missionary Society in Uganda.* London: Mission Book Service, 1999.

Opia, Opolot. *Communal Labor in Colonial Kenya: The Legitimization of Coercion, 1912–1930.* New York: Palgrave Macmillan, 2012.

Orobator, Agbonkhianmeghe E., ed. *The Church We Want: African Catholics Look to Vatican III.* Maryknoll, New York: Orbis, 2016.

———. "Ethics of HIV/AIDS Prevention: Paradigms of a New Discourse from an African Perspective." In *Applied Ethics in a World Church: The Padua Conference*, edited by Linda Hogan, 147–54. Maryknoll, NY: Orbis, 2008.

———, ed. *Reconciliation, Justice, and Peace: The Second African Synod.* Nairobi: Acton, 2011.

———. *Theology Brewed in an African Pot.* Maryknoll, NY: Orbis, 2008.

Parsitau, Damaris. "'Arise, Oh Ye Daughters of Faith': Women, Pentecostalism, and Public Culture in Kenya." In *Christianity and Public Culture in Africa*, edited by Harri Englund, 131–45. Cambridge: Cambridge University Press, 2011.

Parsitau, Damaris, and Philomena Njeri Mwaura. "God in the City: Pentecostalism as an Urban Phenomenon in Kenya." *Studia Historiae Ecclesiasticae* 36, no. 2 (2010): 95–112.

Parsons, Timothy H. *The Second British Empire: In the Crucible of the Twentieth Century*. Lanham, MD: Rowman & Littlefield, 2014.

Pawelczak, Marek. *The State and the Stateless. The Sultanate of Zanzibar and the East African Mainland: Politics, Economy and Society, 1837–1888.* Warsaw: University of Warsaw, 2010.

Peterson, Derek R., ed. *Abolitionism and Imperialism in Britain, Africa, and the Atlantic*. Athens: Ohio University Press, 2010.

———. "Culture and Chronology in African History." *The Historical Review* 50, no. 2 (2007): 483–97.

———. *Ethnic Patriotism and the East African Revival: A History of Dissent, c. 1935–1972*. Cambridge: Cambridge University Press, 2012.

Pickens, George F. *African Christian God-Talk: Matthew Ajuoga's Johera Narrative*. Dallas: University Press of America, 2004.

Pierli, Francesco, Terry W. Mwaniki, and Peter Mbuchi Methu, eds. *The Pastoralists: A Challenge to Churches, State, Civil Society*. Nairobi: Paulines Publications, 2006.

Pirouet, Louise. *Black Evangelists: The Spread of Christianity in Uganda, 1891 to 1914.* London: Collins, 1978.

———. *Historical Dictionary of Uganda*. Metuchen, NJ: Scarecrow, 1995.

Porter, Arthur T. "University Development in English-Speaking Africa: Problems and Prospects." *African Affairs* 71, no. 282 (1972): 79–80.

Porter, Philip W. *Challenging Nature: Local Knowledge, Agroscience, and Food Security in Tanga Region, Tanzania*. Chicago: University of Chicago Press, 2006.

Poucouta, Paulin. "Meinrad Pierre Hebga: Theologian and Healer." In *African Theology: The Contribution of the Pioneers*, vol. 2, edited by Bénézet Bujo and Juvénal Ilunga Muya, 70–92. Nairobi: Paulines Publications, 2008.

Presley, Cora Ann. "Wambui Waiyaki Otieno Mbugua (b. 1928): Gender Politics in Kenya from the Mau Mau Rebellion to the Pro-Democracy Movement." In *The Human Tradition in Modern Africa*, edited by Dennis D. Cordell, 209–29. Lanham, MD: Rowman & Littlefield, 2012.

Prevost, Elizabeth E. *The Communion of Women: Missions and Gender in Colonial Africa and the British Metropole*. Oxford: Oxford University Press, 2010.

Prince, Ruth. "Public Debates about Luo Widow Inheritance: Christianity, Tradition, and AIDS in Western Kenya." In *Christianity and Public Culture in Africa*, edited by Harri Englund, 109–30. Cambridge: Cambridge University Press, 2011.

Prosén, Martina. "Pentecostalism in Eastern Africa." In *The Routledge Companion to Christianity in Africa*, edited by Elias Kifon Bongmba, 297–316. New York: Routledge, 2016.

Pui-lan, Kwok, Cecilia González-Andrieu, and Dwight N. Hopkins, eds. *Teaching Global Theologies: Power and Praxis*. Waco, TX: Baylor University Press, 2015.

Ranger, T. O. "Missionary Adaptation of African Religious Institutions: The Masasi Case." In *The Historical Study of African Religion*, edited by T. O. Ranger and Isaria Kimambo, 221–51. London: Heinemann, 1972.

Ranger, T. O., and Isaria Kimambo, eds. *The Historical Study of African Religion*. London: Heinemann, 1972.

Ray, Benjamin C. *African Religions: Symbol, Ritual, and Community*. Englewood Cliffs, NJ: Prentice-Hall, 2000.

———. *Myth, Ritual, and Kingship in Buganda*. Oxford: Oxford University Press, 1991.

Reed, Colin. "Denominationalism or Protestantism? Mission Strategy and Church in the Kikuyu Conference of 1913." *International Bulletin of Missionary Research* 37, no. 4 (2013): 207–12.

———. *Pastors, Partners, and Paternalists: African Church Leaders and Western Missionaries in the Anglican Church in Kenya, 1850–1900*. Leiden: Brill, 1997.

Renner, Frumentius, ed. *Sheltered by God in His Service: Brother Michael Hofer's Memoirs*. Translated by Matilda Handl, OSB. St. Ottilien, Germany: EOS Editions, 2008.

Robert, Dana. *Christian Mission: How Christianity Became a World Religion*. Chichester, UK: Wiley-Blackwell, 2009.

Rotich, Cathleen Chepkorir, and Richard Starcher. "Traditional Marriage Education among the Kipsigis of Kenya with Application to Local Church Ministry in Urban Africa." *Mission Studies* 33, no. 1 (2016): 49–65.

Rweyemamu, S., and T. Msambure. *The Catholic Church in Tanzania*. Ndanda and Peramiho, Tanzania: Benedictine Publications, 1989.

Rwiza, Richard. "Laurenti Magesa: An African Liberation Theologian." In *African Theology: The Contribution of the Pioneers*, vol. 2, edited by Bénézet Bujo and Juvénal Ilunga Muya, 231–58. Nairobi: Paulines Publications, 2008.

Ryan, Patrick, ed. *New Strategies for a New Evangelization in Africa*. Nairobi: Paulines Publications, 2002.

Sabar, Galia. *Church, State and Society in Kenya: From Mediation to Opposition, 1963–1993*. London: Frank Cass, 2002.

———. "'Was There No Naboth to Say No?' Using the Pulpit in the Struggle for Democracy: The Anglican Church, Bishop Gitari, and Kenyan Politics." In *Religion and Politics in Kenya: Essays in Honor of a Meddlesome Priest*, edited by Ben Knighton, 123–42. New York: Palgrave Macmillan, 2009.

Sandgren, David P. *Christianity and the Kikuyu: Religious Divisions and Social Conflict*. New York: Peter Lang, 2000.

Scherz, China. *Having People, Having Heart: Charity, Sustainable Development, and Problems of Dependency in Central Uganda*. Chicago: University of Chicago Press, 2014.

Sheriff, Abdul. *Slaves, Spices and Ivory in Zanzibar*. London: James Currey, 1987.

Sheriff, Abdul, and Ed Ferguson, eds. *Zanzibar Under Colonial Rule*. London: James Currey, 1991.

Shetler, Jan Bender. "Historical Memory and Expanding Social Networks of Mennonite Mission School Women, Mara Region, Tanzania, 1938 to the Present." *Studies in World Christianity* 18, no. 1 (2012): 63–81.

———. *Imagining Serengeti: A History of Landscape Memory in Tanzania from the Earliest Times to the Present*. Athens: Ohio University Press, 2007.

Shorter, Aylward. *African Recruits and Missionary Conscripts: The White Fathers and the Great War (1914–1922)*. Maryknoll, NY: Orbis, 2007.

———. *Cross and Flag in Africa: The "White Fathers" during the Colonial Scramble (1892–1914)*. Maryknoll, NY: Orbis, 2006.

———. *Jesus and the Witchdoctor: An Approach to Healing and Wholeness.* London: Geoffrey Chapman, 1985.

Sivalon, John C. "Roman Catholicism and the Defining of Tanzanian Socialism: 1955–1985." PhD diss., University of Toronto, 1990.

Small, N. J. "UMCA (Universities Mission to Central Africa): The Early Work in Education, 1876–1905." *Tanzania Notes and Records* (1980): 86–87, 35–55.

Smith, James Howard, and Rosalind I. J. Hackett, eds. *Displacing the State: Religion and Conflict in Neoliberal Africa.* Notre Dame: University of Notre Dame Press, 2012.

Smythe, Kathleen R. *Fipa Families: Reproduction and Catholic Evangelization in Nkansi, Ufipa, 1880–1960.* Portsmouth, NH: Heinemann, 2006.

Soldati, Gabriele. *The Pioneer: The African Adventure of Benedict Falda.* Rome: Istituto Missioni Consolata, 1991.

Spear, Thomas. *Mountain Farmers*. Berkeley: University of California Press, 1997.

Spear, Thomas, and Isaria N. Kimambo, eds. *East African Expressions of Christianity*. Oxford: James Currey, 1999.

Ssempala, Cornelius. "Back to the Future in Africa; Relocating Water and Food Sovereignty among Local Communities." In *Africa Is Not Destined to Die: Signs of Hope and Renewal*, edited by Ambrose John Bwangatto, 225–39. Nairobi: Paulines Publications, 2012.

Stambach, Amy. *Faith in Schools: Religion, Education, and American Evangelicals in East Africa.* Stanford: Stanford University Press, 2010.

Stenger, Fritz, Joseph Wandera, and Paul Hannon, eds. *Christian-Muslim Co-Existence in Eastern Africa*. Nairobi: Paulines Publications, 2008.

Stephens, Rhiannon. *A History of African Motherhood: The Case of Uganda, 700–1900.* Cambridge: Cambridge University Press, 2013.

Stinton, Diane B. "Africa's Contribution to Christology." In *African Theology Comes of Age: Revisiting Twenty Years of the Theology of the Ecumenical Symposium of Eastern African Theologians (ESEAT)*, edited by Laurenti Magesa, 13–34. Nairobi: Paulines Publications, 2010.

———. *Jesus of Africa: Voices of Contemporary African Christology*. Maryknoll, NY: Orbis, 2004.

Stoner-Eby, Anne Marie. "African Clergy, Bishop Lucas and the Christianizing of Local Initiation Rites: Revisiting 'the Masasi Case.'" *Journal of Religion in Africa* 38, no. 2 (2008): 171–208.

Straight, Bilinda. *Miracles and Extraordinary Experience in Northern Kenya*. Philadelphia: University of Pennsylvania Press, 2007.

Strayer, Robert W. *The Making of Mission Communities in East Africa: Anglicans and Africans in Colonial Kenya, 1875–1935*. London: Heinemann, 1978.

Sundkler, Bengt, and Christopher Steed. *The History of the Church in Africa*. Cambridge: Cambridge University Press, 2000.

Sunseri, Thaddeus. *Vilimani: Labor Migration and Rural Change in Early Colonial Tanzania*. Portsmouth, NH: Heinemann, 2002.

———. *Wielding the Ax: State Forestry and Social Conflict in Tanzania, 1820–2000*. Athens: Ohio University Press, 2009.

Swantz, Marji Liisa. *Beyond the Forestline: The Life and Letters of Bengt Sundkler*. Leominster, UK: Gracewing, 2002.

Tablino, Paul. *Christianity among the Nomads: The Catholic Church in Northern Kenya*. 2 vols. Nairobi: Paulines Publications, 2004–2006.

Taylor, John V. *The Primal Vision: Western Christendom and the African View of Life*. Philadelphia: Fortress Press, 1963.

Tebaldi, Giovanni. *Consolata Missionaries in the World (1901–2001)*. Nairobi: Paulines Publications, 1999.

Tengatenga, James. *The UMCA in Malawi: A History of the Anglican Church, 1861–2010*. Zomba, Malawi: Kachere, 2010.

Tucker, Alfred R. *Eighteen Years in Uganda and East Africa*. Westport, CT: Negro Universities Press, 1970.

Tuma, Thomas. *The History of Christianity in Uganda*. Kampala: Makerere University, 1975.

Twaddle, Michael. *Kakungulu and the Creation of Uganda*. London: James Currey, 1993.

Twesigye, Emmanuel K. *Religion, Politics and Cults in East Africa: God's Warriors and Mary's Saints*. New York: Peter Lang, 2010.

Uzukwu, Eugene Elochukwu. *A Listening Church: Autonomy and Communion in African Churches*. Maryknoll, NY: Orbis, 1996.

Vähäkangas, Auli. Christian Couples Coping with Childlessness: Narratives from Machame, Kilimanjaro. Helsinki: University of Helsinki, 2004.

Vähäkangas, Mika. "Babu wa Loliondo—Healing the Tensions between Tanzanian Worlds." *Journal of Religion in Africa* 45, no. 1 (2015): 3–36.

———. "Ghambageu Encounters Jesus in Sonjo Mythology: Syncretism as African Ritual Action." *Journal of the American Academy of Religion* 76, no. 1 (2008): 111–37.

Vaughan, Megan. *Curing Their Ills: Colonial Power and African Illness*. Stanford: Stanford University Press, 1991.

Vokes, Richard. *Ghosts of Kanungu: Fertility, Secrecy, and Exchange in the Great Lakes Region of East Africa*. Woodbridge, UK: James Currey, 2009.

Waliggo, John Mary. "The Bugandan Christian Revolution: The Catholic Church in Buddu, 1879–1896." In *Christianity and the African Imagination: Essays in Honour of Adrian Hastings*, edited by David Maxwell with Ingrid Lawrie, 63–92. Leiden: Brill, 2002.

———. "The Catholic Church and the Root Cause of Instability in Uganda." In *Religion and Politics in East Africa*, edited by Holger Bernt Hansen and Michael Twaddle, 106–19. Athens: Ohio University Press, 1995.

———. "The Catholic Church in the Buddu Province of Buganda, 1879–1925." Diss., Cambridge University, 1976.

———. *A History of African Priests: Katigondo Major Seminary, 1911–1986*. Kampala: Marianum, 1988.

Waller, Richard. "They Do the Dictating and We Must Submit: The Africa Inland Mission in Maasailand." In *East African Expressions of Christianity*, edited by Thomas Spear and Isaria N. Kimambo, 83–126. Oxford: James Currey, 1999.

Walls, Andrew F. *The Cross-Cultural Process in Christian History*. Maryknoll, NY: Orbis, 2001.

Wandira, Asavia. *Early Missionary Education in Uganda: A Study of Purpose in Missionary Education.* Kampala: Makerere University Department of Education, 1972.

Ward, Edwina, and Gary Leonard, eds. *A Theology of HIV and AIDS on Africa's East Coast.* Uppsala: Swedish Institute of Mission Research, 2008.

Ward, Kevin. "Archbishop Janani Luwum: The Dilemmas of Loyalty, Opposition and Witness in Amin's Uganda." In *Christianity and the African Imagination: Essays in Honour of Adrian Hastings*, edited by David Maxwell with Ingrid Lawrie, 199–224. Leiden: Brill, 2002.

———. "The Church of Uganda and the Exile of Kabaka Muteesa II, 1953–1955." *Journal of Religion in Africa* 28, no. 4 (1998): 411–49.

———. *A History of Global Anglicanism.* Cambridge: Cambridge University Press, 2006.

Waruta, Douglas W., and Hannah W. Kinoti, eds. *Pastoral Care in African Christianity: Challenging Essays in Pastoral Theology.* Nairobi: Acton, 1994.

Wijsen, Frans. "Mission Practice and Theory in Africa." In *The Routledge Companion to Christianity in Africa*, edited by Elias Kifon Bongmba, 189–200. New York: Routledge, 2016.

Wijsen, Frans, and Ralph Tanner. *Seeking a Good Life: Religion and Society in Usukuma, Tanzania.* Nairobi: Paulines Publications, 2000.

Wild-Wood, Emma. "A Biography of Apolo Kivebulaya." *International Bulletin of Missionary Research* 38, no. 3 (2014): 145–48.

Wilkens, Katharina. *Holy Water and Evil Spirits: Religious Healing in East Africa.* Berlin: Lit Verlag, 2011.

———. "Mary and the Demons: Marian Devotion and Ritual Healing in Tanzania." *Journal of Religion in Africa* 39, no. 3 (2009): 295–318.

Willis, Justin. "The Nature of a Mission Community: The Universities' Mission to Central Africa in Bonde." In *Missionary Encounters: Sources and Issues*, edited by Robert A. Bickers and Rosemary Seton, 128–52. Richmond, UK: Curzon, 1996.

Wright, Marcia. *German Missions in Tanganyika, 1891–1941: Lutherans and Moravians in the Southern Highlands.* Oxford: Clarendon, 1971.

———. "Maji-Maji: Prophecy and Historiography." In *Revealing Prophets: Prophecy in Eastern African History*, edited by David M. Anderson and Douglas H. Johnson, 124–42. London: James Currey, 1995.

———. "Mama Adolphina Unda (c. 1880–1931): The Salvation of a Dynastic Family and the Foundation of Fipa Catholicism, 1898–1914." In *The Human Tradition in Modern Africa*, edited by Dennis D. Cordell, 123–38. Lanham, MD: Rowman & Littlefield, 2012.

Wuthnow, Robert. *Boundless Faith: The Global Outreach of American Churches*. Los Angeles: University of California Press, 2010.

Yates, Timothy, with Stephen Skuce. *Twentieth-Century Missiology: Issues and Thinkers*. Calver, UK: Cliff College Publishing, 2014.

Index

Lightning Source UK Ltd.
Milton Keynes UK
UKHW02f1557100918
328652UK00005B/227/P

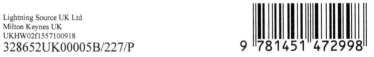